STRONGER THAN SPINACH

THE Secret OF THE Appeal

Famous Studios
POPEYE
Cartoons *by Steve R. Bierly*

Stronger Than Spinach: The Secret Appeal of The Famous Studios Popeye Cartoons
© 2009 Steve R. Bierly. All Rights Reserved.
No part of this book may be reproduced in any form or by any means, electronic, mechanical, digital, photocopying or recording, except for the inclusion in a review, without permission in writing from the publisher.
Popeye © King Features Syndicate

Published in the USA by:
BearManor Media
P O Box 71426
Albany, Georgia 31708
www.bearmanormedia.com

ISBN 1-59393-502-1

Printed in the United States of America.
Book design by Brian Pearce.

Table of Contents

Childhood Daze... 9
I Yam What I Yam.. 11
Popeye the Complex Man............................... 21
"What a Feminine Female!"............................ 31
"Ooohhh, You Handsome Samson!".................... 41
Lights! Camera! Violence! Suspense!.................. 51
"I'm In the Mood for Love"............................ 57
Shades of Gray Amid White and Blue Sailor Suits...... 67
The Island Fling (1946).................................. 73
The Royal Four-Flusher (1947)......................... 85
A Wolf in Sheik's Clothing (1948).................... 101
Snow Place Like Home (1948)......................... 121
Symphony in Spinach (1948).......................... 133
Beach Peach (1950).................................... 141
Jitterbug Jive (1950).................................. 157
Vacation with Play (1951)............................. 167
Beaus Will Be Beaus (1955)........................... 181
Mister and Mistletoe (1955).......................... 193
Parlez Vous Woo (1956)............................... 203
The Rest of the Cartoons............................. 211
The Paramount KFS Popeye Cartoons................ 297
Under The Influence.................................. 303
Sources.. 307
Availability... 309
Endnotes.. 311
Index.. 319
About the Author..................................... 325

Dedicated to Deborah Bierly, the "Famous Studios Olive Oyl" in my life, and to the memory of my parents who let me love cartoons as I was growing up.

ACKNOWLEDGEMENTS

My sincere thanks to:

Frank Grandinetti, the world's #1 expert on all things Popeye, and a friendly, accommodating guy.

Richard Ranke, who got me into Segar, gave me information on the Popeye comic books, and shares my appreciation for the Famous Studios Olive Oyl.

The writers of the *Official Popeye Fan Club News-Magazine* who have enlightened me over the years, most notably Mike Brooks, Chuck Anders, Tim Hollis, Leonard Kohl, and Donny Pitchford.

Charles Brilvitch, my consultant on Bluto and bodybuilders.

All those who have contacted me via the NET to share their Famous Studios Popeye-related thoughts. Especially Neil Tenczar, Michael Beherest, Jefferson Blackburn III, Shade J Ford, Rayna/*aka* Sparki/*aka* Sparkina, Ken Layton, and Phil "The Professor" Mann.

Jerry Beck and Barry Mills, who gave me encouragement in the past about my Popeye writing.

Nathan Willats and Jack Copley, Archie comics fans who helped me track down a story.

Ben Ohmart, for giving me the opportunity to write this book.

My wife and daughter — editors, typists, and encouragers — without whom this book couldn't have been written.

INTRODUCTION
Childhood Daze

When I was a young boy, my parents controlled what I watched on television. I wasn't allowed to watch scary horror movies or science-fiction films that they thought would give me bad dreams. I could, however, watch Popeye get disintegrated by an alien who declared, in an eerie, menacing, powerful, otherworldly voice, "I'll wipe you out!" in the cartoon *Rocket to Mars*. And I could sit glued to our TV set in shock as Popeye was pounded into a steak and fried over a fire by a tribe of cannibals *(Pop-Pie A La Mode)*.

I wasn't allowed to watch movies or television shows which dealt with "adult stuff," or had too many "mushy" scenes that I supposedly wouldn't be interested in. I could, however, watch a rich playboy ogle Olive Oyl's rear, invite her up to his penthouse, and trap her in a straitjacket *(The Royal Four-Flusher)*. I was allowed to watch a caveman repeatedly kiss a helpless Olive so passionately that the two of them seemed to merge into one being *(Pre-Hysterical Man)*. As an elementary schooler, I saw castaway Olive Oyl and Robinson Crusoe sit together on a couch, in the mood for love, as he rubbed his hands over her and wooed her with, "L'amour, l'amour, it's you I adore!" *(The Island Fling)*.

Why didn't my parents' censorship extend to the Popeye films? Probably they didn't pay that much attention to the cartoons, trusting the local TV stations which had deemed the films suitable to broadcast on children's shows.

But what my parents didn't know, or had forgotten, was that the Popeye cartoons had been originally created with adult theatergoers in mind. The cartoons made their debuts in cinemas across America, paired with feature films and other short subjects. Only later were the cartoons marketed, sold, and syndicated as fare for kid's TV. So as I watched Popeye, I was being exposed to adult themes, grown-up humor, and mature thinking.

My parents might have shrugged off whatever was questionable in a Popeye film by saying, "It's only a cartoon." But the characters and situations in cartoons were very real to me, and, indeed, to every little kid I've ever known. And the Popeye cartoons wove their spell on me, informing my dreams, tantalizing me, titillating me, teaching me, entertaining me, frustrating me, mystifying me, challenging me, and, at times, scaring me. These cartoons will never be exorcised out of my heart and mind. Truthfully, I wouldn't want them to be. I love these cartoons which have insinuated themselves into my soul. And because the cartoons were originally made for adults, the older I got - through my adolescent, teen, and young adult years, and up to today - the more they grabbed hold of me, and the more my appreciation for them grew. And I'm not alone. Other fans who grew up with the cartoons and still love them today have said such things to me as: "Those cartoons jump-started my puberty"; "The creators did a boogie-woogie on my psyche"; "I alternate between wanting to bless the creators and to curse them for playing with me as they did" and "Certain scenes are permanently engraved on my inner eyes."

The Popeye cartoons that the fans and I rhapsodize about are those that were produced by Famous Studios. It's only been recently, as I read animation books and surfed the NET, that I learned that, according to the "experts," I'm not supposed to like the Famous Studios cartoons because they are allegedly "inferior" to the earlier Fleischer ones which are considered to be classics of animation.[1] All I can do is echo Popeye and say, "I yam what I yam" and "I likes what I likes." Well, okay, actually, I can also say that the Famous Studios cartoons *aren't* inferior to the Fleischer films, they are just different. And, "Viva la difference!" The Fleischer films concentrated on humor, and I still like to watch them to get a laugh, but while the Famous Studios cartoons are funny and contain puns and sight gags and characters contorting in cartoony ways, their real magic and strengths lie elsewhere.

In Part One of this book, we'll talk about the Famous Studios Popeye cartoons and the forces that shaped them. Then we'll look at the elements that went into producing such affecting cartoons. Later, in Part Two, I'll take in-depth looks at eleven specific Famous Studios cartoons in which the creators worked their magic to near-perfection. Then, we'll take a whirlwind tour through the rest of the Famous Studios Popeye films.

As Popeye might say, "Batten down yer hatches, Matey! We're settin' sail!"

CHAPTER 1
I Yam What I Yam

For someone whose motto and personal philosophy was "I yam what I yam," Popeye sure changed a lot over the years. So did his cast of supporting characters and the ways in which his adventures, and misadventures, were portrayed.

Tracking these changes and reflecting on the Famous Studios' world will enable us to answer the question, "Where did the Famous Studios Popeye cartoons, with their particular ways of portraying characters and situations, come from?"

Accentuating the Positive

When Popeye first appeared in the *Thimble Theatre* comic strips by E.C. Segar in 1929, he was a rough-and-tough son of the sea who gambled, cheated, and brawled. Though his more admirable qualities, such as his perseverance and self-reliance, were also on display, he was a hot-tempered little guy who would just as soon sock you in the mouth as look at you. He would punch first and ask questions later.

Because young children were fascinated with Popeye, who was a rather coarse individual, the distributors of Segar's strip told E.C. to tone Popeye down. This turned out to be a plus for The Sailorman, because, over time, Segar morphed Popeye into the All-American hero we know and love. This later Popeye was still a fighter, but now he fought for what was Right and stood up for the downtrodden and the oppressed. And often he would no longer be the one who threw the first punch.

In his early animated adventures from Fleischer Studios,[1] Popeye was modeled after Segar's first incarnation of The Sailorman. He was bopping and whamming seemingly everyone and everything in sight. As time passed, in keeping with the changes taking place in Segar's comic strip, the animated Popeye's hot temper cooled off somewhat. He had more self-control and would often wait until near the end of a cartoon to take personal action against his "emenies."

The "self-controlled sailor who waits to take action" would become the standard way Popeye was depicted later in the Famous Studios films.

The Coming of the Spinach

Even though the words "spinach and Popeye" go together in most people's minds today like "Brad Pitt and Angelina Jolie" or "pizza and college students," Segar's Popeye rarely had to imbibe a "booster shot" of spinach in order to perform a super stunt. It's true that Segar gave spinach as one explanation for why Popeye was so strong, resilient, and invulnerable, but Segar's Popeye just regularly ate it at his meals. He didn't always have to gulp down a can when the going got rough.[2]

Spinach wasn't the only reason Segar gave for Popeye's vitality. In his very first comic-strip adventure, Popeye survived being shot multiple times by Jack Snork and being left for dead by rubbing the head of the magic Whiffle Hen all night long. And often in Segar's stories, the only reason apparent for Popeye's superhuman strength and constitution was simply that he was Popeye. Popeye was tough enough to take whatever was thrown at him and come back swinging.

But instead of just relying on himself as the Segar Popeye often did, the animated Popeye from Fleischer Studios came to rely on spinach. He would have to chow down on the green veggie to get the strength and "vitaliky" he needed to finally overcome whoever or whatever was threatening him or his friends. This made for a good gimmick that could be used, and played with, over and over in the cartoons. And the Fleischer cartoons took the "Popeye needs spinach" idea in a new direction. They turned Popeye into an incompetent bungler when he was without his green vegetable in films like *The Dance Contest, The Spinach Overture, Learn Polikeness, The Mighty Navy, Blunder Below,* and *Many Tanks.* Also, the Fleischer creators reinforced this idea of Popeye's basic incompetence by making cartoons where Popeye was done in by small animals *(Flies Ain't Human, I'll Never Crow Again)* and his little nephews *(Pip-eye, Pup-eye, Poop-eye, and Peep-eye).* If he couldn't handle insects, crows, and kids, without spinach, how was he going to be able to deal with any serious threats?

As we shall see, in contrast to Segar's original version, but in harmony with some of the Fleischer films, the Famous Studios Popeye was often desperately dependent on spinach and could be almost totally useless and helpless without it.

"Me Goil, Olive Oyl"

The comic strip Olive Oyl went through changes whenever the whim struck her creator, E.C. Segar. For the most part, Segar's Olive Oyl was exactly what most people think of when they think of Olive Oyl — a rail-thin, ugly, fickle, exaggerated caricature of a stereotypical female personality. She was unattractive, except for when Segar needed her to be suddenly irresistible to men in order to make a plotline or a gag work.[3] Then she became a "guy magnet." Some of Segar's funniest Sunday strips centered around Popeye competing with other guys for her affections. And when she dolled herself up to vamp King Blozo and Popeye to save them from a *femme fatale* spy, Segar drew her as fairly good looking.

The Fleischer Studios animated version of Olive Oyl followed Segar's template. Their Olive Oyl was a homely, hyperemotional woman who was somehow, nonetheless, attractive to men. In her screen debut, for example, we see sailors on shore leave hitting on her. And the Fleischer crew, too, could doll up Olive Oyl when they wanted. It's just that they seldom ever wanted to. But in some frames of certain cartoons, they drew Olive with softer facial features and long eyelashes. For a fleeting second here and there, her face could even be described as sort of pretty! And in the cartoon, *Shoein' Hosses*, the Fleischer Studios creators even drew her with breasts throughout the entire film!

So when Famous Studios later decided to glamorize Olive Oyl, what they did really wasn't unprecedented. But the way they did it was. They turned Ms. Oyl into a sexy beauty who could hold her own against any other attractive animated female. Hubba, hubba!

Popeye's Main "Emeny"

Bluto, too, went through changes. In the original comic-strip series, Segar had only used Bluto once. In that story, Segar's Bluto was a big, mean, supertough pirate who gave Popeye a violent, prolonged battle. But the fight wasn't over Olive Oyl (in fact, she wasn't even in that adventure), and Popeye never gobbled down a can of spinach to save the day.

When the Fleischers got hold of Bluto, they made him into Popeye's main, and continuing, antagonist. Usually Bluto was portrayed as a blowhard bully who would spend most of the cartoon fighting, or competing with, Popeye. But the Fleischer cartoons sometimes couldn't decide whether or not Bluto was really Popeye's enemy or just a battling buddy *(Let's Celebrake, Fightin' Pals)*. And in *Olive Oyl and Water Don't Mix*, his last Fleischer appearance, Bluto is more of a buffoon than he is a serious threat.

The Fleischers also introduced the idea that Bluto, Olive Oyl, and Popeye were in a love triangle, if "love" was the right word for it because romance and wooing played little part in their cartoons. Instead, Bluto would usually just grab a struggling Olive to try to get a kiss. However, once in a great while, Bluto and Olive could share some quality intimate moments. For example, in *Learn Polikeness*, a pseudo-sophisticated "Professor Bluteau" pours on the charm with Olive, and she loves it.[4]

When Famous Studios began producing the Popeye films, they used the goofier and more friendly Bluto in some of their early cartoons, such as the war-themed *Seein' Red, White, 'N' Blue*, and *Too Weak to Work*, and in homages to the Hope/Crosby *Road* pictures — *Alona on the Sarong Seas, We're On Our Way to Rio* — but soon returned him to his earlier, more sinister ways, making him more of a threat to Popeye than ever. They gave him muscles on top of his muscles, a handsome face, and a sly, tricky nature. Also, he became even more of a charmer than he had been in Fleischers' *Learn Polikeness*, getting plenty of screen time alone with Olive Oyl in which to apply his charm to win Ms. Oyl's heart. He was such a dashing lover that viewers found themselves rooting for him, instead of Popeye, in the battle for her affections!

Days of Infamy and Bravery

Animated Popeye cartoons weren't made in a vacuum. In the late 1930s and into the early 1940s, the world was threatened with the rise of the Axis powers. And so, the Fleischers did something Segar never did. They put Popeye in the United States Navy. After all, the world was going to war, so how could Popeye be left behind?[5]

And in the very beginning of the Famous Studios era (1942-1957), The Sailorman kept fighting our nation's enemies. But later, after having been at war, how could Popeye, or anyone, or the world itself, ever be the same?

The world had seen the horrors of concentration camps, landmarks and famous cities lying in ruin, oppressed refugees, Pearl Harbor, and the development and the dropping of the atomic bombs. Our boys had been to foreign shores and had seen brutal combat on land, in the air, and on the sea. Some had even seen the insides of prison camps. On the home front, women and families had sacrificed and put in long hours to help the war effort. All of this made some of Popeye's earlier animated adventures under the Fleischers seem rather quaint in comparison. If audiences were going to stay interested in Popeye, changes would have to be made. There were two options for the Famous Studios creators. Either they had to push the envelope and up some antes in the realms of adventure, violence, horror, and suspense, or go another route altogether.

At first, Famous Studios seemed to want to experiment with going that other route by eliminating the fighting and the danger in their films and making Popeye just another goofy male cartoon character. So they had him bumble around with a goat, a woodpecker, his nephews, and his annoying little pal, Shorty, all of whom bugged him and got the better of him. But something was definitely missing from these Famous Studios cartoons and Popeye wasn't really Popeye. After all, what's a Popeye cartoon without spinach and fights? There needed to be some action!

But fisticuffs, violence, and horror weren't the only kinds of action post-WWII America craved. Sex was also very much on Americans' minds. Servicemen had taken posters of their Hollywood pinup girls with them when they were stationed overseas during the war, and they longed for the sweethearts and the wives they left behind. Many women, having had to take the men's jobs while our boys were gone, or having served side-by-side with them in the service, gained a new confidence in themselves and thus became even more attractive than they had been.

So, Hollywood movies of the 1940s and 1950s were filled with flirting, wooing, and as many double-entendres and as much sexual symbolism as the

An example of how WWII changed the Popeye cartoons. Here, a horse's rear end is disguised to look like the house painter — Adolf Hitler! (From *Her Honor the Mare*.)

censors would let them get away with. After all, as a popular song of the time asked, how were we going to keep the boys down on the farm after they'd seen Paris? And other animation studios, such as Warner Brothers, MGM, and Terrytoons, made some films during this time period which could be considered downright racy. Bugs Bunny went crazy over a female rabbit, Tex Avery's Wolf got turned on by Red, and Mighty Mouse saved scantily-clad anthropomorphic female mice from hungry cats seeking to devour them. The Fleischer brand of "romance" — Popeye yelling, "She's my goil!" as Bluto advanced menacingly on Olive — just wouldn't cut it anymore!

And if the animated Popeye and Bluto, like many real servicemen who had fought our nation's enemies, found their desires turning now toward the more domestic concerns of finding a mate and getting a job, who could blame them? They had done their time.

Focusing In On Famous Studios

The early Famous Studios cartoons were much like the last group of Fleischer films (1941-1942) that had preceded them. After all, the same sets of creators were involved with both.[6] But there were signs that these creators, building on the changes to the characters that had previously taken place and understanding the new WWII-shaped world, knew that things couldn't be exactly the same.

So, the Famous Studios creators pushed the envelope of acceptable violence when a giant chewed away on Popeye *(Ration for the Duration)*, and when Popeye intentionally shot his little buddy, Shorty, with a revolver at the end of a cartoon *(Happy Birthdaze)*.[7]

And that envelope of cartoon violence continued to be pushed. In *Puppet Love*, Popeye makes an unconscious Bluto, whom he has turned into a marionette, hold a knife to Olive's neck and threaten to cut her head off. Later, an awakened Bluto punches Popeye into a street lamp where it looks like Popeye is being electrocuted.[8]

Pop-Pie A La Mode finds the sailor on an island of hungry cannibals who force-feed him to fatten him up in a sequence that makes some viewers nauseous. The tribe then uses a mallet to pound him flat, shaping him into what looks like a steak. Poor Popeye appears to be literally (excuse the pun) dead meat! When spinach finds its way into his mouth, something happens that can be interpreted one of two ways. Either the spinach begins working to spring Popeye back into shape, or the sailor steak begins to bubble and sizzle and rise and fall as it cooks above the flames before the spinach takes effect. Gross, isn't it? In *She-Sick Sailors*, a physically-fit Bluto, posing as Superman, challenges Popeye to deflect bullets. Popeye gets all rubber-limbed and scared, but stands there as Bluto machine guns him and leaves him for dead! These weren't the Popeye cartoons of old!

Also, love, lust, romance, and sex began to come to the forefront in these new cartoons. Even though Olive Oyl was drawn in a Fleischeresque style in *We're on Our Way to Rio* and *The Anvil Chorus Girl*, Popeye and Bluto have lustful reactions to her that would do Tex Avery's Wolf proud. Bluto has another wolf reaction to Olive Oyl in *Pitchin' Woo at the Zoo*, a cartoon notable because it gave Bluto and Olive more screen time alone together than any other Popeye cartoon had ever given them before. And in that cartoon, after Popeye is humiliated and left unconscious, Olive happily goes off with Bluto. It's only by accident that Olive later is endangered and Popeye saves her. Up until that point, she wasn't about to reject the charming Bluto at all!

Tops in the Big Top is another significant early Famous Studios cartoon. In it, Bluto's reaction to Olive Oyl morphs him temporarily into a real wolf as he gives her a close once-over and leers hungrily at her derriere. Maybe Bluto has a good reason to go all lupine because, although Olive is very Fleischeresque in appearance, she does have an hourglass figure.[9] Also, her face is cute in some frames, particularly when she despairs, "Now the show can't go on!" As the story continues, ringmaster Bluto saves the day and becomes Olive's new partner so her act can continue. He whips off his ringmaster's suit and reveals a devastating bodybuilder's physique in an acrobatic costume. Olive swoons. However, Olive soon regrets teaming up with Bluto, as he binds her, makes a yo-yo out of her, and kisses her repeatedly against her will on the lips. As for an unconscious Popeye, whom Bluto had craftily framed as being a dangerous drunk, he gets thrown on

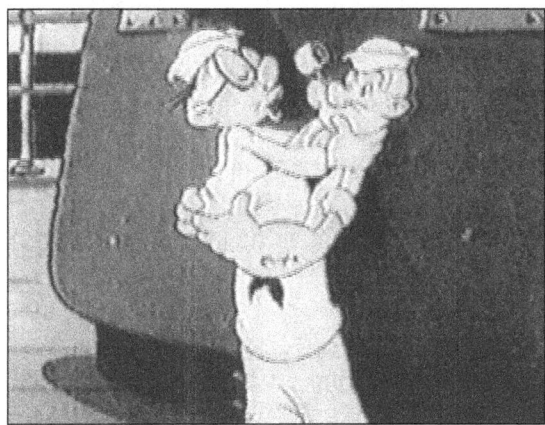

In an attempt to figure out what to do with Popeye, the creators introduced his irritating pal, Shorty (from *Happy Birthdaze*).

top of a cage of apes who reach up through a small hole and begin stretching and pulling Popeye down through it, accompanied by a sickening sound effect. Then they each grab a limb in an effort to tear Popeye apart! Horror, violence, sex, and romance — something for everybody!

Famous Studios was now on its way to finding its voice and tapping into the human heart, mind, and psyche. The ingredients that would enable the creators to cast their spells on us were there. The creators just needed time to learn how to combine them, how much of each to use when, and how to strengthen their potencies in order to enchant us. One other important ingredient in the cartoons' magic came later on and it, too, involved change.

Popeye the TV Man

In the late 1950s, Popeye went from being a movie star to being a TV star. The library of Popeye theatrical cartoons from both Fleischer and Famous Studios was sold for syndication and eagerly snatched up by television stations across the country. Popeye was a big hit on the small screen. Some stations continued to broadcast his cartoons until well into the '70s and '80s. Then the cartoons were seen on cable and satellite stations such as Superstation TBS, WSBK, TNT, Cartoon Network, and Boomerang!

Many viewers grew up having Popeye cartoons imprinted on their minds, having seen them over and over and over again. We viewers were also able to consider the Famous Studios cartoons as a body of work. Because of this, certain repeating themes became associated in our minds with the cartoons, so much so that if the cartoons shown on a particular day's Popeye program were the rare ones that deviated from, or downplayed, those themes, some of us felt cheated. We hadn't seen "real" Popeye cartoons!

Repeated viewings enabled us to come to conclusions about who the characters were. For example, since we repeatedly saw so many cartoons or scenes in which Olive Oyl was portrayed as a sweet-natured sex symbol, when we saw cartoons or scenes where she wasn't, we still tended to think of her that way. Or we wrote off those cartoons or scenes as aberrations, or we figured that Olive was having a really bad day in them. If Bluto reverted to being a bully instead of a sly manipulator in a particular cartoon, we figured he hadn't gotten enough sleep the night before.

Some of us began to ask questions of the cartoons and we tried to harmonize them. For example, how could Popeye and Bluto be meeting Olive for the first time in several different films? We each had our theories. Maybe some cartoons took place in alternate universes. Maybe some were apocryphal.

And repeated viewings of the films enabled viewers to notice things that might flash past someone watching a cartoon for the first, second, or even fifth time. So, we'd be in front of our TV sets and suddenly realize, "Hey! Cupid just ogled Olive Oyl before he made her and Dan fall in love!" or, "The way Olive's mouth is moving as she yells at Bluto makes it look like she's actually trying to kiss him!" Today, with VCRs and DVDs and "slow motion," "pause," and "frame advance" buttons, we can discover even more such "buried treasures."

Certainly the creators of the cartoons never dreamed that their films would ever be watched in this fashion. They couldn't have known that one day we would have access to the cartoons in our homes on our own equipment that would turn technicians of the past green with envy. And never in a million years would they have imagined that kids would be fed their cartoons over and over again. All they knew was that they were making theatrical shorts that would be shown in cinemas before feature films and that their cartoons should, therefore, appeal to adults. And after each cartoon had run its course, it would be shelved. Maybe it would be re-released for a short while in theaters again later, or maybe it would just gather dust. Its future was uncertain. So the creators were essentially making "one-shot" cartoons, not episodes of a TV series that had to fit into a strict continuity.

Nevertheless, the cartoons did have a sort of continuity of their own and they gave us glimpses into the minds of their creators and into the times which birthed them. And because we watched the cartoons over and over, we got chances to notice the little details the creators had slipped into the films probably as "in-jokes" to please themselves, or as ways to subtly enhance the audience's engagement with, and enjoyment of, the storylines, or as ways to thumb their noses at the censors.

Join me now as we examine the shelves of the Famous Studios alchemists and look a little more closely at the ingredients they stirred into their potent cartoons.

As this trade ad shows, the Famous Studios Popeye cartoons were very popular on TV. In fact, they are the longest-running cartoons in syndication.

COURTESY OF FRED GRANDINETTI

CHAPTER 2

Popeye the Complex Man

Many very young Baby Boomer boys, myself included, wanted to be Popeye when we grew up. However, as we aged, many of us suddenly found that we would rather be Bluto! This was due to the schizophrenic, or maybe a better word is "complex," way Popeye came across to us in the Famous Studios cartoons. And after years of watching those cartoons, we found that Popeye had become both the hero we loved and the guy we loved to hate at the same time!

Popeye the Reflecting Man

The Famous Studios Popeye works as a character who is a wish-fulfillment fantasy for his viewers. He reflects our dreams back at us. He is what we'd like to be.

He is the guy who can stand up to any bully.

He's the David who can defeat the Goliaths.

He can come back from any physical punishment and any personal humiliation. He can even return from the dead (or at least from "near-death" states)!

He's the nerdy little guy who, nonetheless, wins the beautiful girl away from the confident hunks.

He continually saves the day for his friends and loved ones.

He has super-strength.

He's got his own personal "genie in a bottle" — though in his case it is actually "spinach in a can" — which can transform him into whatever he needs to be in order to make everything turn out okay at the end of every story. The "genie" can even "cast a spell" on Popeye's enemies and make them do his bidding.[1]

And he's loved by little kids and dogs!

Who wouldn't want to be Popeye? But, read on!

Popeye the Nice Guy Man

Popeye can be a genuinely nice guy. He buys a television set for the local orphanage in *Punch and Judo*. He refuses to shoot the cute little gopher who has caused him nothing but trouble *(Gopher Spinach)*. When he is tricked into thinking he's killed Bluto, he throws his spinach away *(Friend or Phony)*.

In two cartoons, Popeye portrays heroes of the people. In *Robin Hood-Winked*, he's, appropriately enough, Robin Hood, who defeats the tax man and returns the money to the peasants. *Greek Mirthology* finds Popeye telling his nephews the story of his ancestor Hercules (played by Popeye in the flashback, of course) who went around doing good deeds all day long using his great strength.

Instead of being a bully, often Popeye is not looking for any trouble, just going about his daily life, at the beginning of a cartoon. He's watching Swee'Pea or his nephews when disaster strikes. Or he's just spending time with Olive Oyl when some guy will try to get rid of him and take Ms. Oyl for himself. Popeye didn't want to start anything, but he will have to finish it.

And the ultimate proof that Popeye is one heck of a nice guy is that he keeps coming to Olive's rescue even after she has thrown him over. He's the chivalrous knight who will always respond to the cries of a damsel in distress.

So, who wouldn't want to be Popeye? But, I repeat, read on!

Popeye the Victim Man

Some Popeye cartoons followed formulas that were also used in two other series produced by Famous Studios/Paramount. The *Casper the Friendly Ghost* cartoons often began with a lonely Casper desperately wanting a friend. He finds one and things are going along swell until the friend rejects him for some reason. A dejected Casper is alone again and our hearts go out to him until the friend gets into danger. Casper saves the friend, the two are reunited, and all is well as the cartoon ends. This familiar plot certainly echoes the Popeye/Olive Oyl relationship. Popeye and Olive will be together at the beginning of a cartoon. But another guy outclasses, dupes, defeats, dooms, and/or humiliates Popeye, so Olive rejects him and is now with her new boyfriend. Our hearts go out to Popeye. Then Olive gets into trouble. A spinach-powered Popeye comes to her rescue and then all is right with the world. Popeye is very much like Casper.

He's also a lot like Baby Huey, the gigantic, indestructible duck who has super-strength. In some Baby Huey cartoons, other ducks don't have much use for the big guy and try to ditch him until they get into a jam. Then Baby Huey saves them and is suddenly their hero. In the course of these cartoons, our hearts have gone out to Huey. In the cartoon *Patriotic Popeye,* Popeye's nephews don't want anything to do with their uncle and his "no fireworks" rule. Until, of course, their recklessness puts them in jeopardy and they need Uncle Popeye to save them. And our hearts go out to Popeye, who had been right all along.[2]

Poor Popeye not only was victimized by his friends and family members, but also by ruthless enemies. Jack Mercer, the actor who voiced Popeye and wrote some of the scripts, seemed to sum up the Famous Studios view of The Sailorman when he said that Popeye is essentially a nice guy who only strikes back as a last resort when he is pushed up against a wall. But, unfortunately for Popeye, his antagonists knew how to push and push and push. And this pushing sometimes had an unintended effect on us viewers. Instead of making us sympathize, and empathize, with Popeye or respect him for his restraint, it could make us despise him as a weakling. When, oh when, was he going to stand up for himself and stop all of the abuse?!

And we could easily label him as an idiot. If the villain has already tried several times in a cartoon to dispose of Popeye, shouldn't The Sailorman be suspicious when the guy is now seemingly offering to help him? But, no, Popeye always walks right into the traps set for him. And when is Popeye going to wake up, smell the coffee, and realize that Bluto isn't really his friend?

Instead of choosing to turn the other cheek, which would have been a selfless and noble thing to do, it often seemed as though the Famous Studios Popeye had no choice BUT to turn the other cheek, either because he didn't realize what horrible things were happening to him, or because he was helpless to really change anything before he ate his spinach.

Popeye the Addict Man

The Famous Studios Popeye could do amazing things without eating any spinach — or could he? While it is true that he performs incredible stunts like wrestling a polar bear, tunneling the length of an island, carrying a piano and Olive Oyl on a tightrope, surviving getting hit by a train, and matching Hercules feat for feat without viewers seeing even a glimpse of a spinach can, it's also true that in *Rodeo Romeo*, *Popeye the Ace of Space*, and *Toreadorable* Popeye has to put away a mouthful of the green veggie each and every time he does anything out of the ordinary. In *Punch and Judo*, he doesn't have any biceps and his arms are limp and droopy like soggy spaghetti before he eats spinach. And in *Popeye and the Pirates*, Popeye's pre-spinach punches don't affect Captain Pierre at all. After Bluto destroys the world's spinach crop in *How Green Is My Spinach*, Popeye has no super-strength and is helpless before Bluto's punching onslaught. And Popeye can't take much punishment after Bluto tricks him into throwing his spinach can away in *Friend or Phony*. Thus, we viewers came to suspect that it was spinach that was really special, and not Popeye himself. After all, when Swee'Pea, Olive Oyl, and animals ate spinach in a few cartoons, they gained Popeye's powers. So, maybe when we saw him do stunts without first eating spinach, he was actually secretly imbibing some off-camera.

His romance with Olive Oyl also seemed to depend on spinach. In *Jitterbug*

Popeye's spinach dependency reached absurd levels in cartoons like *Rodeo Romeo* where he couldn't do anything without first eating some.

Jive and *Parlez Vous Woo*, he can't turn her on at all or even be compatible with her without first gulping down a can. And when Olive dreams that she and Popeye are getting married in *Bride and Gloom*, she can't imagine Popeye working up the courage to say, "I do," without ingesting some spinach.³

The Famous Studios reliance on the spinach gimmick begged us to ask certain questions. Why doesn't Bluto always carry around a can of spinach so he could defeat Popeye? Why doesn't everyone in that cartoon universe routinely eat the green stuff and become supermen and superwomen? If spinach is what Popeye needs in order to gain the upper hand, why on earth does he wait until near the end of the cartoon to chow down on it? And why does he sometimes not have any on him? Yes, the delayed appearance of spinach increases the suspense in the cartoons, but it also makes Popeye appear to be not too bright.

Popeye the Childlike (or Childish) Man

In every one of his incarnations in print and on film, Popeye always had a childlike quality about him which is one of the reasons fans like him so much. Popeye takes pleasure in simple things and he views the world in his own unique way, much as a child would.

However, children can be annoying as well as endearing, and the Famous Studios Popeye could be very annoying indeed. He could repeat the same action over and over again, expecting Olive Oyl to be amused by it *(Quick on the Vigor)*. He insists on everybody doing things his way at a party even though Olive planned and hosted it *(Jitterbug Jive)*. He even horns in on other people's acts so that he can be the center of attention *(Rodeo Romeo, A Balmy Swami, Quick on the Vigor)*.

And, like someone who has not yet hit puberty, Popeye often acted as though he had no interest in romance and didn't even know what sex was.[4] So in *The Island Fling* and *Mister and Mistletoe*, he seems oblivious to that fact that Robinson Crusoe and Olive, and Santa Claus and Olive, respectively, are all wrapped up in, and around, each other. While it is true that Popeye and Olive Oyl share many lovey-dovey moments together in the Famous Studios cartoons, it is also true that Olive initiates some of them and that, in many cartoons, Popeye shows no interest in Olive as a woman at all. He acts like her brother or someone who is "just good friends" with her.

This might not be a problem, except that Bluto ardently pursues Ms. Oyl and has more intimate scenes with Ms. Oyl than Popeye does, and the plots of many of the cartoons revolve around romance. So, Popeye sometimes seems as though he doesn't belong in his own cartoon. He is like the kid brother hanging around while his sister and her boyfriend want to be alone. We viewers wished someone would give him fifty cents to go outside and play.

Popeye the Establishment Man

Q: What do Popeye and Arthur "The Fonz" Fonzarelli of *Happy Days* fame have in common?

A: They started out as counterculture figures but, over time, became spokesmen for the status quo. Early in their "careers," they would have joined kids and teens who were skipping school or thumbing their noses at authorities or staying up to all hours partying and making a racket. Later on, though, they became the ones trying to convince youngsters and teenagers to stay on the straight and narrow.

In the case of the Famous Studios Popeye, he became the one who tried to get his nephews to stop playing music and go to bed *(Me Musical Nephews, Riot In Rhythm)*, to eat spinach instead of hamburgers *(Spinach vs. Hamburgers)* or ice cream *(Greek Mirthology)*, to sit quietly *(Popeye Makes A Movie)* and stay out of his way *(Tots Of Fun)* while he was working. But when these cartoons were sold to television, the audience for the films was primarily children and young people, and we didn't want to be told, "Sit down and shut up! Eat nutritious foods! Go to bed early!" It was like watching cartoons about our parents and teachers!

And Popeye became the one who would try to stop the fun before someone got hurt. So he wouldn't let the nephews keep a horse they rescued from the glue factory *(Her Honor the Mare)*, or play with fireworks on the Fourth of July *(Patriotic Popeye)*. He tried to talk Olive out of enjoying her romantic fantasy *(Parlez Vous Woo)* and tried to take her away from the adventure and romance she craved *(Popeye and the Pirates)*. But in the world of animated cartoons, aren't characters supposed to be wild and wacky and devil-may-care? Popeye became a foil for other, more dynamic characters — including Bluto. He became the Squidward to everyone else's SpongeBob, and Porky Pig to everyone else's Daffy Duck.

Popeye's penchant for preferring old-fashioned things didn't help endear him to us either. He liked sedate classical music, old style dancing, and quaint party games *(Jitterbug Jive)*. He wore bathing suits that seemingly belonged to some other century *(Beach Peach, Beaus Will Be Beaus)*. And his idea of an exciting Fourth of July was watering his garden *(Patriotic Popeye)*. Even though he was drawn younger looking than he had been in the Segar and early Fleischer days, the Famous Studios Popeye acted like he was someone's elderly grandfather. We viewers related to Olive Oyl in the cartoon *Vacation with Play*, when she disparagingly called him "Grandpa" after he made it clear that all he was planning to do on their vacation was sleep. If Popeye had gotten his desire in that film, nothing exciting would have happened at all. We would have been treated to six minutes of Popeye snoring on screen![5]

Popeye the Cartoony Man

Popeye has always been a funny-looking character. That's part of his appeal. His adventures remind us that looks aren't everything, and that you don't have to be a matinee idol in order to have value or to find love.

But as Famous Studios gave Olive Oyl and Bluto makeovers and even drew them at times to be more realistic[6] than they had been in the past, the cartoony Popeye stuck out like a sore thumb. Did he belong in the same universe as those characters?

And Popeye, like many cartoon characters, could morph into other things and contort his body in strange ways. All well and good except that, as we shall see in later chapters, the Famous Studios cartoons seemed to want us to take their suspenseful situations and their romances seriously. Pretty hard to do when Popeye would pull on his facial features and ears, distending them so he looked like a dog *(Nurse To Meet Ya)*, or when Popeye made a golf tee out of his own bicep, then twisted his neck round and round like he was trying out for *The Exorcist* and unwound to get up the momentum to hit the golf ball using his pipe as a club *(Vacation with Play)*. As kids we might find such things funny, intriguing, or even a little gross and disturbing. As young adults we could appreciate the humor and inventiveness in those scenes, but feel as if they temporarily took us out of the romantic and suspenseful plotlines by reminding us that we were just watching a cartoon.

Spinach morphed Popeye even further. It turned him into a rocket *(Popeye Meets Hercules)*, a torpedo *(Beach Peach)*, a steel sculpture *(Friend or Phony)*, and turned his arm into a jackhammer *(Cops Is Tops)* and a two-thousand-pound

Spinach morphed Popeye into strange things, like this torpedo in *Beach Peach*.

weight *(Gym Jam)*. While it was cool to see what Popeye would be transformed into in order to turn the tables on the villain, this also made him seem like something other than human. Was he an alien, or a being from another dimension, or a changeling from folklore?

The scenes of wooing between Bluto and Olive Oyl, despite the slapstick, puns, and cartoon logic and cartoon universe physics sometimes employed in them, often came across as scenes between two human beings, a "real" man and a "real" woman. So, once again, Popeye sometimes seemed as though he, being a total and complete cartoon character, didn't really fit in his own films!

And Famous Studios would sometimes have Popeye open both of his eyes! Segar's Popeye lost an eye during the most terrible fight (and most fun) Popeye ever had. But the Famous Studios Popeye evidently had two good peepers. He just walked around with one squinted shut most of the time. Hardly an attractive thing to do!

Popeye the Cross-Dressing Man

Males dressing as females have been a staple of comedy since forever. But the Famous Studios Popeye took this to new levels.

In *Too Weak to Work* and *Popeye and the Pirates*, the sailor dresses as a woman in order to trick, and get the best of, his foes. Bugs Bunny used to do this sort of thing, too, but Popeye was supposed to be a rugged he-man with super strength. It shouldn't have been necessary for him to have to resort to this. In *Popeye and the Pirates*, Captain Pierre is Popeye's physical superior, but instead of chowing down on spinach to get more strength, Popeye dons a dress, hat, and petticoats to vamp him and his crew. While there is something humorous about a supposed man's man having to resort to using his softer side to face the villains, and the pirates going all gaga over Popeye's non-existent sex appeal (they must need glasses!), there is also something a little creepy about this.

And creepy describes the scene in *Popeye's Pappy*, in which Popeye dresses as a native girl to seduce his own father into leaving an island paradise and returning to civilization with him!

Add to this the scene in *Puppet Love* where Popeye paints his toenails and the one in *Cops Is Tops* where he, as a male, joins the women's division of the police force wearing a skirt and a blouse, and we could come to the conclusion that maybe Popeye enjoys being a girl![7]

Popeye the Pseudo-Bluto Man

The Famous Popeye sometimes had a hard time winning Olive's heart, or even attracting her and turning her on, until spinach turned him into a sort of "mini-me" version of Bluto, the guy who can get Olive's motor running just by acting naturally. So, since cool hipster Bluto sweeps Olive off her feet in *Jitterbug Jive* and dances up a storm with her, Popeye's spinach has to transform him into a "reet neat" zootsuiter. And when Bluto imitates the suave, sophisticated TV star, The International, that Olive has a crush on in *Parlez Vous Woo*, spinach gives Popeye a tuxedo and a more refined manner. Bluto is a rodeo performer in *Rodeo Romeo*, a matador in *Toreadorable*, and a magician in *A Balmy Swami*. In each cartoon, he has Olive's attention. Spinach gives Popeye the ability to match Bluto's stunts and, in the latter two cartoons, even gives him new duds to go along with his new skills.

But if Popeye needs to become Bluto in order to win Olive and has to have the "magical" help of spinach to do so, who really is the guy that Olive is in love with? Who is the most naturally compatible with Ms. Oyl — Popeye or Bluto? And what is poor Popeye going to do when the effects of the spinach wear off and he reverts back to being himself?

Looked at one way, these cartoons show us that Popeye can beat Bluto at his own game. Looked at another way, these cartoons prove that Bluto, without having to rely on strength and ability enhancement from an outside substance, is really the better man, and is Olive's ideal mate. So how were we supposed to feel relieved when Olive ended up with The Sailorman at the end of the cartoons?

The Famous Studios cartoons made us viewers sometimes want to cheer Popeye and sometimes want to jeer him, often during the course of a single film! And they could make us sick of Popeye. But that was okay because there were more interesting characters to watch on the screen — Olive Oyl and Bluto, two of the hottest animated stars of all time! Let's turn our attention to them now.

Spinach gives Popeye a tuxedo so he can compete with the sophisticated Bluto in *Parlez Vous Woo*.

CHAPTER 3

"What a Feminine Female!"

"You're probably going to think I'm crazy," my friend at college sheepishly said to me one night as we were discussing TV and movie stars we had crushes on, "but I used to lust after Olive Oyl." I didn't think he was crazy at all. In fact, I knew exactly how he felt.

But maybe you don't know how he felt. Maybe after you read that first paragraph you concluded my friend and I *were* crazy! If so, you probably have in mind the whiny, flat-chested, rail-thin, dowdy, spinsterish Olive Oyl with the big nose, plain face, and severe ponytail hairstyle who has appeared in comic strips and comic books for decades and who starred in the Fleischer and Hanna-Barbera cartoons.

But let me introduce you to a different incarnation of Olive Oyl who was very attractive indeed and who was a big part of the appeal of the Famous Studios cartoons. Ladies and Gentlemen, may I present the Famous Studios Olive Oyl, The Sexiest Cartoon Woman of All Time!

Extreme Makeover: The Olive Oyl Edition

In the 1945 Famous Studios cartoon, *Mess Production*, a different Olive Oyl debuted. This Olive Oyl had fuller, fluffier hair, a young pretty face, curves where there should be curves, and even a shapely bustline! For maybe the first time in history, viewers could truly relate to Popeye and Bluto as they went crazy over her, and we didn't doubt that she could make a factory whistle come to life to give her a "wolf whistle." And this Olive Oyl wasn't a one-shot fluke.

Though a few more films would be released that featured the plainer Olive, the new, more alluring version eventually became Famous Studios' normal way of depicting Ms. Oyl. So, audiences watching a Popeye cartoon would usually be treated to an Olive Oyl who had a face that was never less than cute and often was quite gorgeous. Chances are she might also have curvy hips, and/or an hourglass figure, and/or luscious legs, and/or a beautifully shaped derriere, and/or a well-endowed chest. Sometimes even her trademark big feet would be gone, replaced with dainty ones in high heels.

Why did Famous Studios give Olive Oyl a makeover? As was said in an

The new version of Olive Oyl makes her debut in *Mess Production.*

earlier chapter, the times were changing and the creators had to compete with the cartoons from studios on the West Coast which featured pretty girls. Also, perhaps the creators wanted to really "sell" their plots that had Popeye and Bluto competing for Olive, and the stories where a guy would spot her and it would be love (or at least lust) at first sight. And Olive's new appearance added to the suspense of the cartoons by raising the stakes. If Popeye lost her now, he'd be losing a real prize, not a strange character whose appearance and mannerisms were off-putting, to say the least. Jack Mercer, the voice of Popeye and the writer of some of the cartoons, said that the studio got complaints from females who wanted to see Olive Oyl get better treatment. And Famous Studios did employ some animators who loved to draw "off-model," that is, they would ignore the sheets of drawings they were given which were supposed to be models for them to follow, and put their own exaggerated spins on the characters.

Whatever the reasons, the "babe version" of Olive Oyl was here to stay during the Famous Studios era, and beyond. When the made-for-TV Popeye cartoons from King Features Syndicate followed in the early 1960s, their Olive had the Famous Studios' hairstyle and pretty face. Once in a great while, their Olive was even drawn with curves, a figure, and nice legs. So, the influence of Famous Studios lingered on.[1]

The Amazing Morphing Olive Oyl

Young male Baby Boomers who tuned their television sets to Famous Studios Popeye cartoons in order to girl-watch were sometimes disappointed, or at least confused. A film might showcase the pretty Olive Oyl for a scene, or

Olive's makeover reached its zenith in *Parlez Vous Woo*.

some frames, only to then switch over to a somewhat plainer-looking Olive for another scene or other frames, then suddenly the gorgeous Olive would be back. And so on and so forth. What was going on? Was this a curse from the Sea Hag? Not exactly.

More than one artist worked on each cartoon. Some artists' Olives were more attractive than others'. Also, cartoon characters tend to change during the course of a film depending on the needs of scenes, situations, and gags. So when characters scream, their heads and mouths might suddenly become gigantic, or when short characters get courage, they might swell to gargantuan proportions. Likewise, when characters are humiliated or scared, they might shrink down to the size of a mouse. So when Olive Oyl needed extra sex appeal, the Famous Studios artists would give her some. If she needed to show a little leg or some cleavage to get a guy's attention, they gave her a leg and some cleavage to show. And, when the creators needed Olive to be dumbstruck, or ripping mad, or flabbergasted, or even to fade into the background for a moment or two in order to make a gag or scene work, they would draw her accordingly.

Another reason scenes and frames of a less-dazzling Ms. Oyl found their way into cartoons featuring the Olive who made males' eyes pop out of their sockets might be that the creators wanted some continuity between the older, more traditional Olive of Segar, the Fleischers, and the printed page, and the newer pulchritudinous Olive Oyl. After all, the Famous Studios cartoons were originally made for movie theaters. So, there was a chance, in the 1940s and '50s that someone seeing a Famous Studios film hadn't viewed a Popeye cartoon in quite awhile. The creators may have wanted that audience member to be able to recognize Olive Oyl as Olive Oyl, and not think that Popeye had found a new girlfriend. An example of this might be the first time Olive appears in the cartoon *Wigwam Whoopee*. She's taking a shower in a waterfall and we're seeing her silhouette. (And, don't worry, censors, that's all we see!) At times the silhouette is as curvy and appealing as a Hollywood starlet's would be. At other times, it is painfully thin. The cartoon's creators may have wanted viewers to realize that the maiden in this natural shower was Olive Oyl and not a new character invented for the cartoon.

There were cartoons in which Olive was pictured as being beautiful from start to finish. The supreme example of this is 1956's *Parlez Vous Woo* with an Olive Oyl who could hold her own against any other past, present, or future animated beauties.

But even while watching scenes or frames of the blander-looking Olive, viewers could still find themselves attracted to her. This is because the Famous Studios creators had given her another kind of makeover to match her new lovely looks.

The Reincarnation of Betty Boop

Olive's looks weren't the only thing that made male characters in her films (and viewers as well) exclaim, "What a doll!" Her creators had given her a personality transplant.

Traditionally, Olive Oyl had been whiny, complaining, nagging, and overwrought. But the Famous Studios Olive was cheerful and fun-loving, enjoying life by throwing herself completely into it. She sang and danced and skipped, even when she was doing mundane tasks like the laundry, or giving her dog a bath, or setting the table. Her motto could be summed up by a line she said in *Vacation with Play*, "Let's live!"

Over time in the Famous Studios cartoon, Olive's personality became an appetizing mixture of the sweet young thing and the saucy siren. She was the tantalizing paradox of a totally innocent total flirt. So, on one hand, she could be happily overwhelmed by the attentions of Robinson Crusoe *(The Island Fling)* or a handsome lifeguard *(Beach Peach)*, as if initially not believing they could be interested in little ol' her. She could naively believe that Crusoe invited her alone to his place and got her on the couch, just so he could show her his etchings. She could be unaware that a rich count was ogling her *(The Royal Four-Flusher)*. But, on the other hand, she could also do a "Claudette Colbert" and strike a pose by the side of the road, lifting up her skirt to show off her legs, in order to stop a fleeing bank robber in *Cops Is Tops*, and confidently compete for the attention of an athletics instructor against other girls in *Vacation with Play*, use body language to convey her interest and availability to a hot air balloonist in *All's Fair at the Fair*, and give a masculine Santa Claus a suggestive, submissive giggle while inviting him to "Drop in any time at all" in *Mister and Mistletoe*. Her personality was that of the childlike, yet all-woman, sexy characters that Marilyn Monroe

A Betty Boop-like Olive Oyl from *Olive Oyl For President*.

portrayed in such films as *Some Like It Hot* and *The Seven Year Itch*. In fact, Olive became much like the very first animated sex symbol, Betty Boop, who may have inspired Miss Monroe's sexpot persona.

Betty and Olive enjoyed flirting and being romanced and even getting physical to some degree with men, but they weren't going to share their full "Boop-Oop-A-Doop" with just anybody or everybody, though it seemed as though almost every male in their worlds wanted them to. This sense of morality endeared them to viewers.

Both Betty Boop and Olive Oyl caused inanimate objects to come to life to wolf whistle at them and ogle them. And, stepping in to preserve and protect Ms. Boop's and Ms. Oyl's modesty and virtue were helpful, observant small animals and other objects that suddenly came to life. It was as though the universe itself was in love with these women and was watching out for them, keeping the slobbering males of their worlds from succeeding in compromising them.

And, like Betty Boop, Olive's mannerisms were ultra-feminine. She would blink her long-lashed eyelids, wiggle her hips as she walked, hug herself with delight, curtsy, coyly withdraw a little from a guy's advances while still letting him know his affections were definitely welcome, put her hands on her hips, give a cute little pout when things were going wrong, etc.

The connection between Betty Boop and the Famous Studios Olive Oyl is actually a direct one. Many of the Famous Studios creators had started out at the

Fleischer Studios where the Boop cartoons were made. Some had even worked on the Boop cartoons. So, when they thought of sexy animated females, they would naturally think of Betty and model the new Olive Oyl after her. And with 1944's *The Anvil Chorus Girl*, the woman who had been the main voice of Betty Boop, Mae Questel, returned to voice the Famous Studios Olive Oyl for the rest of the run of the Popeye series.

Now, if you only know the older Mae Questel as Aunt Bluebell from the Scott Towels commercials, or as the actress who portrayed Woody Allen's mother, or as senile Aunt Bethany in *National Lampoon's Christmas Vacation*, you might have a hard time believing that she could pull off the part of a vivacious fair maiden. But she was quite pretty when she was younger and got her start in show business by imitating, and looking like, singer Helen Kane, who was the real-life inspiration for Betty Boop. Mae once said that, when she was younger, she *was* Betty Boop, in that she was always joyfully singing and dancing and bopping around. Perhaps Mae's advent at Famous Studios was one of the reasons the creators eventually changed Olive Oyl and put the character in more and more Boop-like plots and situations. After all, if Betty Boop herself is working for you, why not use her to full advantage?

Upon her arrival at Famous Studios, Mae began by using the traditional Olive Oyl voice that she had used when she had earlier voiced Popeye cartoons featuring the homely Olive for Max and Dave Fleischer. But as Olive's looks and personality changed, so did Olive's voice. Sometimes Mae would give the voice a Boop-like quality for some lines, but use traditional Olive tones for other lines in the same cartoon. In other films, Olive's voice became an appealing mixture of Betty Boop and traditional Olive Oyl. And sometimes Olive's voice would just be pure, out-and-out Betty Boop. Nobody could vocally convey both innocence and sex appeal like Mae Questel! She enhanced Olive's allure considerably and some of her lines, like the breathy, "I don't believe it!" in *A Wolf In Sheik's Clothing*, or the sneeze under the waterfall in *Pre-Hysterical Man*, are among the sexiest ever recorded on film.

O.O.O.P.S. and Other Considerations

Another reason audiences bought into the idea that Olive Oyl was attractive was what I call the Olive Oyl Outfits Psychological Syndrome, or O.O.O.P.S., for short. Famous Studios dressed Olive in the kinds of clothes that audiences saw movie starlets, pretty sitcom stars, pinup queens, models, and beautiful dramatic actresses wearing — evening gowns, short shorts, bikinis, two-piece swimsuits, cowgirl duds, blue jeans, nurses' uniforms, slinky songstress dresses, revealing hillbilly and island castaway togs, etc. And the male characters in the cartoons and the plots of the stories always treated Ms. Oyl as though she was just as stunning in those outfits as her real-life counterparts were. So viewers began to see Olive in this light as well. And we began to associate Ms. Oyl with those other women and put them all in the same category — "Glamour Girls." Even if she was drawn Fleischeresque in some scenes, as long as she was wearing those outfits, her appeal for us was increased. And the Famous Studios artists could draw a "babe version" of Olive Oyl that belonged in those clothes when they wanted to. Check out Olive's long shapely legs displayed as she's wearing short, short, short shorts at the end of the archery scene in *Vacation with Play*, or the way her safari pants and harem girl outfit show off her figure in *A Wolf In Sheik's Clothing*, or her evening gown clinging to her shapely derriere as she grooves to Popeye playing the cello in *Symphony In Spinach* and falling down off her shoulders when she's at the piano with Bluto, or another evening gown showing off her voluptuous chest in *Parlez Vous Woo*, for a few examples.

The fact that practically every male in the Famous Studios Popeye universe desired her also made Olive Oyl attractive to viewers. Since television viewers from the 1950s through the 1970s day after day watched guys in the cartoons salivate over Olive, it was easy for them to convince themselves that she was desirable. The guys in the films that desired her were strong male figures, in many cases cultural icons of masculinity — Bluto, Superman, Hercules, Tarzan, rich playboys, sheiks, lifeguards, athletic instructors, body builders, romantic French men, pirates, cowboys, etc.[2] If these types of guys found Olive Oyl irresistible, who were we to argue with them? Instead, we found ourselves in agreement. And there were cartoons where those guys choose Olive Oyl over other beautiful women. (See *Popeye Meets Hercules*, *Vacation with Play*, and *Beach Peach*.) Olive, therefore, had to be something special.

And when those guys got together with Olive, sparks would fly, and how! It's a wonder that the film in the movie projectors didn't melt! I'll talk more about the hot, passionate, and romantic situations and locales Olive found herself in when we come to Chapter Six. For now, though, sexy is as sexy does, and the fact that Olive was the female lead in sexy storylines increased her sex appeal beyond that of animated babes from other studios who tended to be just eye candy inserted into the middle of cartoony situations. Take for instance, Tex Avery's Red character in MGM's justly famous *Red and the Wolf* films. Though Red attracts males and does provocative dances, we never see anybody wooing her or getting intimate with her. The focus in those cartoons is on the males' exaggerated reactions to her and their frustrations when she proves to be unattainable. But in the Famous Studios Popeye cartoons, males would not only react to Olive Oyl, but then they'd spend the bulk of the cartoons trying to seduce her — and succeeding admirably! Consider Pearl Pureheart in the *Mighty Mouse* cartoons. Yes, Oil Can Harry lusted over her, but never did much to win her. His idea of romance was to kidnap her, sing threats to her, and listen as she, in turn, sang out to call on Mighty Mouse for help. One of the most popular modern cartoon beauties, Jessica Rabbit, of *Who Framed Roger Rabbit?* fame, turned guys on, but they didn't do the same for her. She was a "one rabbit woman." And when Marvin Acme played "pattycake" with her, that's literally what he did. If Bluto ever invited Olive to play "pattycake," viewers would know that he meant something else entirely!

The males in the Famous Studios cartoons addressed Olive Oyl using such terms as Babe, Sugar, Beautiful, Doll Face, Sunshine, Angel, and even the provocative and racy Bait. And the titles of the cartoons sometimes signaled to us that Olive Oyl was a woman who caught the eye of males around her — *The Anvil Chorus Girl, Shape Ahoy, Beach Peach, The Farmer and the Belle*. Males would make comments about her looks and parts of her anatomy:

> "Dem pins [legs] sure bowls me over."
> "I'd like to teach that figure a trick or two."
> "My weakness is a pretty face!"
> "What a doll!"

Hearing these kinds of words and phrases applied to Olive led viewers to want to use some appealing adjectives of their own to describe Ms. Oyl.

But some members of the general public might have less complimentary things to say about Olive Oyl. This is because they don't understand her as she is in her Famous Studios incarnation.

Accentuate The Negative?

The stereotypical view of Olive Oyl goes like this: "She's a man-crazy, fickle flirt who is always dumping poor Popeye for another guy. But then when the other guy just wants a kiss, she rejects him and yells for help."

It is true that, in every one of her incarnations, Olive could throw Popeye over in an instant, and that she enjoyed guys and getting all romantic with them. It's also true that she can scorn her new lovers and scream for Popeye to come to her rescue. But these aren't necessarily negative traits. In fact, the Famous Studios cartoons found ways to turn them into pluses and enhance Olive's appeal even more.

Far from being committed to Popeye and breaking that commitment whenever a cute guy winks at her, the Famous Studios Olive Oyl seems to view Popeye as just one possible steady boyfriend among many. So she happily dates Bluto in *Puppet Love, Cookin' With Gags, Beaus Will Be Beaus*, and *The Crystal Brawl*. And it was the case that whichever guy, Popeye or Bluto, asked her first got the date (*Mister and Mistletoe, Parlez Vous Woo*), and that she couldn't decide between the two of them when they were asking for her hand in marriage *(Nearlyweds)*! In many cartoons, Popeye and Olive seemed more like "just good friends," or like "brother and sister," than sweethearts. So in her view and in the minds of viewers, Olive was free to hook up with someone else.

And most of the time in the Famous Studios films, the creators gave Olive good reasons to leave Popeye. He would reject, ignore, snub, endanger, or make fun of her. Popeye would take it for granted that he had a relationship with Olive Oyl and not put any effort into it at all. Or he would prove himself to be incompatible with her. She would move on to another guy, and then Popeye would suddenly want back into her life.[3]

The roving eye of the Famous Studios Olive could also be seen as an aspect of her appealing personality, rather than as a character defect. Her love of life, her big dreams and willingness to pursue them, and her desire to throw herself totally into what she was doing meant that she could get swept up in romantic fantasies and swept off her feet by guys who seemed to be willing and able to offer her more, more, more, more of life and love.

When she would later reject those same guys, Famous Studios usually made us feel that she was justified.[4] A guy might get too violent or mean with Popeye in front of her.[5] Or a guy would try to force her into things and situations she wasn't ready for.[6] Or she'd find out that her date had lied to her. And so Olive would stand up to these men, which further enhanced her appeal to the audience. Olive wouldn't be pushed around by males, no matter how attractive they were.

Olive the Feminist?

Some feminists and groups that promote women's rights and women's health issues have used Olive Oyl as one of their icons. If they had in mind the Famous Studios version, it's easy to see why.

The Famous Studios Olive Oyl ran for president long before any real-life woman ever thought of doing so. Despite Popeye's concern for her safety and his belief that she couldn't handle it, Olive also served as a policewoman, and an extremely competent one at that. And she refused to let Popeye mock her desire to learn how to drive. She also owned and managed a farm and a ranch, was co-owner of a saloon, and was the singer/leader for her own band, doing her own hiring and firing.

Even though every incarnation of Olive Oyl has yelled for help, it's been an ongoing joke, from the Segar era up through today, that she doesn't always need it. In the Famous Studios cartoon, *Beaus Will Be Beaus,* Olive punches Bluto out by delivering an uppercut. In *I'll Be Skiing Ya,* while she's screaming for Popeye, she's keeping Bluto at bay by using his head as a punching bag and giving him a few kicks as well. And in *Jitterbug Jive,* she's fending off Bluto, who is suddenly all lips, hands, and arms, quite well until she becomes ensnared in a string of hot dogs.

And then there are the fan-favorite cartoons in which Olive Oyl eats the spinach and saves the day.[7] In *Fireman's Brawl*, she downs a can of the green stuff to save herself and the boys when her boiler blows up after Popeye and Bluto have

A spinach-powered Olive Oyl prepares to battle Possum Pearl in *Hill-billing and Cooing*.

failed to stop a fire from consuming her house. Olive also eats spinach in *Hill-billing and Cooing* to escape from a trap and stop a burly, homely hillbilly gal, Possum Pearl, from marrying Popeye. The idea of Olive Oyl, a character traditionally portrayed as being thin, suddenly sprouting muscles and gaining super strength has intrigued fans of female bodybuilding. Maybe Olive even inspired some early female bodybuilders, because the "Olive eats spinach" cartoons came out long before there even was such a thing as female body building. One can find pictures and stories done by fans on the Internet of an Olive Oyl bulked up to degrees far beyond anything the animated cartoons ever attempted. Fans have taken the idea of a muscular Olive Oyl and have run with it, or should I say, "pumped it up?"

The various ways that the Famous Studios Olive Oyl was depicted as being empowered make her seem much more contemporary than the earlier Fleischer version was. Despite the '40s and '50s slang, styles of dress, cars, and decor, many Famous Studios cartoons seem like they are taking place today. Olive seems like a thoroughly modern girl, and so modern viewers are drawn to her.

But enough about The Sexiest Cartoon Woman. Let's now turn our attention to the second sexy member of the Famous Studios Popeye love triangle — Bluto.

CHAPTER 4

"Ooohhh, You Handsome Samson!"

When Bluto debuted in the Thimble Theater comic strip by E.C. Segar, he was said to be "lower than bilge scum, meaner than Satan, and stronger than a small ox." Anyone who read this strip, and saw the hard-edged pirate swear to kill Popeye, had little trouble believing that Segar's description was true. Likewise, viewers of the earliest Fleischer Popeye cartoons, seeing the gruff, tough bully beating on Popeye or angrily advancing on Olive Oyl, could say, "Amen!" to Segar's words. About the only redeeming feature the character had was his ox-like strength. Aside from that, he was rotten to the core. And his scruffy appearance and black heart gave him absolutely zero sex appeal. Bluto was just someone for the viewers to root against.

However, viewers of the Famous Studios cartoons might come up with other ways to describe the version of Bluto that appeared in those films. Let's let Popeye and Olive Oyl themselves describe him as they lead us into the next section of this chapter.[1]

"What a Chunk of Beef, Olive! What developkment! What Eye-Tomic Energy!"

"Hubba, Hubba! Woooo! What a Physical Phenonemum! Mmm, That's My Meat!"

The Famous Studios creators would have fit right into today's health-conscious culture because when they took over the character of Bluto, they began slimming him down. And as his waist got smaller, his chest and arms began to gain more definition. And what definition! It was obvious that Bluto had been working out and could rely on his powerful muscles, not just on throwing his weight around, to defeat his enemy — namely Popeye. And he could make the ladies, especially Olive Oyl, swoon.

Bluto's spectacular, devastating physique is notably on display in films like *She-Sick Sailors, Tops In The Big Top, Shape Ahoy, Safari So Good, Pre-Hysterical Man, Popeye Meets Hercules, Snow Place Like Home, Beach Peach, Quick On*

An example of the bodybuilding Famous Studios Bluto from *Swimmer Take All.*

The Vigor, Vacation with Play, and *Swimmer Take All.* Bodybuilders looking for inspiration can find it by viewing these cartoons. In fact, many boys growing up watching cartoons featuring the Famous Studios Bluto were indeed inspired to try and match his look by weight training and/or bodybuilding.

Speaking of which, the Famous Studios Bluto predicted with remarkable precision what chemically-enhanced bodybuilders would look like a half-century later. The Famous Studios creators seemed to thoroughly understand the potential for human muscular development. And just as they seemingly intended Olive Oyl to be the sexiest girl in her cartoon universe, so they wanted Bluto to be the universe's best-built man — and a decided contrast to Popeye.

Aside from his huge forearms,[2] the pre-spinach Popeye often has no muscular definition at all. Bluto, though, had thick, broad shoulders and exaggerated deltoid muscles; a 2-1 waist-to-chest differential; a pyramid shape set off by well-developed latissimus dorsii and an expanded ribcage; huge arms with bursting biceps and defined triceps.

Clearly the prototype for this new Bluto was the bodybuilder John Grimek. Grimek won the Mr. America title in both 1941 and '42 and, much like Arnold Schwarzenegger in a later era, changed and heightened public perception of bodybuilding. He had the developed "traps" and "lats" that were almost entirely lacking in earlier physique culturists. His massive chest and small waist were also somewhat revolutionary for their day and almost certainly were major influences in the creation of Bluto the bodybuilder.³

But the creators of the Famous Studios Bluto had other inspirations as well. They looked at the handsome leading men of the silver screen and began drawing Bluto accordingly. In fact, in *Shaving Muggs*, after Bluto shaves his beard off, he

The Rock Hudson Bluto of *Shaving Muggs*.

looks like Rock Hudson! But bearded or not, the Bluto in the Famous Studios cartoons was very different than the Fleischer Bluto had been. The earlier Bluto appeared to be as old as the Fleischer Popeye and to have had a very rough life. He looked like he was spoiling for a fight and had already been in one too many of them. His countenance had a dark, edgy quality to it. In the last of the Fleischer cartoons, his appearance changed to be that of a big goofball. Though some early Famous Studios featured the goofy Bluto, and the Famous Studios Bluto could indeed wear expressions of pure hatred and evil on his face, in most of his films and scenes he had manly good looks and a swashbuckling twinkle in his eye. He was the attractive rogue to Popeye's clueless, cartoony-looking Boy Scout. And he knew how to use the chiseled features of his face and body to full advantage. This Bluto was The Handsomest, Sexiest Cartoon Male of All Time!

A Bluto By Any Other Name

Before we go any further in our discussion of Bluto, I need to clarify just who I'm talking about when I use the name "Bluto," because there are many males in the Famous Studios cartoons who could go by that moniker.

There is the Bluto who's a sailor, like Popeye, and who either travels with him, or lives in the same town of Bridgeport, Connecticut, that Popeye and Olive do.

But there are cartoons where Bluto is playing other characters in the storylines. He's not a sailor and is meeting Popeye and Olive Oyl for the first time. These characters may have names that contain the word "Bluto" in them. Examples would be Bluto the Bravo in *All's Fair at the Fair*, Dangerous Dan McBluto in *Klondike Casanova,* and Señor Bluto from Brooklyn in *Toreadorable.*

Some of Popeye's antagonists, like Mr. Lifeguard from *Beach Peach,* aren't Bluto.

Or they may not and instead be called something else entirely, such as Robinson Crusoe in *The Island Fling*, Mr. Instructor in *Vacation with Play*, Count Marvo in *The Royal Four-Flusher*, and Hercules in *Popeye Meets Hercules.*

And then there are Popeye's rivals who aren't Bluto. They usually have been blessed with good looks and super strength like Bluto, but if the Famous Studios cartoons were live-action films these characters would be portrayed by different actors than the actor who plays Bluto. So Famous Studios gave us Pierre the trading post proprietor in *Snow Place Like Home*, the sheik in *A Wolf in Sheik's Clothing*, Mr. Lifeguard in *Beach Peach*, Count Noah Count in *Double-Cross-Country Race*, etc. All of these men have "the spirit of Bluto" and are cut from the same cloth as Bluto, even though they aren't, in fact, Bluto.

In this chapter I am referring to all of Popeye's antagonists when I use the name "Bluto." It makes things easier for you and for me. You would get tired of reading things like, "Bluto, the guy who lives in Bridgeport, and all of the other various characters he plays, and Pierre the pirate captain, Chief Shmohawk, Mr. Lifeguard, etc. were all sneaky." And I would get tired of writing long, long sentences. Plus, our heads would hurt.

Being headachy and tired is no way to appreciate all of the aspects of "Bluto." So, let's understand that "Bluto" in this chapter stands for a lot of characters, take some aspirin, and get back to having some fun as we examine the personality that amped-up Bluto's sex appeal even more.

"You're So Vigoroso!"

The Famous Studios Bluto, like its Olive Oyl, pulsates with life. He throws himself completely into whatever he's doing, and enjoys it thoroughly, whether it be making love to Olive or trying to obliterate Popeye. He will tolerate no distractions and will let nothing keep him from his goals. And he's willing to overcome any and all obstacles to get what he wants. We hardly ever see Bluto giving up. By contrast, in *All's Fair At The Fair*, *Alpine For You*, and *The Royal Four-Flusher*, we see Popeye hanging out by himself, dejected, depressed, and frustrated after being dumped by Olive Oyl. If Bluto were in that situation, he wouldn't waste time moping. He'd be planning his next move. And there are easier conquests in the Famous Studios universe than a girl who has a protector with a magic green vegetable that makes him invincible, yet Bluto keeps coming back to Olive again and again. Though other women throw themselves at him, he wants, and thinks he deserves, The Sexiest Cartoon Female of All Time, and he won't stop until he wins her.

Bluto is a self-made man. He doesn't resort to spinach in order to get his physique, or his skills, or his mannerisms and personality, or his wealth, or his new clothes, or his passion the way a certain one-eyed sailor, whose name we won't mention, does. No, Bluto works for these things, and, obviously, if his massive muscles and his dance moves and musicianship are any indication, he works really hard. The aforementioned one-eyed sailor just reaches for a can opener! And there are cartoons in which Bluto, without chemical enhancement, is a formidable opponent for the sailor even after the latter consumes his spinach. In these, Bluto puts up quite a fight, and it's only the sailor's boxing skills, or maybe a lucky punch, that defeats the he-man. In *The Island Fling*, for example, Robinson Crusoe not only holds his own against a spinach-powered Popeye (oops, I said the name), but actually belts the sailor away and leaves him momentarily stunned! It's only as Mr. Crusoe is plunging down a waterfall that Popeye, standing on a ledge, manages to land a superpunch that sends Crusoe flying.

And Bluto was an ardent, supremely passionate lover.[4] He was attentive because he focused right in on Olive Oyl. And though he could be the very picture of consuming male lust, he could also be very gentle and tender.[5] Sometimes he might act as though he was trying to pick up a girl at a bowling alley, but he could also be very suave, sophisticated, and charming. Olive gets him turned on in ways few cartoon males ever get turned on. And, in many cartoons, he is willing to enter Olive's world and fulfill her dreams and fantasies. He's ready, willing, and totally able to be anything she needs him to be. Rather than this being a sign of a weak man at the mercy of a woman's whims, in Bluto's case it demonstrates his strength. He is purposely choosing to become Olive's dream man as a way of getting exactly what he wants — namely Ms. Oyl. And in the majority of cartoons, he fulfils her dreams just simply by being himself. He's the dynamic type of guy who will overwhelm Olive — and she will love it!

All of these things make Bluto a very real threat to Popeye. But there's another factor which seemingly dooms the sailor — Bluto's cunning.

"That Sneaky Snake!"

The Famous Studios Bluto can manipulate Popeye and Olive Oyl because he is smarter, and worldlier, than they are. He knows how to use their basic psychologies. Bluto can count on Popeye's "nice guy-ness" to ensure that the unsuspecting sailor will walk right into a trap. And Bluto understands, and shares, Olive's lust for life and excitement. So, since he is in tune with her, if he offers her the kind of zestful relationship she craves, she will fall for him.

Instead of just going around bashing and bopping people and things, the Famous Studios' version of Bluto often relied on trickery. And he could pull off his deceptions with all of the glibness and skill of a seasoned con man. So, cartoons could feature Bluto framing Popeye as an incompetent drunkard (*Tops in the Big Top*), or as an uncaring, unfeeling lout of a jokester (*Nearlyweds*), or as a two-timer (*Abusement Park*), or as the one who endangered Olive's life (*Beach Peach*). The films weren't only about Bluto dropping anvils on Popeye's head.

Bluto was also a quick study and could improvise on the spot. He was keenly aware of his environment at all times. He would readily use objects around him to fool, and/or eliminate, Popeye, and to flirt with, and seduce, Olive Oyl. For example, he turns a tennis game with Olive into a sexy give-and-take, and maneuvers her into position for a kiss in *Vacation with Play*. He then unscrews the metal knob off a pole and uses it as a "tennis ball" to defeat Popeye and send the sailor off to slumberland.

Perhaps the supreme examples of Bluto showing his superior intellect are found in those cartoons where he takes away Popeye's spinach (*Taxi-Turvy, Toreadorable, Rodeo Romeo, Cookin' With Gags, How Green Is My Spinach, Lunch With A Punch*). Although, it doesn't really take a rocket scientist to figure out that if there's no more spinach, there's no more Popeye.

"Start Sizzlin', Sister!"

Cartoons that feature Bluto and Olive Oyl getting romantic can serve as cautionary tales to illustrate the moral that all that glitters is not gold. Bluto seems like the ideal date, and even ideal mate, until he reveals his darker side, usually toward the end of a cartoon.

Bluto, you see, like many of Shakespeare's fictional characters, has a "fatal flaw," an aspect of his makeup which will ensure that he will never totally succeed at keeping the hand of the fair Olive Oyl. In Bluto's case, his fatal flaw is impatience.

Badlands Bluto wises up and pours out Popeye's spinach in *Rodeo Romeo*.

In film after film, Bluto is doing a fine job of getting rid of Popeye, at least temporarily, using a series of successful gambits, when suddenly he will get sick and tired of The Sailorman popping up again and again. Letting loose his rage, Bluto will then blatantly try to eliminate Popeye right in front of Olive. She becomes horrified, tries to stop the violence, and utterly rejects Bluto. Bluto loses Olive in this manner in cartoons like *Snow Place Like Home*, *A Wolf In Sheik's Clothing*, *Beach Peach*, and *Jitterbug Jive*. If Bluto had just kept subtly moving Popeye aside, one of his ploys would have worked permanently and Popeye wouldn't be back to interrupt again or Olive would have forgotten all about The Sailorman or would have been fooled into giving Popeye the heave-ho. And Olive would have been Bluto's girl forever.

In other cartoons, Bluto is doing just fine with Olive Oyl, wooing and winning her, even getting intimate with her, when suddenly his lust gets the better of him and he speeds up the process. As Bluto tries to force her to do things she's not ready for yet, he loses her heart — and the rest of her, too, for that matter. If only Bluto had continued to take his time with her, the endings of the cartoons would have been very different. An example of Bluto's impatience losing him the girl can be found in *Klondike Casanova*. Dangerous Dan McBluto and Olive Oyl are already attracted to each other when Cupid appears and bops each of them over the head with his mallet, infusing them with love. Then, in a racy, yet sweet, scene that some fans think is filled with visual double-entendres, Bluto and Olive playfully "fight" and flirt over the cherry from an ice cream soda. Both are reveling in the provocative process, when Bluto suddenly grabs Olive and his message to her appears as words on his teeth, "Start Sizzlin', Sister!" Olive tries to escape by "remembering" that she has a mah jong appointment. And we don't blame her. Another example is Count Marvo getting a willing Olive alone in his penthouse apartment in *The Royal Four-Flusher*. She's putty in his hands. That is, until he tricks her into putting on a self-locking straitjacket! Then she's justifiably scared. If he had skipped the bondage bit and kept up the wooing, Olive would have soon given him all the kisses he ever wanted.

When viewers see Bluto blowing it, they shake their heads and sigh over what might have been. Some even make up their own endings for the cartoons and have Bluto controlling himself so that he, not Popeye, ends up with Olive Oyl. After all, two such dynamic, seemingly made-for-each-other characters like Bluto and Olive *should* wind up together! And Bluto's impatient actions seem somewhat out of character and beg to be erased. Would hardworking, hard-exercising, self-disciplining, meticulously planning, sly, romantic Bluto really throw everything he had been building toward away in a few seconds of uncontrolled rage or lust? Maybe not.

But maybe he would. Bluto, even though he is a cartoon character, is also only human. Tragically, he may be one of the most human of all the cartoon characters. This is one reason why we humans can relate to him so much and wish things could be different for him.

And speaking of humans...

The Man Behind The He-Man

Credit for making the Famous Studios Bluto such a memorable character must go to the animators, writers, and directors, of course, but also to the voice artist and character actor, Jackson Beck.

Beck had a long career in show business doing everything from being the announcer on the *Superman* radio program and playing various roles on that show, to narrating Woody Allen's *Take the Money and Run*, to doing the voice-overs for Dominos Pizza commercials.

Beginning with 1944's *The Anvil Chorus Girl*, Beck voiced Bluto for the rest of the Famous Studios era and went on to perform Brutus' lines in the King Features Syndicate made-for-TV cartoons. Jackson was actually smaller in stature than Jack Mercer, the man who voiced Popeye, but you'd never know it listening to Beck's confidently male Bluto voice. Also, though this may come as a disappointment to Popeye cartoon fans, Beck and Mercer liked, respected, and trusted each other in real life and were friends. And, no, they didn't fight over Mae Questel.

Jackson Beck expertly portrayed every vocal nuance from A-Z that the creators and their storylines required of Bluto. He could have a macho swagger in his voice, or sound genuinely bewildered. He could be lascivious, or romantically tender and gentle. He could put a dangerous edge to his voice, or drip with sincerity. And when Bluto was selling Popeye or Olive on one of his schemes, Beck sold the audience on the con as well! Beck's Bluto also had the most cruelly evil laugh in cartoon history.

It has been said that a hero is only great if he has a great villain to overcome. If that's the case, then Popeye is truly great, because Bluto is the greatest animated villain of them all.

In our next chapters, we'll examine what happens to Popeye, Olive Oyl, and Bluto in the Famous Studios cartoons, how they were used in the storylines, and what effect this all had on the viewers.

CHAPTER 5

Lights! Camera! Violence! Suspense!

Perhaps Famous Studios should have been more appropriately named "Infamous Studios" because it became infamous for the levels and types of violence that it portrayed in its cartoons.[1] And its Popeye films certainly weren't exceptions to the rule.

Well, Blow Me Up...Er, I Mean... Blow Me Down!

The characters of Popeye and his supporting cast certainly were no strangers to violence. Segar's Popeye was a rough-and-tumble old sailor who frequently found himself in life-threatening situations. But the violence in Segar's comic strips was very surreal. Though it would grab the readers' attentions and sometimes their emotions as well, it was of such an exaggerated nature that, though the reader may gulp when first confronted by it, the laughs wouldn't be far behind. So, Segar's Popeye walks around with multiple bullet holes in him and the only time this bothers him is when he takes a drink, because then he leaks. He plugs up the holes with corks and then has no problems. Or Popeye has his neck broken in a fight, so he jams a broom handle down the back of his shirt to provide him with stability enough to continue the battle and win. Or Popeye can be literally wrapped around a ship's mast by Bluto, but recover to beat the big pirate using his "twisker punch."

But, while watching a Famous Studios Popeye cartoon, viewers may not only gulp at some of the violence, but gag because of it as well. The violence can be utterly shocking, even sickening. And rather than provoke laughter, it causes us to shake our heads because it comes across as something that somebody thought would be hilarious, but instead is just a failed joke that sits there inert, like a lead balloon. We don't turn away from it, though, because as a failure it succeeds as a monument to the way in which humans can thoroughly miss the targets they are shooting at. Characters in the Famous Studios cartoons, by contrast, would rarely miss when they shot actual guns or cannons at each other. And even though the violence could be horrifying at times, we viewers wouldn't turn away from it any more than we could turn away from watching a train wreck. Extreme violence and destruction fascinate us.

So, our television sets would be like the eyes of a snake, hypnotizing us with images of Popeye being munched on by giants and dinosaurs, or Bluto's internal

The Popeye steak frying over the fire in *Pop-Pie A La Mode*.

skeleton shattering into hundreds of little pieces, or a tribe of cannibals overcoming and binding Popeye and then literally pounding him into a steak and frying him in a pan over a fire, or a lion chomping down on Popeye's neck, forcing the sailor to fill the inside of its mouth with smoke from his pipe, which causes both the lion and the orchestra on the soundtrack to turn a sickening shade of green, or a strangled Popeye being stuffed into a piece of artillery and fired into the mouth of a deep tomb because he's seemingly dead and will be buried forever, or the symbols of Bluto's pain and unconsciousness — stars — being used to decorate Popeye's Christmas tree, or Bluto gleefully and mercilessly machine-gunning Popeye down in cold blood.

The Famous Studios brand of violence had a more visceral impact on viewers than did the violence in the Segar strips and the mayhem from other animation studios. This is because Famous Studios often took things a step or two or three beyond "slapstick" into another indefinable territory altogether. Also, the Famous Studios cartoons seemed to take place in a world that looked more realistic than the world of Segar's comic strip and the Great Depression-inspired world of the Fleischer films. And the Popeye characters were human beings trying to do each other in, not anthropomorphic cats and mice, roadrunners and coyotes, etc.

Animation historian Leonard Maltin has said that a weakness of the Famous Studios Popeye cartoons is that they took themselves too seriously. But what he views as a weakness, others see as strength, particularly in the areas of violence and romance. The underlying tone of seriousness in the cartoons, in spite of the puns, spoofs, and slapstick, increased the suspense of the films, which added to the viewers' pleasure immensely.

"Ooohhh, What a Whale Of A Spot I'm In!"

Nobody watching a Bugs Bunny cartoon was ever on pins and needles wondering whether Yosemite Sam was really going to kill Bugs or not. But, like the animated feature-length films from Disney, the Famous Studios Popeye cartoons made us care about the fate of make-believe characters and to feel for them. A Famous Studios cartoon got us to suspend belief and to worry if perhaps Popeye really was a goner because he wasn't going to get his spinach in time and/or if Bluto was actually going to succeed in forcibly having his way with a helpless Olive Oyl. And we would get feelings of suspense and tension even when we were watching a cartoon for the third, fourth, or five-hundredth time!

Partial credit for this must go to Musical Director Winston Sharples. His orchestra took the menaces very seriously, and he would arrange and compose music for the cartoons as though he was scoring thrillers.

Credit must also go to the writers who kept coming up with effectively dire straits for Popeye and Olive to find themselves in, and to the animators who gave the characters convincing expressions of terror, pain, sorrow, desperation, hopelessness, and, in the case of the villains, malevolence, and lust-about-to-be-sated.

And certainly credit must also go to the voice artists and the emotions they conveyed. A word must be said here about Jack Mercer, the voice of Popeye.[2] No one could groan and moan in pain and futility the way he could. And when Popeye yelped, "Yeow!" Mercer put his heart and soul behind it. Even Popeye's "Huh?" when he realized he was in trouble didn't just express dawning understanding, but also that he was feeling as though he was overwhelmed, outclassed, and doomed.

Popeye's world was a world full of threats. During the World War II years, those threats mainly took the form of exaggerated, stereotypical, offensive caricatures of our nation's enemies shooting at Popeye or trying to torpedo him or otherwise subdue him. But it was hard to feel much of anything while watching those cartoons, because the enemies were portrayed as such complete blundering goofballs that viewers knew it was only a matter of time before All-American Popeye would defeat them. Which, of course, was the point of those cartoons: We were going to win the war, Audiences, so don't worry. When Popeye worked or relaxed on the homefront during the war, the threats came from his nephews, or small animals, or his slacker pseudo-buddy, Bluto. Once again, it was hard to take these threats seriously because Popeye's antagonists were tiny and cute, or large and not overly bright. And nearly everything was played for laughs. But when the new version of Bluto began coming onto the scene,[3] Popeye was faced from then on with enemies who wouldn't hesitate to

Popeye gets stabbed in the chest by Bluto in *Parlez Vous Woo*.

trap, incapacitate, injure, kill, or even totally obliterate him. With this new male force loose in the world, viewers knew that Popeye had better watch his step. Each one could be his last. The cartoons perfectly conveyed this and heightened the viewers' suspense.

But the new Bluto wasn't just a formidable physical threat to The Sailorman. He was a romantic rival as well. And this, too, upped the level of suspense.

"You Won Me Heart, Babe!" "Oooo! Likewise, I'm Sure!"

In the Fleischer cartoons, Olive Oyl would have had to be a complete idiot to fall for the unsavory Bluto, and viewers knew that she wouldn't ultimately choose him over Popeye. But in the Famous Studios cartoons, it often seemed as though Olive would be a complete idiot *not* to fall for Bluto and choose him over Popeye! And Olive, though sweet and naive, was no idiot! So, while watching the Famous Studios cartoons, viewers could fear that Popeye really was going to lose Olive Oyl forever. And though we viewers were privy to scenes that revealed Bluto's black heart, Olive wasn't. So Olive was about to give herself to The Wrong Guy! The villain was going to win! And viewers would get anxious feelings whether they were watching a cartoon for the first, third, or three-hundredth time.

But the viewers' anxieties would sometimes do a 180-degree turn. Because Olive Oyl and Bluto were so smoking hot together and were so perfect for each other, viewers started to get anxious that Bluto and Olive wouldn't end up together! Maybe Popeye was actually The Wrong Man! The Better Man, Bluto, was going to lose! So viewers found themselves hoping against hope that maybe this time Popeye *wouldn't* eat the spinach! Yes, Bluto did nasty things to Popeye, but Popeye also did nasty things to Bluto. And besides, Bluto was just playing by the rules of the cartoon universe where characters are allowed to beat each other silly. So viewers started to root for Bluto.[4] And these thoughts and feelings kept returning with multiple viewings of the cartoons.

Credit for this romantic tension once again goes to the writers, directors, animators, and voice artists. And Musical Director Winston Sharples, whose scores and choices of background music for scenes involving Olive Oyl and Bluto could be tenderly amorous or saucily sexy, leading us to believe that the two characters belonged together alone somewhere with their love and their passion.

Speaking of these things, let's now focus our attention on the sexy and romantic elements of the Famous Studios Popeye cartoons. Have a cold shower standing by as you read the next chapter. You're going to need it!

CHAPTER 6
"I'm In the Mood for Love"

Some years ago a poster on the Internet mourned the state of current animated cartoons. He lamented that they weren't sexy, like the old Popeyes were.

Sexy? Popeye cartoons?

If the poster had in mind the Famous Studios films, the answer is, "And how!" Many Famous Studios fans have said that the cartoons helped jump start their puberty and that even today the films put them in the mood for love. And the cartoons accomplish this despite slapstick, visual and verbal puns, and hyper-exaggerated characters and situations.

So, light some candles, break out a bottle of wine, slip into something more comfortable, and come with me to the Casbah, as we experience the romantic side of Famous Studios.

"I Wish I Could Meet A Big Strong Sheik Who'd Kiss Me All To Pieces And Leave Me Soooo Weak!!"

The plots of many Famous Studios cartoons are taken right out of America's sexual fantasies:

> *A sheik sweeps a girl off her feet and carries her off across the desert to be his mate*
> *A beach bunny and a lifeguard cuddle on a blanket*
> *A magician hypnotizes a beautiful woman*
> *A rich, dynamic playboy overwhelms a young miss and invites her up to view his "penthouse in the clouds"*
> *Two castaways are alone on an island*
> *Tarzan finds his "Jane"*
> *An athletics instructor gives private lessons to a female vacationer*

A cute carnival/fair-goer and a performing strongman fall for each other
A sailor on leave gets a girl alone in a photo booth
A handsome, sophisticated TV star shows up at the door of his biggest fan
A pirate captain captures a boat and the heart of a fair maiden
A lumberjack takes the new camp cook for a canoe ride
A dashing Santa Claus gives a pretty girl a very Merry Christmas
A rodeo star lassoes a cowgirl
Hercules out-muscles the competition and moves in on a Greek miss
And many more!

These stories reflected, and sparked and teased, the dreams of adult viewers and introduced kids coming of age to cartoon plots that didn't have to involve wisecracking rabbits outwitting hunters in order to be thoroughly intriguing in new ways. And young people found their thoughts hurriedly going down these delightful and mysterious new pathways. While watching the films, the young had new emotions and feelings kindled, while older audience members had their fires stoked again.

"Must Have Class and Double In Brass"

Some of the credit for the romantic and sexy feel of many of the Famous Studios cartoons must go to Musical Director Winston Sharples. No matter what goofy, cartoony things were happening in the films, he and his orchestra took the romance seriously.

He employed many popular love songs of the day, some of which have become standards over the years: *I'm in the Mood For Love, Love In Bloom, To Each His Own, Cocktails For Two, June In January, Frankie and Johnny, By a Waterfall, Too Romantic, I Don't Want To Walk Without You, Welcome Sweet Springtime, Let's Get Lost,* and *Louise.*[1]

And Sharples would use soft or saucy versions of other well-known melodies and musical themes to convey amorous moods. For example, listen to the subdued, yet lively, rendition of *Jingle Bells* playing on the soundtrack as Bluto and Olive come together on the couch, and the tender, sensual version of *Deck The Halls* that accompanies them as they light the candles on the Christmas tree while flirting with a different kind of fire in *Mister and Mistletoe.*

Sharples would write or arrange themes that added spice when characters were initially attracted to each other, or that built to a pleasurable climax while Bluto[2] and Olive were coming together.

When the talents of Mr. Sharples were added to those of the artists, writers, directors, and voice artists who could expertly depict masculinity, femininity, lust, love, passion, tenderness, desire, satisfaction, flirting, desire — everything related to romance from A to Z — the result was cartoons full of sexual tension, and much of it centered on whether a guy would kiss Olive Oyl on the lips or not.

In cartoon after cartoon, Bluto and Olive would be interrupted before they could kiss on the lips. Here, Popeye comes between them in a scene from *The Island Fling*.

"Howzabout A Kiss, Babe?"

Looked at from one perspective, the whole question of whether Olive Oyl will get kissed or not can seem sweetly naive and old-fashioned to people in the 21st Century with our "enlightened" ideas, something that would scandalize only those of a bygone era, or excite children who have no experience with lovemaking. But looked at from another perspective, maybe the cartoons' creators knew something we have forgotten — that physical intimacy is supposed to be reserved for committed relationships and that even a kiss can link two hearts together in ways that we can't explain. Every kid watching Popeye cartoons knew instinctively that if Bluto kissed a willing Olive Oyl, it meant that she was now his girlfriend, not Popeye's, forever! So Popeye, or concerned small animals, or circumstances, would have to interrupt Bluto and Olive before that magic moment occurred, or all was lost! And the creators, in order to build up and prolong the tension and suspense, would sometimes wait until Bluto and Olive's lips were just starting to touch, or couldn't have fit anything but a sheet of paper between them, before the interruption came. And to make matters even more complicated and deliciously anxious, viewers often were actually rooting for Bluto to kiss Olive, so we kept impossibly hoping, even after seeing a cartoon umpteen times, that he'd taste those lips before Popeye got there.

The creators would let Bluto kiss a smitten Olive on the cheek, chin, forehead, shoulder, hand, arms, and neck, and would let him tickle, stroke, caress, and hug her. The couple could snuggle and hold hands. But the one thing that normally the couple couldn't do is kiss on the lips. Because this activity seemed to be forbidden, and it implicitly implied long-term commitment and an end to Popeye's chances with Olive, many viewers have wondered whether or not the creators meant for a kiss on the lips to symbolize sexual intercourse. If true, suddenly Popeye's desperate interruptions make even more sense. And we do know that in the '40s and '50s, movie studios took advantage of the new attitudes toward sex that were prevalent in America after the war. In films, sex could be hinted at, symbolized, euphemized, celebrated, and talked around and talked about, as long as things didn't get too explicit and as long as words like "sex" and "intercourse" were never uttered. So it is indeed entirely possible that Bluto kissing Olive on the lips was meant to convey that he was taking her "Boop-Oop-A-Doop" away.[3]

This may explain the feelings of horrified fascination that capture viewers watching those few and far between scenes in which Bluto actually does forcefully have his way with an unwilling Olive, repeatedly kissing her on the lips.[4] Our reaction to these scenes goes beyond just seeing a cad stealing some kisses from an innocent miss. We seem to know that we are watching something *verboten*, something we shouldn't be seeing, something that shouldn't be taking place.

It is true that, once in a great while, the Famous Studios creators let a guy kiss a willing Olive Oyl, but these instances are so rare that they stand out in our minds. And the unique circumstances surrounding the kisses could still support the ideas that kisses are something special and that they can symbolize long-term relationships (true love) or sex. In *Happy Birthdaze*, Olive gives Popeye's friend Shorty a friendly kiss and inadvertently turns him on in the process. Shorty kisses her in *The Marry-Go-Round* because he's demonstrating to Popeye how to be a great lover and how to get Olive to marry The Sailorman. Shorty's plan backfires as Olive then returns the favor, wanting him for her new permanent boyfriend. In *Puppet Love*, Bluto and Olive kiss, but she thinks she is kissing Popeye, so this doesn't seem so wrong to the viewers. (Both Olive and Bluto really enjoy that kiss!) *The Royal Four-Flusher* gives Olive a kiss that literally lifts her off her feet. She's happily overwhelmed by him and quickly forgets all about Popeye. In *The Fistic Mystic*, a fakir sweeps Olive into his arms, leans her back, and gives her such a passionate kiss that she literally melts. This is after he has asked her to stick with him and she agrees. Finally, in *Parlez Vous Woo*, the creators sneak in a quick sweet kiss between Olive Oyl and "The International" while they are waltzing together. It fits the film's context as Olive and "The International" are head-over-heels in love with each other and the cartoon is all about romantic encounters. And besides, you have to view the scene in slow motion/frame advance mode to really catch it.

In other cartoons, guys had chances to kiss a willing Olive Oyl on the lips,

The creators sneak a rare on-the-lips smooch between Bluto and Olive into *Parlez Vous Woo*.

with no Popeye around, and passed them up! The sheik kisses Olive on the forehead, and later on the chin, instead, in *A Wolf in Sheik's Clothing*. And the Magical Hypnotist kisses her on the cheek in *A Balmy Swami*. It's as though the creators suddenly woke up in those scenes and said to themselves, "Uh oh! We can't let happen what is about to happen, so we'll cop out instead!"

Of course, there are many cartoons in which tension and suspense surround Bluto's attempts to kiss an unwilling Olive. These scenes can sometimes be as appalling as the ones where he succeeds, because we still know that he is about to take something that isn't his to have. We want Popeye to rescue her. But...to be honest, sometimes we don't. Because sometimes it seems as if Bluto is taking the Rhett Butler approach to Olive Oyl. He's going to kiss her like she's never been kissed and she's going to find out that she likes it — and him! And maybe this wouldn't be so bad! The supreme example of this is found in *Vacation with Play* as the squirrels try to act out for Popeye what is going on in Bluto's cabin. The squirrel representing Bluto is repeatedly kissing the cheek of the upset squirrel representing Olive. Suddenly, the Olive squirrel dreamily gives in and enjoys the smooching. The implication is that this is what will happen between the real Olive Oyl and Bluto. She will eventually, happily surrender to him. (And Popeye is such a selfish jerk in that cartoon, that Olive would probably be happier, and better off, if she did!)

Love Knots or Nots

In order for Bluto to be able to at least start to kiss a rejecting Miss Oyl, Olive has to be helpless before him and incapacitated in some way. Therefore, Olive Oyl became the most tied up, bound, and immobilized cartoon female in history. And the creators came up with new ways to trap her as the wolf closed in for the kiss.

Sometimes Olive would just be tied up or encumbered with rope as in *The Island Fling, Rodeo Romeo, Tops in the Big Top,* and *Alpine For You*. But she was also lassoed by a string of redhots (*Jitterbug Jive*), stuck in a stove pipe (*Snow Place Like Home*), embedded in a block of wood (*Lumberjack and Jill*), locked in a straitjacket (*The Royal Four-Flusher*), sucked up into a vacuum cleaner's bag (*Silly Hillbilly*), and netted like a fish (*Vacation with Play*).

Sometimes Olive just couldn't escape from Bluto's strong arms (ex. *Symphony in Spinach, Pre-Hysterical Man,* and *Gym Jam*), or he would just carry her off to his place as she hopelessly struggled to get away (*Klondike Casanova, The Fistic Mystic, Safari So Good,* and *Robin Hood-Winked*.)

At other times, the creators would place Olive and Bluto in close quarters so she'd have nowhere to escape to. The couple winds up on the chair of a ski lift in *I'll Be Skiing Ya,* in the basket of a hot air balloon in *All's Fair at the Fair,* on a girder high above a construction site in *A Balmy Swami,* and stuck at the top of a Ferris wheel in a small seat in *Quick on the Vigor*.

In at least one instance, the creators' desire to get Bluto and Olive alone when she was seemingly helpless went way too far.[5] After Popeye is dispatched in *The Anvil Chorus Girl,* Bluto trusses Olive up on a pole, as though she were a side of beef, and then swaggers away with her, presumably to do anything he wants to her.

And speaking of scenes and cartoons which probably went too far...

"Wow! I Hopes Olive Ain't Overexposed!"

Famous Studios Popeye cartoons could convincingly portray tender romantic scenes. They could also explore the mysteries of the ways between a man and a woman. They could ignite some fun and harmless sexual fantasies. They could actually provide lessons and food for thought about what, and what not, to do while wooing. But like all human creative endeavors, they could also push the envelope until it ripped, and take things a step or two or twenty beyond good taste. There is something disturbingly human about the tendency to see how much can be gotten away with and the temptation to pull good things down into the gutter. The Famous Studios creators, alas, were human.

The "Wolf Reactions" that guys had to Olive Oyl were always a little risky, with the guys' bodies often stiffening and stretching out toward her, but in *The*

Royal Four-Flusher and, to a lesser extent, *A Wolf in Sheik's Clothing*, they are risqué, as well. In the former film, as The Count ogles Olive, the cigarette holder in his mouth points straight up. In the latter, when the sheik first sees, and reacts to, Olive, the sword sticking out from his waistband from his pants suddenly becomes visible and pronounced.

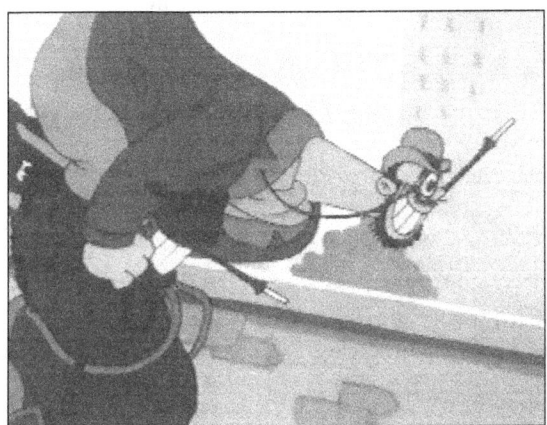

As the Count leans up and over his horse to ogle Olive Oyl, his cigarette holder rises *(The Royal Four-Flusher)*. An example of how the creators snuck things past the censors.

And Mr. Crusoe and the lifeguard ought really to watch their hands, and what those hands are doing and where they are going on Miss Oyl, as they snuggle with her in *The Island Fling* and *Beach Peach*![6]

The closest a Famous Studios cartoon ever came to doing everything short of spelling out the fact that Bluto was taking Olive to bed was in *Robin Hood-Winked*. Bluto carries Olive up a spiral staircase to his chambers in a castle as a resigned Olive yells to her lover, Popeye, "Farewell, Robin Hood, my beloved! Farewell!"

Some of the verbal puns in the films also stretched the limits of what could, and couldn't, be said. The title of this section of the chapter is a line Popeye says in *Pre-Hysterical Man*. It comes after he has tried to take Olive's photograph and she has fallen into a valley that time forgot. Rescued from death by a caveman, a swooning, willing Olive is being dragged back to his cave apartment to be his mate. She teasingly dangles one of her shoes from her foot. Popeye looks up from his camera and down into the valley and exclaims, "Wow! I hopes Olive ain't overexposed!" Maybe not yet, Popeye, but if you don't hurry she's going to be! In *Tar with a Star*, Olive needs help because Bluto is manipulating the piano she's hiding in, making her pop in and out as he goes for the kiss. She yells that he is "soft pedaling" her.[7]

These moments surprised and shocked me in the cartoons. You, however, might think my examples of the creators going too far are actually just cute, or even hot. And I might think any examples you would come up weren't dirty at all. But, if you watch the cartoons, I'm sure you'll at least agree with me that the gang at Famous Studios sometimes slipped some things past the censors — and that often the Famous Studios cartoons are actually red hot.

"Let's Make This A Hot Picture, Babe, and Burn Up the Camera!"

Many of the scenes between Bluto and Olive are smoking hot, or at least smoldering.

There's the scene in *Klondike Casanova* in which they are playfully fighting over Olive's cherry from a soda they shared. They look at each other with hearts in their eyes, they make goo-goo eyes at each other, and their foreheads rub together. The cherry becomes trapped between their two straws. They each pull their straws with their mouths, until they become like one being, each person bound to the other by the stretching straws, the elongating cherry, and their efforts which give them a measure of pain and of pleasure. Suddenly the suction joining them gives way and the cherry rolls down Olive's straw to her mouth. She drops the straw and balances the cherry on her puckered lips, offering the cherry, her lips, and herself to Bluto.[8] But, of course, Popeye has to intervene.

Then there's the tennis lesson scene in *Vacation with Play*. The back-and-forth of the ball over the net symbolizes the give-and-take between Olive and Bluto. They share the rapture of the game and of being together. Each volley brings them closer to the net and to each other until their rackets meet as though they are being linked together, trapping the ball between them over the net, as Bluto pronounces the score to be, "Love," and moves in toward Olive for a kiss. When she realizes what's going on, she doesn't duck or move away. She happily awaits the kiss and the match with Bluto. But, of course, Popeye has to intervene.

And there's the time Bluto is holding Olive suspended in water at the beach. His hands move up and down her as she tries out a new swimming technique. He tenderly, with a voice that nonetheless conveys desire and an invitation, says, "I'll show ya how to improve your stroke, Baby Face." But, of course, Popeye has to intervene.

Notice the pattern on display here?

The problem is that we viewers were having our fires lit along with Bluto and Olive, but Popeye came along and poured cold water on everything and everyone. We have felt the love and the sexual tension along with Bluto and Olive Oyl. Then we felt their frustration as well.

Many Popeye cartoons seem like a piece of music that finishes with an unresolved chord. Listeners wish someone would run to the piano and strike a few notes that would properly end it. Viewers of Popeye cartoons have followed plotlines that centered on Bluto and Olive coming together. But then the stories end with them apart?!?!? Where's the satisfaction in that? And so we composed new endings for the cartoons in our minds, or turned off our televisions, or stopped our VCRs, before Popeye's jarring notes could be struck.

It was so easy to root for Bluto in those films. The next chapter will examine some more of the reasons why.

CHAPTER 7

Shades of Gray Amid White and Blue Sailor Suits

While watching Popeye cartoons, who should the viewer be rooting for? The answer might seem obvious because "Popeye is the hero and Bluto is the villain." But in the Famous Studios cartoons, things aren't always so clear cut and black and white. There are shades of gray in the films, and because of this, viewers can find themselves switching loyalties continuously and can have endless debates with each other. The cartoons stay fresh because the viewers' perspectives constantly change, and there always seems to be another point of view to consider.

In this chapter, we'll look at the Famous Studios' incarnations of Popeye and Bluto a bit differently and be introduced to some of the fan debates.

"Eenie, Meenie, Meinie, Moe, I Shall Choose This Here Beau!"

First, let's ponder the reasons why Bluto[1] is considered a villain and compare the supposedly heroic Popeye to him.

1. Bluto is a villain because he won't take "No!" for an answer and tries to force Olive Oyl to do things she doesn't want to do. But in *Jitterbug Jive*, Popeye tries to completely take over Olive's party even though she protests, and her views and his aren't the same. In *Alpine for You*, Popeye refuses to employ a guide, though Olive wants one. In *Pitchin' Woo at the Zoo*, Popeye forces Olive to move along before she's ready.

2. Bluto is a villain because he resorts to violence to solve everything. But *Beaus Will Be Beaus*, *Cookin' with Gags*, and *The Royal Four-Flusher* show us that Popeye's first resort is to violence in order to handle problems.

3. Bluto is a villain because he steals another guy's girl. However, in *Wigwam Whoopee* and *Silly Hillbilly*, Olive is actually Bluto's girl until Popeye shows up on the scene. And in numerous cartoons, Olive rejects Popeye and is happy

with her new boyfriend when The Sailorman tries to horn in and break the couple up.

4. Bluto is a villain because he leaves Popeye in dangerous, humiliating, life-threatening situations. But in cartoon universes, characters are always trying to destroy one another. It's just standard operating procedure! Popeye does this, too. He leaves Bluto trapped in a flooded lighthouse with an angry swordfish *(Swimmer Take All)*, embedded in a stone wall as part of a mural portraying love slaves *(A Wolf in Sheik's Clothing)*, being chased by a giant buzz saw *(Lumberjack and Jill)*, and running from an amorous female gorilla *(The Island Fling)*, just to give a few examples.

5. Bluto is a villain because he cheats and lies and plays tricks in order to get what he wants. Again, this is normal behavior for cartoon characters, and Popeye himself uses deceit to win in *Beaus Will Be Beaus, Cookin' with Gags, Fright to the Finish, The Crystal Brawl,* and *Nearlyweds.*

6. Bluto is a villain because he stops Popeye from marrying a willing Olive Oyl. But Popeye stops Olive from willingly marrying Bluto in *Nearlyweds*. And Popeye interferes after Olive had accepted implicit, or explicit, proposals and is going off to mate with another guy in *The Fistic Mystic, Popeye and the Pirates, Pre-Hysterical Man,* and *A Wolf in Sheik's Clothing.*

7. Bluto is a villain because he endangers Olive's life. However, it's Popeye who places her in harm's way in *A Balmy Swami*. And both of the boys' antics and competitions put Olive in jeopardy in *Lumberjack and Jill* and *Fireman's Brawl*.

Hmm, Popeye isn't coming across as being much better than Bluto, is he? If Popeye does the same things, and exhibits the same attitudes, that define Bluto as a villain, what does that make Popeye?

How about if we try another tactic? Let's list some reasons why Popeye is a hero and compare Bluto to him.

1. Popeye is a hero because he saves Olive Oyl from danger. But actually, it's Bluto who saves Olive from drowning in *Beach Peach*, from being eaten by a crocodile in *Safari So Good*, from a dinosaur in *Pre-Hysterical Man*, from freezing to death in *Snow Place Like Home*, from going over a waterfall in *Lumberjack and Jill*,[2] from walking off a girder high above a construction site in *A Balmy Swami*, from Popeye's incompetence in *I'll Be Skiing Ya*, and from The Sailorman's boorishness in *Jitterbug Jive*. Bluto is preparing to rescue Olive from leopards in *Pitchin' Woo at the Zoo*, but Popeye stops him.[3]

2. Popeye is a hero because he liberates Olive Oyl from relationships with wrong guys and from abusive situations. But so does Bluto! He liberates her from…Popeye! The Sailorman is abusive, and/or selfish, and/or neglectful, and/or self-absorbed to the point of not even noticing whether Olive is there, and/or completely incompatible with her in films like *Vacation with Play, Jitterbug Jive,*

Parlez Vous Woo, She-Sick Sailors, A Balmy Swami, Quick on the Vigor, All's Fair at the Fair, and *A Wolf in Sheik's Clothing.*

3. Popeye is a hero because he stands up for the underdog. Well, Bluto is never seen doing that, but he did put aside his rivalry with Popeye to help fight our nation's enemies in *Seein' Red, White, 'N' Blue.* And the Famous Studios Bluto

Olive wants to have a swinging party in *Jitterbug Jive,* while Popeye just wants to force her to play old-fashioned games. It's up to Bluto to rescue Olive. This kind of thing happens frequently in the Famous Studios cartoons.

is generally a nicer guy than other incarnations of the character are. He rarely went around causing pain and destruction just for the fun of it. Instead, he was a guy going all out with a special goal in mind — getting a job, winning Olive, triumphing over his archenemy, etc.

4. Popeye is a hero because he's nicer to Olive Oyl than Bluto is. Well, Bluto can be *plenty nice* to Olive. That's how he wins her in the first place! And Popeye can be downright mean to Ms. Oyl. Popeye mocks her dreams and stands in her way of fulfilling them in *Olive Oyl for President, Cops is Tops,* and *Car-Azy Drivers.*

So who is the hero and who is the villain? Popeye and Bluto are like real human beings. Neither is perfect, but they are defined by which side — "The Light" or "The Dark" — wins out in their lives, or in a specific cartoon, most often. But granting this point makes it easy to root for Bluto in those cartoons in which he is demonstrating more heroic, "Light" side traits than Popeye is! And the debates rage over about who is the most heroic at any given moment and why.

Likewise, spirited discussions take place over which of Olive's suitors is really the best man for her in any specific cartoon, or if the Famous Studios films are considered as a whole.

Sometimes is seems as though the Famous Studios creators themselves were going back and forth in their minds about who the real hero of their cartoons was.

Sympathy for a Devil?

Three Famous Studios cartoons start out by focusing on Popeye's rivals. Two of the films show us how desperate these guys are for a woman and for some loving. A caveman carves pictures of beautiful girls in stone and then puckers up and kisses them, only to have them crumble away *(Pre-Hysterical Man)*. Robinson Crusoe spends his day reading a book of "Lovey Dovey Stories" and has pictures of pinup girls plastered all over his walls *(The Island Fling)*. Friday sings, "No one needed a gal like he did, he wanted to woo so." These guys achingly need Olive Oyl in their lives, and she soon arrives. Sympathy has been built up for these men, and the plots of their cartoons center on whether or not they will win the one they long for and get to "woo so" when they are alone with Ms. Oyl. Popeye's presence in the films seems unnecessary. The audience members (and, seemingly, the creators) are actually rooting for the caveman and Crusoe! Popeye is the interloper causing these guys to suffer. And *How Green Is My Spinach* opens with Bluto lamenting the number of times he's been beaten by Popeye and wishing things could be different. Audiences feel sorry for the big, beat-up lug. Later in the cartoon, when we find out that Popeye can't do anything at all without spinach, and Bluto displays his all-natural, incredible muscles with manly confidence, we want Bluto to pulverize The Sailorman. In this film, the creators seem to be pouring out their contempt for Popeye and their love of Bluto, until, of course, the obligatory "happy ending."

Winston Sharples' orchestra would often seem to be rooting for Bluto in the Bluto/Olive/Popeye love triangle. It would really put its heart and soul into the romantic music that enhanced the scenes of Bluto and Olive getting intimate. Often the orchestra was building its romantic themes to a satisfying climax as Bluto and Olive got closer and closer together. And the musicians would urge Bluto to hurry along and seal the deal with Olive before Popeye stuck his nose in where it didn't belong. But then jarring, even angry, notes would sound when Popeye, or something else, interrupted the love birds. The orchestra didn't believe that it was right for the wooing to end. Sometimes when Popeye did make the scene, or was compared to Bluto as the big guy was winning the heart of the fair maiden, goofy, or even embarrassed, versions of Popeye's themes could be heard on the soundtrack. The orchestra knew that Popeye was no match for Bluto in the lovemaking department. And the orchestra plays a happy tune as Bluto and Olive go off together after Bluto has finally gotten rid of his nemesis in *Beaus Will Be Beaus*. A jaunty, expectant version of "Here Comes the Bride" is heard as a tuxedoed Bluto and a wedding-gowned Olive Oyl head to the Justice of the Peace to get married in *Nearlyweds*. In those two films, the orchestra gives no hint at all that there's anything wrong with Bluto and Olive being together, and with Popeye being finally and completely out of the picture. The orchestra celebrates what's happening!

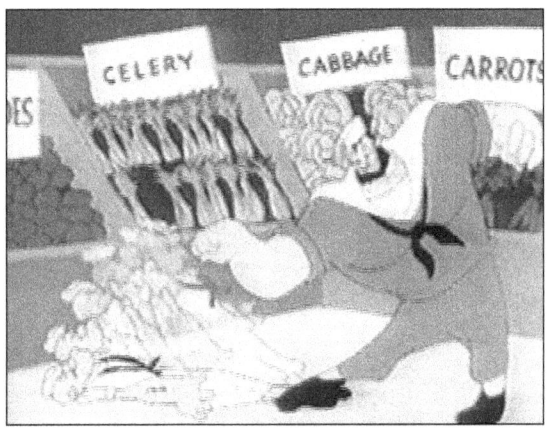

Bluto uses Popeye as a punching bag as the creators may be expressing their true feelings about Popeye in *How Green Is My Spinach*.

So, who did the creators like better? Who were they secretly rooting for? Popeye or Bluto? Let the fan debates continue!

Having examined the ingredients that went into the Famous Studios films, I'll now examine some specific cartoons in depth, keeping an eye on the characters, the violence and suspense, the romance, and the shades of gray and shifting loyalties in each film. Then we'll take a whirlwind tour through the rest of the Famous Studios Popeye cartoons, paying attention to those same elements.

Onward to Part II!

CHAPTER 8

The Island Fling (1946)

The Island Fling is one of the many films which features both the cute version of Olive (shown here) and the plainer version of Ms. Oyl, depending on the scene.

If you were seeking proof that the Famous Studios Popeye cartoons weren't made for children, you would have to look no further than this film. Though it features Popeye cheerfully overcoming obstacles and performing superstunts, sex and romance are the real themes of this cartoon. And most of the tension in it surrounds whether or not Mr. Crusoe will be able to make out, and mate, with Olive Oyl before Popeye interrupts.

The title card for the cartoon isn't anything special, but the title itself is. A "fling" implies an affair, a dalliance, a party, a time of joyfully abandoning yourself to love. A fling can be fun, but it can be dangerous, too, as during a fling a person may do what he or she normally wouldn't. And in this cartoon, it's Crusoe and Olive who have the fling. The title is all about them. The film was named for them. So where does this leave Popeye? Pretty much nowhere, as we will see.

The camera irises in on a tropical island in the middle of the vast ocean. There's a compound that's been built up on it. A closer look reveals that there are two mailboxes in front of the compound marked "Robinson Crusoe" and "Friday." The flags on them are down because this island is far off any delivery route. There's also a "Post No Bills" sign on the fence and a locked area labeled "Garage." The whole thing has been built out of logs, and pieces of wood and boards that no doubt drifted ashore from shipwrecks.

We're taken inside the compound to see Friday busily tidying up the place, sweeping dust under the rug while winking at us. Herman Mouse, in a cameo, emerges from beneath the carpet, angrily sweeping the dirt back out again. The compound is an appealing mixture of poverty, opulence, simplicity, and castaway ingenuity. Obviously some nice stuff has washed ashore over the years.

A word must be said about Friday. While he is drawn as a stereotypical caricature of a short Black tribesman and talks in a Buzzy the Crow[1] voice, he's not really offensive. He's more like the character of Rochester in the Jack Benny programs. Yes, he is an employee and a sort of servant to a white man, but at times in the cartoon it appears that he's wiser than his boss and may indeed just be playing whatever role is necessary for his own advantage.

These opening scenes are accompanied by a bright jazzy score featuring a song sung by Friday:

> "Oh Robinson Crusoe! Oh Robinson Crusoe!
> No one needed a gal like he did,
> He wanted to woo so!
> His faithful man Friday — that's me
> kept everything tidy.
> Yet he'd sigh for
> some Hidey-Ho-Oh
> Oh, Robinson Crusoe!"[2]

The orchestra and Friday obviously believe it would be a good thing if Robinson Crusoe could somehow get a girl. And the audience's sympathy is already aroused for Crusoe, even though we haven't met him yet. He's in the middle of nowhere, and according to the song, he's lonely, he's sexually frustrated, and there seems to be no hope of him ever getting a mate.

But wait! Friday is cleaning a window and then starts to walk away, but does a double-take. He looks out of the window again. Then he hurries to a phone and dials. The orchestra makes us feel that progress is being made.

We see Robinson Crusoe in a hammock[3] reading a book of *Lovey Dovey Stories*. Hanging up on the wall behind and beside him are pictures of glamour girls from magazines. One picture is just of a shapely female leg! The phone next to him rings. Friday's voice says, "Hey, Boss! Hey Boss!" Crusoe, still caught up in his romantic fantasies asks, "Who is it?" "Is you kiddin' Boss? There's only the two of us on this island. Look, there's a raft on the horizon!" Friday responds. A surprised Crusoe says, "A raft?" Then, while unconsciously showing off his muscular physique, he says, "Bring me telescope!" We see that Friday and Crusoe are actually standing right next to each other. "Here 'tis!" Friday hands it to him. Happy with anticipation, Crusoe brings it to his eye and leans out of an open window.

What he sees makes his eyeball sail out of the telescope to get a closer look. It then returns, and we get his view from inside the scope looking out. Olive Oyl and Popeye are on a raft. Olive is standing up, hopefully gazing off to the horizon. Popeye is sitting down with a disgusted look on his face. Even when Olive and Popeye are all alone together, they aren't really together in spirit. And Olive's apparent optimism here is a very endearing trait. As the orchestra arpeggios into a straight-forward version of *I'm in the Mood for Love*, the telescope changes into the shape of a heart and focuses in on Olive. To Crusoe, and to us, Popeye is unimportant. Mr. Crusoe uses the telescope to give Olive a close once-over while saying, "Ahhh! Mmmm! Dem pins sure bowls me over!"

Though Olive Oyl is drawn very Fleischeresque in this scene, the O.O.O.P.S. factor[4] kicks in, as she's wearing a tube/halter top, a short ripped skirt, and high heels. She's showing plenty of skin and leg. Girl-watchers who are disappointed with this scene need only wait a short while. Soon Olive will be drawn much, much, much better in this film.

Crusoe continues to react to, and be moved by, Olive. He leaps out of the window so that his toes land on its sill, which then supports his weight. His body stiffens, elongates, and stretches toward Olive while his face morphs into a wolf's. He lets out a long howl and then keeps on making lupine sounds of hunger, pleasure, and life. The telescope either acts as an extension of his male desires, or comes to life itself, as it, too, stretches out and then forms lips to sort of blow kisses toward Olive and give out an ecstatic expression of lustful appreciation — "A hubba hubba hubba hubba!" Wearing a look of famished, but enraptured, anticipation, Crusoe superzooms back inside.

He digs a sketchbook of etchings out of his Hope chest, which is next to his Crosby chest, and puts it on the table next to a couch. Then he superspeeds around the room bringing huge comfy pillows to the couch, so that whatever positions he and Miss Oyl will find themselves in later, whether seated, reclined, or lying down, they will both be extremely comfortable. He whisks a champagne bucket, filled with ice and a bottle, over. Then he brings a coffee table with glasses, flowers, and plates. Suddenly he gets an idea of how to top everything off. He winks at us and runs out of the picture.

We see him zoom over to his dresser where atomizers contain aftershaves labeled "Night in Paris," and "Morning in Brooklyn." Choosing a third one, he sprays its contents over himself saying, "Ahh, this scent'll send her, 'Schlemiel Number 49'!" He also dabs some behind his ears and, putting a finger to his lips, inhales some to freshen his breath. Then he rears himself up, puffs himself out, and does a "Tarzan flexing muscles" pose, quivering with barely-contained male energy. He whinnies like a champion stallion feeling his oats and ready to be a stud. All this has taken place while the soundtrack has kept on playing *I'm In the Mood for Love*. I'd say the orchestra was understating things! And we're about a minute and eighteen seconds into the cartoon and, so far, the emphasis has been almost exclusively on Mr. Crusoe and his desire for Olive. Popeye barely appeared for just a second or two.

Crusoe zips out of the picture. We then see him sliding down a twisting ramp and landing in the back seat of a convertible. "Hurry up, Friday!" he commands. "I'm jumpin', Jackson!" Friday replies and, bouncing off Crusoe's umbrella, lands in the driver's seat. Friday turns the label on his hat from "Stooge," past "Cook" and "Dish Washer," to "Chauffeur." He then propels the vehicle along Flintstones' style, using his feet. The car is actually only a few steps away from the beach. As Friday brakes with his feet, Crusoe has another wolf reaction to Olive, his eyes bulging out of his head.

And this time we can see why. Popeye and Olive are wading ashore. Popeye is in the lead, but the audience can be forgiven for not noticing him. Olive has a cute face, an attractive hairstyle, shapely breasts, and an hourglass figure in some frames. At one point, a beautiful blue butterfly appears briefly beside her. Popeye comes up onto the sand, but Olive stays just in the water. She draws herself up to her full height and puts her hands and arms behind her, waiting for Mr. Crusoe's welcome and being wide open to whatever he will suggest. And it's interesting to note that Olive makes the eager guy come to her. She doesn't rush toward him.

Popeye is approaching Crusoe, though. "Oh boy!" he had said while coming ashore. "Human inhabitants!" He offers his hand on an outstretched arm for a shake. Crusoe has his hand and arm out, too. He says in a sexy, playful voice, "Welcome to the island of Robinson Crusoe!" But he's not addressing Popeye. He walks right past The Sailorman, who has his eyes closed. Popeye strolls up to a monkey hanging from a tree branch and shakes its hand. The monkey promptly gives Popeye a big kiss on the cheek. Startled, Popeye realizes what has happened and looks toward where Crusoe and Olive are.

Speaking of Crusoe and Olive and of kissing, Olive is now standing in a flirty pose which shows off her curves. Her one hand is on her hip, her other arm has been offered to Crusoe. Her one knee is bent and she's up on the toes of one foot. The other leg anchors her to the ground, while the toes on its foot point right at Crusoe. He has gently taken her hand in his own left one, while his right hand walks its way up Olive's arm, accompanied by his lips. Yes, Crusoe is kissing his way up Olive, enjoying every second of it, and every inch of her! And Crusoe wants more and more. A pretty and cute-faced Olive is thoroughly enjoying herself, too, though she coyly asks, "Mr. Crusoe, must you schmooze so?" She gives a little laugh. She wants to be wooed, likes what he's doing, wants more, but doesn't want to be rushed either. She's telling him she's definitely interested, but that she's not a pushover. This makes her even more attractive to the audience. *I'm in the Mood for Love* is on the soundtrack again.

Crusoe has reached the top of Olive's shoulder as Popeye speeds into the picture. He pushes Crusoe away from Olive just as the next kiss would have landed on her cheek. Crusoe keeps trying to kiss Olive, but Popeye is between them now, shoving them apart. A couple of the smooches would have found Olive's mouth. Both Crusoe and Olive are upset and concerned by Popeye's sudden intrusion, and the orchestra inserts his theme song as an interruption. But Popeye doesn't seem to be reacting at all to the fact that Crusoe was sampling the delectable Ms. Oyl. He only wants a turn to be greeted! In fact, in this cartoon, Popeye shows no romantic interest in Olive at all. He just seems to be her good friend. Popeye never has a clue what Crusoe and Olive are doing. Seeing as how this cartoon is all about desire and whether or not it will be fulfilled, who should we root for to "win" — the passionate Crusoe or the passionless Popeye?

The Sailorman happily offers his hand again and says, "Popeye's the moniker. Shake!" We see that Popeye is wearing black socks. Remember this, as it will be important later on. Trust me! Anyway, Crusoe grabs Popeye's hand with a superior sneer and crushes it in a literal vice grip. Popeye writhes in pain. Then Crusoe lifts him off the ground and repeatedly shakes him in the air so hard that it sounds like Popeye's bones are coming loose and rattling inside of him. Then Crusoe smashes Popeye face-first to the ground and leaves. The orchestra has believed that Popeye was being done in, but after being momentarily stunned, Popeye starts lifting himself up and says with a smile, "A real friendly handshake!"[5] Then he's surprised because Friday, now with a Chef's hat on, is tinkling a triangle and calling, "Come and git it!"

Now we're treated to a scene that is a masterpiece of comic timing, as well as being sweet and sexy and pushing the envelope a little. As a romantic, tropical version of, you guessed it, *I'm in the Mood for Love* plays on the soundtrack, Crusoe is pushing Olive's chair up to a small round table set for an intimate dinner for two. Olive, who had been adrift at sea with no provisions, is delighted. "Good, good, good! It's food! It's food!" she squeals. Crusoe is thinking the same thing, although he has a different kind of appetite to take care of because he never takes his eyes off Olive as he sits down across from her. Olive can easily fall for Crusoe. Not only is he handsome and attentive and appreciative, but he's also providing for her needs and, in a sense, is saving her life. He puts a finger tenderly under the chin of her pretty face. He leans romantically and longingly over to her, rubbing his cheek against hers as he begins, "Ahh, your eyes are like limpid pools of..." "Clam chowder!" a delighted Olive finishes as she lifts the cover off of a dish. The orchestra and Crusoe are temporarily and unpleasantly stymied and frustrated, but they won't be deterred and begin again. Crusoe now is holding Olive's head in his hand and is caught up in ecstasy as he says, "Ohh, your lips are soft as..." Olive takes another cover off and exclaims, "Liverwurst!" As she does so, her lips do sort of kiss Crusoe's. A ravenous Crusoe now climbs up on the table top, using it like a bed, to sort of crawl his way to Olive, get leverage, become even more turned on, and be ready for lovemaking. Once again, he takes Olive's head in his hand. He gently lifts it up so she's no longer looking at the table. She doesn't resist. She's finally realized that this isn't about eating supper. And she's happy about it! She puckers up a couple of times and her face gets cuter and cuter as Crusoe gets closer and closer and begins pressing his face against hers. Olive is now totally in an enraptured spell and standing up from her chair. Crusoe murmurs, "Let's make with the kisses!" And that's exactly what's going to happen!

Except that Popeye rushes into the picture, comes between them, and separates them with his outstretching arms. But Popeye's hand first goes to Crusoe's, er, male area, and keeps that away from Olive! Not that Popeye is conscious of this. Again, he acts as though he doesn't know what Crusoe and Olive are doing. And he's only concentrating on the food. "Wow! Chow!" An embarrassed orchestra ends the romantic mood.

Then Popeye continues as he looks around, "Dis is some huntin' lodge!" Jumping up from the table, a frustrated and angry Crusoe snarls, "You like huntin'?" As Popeye says, "Well, uh..." Crusoe grabs him away from Olive and says, "Good!" He then superpiles Popeye up with snowshoes, a canteen, binoculars, a backpack, sleeping bag, net, etc. Obviously he's preparing Popeye for an extended stay elsewhere. He then gleefully throws Popeye out the door and down the ramp, commanding him, "Okay, Runt, start to hunt!"

I'm in the Mood for Love instantly starts up again as Crusoe speeds to Olive. She's now sitting on the couch Crusoe prepared and is puzzling over his sketchbook. Sweet, innocent Olive really believes that Crusoe wants her to look at his etchings. She's quite an etching herself as she's drawn in this scene with full, rounded breasts! Crusoe gently sits down beside her. In a tender, but masculine and sexy voice, he enthuses while touching his heart, "L'amour! L'amour!" He then circles his arms around her and presses his hands against her breasts! "It's you I adore," he continues. Experiencing the pleasurable sensation, Olive happily turns toward him and lets him pull her close. Then his hands massage her bare midriff! The two lovebirds come cutely apart while still staring at each other, smitten and longing for more, but not wanting to push things. Crusoe has an "I know I was naughty, but didn't you like it, and besides I love you" look on his face. Olive has a fun-loving "You bet I enjoyed it, but I probably shouldn't have, but what the heck, I did" look on her own countenance as she says, "Mr. Crusoe! Such high falutin' language!" and strikes an enraptured, flirty pose. The two lovers enjoy gazing at each other for a moment. But only for a moment because...

"Yoo Hoo! Mr. Crusoe!" Popeye's jarring voice interrupts, and cuts short, their time on Cloud Nine. They react with shock and dismay. And Crusoe acts like someone just ran fingernails over a chalkboard. Together, Crusoe and Olive turn, put their knees up on the couch and lean against the back of it as they look out the window. Speaking of backs, the creators have drawn Olive with an exceptionally shapely derriere.

And the girl-watching continues. Though Olive and Crusoe's heads and faces and eyes contort as we see them framed in the window, Olive is still baby doll cute and has an hourglass figure. The orchestra is alarmed as we see what has stunned them. Popeye is waving "Hello" with a huge pile of captured, or dead, animals on his back, including a lion, a hippo, a bear, an elephant, and a gigantic sea serpent! "A-Hunting We Will Go" plays on the soundtrack.

Then the music turns ominous as the scene changes and time passes, and Crusoe is now holding a map and saying under his breath, "This phony treasure map oughtta get 'im!" He's next to Popeye, who is standing, shovel in hand, above a big "X" on the ground. "Yeah," Crusoe says, "you're on the spot all right, so keep diggin' and dig deep!" Popeye does so, going to town, and dropping into the hole he's making. As the death knell sounds on the soundtrack for Popeye, Crusoe levers a huge boulder into the hole and quickly piles other sizeable rocks around, and on top of, it. Popeye is buried! But the orchestra now doesn't seem to mind. As we see Crusoe superspeeding across the island, it keeps building up to a sweepingly triumphant version *of I'm In the Mood for Love*. He races back to the compound and into the small bungalow where Olive is seated on another couch. He slams the door shut, blocking it with his body. But he needn't have bothered. Olive doesn't want to go anywhere. After being initially startled, Olive sees who it is and is quite happy to be alone with him. As a soft version of *I'm In the Mood* is heard, she strikes a welcoming, seductive pose and telegraphs a message to Crusoe, using her doe eyes, to come ahead, as he says, "Ah, My Little Peach Blossom..." He goes down on his knees before her, cradles her head in his hands, stretches his lips out toward her and gets closer, ever closer, ever closer, until, to paraphrase Hawkeye Pierce from *M*A*S*H*, if he were any closer, he'd be behind her. "At last we are alone!" And, indeed, at last they are. This is what the whole cartoon has been building toward as Crusoe and Olive have had scene after hot scene together. Unless you are a diehard Popeye fan, Crusoe and Olive are the couple you have been rooting for. So far, Popeye and Olive aren't even really a couple in this film. Crusoe and

Olive's romance has been proceeding at a nice pace — at least for a romance self-contained in a short cartoon. Now it's time for them to be together. Now we'll have satisfaction.

But wait! The floor boards are bulging! As the startled couple looks on, Popeye comes up through the floor with a treasure chest. An embarrassed orchestra signals that the romance is over and Crusoe's dreams have been dashed. But is the orchestra right? Though Crusoe is seething, as Olive has stood up, she has wrapped her hands around Crusoe's massive arm. And she stands there like that, having chosen her man and being willing to stick with him come what may, even in front of Popeye. Popeye, of course, doesn't even notice and is focused solely on the gold he's pouring out on the floor, and looking for Olive and Crusoe's (Mommy and Daddy's?) approval. "Gee, thanks for the tip, Pal!" he says to Crusoe.

Crusoe slaps, grabs, and stretches his own face in total frustration. "So, ya found the treasure." He grabs Popeye and slams him into the chest. "Well, find your way outta dis!" Popeye's body takes on the shape of the interior of the chest. The lid slams shut, locks, and Crusoe repeatedly jumps up and down on the treasure chest, crushing it and Popeye. The orchestra is worried. Crusoe then angrily hurls the chest into an alligator pit. But, Popeye has managed to spring the chest back into shape, and we see it bouncing around as he struggles inside it. "Why dat dirty double-crossin' Crusoe! Let me outta here!"

While we certainly relate to how Crusoe is feeling and kind of wanted to do that to Popeye ourselves, we're still appalled at his extreme measures. And we're sorry for Crusoe, because he had actually won his dream girl, Olive, but now he's blown it and lost her. We know Olive won't approve of what he's just done.

Speaking of Olive, the very shapely Miss is now trapped and backing away from Mr. Crusoe inside a round bungalow. A desperate, "all-is-lost" version of *I'm In the Mood* is playing. Crusoe is all anger and lust, and no romance. "Keep away, you wolf in cheap clothing!" she pleads. But she's up against a wardrobe. Crusoe lunges at her. But she jumps up on top of a nearby lamp. He comes at her again, and this time the two of them race around and around, sticking to the circular walls as only cartoon characters can do. Furious chase music plays, and car racing sound effects are heard.

Back in the alligator pit, Popeye manages to push his legs, neck, and head out of the treasure chest. The bottom of his right leg is all red. But this is where a black sock had been in an earlier scene. Are we actually seeing Popeye's blood from the injuries he sustained while being stomped on by Crusoe?!?!?! Yuck! An alligator comes out of its cave and opens its wide mouth to consume The Sailorman. Panicking, Popeye runs away, as best as he can while still in the chest. The orchestra joins him. But he isn't watching where he's going, and he runs right into the gaping jaws of another gator, and right down its throat into its stomach and back to its tail! Then the alligator bulge that is Popeye and the chest backtracks a little. We see Popeye inside the alligator. He's looking around. A mournful version of Popeye's theme is playing. He hears Olive scream in terrified desperation, "Help, Popeye! Popeye, help!" Popeye looks out through the alligator's teeth.

Popeye at the mercy of wild, hungry animals was a frequent theme in the Famous Studios cartoons.

Crusoe is just finishing tying Olive to a post. He has her immobilized now, and he clamps a hand over her mouth.

Back inside the alligator, Popeye starts squeezing the chest with his legs. He eventually, don't ask me how, squeezes a spinach can right out of his shirt and right out of the chest. He consumes its contents and bursts the chest apart as his "spinach powered" theme plays. He stomps around the interior of the alligator and forms massive biceps. On one, a battleship labeled "Big Mo," the *U.S.S. Missouri*, appears. Popeye then grabs the alligator's tail and turns the beast inside out, freeing himself. He then gives the other one an uppercut, which turns it into a set of shoes and matching luggage.

The orchestra is suddenly worried again as Crusoe uproots the post and runs off carrying Olive. A desperate version of *I'm In the Mood for Love* is playing as he tosses the post in the river and jumps aboard, using it as a raft which he tries to hurriedly row away from Popeye. Is the orchestra worried that Popeye won't catch up? Or about Olive's fate? Or that Mr. Crusoe is going to lose his chance for love because of Popeye? Or all of the above? Popeye jumps on, and he and Crusoe begin a furious fist fight while they keep rolling the post to stay on it. This, of course, means that the bound Olive Oyl keeps getting dunked under the water.

We see a close-up of her, and I wouldn't be doing my job if I didn't point out that her shapely bustline is emphasized, that in some frames she has a cute and more realistic-looking face, and that, at one point, the drops of water on her tummy form a smiling face, maybe to remind us that enjoying Olive's body is what this cartoon is all about. She tries to cheer Popeye on, but of course keeps burbling and blowing bubbles as she goes under while talking.

But now the orchestra is agitated again and signaling danger. We see the post approaching a high waterfall. Crusoe actually punches Popeye right off the post and The Sailorman lands stunned on a lower rock shelf. So Crusoe is not only Popeye's superior when it comes to romance, passion, and intelligence, but he can also hold his own against, and actually defeat, Popeye even after Popeye has eaten his spinach! What a man!

Popeye comes to and snatches Olive off the log as it is going past him, plunging down the waterfall. Then, as Crusoe comes helplessly along, being carried downward by the rushing water, Popeye hauls off and socks him. Olive looks concerned! Because of what she just went through? Because a part of her worries about Crusoe's fate? Because she was anxious that maybe Crusoe would defeat Popeye? All of the above? Anyway, because of circumstances and a lucky punch that Crusoe couldn't avoid, Popeye sends him sailing through the air.

Crusoe lands in bushes and a female gorilla rises up out of them. Here we have an offensive racial stereotype because the gorilla is drawn like the stereotypical caricature of a black woman that was prevalent at the time this cartoon was made. The gorilla says, "Ooo, a man!" She picks Crusoe up and snuggles him. She adds, "And a live one, too!" Crusoe comes to, realizes what's going on, leaps out of her arms, and heads for the hills. "Lemme go!" he commands. "You ain't gonna make a monkey out of me!" The gorilla pursues him. So Crusoe, the man who achingly wanted a mate, now has to try to escape being the love slave of a beast! The less said about this, the better!

We fade in on Olive and Popeye riding in Crusoe's car. And Olive is showing some cleavage! Though she contorts her face and neck in cartoony ways as she says, "From now on, it's Coney Island, no phony island for me!"[6] she is cute in many frames, and we're concentrating on her beautiful chest. She strikes a carefree, feminine, flirty pose — for Popeye this time. Looking at her and smiling is the closest he gets to showing any interest at all in her as a woman in this cartoon. And even in this scene, he could just be a good friend, or someone who is like a brother to her, enjoying her company. So Olive, the romantic creature that she is, winds up with the dispassionate and generally disinterested Popeye. A happy ending? Suddenly, the two of them hear a voice. "How we doin', Boss?" They turn toward the backseat, startled. And from this moment to the final fadeout, Olive has one of the prettiest faces Famous Studios ever gave her! Popeye says, "It's Friday!" as the camera pulls back to show us the car is now on a raft in the ocean, its tires having been replaces by rotating paddles. Friday is in the backseat. Another native pops up, "And I'm Saturday!" Another, "Sunday!" Another, "Monday." And they all join together singing harmony, "And always!"

The Island Fling (1946)

Director: Bill Tytla
Animation: John Gentilella, George Germanetti
Story: Woody Gelman, Larry Riley
Scenics: Robert Connavale
Music: Winston Sharples

CHAPTER 9

The Royal Four-Flusher (1947)

In many cartoons, such as this one, it's Olive Oyl and Popeye's rival that make a handsome couple, not Olive and The Sailorman.

This is the quintessential Famous Studios Popeye cartoon. If I could only write about, or show, one film to someone curious about the Famous Studios era of Popeye, this would be the one. It's got everything. It provides an introduction to the new versions of the characters. It features violence, suspense, romance, some shocking ideas and imagery, and entices viewers to switch their loyalties.

The plot is classic: Popeye and Olive are together; a guy who outclasses Popeye spots Olive and has a wolf reaction; the new guy woos and wins Olive while getting Popeye out of the picture; the guy tries to rush things when he gets Olive alone, and she yells for help; Popeye eats his spinach and comes to the rescue. Sounds simple, doesn't it? But it's how the story is told and embellished that makes this cartoon special.

The title card itself is enough to spark debates, but just wait — there's a lot more combustible material to come. It depicts The Count (Bluto playing a role in this cartoon), Olive Oyl, and Popeye as figures on playing cards. The Count is the King of Hearts, Olive Oyl is the Queen Of Hearts, while Popeye is the Jack. Already we're set up to think of The Count and Olive as the couple that ought to be together and Popeye as the outsider. But Popeye and Olive are smiling, while The Count isn't, hinting that they have something going on and will be the ones getting the happy ending. The hand the cards are a part of is a hand to bluff with in Poker — 10, Jack, Queen, and King of Hearts, Two of Spades — and not a winning combination. If the cartoon's title didn't clue us in to the fact that the member of the nobility in this film isn't all he appears to be and will try to trick others to get his way, the poker hand as depicted would have given us the idea.

The cartoon opens with a scene that has nothing to do with poker, and The Count is not yet in sight. Instead, Olive's realistically drawn hand is offering a peanut to a squirrel who has climbed down a tree trunk. Olive, though, says, "Here bunny, bunny, bunny! Here bunny!" I suppose it sounds better than, "Here squirrely, squirrely…" The squirrel evidently disagrees with me because he rejects Olive and quickly jumps back up the tree.

The camera pulls back to reveal that Popeye and Olive are together in a park located in a big city. We can see skyscrapers in the background. There's a sign pointing "To The Zoo." Olive is bent over and has a cute face in some frames. She's wearing a little red hat and is holding a bag of peanuts.[1] Popeye has a bag, too. The music on the soundtrack lets us know a happy-go-lucky, fun day is unfolding.

Popeye laughs and says, "Feedin' animals is nuttin', Olive. Watch this!" He places a peanut between his lips and bends toward the squirrel, wiggling the nut. The squirrel runs down the tree, up Popeye's back, and under his hat. Peeking out from under the hat, the squirrel grabs the nut, then runs down Popeye and up the tree again.

Olive straightens up a bit and coos in a sweet voice, "Oh, Popeye, you're so familiar with animals!" She's having fun on their date. Though she will soon be tempted by riches, it's good to know that she doesn't need them in order to be happy. Olive's content to feed squirrels in a park. Putting a peanut tenderly between her own lips, she plays with it a second, then turns toward the tree, calling, "Here bunny, bunny, bunny!" while wiggling the nut invitingly. Olive has an extremely cute face in some frames of this sequence. As for Popeye, he's standing with his eyes closed in delight because he impressed the cutey.

Cut to The Count. We see him from about the waist up. He's moving back and forth while riding on something. From the park-like background, it's obvious he's near Popeye and Olive Oyl. He's wearing a fancy coat, an ascot, and a gentlemen's dress hat. There's a monocle in front of his one eye, and he's using an expensive cigarette holder to smoke. His big smile shows off his perfect teeth. His eyes are closed in delight as he's enjoying the day and basking in his high class glory. The orchestra likes him, as it plays a "royal presentation/hunting/parade" theme.

The camera pulls back a bit so we can see that The Count is a dashing figure atop a fine horse, with its own monocle and cigarette holder. The horse is trotting in time to the music. Both the horse and the music are traveling somewhere. The camera moves back a little as The Count's monocled eye starts to open. As the music ends, both his eyes are open in delight. He has reached his destination and really likes what he sees. He pulls back on the reins to halt his steed. Then he sits straight up with both eyes open and riveted on whatever has caught his attention.

We can guess what, or who, it is because he then leans impossibly forward so that his upper body is supported by, and is out in front of, the horse's head. His neck stretches out. He has a hungry, enraptured look on his face as his neck stretches again and thrusts forward. His cigarette holder, which had been parallel to the ground at one point, now rises up at an angle. (This sequence snuck past the censors!) The camera begins to follow his gaze...

There's a quick cut to reveal to us who he's ogling. Olive Oyl, in bending forward to feed the squirrel, is inadvertently showing off her shapely rear. It's what made The Count want a closer look. And Olive's lips are doing some mini-puckering up as she wiggles the peanut in a way that is inviting to both men and squirrels. She has a cute, dreamy expression on her face. Olive is the appealing young miss who is oblivious to the fact that she is the object of a male's desire. But she won't remain oblivious for long.

"Popeye, it works!" Olive exclaims. She turns from The Sailorman and looks off to her left, the direction The Count was coming from. Breathy because of excitement and anticipation, Olive gasps and says, "Lookee! There's another one!" She points.

We see a close-up of a toy squirrel controlled by air which is flowing through a tube leading back into a bush. The pseudo-squirrel jumps up and down and makes squeaking sounds.

Olive comes over and gets down on all fours in front of the "squirrel," with a peanut wiggling in her lips, and she gives her, "Here, bunny!" call again. Leading with her face, head, and lips, her upper body follows the toy into the bush. Suddenly, we hear the sound of a long, passionate kiss. Olive's lower half lifts off the ground and her legs open wide. Her dress swirls around them. Her legs close and open again a few times. Then her body goes straight out as The Count's passion, energy, lust, and prowess pass through her. The music on the soundtrack had been leading up to the kiss and now ends, satisfied. Popeye, however, suddenly realizes what's going on and gets a startled look on his face. As the kiss breaks off with a sound that let's us know The Count and Olive had really merged with a great deal of suction, Olive comes back down to earth. At least her body does. Her emotions never do until near the end of the cartoon.

The Count and the rest of Olive Oyl emerge from the bush. Popeye is now angry because The Count is holding Olive's hand, and both have their eyes closed with looks of love, satisfaction, and delight on their faces. They are cheek-to-cheek as The Count begins kissing his way down Olive's arm. A trombone does a brief comic run, but then the woodwinds tell us that this is sweet, romantic, and cool. After the first arm kiss, The Count looks like he's had a taste of something delicious and is saying, "Ahhh!" Olive, for her part, wants to keep snuggling. The second kiss moves The Count ever closer to her. The third kiss leaves Olive all feminine, demure, and ravished. Then she and The Count bring their cheeks dreamily together again. As he starts his way down the arm a second time, they briefly cuddle and then Olive watches him do his thing. She alternately opens her eyes wide with joy and closes them in ecstasy.[2] Reaching her hand, The Count opens his own eyes and forms a "Wooo!" or a "Whoa!" or an "Ohhh!" with his mouth, as though he is seeing for the first time a part of Olive that's turning him on. Speaking of hands and body parts, Popeye now has clenched fists. The Count begins to kiss Olive's hand, putting his lips around it, like he's sucking her in. She loves this! As he moves away from her, his lips remain stuck there and his mouth stretches out. Sure, it's a typical cartoon gag, but it also conveys the idea that he never wants to let go of Olive. Finally, though, there's a satisfying "Pop!" as his lips come loose.

The Count stands fully upright now. He opens his jacket and holds its sides out as Olive stands open-mouthed at his rich apparel, muscular physique, and male confidence. The Count begins in a suave, sophisticated, slightly British voice, "Allow me to…"

There's a cut to a close-up of his torso. "…introduce myself." The words "Count Marvo Magic King" appear and flash on and off his vest like a neon sign. (It will become evident as the cartoon progresses that The Count is a magician and that he made his fortune selling and inventing trick gadgets.) The music begins a fanfare to herald him, but before it can finish the camera pans over to Olive and Popeye.

A hurried, cartoony-sounding flute accompanies an enraged Popeye as he begins to charge forward saying, "Ya can't kiss me goil and…" But the brass section and Olive interrupt him. She catches him with her left arm under his chin, forming a barrier so he can't reach The Count.

"Popeye!" She gives an embarrassed and cute laugh trying to cover up Popeye's faux pas. "Eh, heh…(gasp!)" She releases Popeye and steps behind him and to his left. "Meet The Count!" Olive takes hold of the edges of her skirt, sticks her chest out while displaying a figure, and demurely curtseys, presenting her whole self to The Count. She's pleased and honored and definitely giving the impression that she is at his service and that it is her delight to dutifully do for him whatever he wants. Sweet flute "Welcome, Royalty…I'm all yours to command" music accompanies Olive. If The Count was hot and bothered before, he's got to be burning up now! But during this whole scene, he acts cool and like he can bide his time because he remains supremely confident in his personal appeal, his plans, and that Popeye poses no real threat whatsoever.

Popeye, for his part, is openmouthed — flabbergasted that Olive's not upset at being kissed. He also seems surprised about his own behavior — that he insulted visiting royalty. Shocked, he then whips his head to look at The Count. "The Count...?!?!?" Popeye exclaims. He gets angry at himself and then fixes The Count with a gaze of joy, excitement, and admiration. Even Popeye thinks The Count is a great guy! Popeye takes his hat off in respect, then self-consciously begins playing with it as he sort of shrinks and hopes for mercy and forgiveness by explaining, "Gee, nobiliky! Er, I didn't know that you were..."

Let's pause a moment here to ask what in the world Popeye is doing? Does he not care that this guy ravished Olive and is winning her? Does he think that normal rules don't apply to royalty? Is he saying that The Count can do anything — even with Olive Oyl — that he wants? Is Popeye, too, offering his services to The Count? Is Popeye being a good American welcoming a visitor? Or is he being the supreme sap? Whatever the answers, things don't look good for Popeye being able to break apart the new couple at all — if he even still wants to!

Back to the cartoon. The Count is assuring Popeye, "...that's perfectly all right, Old Man." Popeye has a silly grin on his face. The Count offers his hand to Popeye, "Shake!" A blissful, forgiven, and accepted Popeye shakes the hand with his eyes closed.

But The Count steps back away from Popeye to reveal that it's not a hand at all. It's a fake, mounted on the end of an extendible/collapsible rack. The Count is holding the other end of the rack. As the smooth royal music comes to an end, The Count's eyes open wide and his smile turns into more of a sneer. A helpless Popeye opens his eyes as The Count first quickly contracts the device, pulling Popeye forward, then squeezes the end of it with super strength, propelling Popeye off his feet, into the air, and out of the picture, accompanied by speed lines, clouds of dust, and appropriate "unwilling travel" music on the soundtrack.

We now see a giant turtle sleeping in the zoo. Popeye comes flying into the picture, knocking the turtle out of its shell. Popeye is now the one under the shell. Popeye rises on all fours, as an utterly embarrassed version of his theme song begins playing. He's just proved to us and the orchestra that he really is a sap. The angry turtle, on its hind legs, strides over to Popeye, lifts the shell up, and dumps him out. Popeye's body is now impossibly folded on itself. He looks to be immobile. But Popeye sticks his neck out in determination toward where Olive and The Count are. He whirls his pipe in anger as a triumphant chord is struck and the Popeye theme song begins.

The camera cuts to Olive and The Count at a hot dog cart in front of a lion's cage. A smiling Count hands a pleased Olive Oyl a hot dog on a bun. Then he opens his monocled eye wide to see how she will react to his gift. He's pleased with what he sees, because not only is Olive a sweet, simple miss who can be grateful for a hot dog, but she goes about consuming it in the most provocative way imaginable. If this is the way she always eats, her male friends probably can't wait to buy her food! Olive receives the hot dog and goes to take a bite, but then, with her mouth open, moves the hot dog sideways in front of her face. She's prolonging her pleasure and is in ecstasy. She plays with the hot dog, teasing it, kissing it, maybe licking it, letting it overwhelm her before it enters her. Olive seems to be just innocently and sincerely enjoying the hot dog, but is she also unconsciously and subliminally trying to turn The Count on by sending him a message? Freud would remind us that sometimes a hotdog is just a hotdog — but that sometimes it isn't!

The Count is receiving another hot dog from the vendor as Popeye dashes into the scene. The Count stands serenely confident as Popeye hauls off to sock him. Pleased and lost in his lust, The Count isn't really paying all that much attention to Popeye. He wants to watch Olive reacting to his gift. And, honestly, he also doesn't believe Popeye is any kind of a threat to him. And, at this point, neither does the audience. He turns toward The Sailorman.

In a close-up of the two of them, The Count ignores Popeye's waving fist, emphasizing again how outclassed and ineffectual Popeye is, then reaches right over top of him for the mustard on the cart while positioning the hot dog under Popeye's nose. The unbelievably easily distracted Popeye, who must have the attention span of a flea, forgets why he's there, as The Count dabs on the mustard under the nose of the suddenly sniffing, suddenly hungry sailor. Popeye'd rather have a hot dog than Olive Oyl! Popeye's theme ends abruptly on the soundtrack. The orchestra knows this isn't one of Popeye's finest moments. Instead, The Count's theme begins.

Magnanimous and jovial, The Count addresses Popeye, "Ah, just in time to join us for a bit of a snack!"

Popeye's tongue is hanging out. He takes the hot dog with two hands. "Thanks, County! I'm much obliged!" Popeye is either wonderfully forgiving or terribly naive. Olive's left hand comes around The Count's right arm. The confident, happy Count then strolls away out of the picture with Olive, as she leads him! And Popeye, entranced by a hot dog, doesn't even realize his girl is gone, in more ways than one! He also doesn't realize that the magical Count has performed sleight-of-hand and has replaced the hot dog in the bun with the tail of the lion in the cage. Popeye hungrily chomps down hard on it, causing the lion to raise up in pain, whirl toward Popeye and roar, and take off running in the cage, pulling Popeye, whose teeth are still locked on the tail, through the bars and into the cage with it!

The lion keeps running around the cage in pain, pulling Popeye along in the air like a kite, and causing The Sailorman to hit every steel bar along the way. Round and round they go, with Popeye looking helpless and unconscious. Then the lion stops and shows Popeye its teeth. Popeye plops down hard on the floor of the cage, seemingly "out of it." A close-up of the lion and Popeye shows us that the beast is opening its mouth as wide as possible in order to kill and devour Popeye. Its teeth are huge and the music is tense. Just as Popeye's head is framed in the lion's jaws, Popeye wakes up. He quickly moves out of the way and lays the lion's tail in its own mouth. A suspenseful snatch of the Popeye theme plays. The lion bites down hard on itself and soars to the roof of the cage in pain. Popeye watches it go up.

Then the scene changes and we go from violence to romance. Olive and The Count are strolling, completely in sync with one another, arm-in-arm in the park, as a romantic version of The Count's theme plays on the soundtrack. The couple is enraptured. Some of the characters' movements seem very realistic. Olive and The Count are quite the handsome couple! And Olive displays a shapely rear and curves in some frames. She gets a look of satisfied submission on her face. At one point, when she is really turned on and satisfied, she has an hourglass figure, and a bush in the background looks like it is The Count's hand around her hip. Olive's faraway expression tells us she's in dreamland. But Popeye rushes in from off camera and he and the music intrude. Popeye skids to a stop in front of The Count and strikes a belligerent pose. "That was a dirty trick!" he exclaims. The Count stops and Olive steps away, both of them smiling and amused all the while. Neither considers Popeye as a threat to their happiness as a couple, and they are still basking in the afterglow of their stroll. Popeye hauls off to sock The Count again.

There's a close-up of The Count as he continues to outclass Popeye. "Why be vulgar?" he asks. "Let's settle this like gentlemen." Still smiling, he reaches into his jacket and pulls out a black box that contains a set of dueling pistols. The music makes his theme sound dangerous. He closes and opens his eyes in anticipation.

We see Popeye still wound up and The Count offering the pistols. Popeye does a scared double-take. He gingerly comes out of it and, looking limp, chooses one by picking it up with just two fingers. He's not totally willing to participate and is slack-jawed with fear. The music shares his concern.

The Count, though, can't wait to get started. He takes a gun and speeds behind Popeye so that they are now in a classic dueling stance, back-to-back. The Count is straight and confident, happily glancing down on Popeye. And while The Count is gripping his pistol, Popeye still seems afraid to handle his. And Popeye is standing in a little girlish, helpless manner. The Count raises his gun in salute and instructs, "At ten paces."

There's a close-up of Popeye as The Count begins counting off the paces. "One...Two...Three...Four..." The orchestra plays a "march of the doomed," building up to a disaster. A worried Popeye now grips his pistol and is holding it straight out in front of him. A thought balloon appears above Popeye showing that he is certain that he's a dead man. His tombstone and freshly filled grave are in the balloon, and his pipe and hat are resting on top of the headstone.

"...Five..." The camera pulls back and we see The Count, with his pistol all ready and cocked and buried into the back of Popeye's head! Rather than pacing away from Popeye, The Count is following right behind him! Why doesn't Popeye respond? Can't he feel the press of cold steel? There doesn't seem to be any way Popeye can cheat death this time! The Count gleefully and expectantly continues to count as he and Popeye keep walking forward.

"...Six...Seven...Eight...Nine...Ten!" Popeye whirls around and pulls the trigger while cringing. A flower pot pops out of the barrel of his gun. The Count pulls his trigger, causing a watering can to come out of his own pistol. It begins to water the pot. A mocking springtime theme is heard as a palm tree quickly grows up out of the flower pot. A slack-jawed Popeye watches, then does a double-take. The top of the tree is now filled with coconuts. They come loose and rain down. There's now a pile of them where Popeye once stood. More drop down. A barely conscious Popeye pokes his head up out of the pile. One last coconut falls right on top of him, embedding itself briefly in his forehead and squishing him. He shakes off the impact, but still seems out of it until he spots Olive and The Count. He's helpless and confused as we hear Olive and The Count burst out in laughter off screen.

The camera cuts to Olive and The Count laughing. Olive's laugh starts out harsh and cruel-sounding, but quickly turns sexy and sweet. Is she mean to laugh at Popeye? Remember that The Count is now her guy and she's sharing in his triumph over an enemy. Also, her laughter is probably one of relief because the duel was won without the shedding of blood. Her guy is so clever! The Count is casually and proudly leaning against a tree. Olive is holding herself and expanding a little as she laughs. What The Count did has pleased her to the core and made her hug herself in inexpressible delight. She shows off some curves and gets a look of pure rapture on her face.

Popeye speeds into the picture and starts to sock The Count again, as the nobleman reaches into his coat and pulls out a large cigar. He shoves it into Popeye's mouth, forcing the sailor backwards and off his feet momentarily. The conciliatory Count says, "Have a five dollar cigar, Chum!" (Expensive for that day!) He then pulls out a cigar for himself. Popeye seemingly believes that The Count now wants to bond with him and be his friend. What an idiot!

The romantic, classy Count's theme begins again as The Count uses his fancy lighter, consisting of a mini-bellows, a wick, and two sticks being rubbed together.

There's a close-up of a goofy-looking Popeye as he receives a light and begins to puff out smoke rings. Popeye is happy and satisfied until one of his clouds of smoke becomes a thought balloon. Looking within it, Popeye sees a trick cigar burning down to its hidden load and exploding.

Popeye turns to The Count with a sly look on his face. The music wonders what Popeye is up to as The Count is contentedly smoking away. Popeye pulls the cigar out of The Count's mouth and sticks his in it. "There, wise guy!" Popeye snarls. The Count looks worried. A triumphant Popeye puts The Count's cigar in his own mouth. Then he bends forward, watching the cigar The Count is now smoking and, waiting for the big boom, Popeye puts his fingers in his ears. The Popeye theme begins on the soundtrack. But suddenly, the end of the cigar in Popeye's mouth acts like a lit fuse. Popeye looks at it in horror. The Count leans forward with a leer and watches Popeye's cigar become a jet engine, blasting Popeye off and out of the picture. The Count happily watches him go.

We see the Popeye jet weaving through the air over the park. The Popeye theme is continuing, but the orchestra is also portraying the flight. Popeye lands in a pool of water at the zoo and stays submerged. His theme music stops. Is Popeye dead? But the music resumes again as Popeye emerges, balanced on the nose of a seal. The seal isn't exactly saving Popeye, though. As the music changes into the accompaniment for a circus act, the seal tosses Popeye over to another seal which balances him and tosses him back. This keeps going on and a stunned Popeye takes no action to free himself. Maybe he will just stay a toy for the seals forever.

There's a quick cut to The Count, looking rich, handsome, and confident, and a pleased Olive, riding on the back of The Count's horse, away from Popeye and the zoo and the park, and toward the city. Olive is riding bareback behind The Count with her hands on the back of the saddle. Her shapely rear is emphasized in some frames as she bobs along.

A sophisticated hunting/marching theme begins. The orchestra is progressing toward a destination and is counting down, via the beat, to a magic time. It emphasizes that The Count and Olive are getting ever closer to being finally, totally alone, and that their relationship is progressing along to its inevitable, pleasurable conclusion.

The camera moves in for a close-up of Olive and The Count. He gets a sly/happy expression on his face as he looks back at Olive. A joyful, expectant Olive never takes her eyes off of him. The Count gives a controlled, cultured laugh, "Haw, haw, haw!" He gestures to a faraway place with his hand. "M'Lady, wouldn't thou view my penthouse in the clouds?" Giving Olive a teasing look, he then faces forward again, satisfied. He knows that Olive is totally his.

The scene dissolves (indicating that time has passed) into a shot of the horse and the couple crossing a city street and going toward a swank apartment building.

Olive now has her hands on The Count's shoulders. The relationship is progressing indeed! They go under the building's awning and through its entrance.

Next we see a very opulent lobby and an open elevator. The horse and the couple enter the elevator, as Olive is now leaning forward, sometimes burying her face in The Count's back, in happy anticipation of what will happen next. The relationship is indeed progressing! The elevator door, made from expensive wood, closes behind them with a sophisticated sliding noise. The Count and Olive are now all alone at last. The arrow indicator above the elevator shaft shows us that the couple is going up to the top of the building away from the rest of the world.

The scene dissolves into a bird's-eye view of the outside of The Count's penthouse. He obviously owns the whole top floor of the building. The elevator is housed in a charming cottage-like structure. The Count and Olive are emerging from it and walking through an archway toward a huge swimming pool. These movements are drawn more realistically than usual. The music ends and then soft notes are heard. The couple have reached their destination and what they, and we, have been waiting for.

And Olive Oyl has taken off her hat. She's letting her guard down and getting comfortable, ready to settle in for the evening with The Count. And let's face it, she has removed an article of clothing. The relationship continues to progress!

Olive and The Count walk to the edge of a golf course. Olive is taking it all in with her hands clasped in front of her, overwhelmed at The Count's wealth and won over by it and him. The Count gestures, both showing off and pooh-poohing, his riches at the same time. He says dismissively and charmingly, "It's small, but it's homey." Olive's curvy hips are emphasized in some frames.

We see an impossibly huge, full-size golf course. Only a rich cartoon character could have one like it in his penthouse. The Count continues, "Now, there's muh golf course…"

"…my archery range…" The camera pans over to a gigantic and classy archery range.

"…and, of course, my swimming pool." Panning again, the camera shows us a mammoth swimming pool with palm trees surrounding it and a fancy fountain in the middle of one end. We hear Olive in an overwhelmed with delight, laughing because it seems too good to be true, enraptured, sexy voice saying, "Oh, oh, it's wonderful!"

But we see that Olive is fixated on a full-length mink coat hanging on a coat rack. The Count is looking away, continuing his tour. Olive lifts the bottom of the coat as he turns toward her. She continues to enthuse, "(Gasp!) It's gorgeous!" Olive displays an hourglass figure and swoons. She stands leaning back somewhat, as though the coat is sweeping her off her feet, with the lower half of her body therefore thrust forward toward The Count in a flirty, inviting position. The music is now dream-like because for Olive, this is all a dream come true. It is for The Count, too. The Count winks. He knows he's gotten to Olive completely. She gets a closer look at the coat. Both Olive and The Count have their mouths open in amazed, rapturous delight — she over the coat, he over her "I'm butter in your hands" reaction. Olive rhapsodizes, "(Gasp!) It's just too, too!!!" The Count turns dramatically toward the coat and lifts it off the hook. With a happy and hungry expression, he opens it for Olive. "Try it on for size, Beautiful!" he says, praising and inviting her, and implying that if she is his woman she'll get the coat as a gift. His face exhibits pure animal lust as he moves the coat toward her. Olive daintily and very femininely steps forward, turning around so The Count can put the coat on her, and gives The Count a happy look, as he struggles to get his own countenance to look more normal. He slips the coat around her in a manner both gracious and voracious at the same time. Then as Olive examines herself in the coat, he gestures magnanimously and looks enraptured while proclaiming, "There! A perfect fit!"

Things continue to be perfect. Olive begins a very feminine fashion model's walk in a small circle, losing herself in the coat. She's not really trying to show off. She's just caught up in the enjoyment of this wonderful dream and the luxurious, super-comfortable coat. But maybe there is a part of her that wants to model for The Count. At any rate, whether intentional or not, as the coat accentuates her shape, she does display curves for The Count, and us. The Count puts his hands together in pleasure as he looks at Olive's body. As she makes a turn in the circle, her shapely derriere is attention-getting, and her face, framed by the coat's high fur collar and her own appealing hairstyle, is one of the cutest, most attractive faces she has ever had.

Freeze frame this perfect moment. The Count has won Olive. If he continues the high class wooing, there's no doubt that the two of them will soon be sharing kisses and each other. But The Count, impatient for his desire to be sated, and showing that he is as much into manipulation and the enjoyment of his power over people as he is into romance, is about to blow it.

Let's let the cartoon continue. As Olive is about to start her second circle, she bends to one side, a look of shock on her face. Then suddenly her rear lower half is violently thrust backwards. She is helpless. The soft music has been disrupted, and the orchestra is now helping to trap Olive. We hear locks snapping shut. Her body snaps again. Her face is cute, but totally shocked. Her body spasms again and she's aghast. Another spasm and the coat shows off Olive's body — curvy hips and spectacular legs. The spasms keep coming until she finally is able to stand up straight again. Olive looks at the coat, trying to figure out what's happened. The Count, who has been gleeful because of Olive's helpless contortions, leers wolfishly, practically pounces forward, and snatches the fur coat off of Ms. Oyl to reveal that she's now totally bound and locked in a straitjacket!

Olive is understandably worried as he throws the coat aside and then turns back to her like a predator — his male lust and dominance on display. "Now, Babe," he says, dropping his accent and all pretense of sophistication, "how 'bout slipping me a little kiss?" It's not really a question. And there's no doubt that's not all he wants.

He leans in as an angry Olive tries to lean away. The orchestra is shocked. Olive shakes her head, "No," then does a double-take as she fully realizes her hopeless fate. As The Count puckers up, she tries to run backwards away from him, but she's off balance and doesn't really have much freedom of movement at all. Half running and half falling out of control, Olive desperately propels herself back. Flute music mimics her. "You keep away from me, you Royal Four-Flusher! Help, oh Popeye!"

Cut to Popeye, still being balanced by a seal. As it begins to throw Popeye to its partner again, Popeye hears Olive's voice, "Help! He's after me! Oh, somebody, help!"[3] Suspenseful music plays. Popeye comes out of his stupor in mid-air. Determined, he begins running at superspeed while suspended above the pool. When he hits the water, he continues running, then gets airborne again, trailing the water — that's been sucked up in his wake — after him. A Popeye victory theme is playing. Popeye swoops across a street and into the apartment building. He races into the elevator and the door shuts. The water spout hits it and disperses, depositing two stunned and confused seals in the vases bordering the elevator.

The last chord of the Popeye theme turns ominous as the scene changes to Olive trying to flee backwards across the tennis court. Frantic, suspenseful music is now on the soundtrack. Olive is almost tipping over. She scolds The Count, "Don't you dare reproach me, you, you…(squeal!)" Olive has stumbled over a golf bag. She lands on her head, bounces back to her feet, back flips again, and lands with her head stuck in one of the golf holes. Her feminine-looking feet kick back and forth and the straitjacket elongates and contracts as she struggles to free herself. But to no avail. The orchestra has emphasized her predicament and let us know that The Count is about to have her. And here he comes, wearing a pleasant, hungry expression.

As he's getting ready to grab her, the elevator suddenly shoots up underneath her, lifting the floor/soil/green/Astroturf up and away from The Count. The doors open and The Count does a quick, shocked double-take as he sees an angry Popeye stepping to the elevator doorway and demanding, "Where's me goil?" Did Popeye use his superpowers to re-route the elevator shaft? Well, it doesn't matter because whatever powers The Sailorman has will be useless. The orchestra dissolves a triumphant Popeye theme into a suspenseful chord. It knows Popeye is no match for The Count. And so does The Count. He's now over his temporary surprise and is acting totally in control again. He grabs the elevator doors with super-strength, bends them outward, and then slams them back on Popeye. Pain symbols and impact lines radiate from The Sailorman as he's smashed between the doors. The Count steps back to survey his handiwork — an unconscious Popeye framed by the doors. The Count cheerfully goes to get something as Popeye falls forward, stiff as a board.

As suspenseful music plays, an expectant Count grabs Popeye's feet, lifts him up, and fits him, like an arrow, to a bow The Count is now holding. The Count pulls the string and the "Popeye arrow" back, but doesn't notice that the sailor's feet are catching on The Count's suspenders. The Count lets the "arrow" fly, and the worried music and the sound effects let us know that Popeye would have traveled for miles and miles because of The Count's great strength. Indeed, we see Popeye flying out over the city. But he's unwittingly dragging The Count along. The Count's body and clothing stretch to ridiculous extremes as he resists. Finally, because The Count's feet have caught on the penthouse's railing and his body and apparel have reached their elastic limit, he springs back to normal and stands on the floor again. A helpless Popeye snaps back to the penthouse, too, shooting over the head of the ducking nobleman.

The Sailorman goes straight through the bulls-eye of an archery target, feet first. (Of course, The Count would score a bull's-eye using Popeye!) Then Popeye's feet and lower body go over the cement railing wall on the far side of the penthouse, but the rest of him crashes into it. Flattened, scrunched, and out of it, Popeye begins to slide down the outside wall. A trombone mockingly accompanies his slide. Finally, only his fingertips show, and they are all that's keeping him from falling.

A humiliating, "all is lost" version of the Popeye theme is playing as we see that The Count has ripped a diving board from its moorings and is bending it back while standing on one end of it. He's aiming it at Popeye. As the board goes back more and more, we see Popeye using his arms to try to climb back up over the wall and onto the floor of the penthouse.

There's a close-up of Popeye looking hurt, exhausted, and almost dead. His torso and head are now showing above the wall. He pulls a can of spinach out of his shirt and gives it a baleful look. It's his last chance and he knows it. And he wonders if even it can defeat The Count. He opens his mouth and tips the can. As its life-giving contents are about to spill into his mouth, The Count lets go of the board and it smashes Popeye in the face, launching him off the wall. The can somersaults and lands upright on top of the wall.

Popeye is not so lucky. He plummets at least 14 stories, as the orchestra follows him down, to smash into the concrete road far below. There's a huge dust cloud from the impact and we hear a tremendous crash. A funereal chord is sounded.

We now see a huge hole in the road. A water pipe, bent by the impact, has Popeye's head sticking out of it. Water squirts around him, and then the pressure forms a waterspout which lifts him slightly above street level. Popeye is limply lying motionless on top of the spout. He's at least unconscious, and maybe he's even dead. A mournful version of his theme song plays in the background.

Cut to Olive still trying to pull her head out of the golf hole as only a cartoon character can. A desperate fanfare emphasizes her plight. Her head finally pops out, but the momentum throws her off of the elevator's roof. She flies toward a flag pole, wraps her feet around it, and spins a few times helplessly. Her momentum abates and she angrily and determinedly bends her body so that her head is now above her feet. She does a double-take as she realizes The Count is coming toward her. With a resigned, worried, "what's the use" look on her face, she clamps her mouth partway up the pole and then shimmies her feet up almost even with her mouth. Then she repeats the process. As The Count makes a dive and a grab for her, she inchworms up and away from him. The Count is frustrated.

Olive continues her climb and the orchestra helps her. Finally she reaches the ball on the top of the pole. Kicking and grabbing with her feet, she maneuvers herself to then sit in a very ladylike manner atop the pole. Suddenly, she's startled as the pole sways to the right, and then violently to the left, and so on and so forth, shaking Olive. She finally comes to a stunned stop, but her pupils keep rattling back and forth in her eyes. She has a gorgeous face, framed by an appealing hairstyle in some frames of this sequence. It all happens again. And again. There's a rhythmic pattern to it.

And brass notes seem both to be counting down, and building up, to some dynamic climax at the same time. After each rhythmic cycle completes, a flute echoes Olive's uncontrollable, over-the-top, sweet reaction. We see that The Count is swinging an axe at the pole. The spinach can is perched nearby. As he swings the axe, there's a look of hunger and glee on his face. As the axe bites into the pole and chips fly off of it, he first looks a little pained, then satiated, but then wanting more. And finally, before the axe leaves the pole, he looks gleeful and enraptured. He pulls the axe back for another mighty swing and everything repeats as the frenetic music matches his blows and keeps building up, and counting down, to something.

So, The Count's rhythmic physical actions are making him ecstatic while affecting, and shaking, a helpless, bound Olive Oyl to her very core. And some sort of climax is being reached. Is it any wonder that some fans think this whole scene is meant to symbolize sex, or that The Count is having his way with her, or that the scene even depicts rape? True, it can all just mean that The Count is about to down the pole and get the unwilling girl, and we're supposed to be worried that this is going to happen. But when the creators have given us a plot about a playboy getting a pretty girl alone up in his penthouse after taking her boyfriend out of the picture, viewers minds will easily go wherever that idea leads them.

Cut to the spinach can on top of the short railing/wall. We see the axe come near it as The Count pulls back to swing again. But the axe misses the can, building up the suspense. However, when The Count swings the axe forward toward the pole, it hits the can, knocking the spinach up and over the ledge. The spinach can falls and tips, spilling its contents into the air.

Popeye, now conscious, looks up, does a double-take, and opens his mouth wide. The column of plunging spinach falls into it. We were hearing the chopping and the rhythmic music until now, but the creators want us to focus on something else. The "spinach eating" theme begins. Popeye chomps on the green stuff and swallows it. We see the glob travel down his throat and out to his left arm, making it huge. A happy, revitalized Popeye makes a bicep and looks at it. The image of an electric dynamo appears on it, crackling with energy as lightning bolts shoot out of it. Popeye stands upright on the waterspout and then superspeeds out of the picture.

A triumphant version of Popeye's theme plays as he runs to a corner of the apartment building. He grabs the corner and rips a whole floor out of the building, shoving it out of the picture to the left of the screen. The rest of the building drops down into place. Then Popeye grabs some window frames of the new bottom floor and muscles the whole floor out of the picture, to the right this time. The building drops down in place again. To the left, to the right — Popeye has his own rhythm going, slightly different than The Count's.

Speaking of The Count, the camera cuts to him still swinging his axe. We can also see the building shuddering because of Popeye's actions. The Count looks more gleeful than ever as he completes each cut. The music is more frantically rhythmic, more intense and hurried, as it speeds toward a climax. We see Olive, still helpless, still gorgeous, and still vibrating on the pole and coming to rest, then vibrating again.

The scene dissolves into Popeye continuing to bring the couple down to earth. He finally rips away the last floor and The Count, the pole — bending as though about to break — and the elevator land at street level. The Count completes his last blow as Popeye rushes up behind him. He becomes aware of Popeye and reacts with surprise. He had been so intent on dethroning Olive that he was unaware the building was being lowered. Popeye hauls off and socks The Count out of the picture. The pole breaks, and Popeye runs past all of the rubble he and The Count have made to catch Olive. And catch her he does. Her hair is pleasantly mussed up.[4] First Olive looks exhausted and out of it, but then she and Popeye smile at each other. Olive has a cute face and feminine features. Popeye and Olive revel in their triumph, but do a double-take and look off-camera to where The Count has landed. As they turn, Olive has a pretty, realistic-looking face, and her hair bob is quite attractive.

Cut to The Count, seemingly unconscious, trapped in the doors of the elevator which has come to rest in the hyena cage at the zoo. The hyena begins laughing uproariously. Soon The Count joins in and we see why. The Count's leg is sticking out through a hole in the elevator and out through the bars of the cage. Popeye is tickling the bottom of The Count's bare foot and laughing himself. The camera pulls back to give us the full scene as Olive, wearing the red hat once again, enters the far left of the picture. She's clasping her hands together and laughing, too. Even the orchestra joins in on the laughter and the mocking of The Count.

But the viewers are left with questions. Who is going to pay for all of the property damage? What about the people who are now homeless or who are left without water? Is there a traffic jam due to the ripped up street? Wasn't anybody injured? Has Popeye never learned to use the stairs? But to those who are involved in a love triangle, the three members of it are the only people in the world, or at least the only people who are important. In the case of The Count/Olive/Popeye, this seems to be literally true.

And The Count at the end of the cartoon has a sophisticated laugh even when he is being manipulated and isn't in control of himself. So maybe he is the real deal after all. If only he didn't have that horrifying character flaw! And if only he could have been more patient with Olive Oyl! Then she could have ended up with the rich, dynamic, passionate, smart guy, instead of the slow-on-the-uptake Popeye. But at least Popeye won't trick her into putting on a straitjacket! And squirrels like him.[5]

Questions and concerns will have to go on the back-burner for now, though, because the cartoon has ended.

The Royal Four-Flusher (1947)

Director: Seymour Kneitel
Animation: Tom Johnson, Frank Endres
Story: Joe Stulz, Carl Meyer
Scenics: Tom Ford
Musical Direction: Winston Sharples

CHAPTER 10

A Wolf in Sheik's Clothing (1948)

Popeye being buried alive, or sent to a literal early grave, is a theme in several cartoons. Here, he's wrapped as a mummy and entombed.

The main theme of this film, even more so than some of the other romantic Popeye cartoons, is the way between a man and a woman. In fact, some of the cartoon's humor is based on exaggerated passion and the way people react and respond when they are feeling the pangs of l'amour.

The cartoon is also about sex appeal. The creative team, including voice artists Mae Questel and Jackson Beck, went out of their way at points in this cartoon to make Olive Oyl and her suitor as attractive as they have ever been in any film. We viewers enjoy watching them so much that we're impatient and disappointed whenever the supposed hero, Popeye, dominates the screen. The O.O.O.P.S. factor[1] is definitely at work in this cartoon, too, as Olive Oyl wears both safari pants and a harem girl costume. Along with dressing Olive in traditionally form-fitting outfits, the artists also gave her, in many frames and scenes, quite a nice form to be fitted!

The title card shows us a scene of midnight at an oasis and gets us in the mood for love. While the words are in a typical cartoon font, the title itself lets us know that this film isn't going to be about Popeye fighting the Nazis or taking Swee'Pea to Little League practice, but about lust, sex, and romance.

As the title card fades out, we iris in first on Olive Oyl, and then Popeye, riding in a rather strange conveyance across the desert sands. The two are seated in the body of a top-down convertible which is mounted on top of a galloping, buck-toothed, fez-wearing camel. An Arabian version of *The Sailor's Hornpipe*, one of Popeye's themes, is playing in the background. Popeye and Olive, both wearing safari outfits including pith helmets, are facing opposite directions. The Sailorman is looking forward, his hands on the steering wheel. Olive is in the back seat, gazing out at the sweeping vista behind them. The characters may be on screen together, but they aren't on the same page. This will become even clearer as the cartoon continues.

Olive, caught up in the moment and in her environment, clasps her hands together and says, "Oh, Popeye, isn't the desert romantical?" She says Popeye's name and "desert" in a tender way and holds out the "cal" in "romantical" in an open-ended, dreaming fashion, as she closes her eyes and puts her head in her hands. Then she puts her hands together again and places them on the side of her face in a feminine expression of delight. Olive's face is very cute while she's doing so. Then, she rests her chin on her hands and continues to gaze wistfully out at the horizon.

Olive has let Popeye know what's on her mind and that she's in the mood to be intimate, and like any red-blooded, American, male sailor, he responds with — a pun?!?!? "Yeah, Olive," he replies in a semi-mocking, teasing voice while leaning back just a little, "it's hot stuff." Then he laughs at his own joke. Is Popeye making fun of Olive and her fantasies? Or does he actually think punning is romantic? The latter is doubtful because, for most of the rest of the cartoon, Popeye doesn't seem to have a romantic bone in his body. And he's about to do something to demonstrate that, to him, Olive and her feelings, thoughts, and needs don't really matter.

As the music winds down and changes into a "gathering of the nomadic peoples" tune and rhythm, Popeye pulls the camel-mobile into a "Desert Filling Station," as the sign on the Middle Eastern building proclaims. A sheik in full desert regalia is seated by the side of the building, reading a racing form and paying no attention to what's going on. A midget Arabian is the station attendant and he springs into action.

Several Famous Studios Popeye cartoons included a short, non-speaking character, like this attendant, who usually starts out aiding, or being employed by, Popeye's rival, but by the picture's end is on Popeye and Olive's side and is traveling with them, or is skulking about, intent on fulfilling a personal goal that the film's antagonist had previously denied him. Fans have dubbed the character "The Little Gnome Guy" (hereafter referred to as T.L.G.G.). In *Snow Place Like Home*, T.L.G.G. was a penguin. *Klondike Casanova* and *Popeye and the Pirates* featured the same character as T.L.G.G. — a goofy looking, buck-toothed dwarf who even sings a few lines and steals a kiss from Olive in the latter cartoon. *Wigwam Whoopee* had a young Indian brave fill T.L.G.G. role, while *Pop-Pie Ala Mode* used a miniature cannibal.

"*Wolf's*" version of T.L.G.G. obeys Popeye's order to "Fill 'er up, Junior." The attendant brings over a pump's hose and begins putting water into the top of the camel's hump. Popeye jumps down from the camel without a word to, or a backward glance at, Olive, as Arabian theme music plays. "And don't forget to change the oil," he instructs the attendant, which is interesting as a joke, but also because Miss Oyl's life is about to change drastically. We watch Popeye enter the "Wash Room" and hear him start to "scat" sing.

An interior shot fades in and we see Popeye in a spacious room as would be found in an ancient bathhouse. Speaking of baths, Popeye has disrobed and is in a walk-in pool, using a back brush and a cake of soap to get clean. It turns out that the "Wash Room" is literally a wash room! Popeye is enjoying himself, proclaiming, "This is soikanly invigorating!" and "scat" singing again as his theme song comes to an end.

One has to wonder why Popeye is indulging himself while Olive is baking out in the sun? And why go off and leave her alone when she's feeling romantic? Why couldn't he have said something like, "Hold that thought, Sweetie! I'll be right back?" Or blown her a kiss over his shoulder? Or laughed, "Here's a refreshin' stop for ya, Olive, so we'll be refreshed to get fresh later!!!" He seemingly cares more about taking care of his own needs, and even the needs of his camel, than he does about caring for Olive! Popeye's defenders may try to say that he was getting clean in order to get ready for some cuddling time with Olive. If only that were so, but, alas, it is not, as we shall see! It will soon become evident that Popeye takes Olive Oyl for granted, assuming that, no matter how he treats her, she'll always be there. (A fatal assumption when it comes to love!)

There's a quick cut to a close-up of a bored Olive Oyl, who is still looking back at the terrain. Soft, wistful, romantic music plays. Olive gives out a deep sigh and, in a scene of masterful animation, begins daydreaming — her actions revealing her heart to us just as much as her words do. She scans the horizon, looking for a fantasy date. She makes a semi-pucker motion with her lips. She scrunches her cute face down into her hand with intense delight, caught up in the throes of an imaginary kiss. And she breaks the "fourth wall" by turning and addressing us a couple of times, inviting us to share her fantasy. And we are more than willing since we've seen Popeye essentially blow her off. When she's speaking to us, the artists have drawn her more realistically than usual and she is very attractive.

This all has the effect of drawing us to her, portraying her as an endearing friend, and asking us the implied rhetorical question, "Won't it be fun to see what happens to this lively, appealing character next?" (It will certainly be more fun than watching Popeye take a bath!) Olive says in hopeful, "I want to go for it" tones, "I wish I could meet a big strong sheik who'd kiss…"

"…me all to pieces and leave me soooo weeaak!!" Then she gasps and lets out a long feminine swoon, "Oooohhh mmmm!" As Olive finishes her sentence, the camera pans over to the handsome sheik, now gazing happily at Ms. Oyl, his racing form forgotten. He does a double-take when he fully realizes what he's seeing and hearing. His body stiffens and leans toward Olive. His eyes are enlarged and his mouth hangs open in amazed, rapturous delight. He scrunches up the racing form in his hand. His moustache also stiffens, elongates, and begins whirling around like a propeller. A sword in his pants is now visible sticking out of his waistband and causing a strategic area of his lower covering to bulge! As his wolf reaction comes to an end, he has a very male look of desire on his face.

Leaping up, the sheik zooms past the entrance of the "gas station" building (he only had to go a few steps, but such is the effect of Olive Oyl on cartoon men that they become superenergized). Then he executes a "Bat Turn" and swoops inside. (Viewing this scene in slow motion reveals that before he turns, his body elongates and, like Mr. Fantastic, he reaches out, nearly grabbing Olive.)

The sheik almost instantaneously exits the building using superspeed and carrying a bunch of stuff. The orchestra shares his impatient frenzy. He runs past Olive Oyl and, at "warp speed," sets up a bazaar-like tent/booth with an Oriental flavor and rich look. (The set-up is great to watch in slow motion.) Hanging a heart-shaped sign on it that reads, "Sheik's Daily Special — 1 Kiss 1 Buck," he then pulls T.L.G.G. up from behind the counter. The little guy begins playing some sort of exotic flute-like instrument as the handsome, muscular sheik strikes a manly, expectant, "I'm going to get the girl," pose. The tune T.L.G.G. plays is a snake-charming melody, and we also hear erotic bongo/jungle drums beating away in the background.

The fact that the racing form was quickly discarded when he eyeballed Olive and heard her fantasy, makes us root for the sheik and Olive to get together. The prospect of wooing Ms. Oyl galvanized him into action, and what he was doing beforehand was no longer important. This guy is hot-blooded, and his pastime, other than racing, seems to be the same as Pepe Le Pew's, who once said, "Everyone should have a hobby. Mine is making love." Contrast the sheik's reaction to, and pursuit of, Olive with Popeye's indifference and neglect. Who (at least at this point in the cartoon) is more compatible with the young, vital miss?

The cartoon fades to a close-up of a pretty-faced Olive, her hair peeking out of her hat and outlining the sides of her head, resting her head on her two hands, and her elbows on the side of the convertible. Her eyes are closed dreamily. As she hears the music at some deep, subconscious level, her left eye opens and its pupil bounces to the top. Then as that eye closes part way, revealing to us that she wears attractive blue eye shadow, her right eye follows suit. The eyes keep at it, alternating in time to the drumbeat. Suddenly, she snaps upright in a hypnotic spell. Her eyes are now wide open, as is her mouth. She turns toward the sheik. Her shoulders start in doing the drumbeat thing. Then, snake-like, she flows down the side of the camel and undulates across the sand toward the booth while moving her mouth in time to the music. The orchestra joins in with notes that let us know that Olive is reaching her destination. She approaches the flute thingy and T.L.G.G. uses it to maneuver her up right in front of the sign. The song ends and we're treated to a close-up of Olive and the sign.

She shakes her cute head as she and the orchestra comes out of the spell. (The sheik won't need hypnosis to win her, but will do so on his own merits, fair and square.) Olive does a double-take with her eyes bulging out as she sees and reads the sign. The romantic desert music starts up again. Olive, in a breathy, innocent, enraptured, "it can't be true, I'm so lucky," voice (one of the sexiest she's ever used in any cartoon) exclaims, "Oh bar-uh-ther!" The camera pulls back to give us a full shot of Olive, so her safari shirt and pants can show off her great figure in some frames. She gasps, and in a soft, overwhelmed, bedroom voice enthuses, "Hubba, hubba, hubba, hubba, hubba!" as she pulls down the corner of her shirt with her left hand, revealing her undershirt, and puts her right hand and arm inside, guiding them all the way down the length of her body and into her left boot. This gives the artists the opportunity, using the bulges and flaps of the safari pants, the bumps made by the incursion of her hand and arm, and the natural shapeliness that Olive has during moments of this cartoon, to draw frames of fashion model legs. Happily, Olive pulls forth a huge stack of money with a flourish. She doesn't want just one kiss, she wants hundreds or thousands or even more! It looks like she's about to give over her life's savings! A giant step forward brings her before the sheik, as she curtseys before him with a pretty look on her face while displaying those legs again. She is bowing to him and humbly presenting herself. Her eyes are closed in rapture. She straightens up in front of the delighted sheik and leans over the counter toward him with her stack of money held out. She then closes her eyes and puckers up. The sheik puts his hands together and gets a look of tender, dreamy desire on his face

We now get a close-up of Olive and the sheik. His facial expressions and movements go from amazed, rapturous delight to lust, to "goofy in love", to "savoring a treasure," to "praising her to the heavens," as he says in a smooth, masculine voice with a French/Arabian/exotic, appealing accent, "Ah, my desert flower, you sand me!!" He takes the money and stuffs it down his shirt. He keeps his cash the same place Olive keeps hers! These two are completely compatible! While the sheik does look at the money happily and determinedly once in a while as he is squirreling it away, he mostly gazes at Olive with a joyous, hungry anticipation. His primary interest is her. Remember that he began wooing her before he even knew she had any money.

The sheik then puckers up, his lips forming the shape of a heart, signifying love and that his heart is going out to Olive. He wants his heart to unite with Olive. The camera moves in a bit as the sheik leans back in order to gain momentum for the kiss, with a wily male look on his face. Moving forward toward the cute, still-puckered, long-lashed, eyelids-closed Olive, the sheik's "heart" lips look joyful. His mouth elongates toward her and his full lips form a cap at the mouth's tip, right before the sheik plants those lips on Olive's forehead. He really squashes them onto her and the skin folds of his mouth and his lips undulate as if he's trying to inject his essence into her, or maybe suck all the sweetness he can from her, or maybe both. An adhering, suction sound is heard and the music emphasizes that the kiss was the climax it was waiting for.

Many viewers don't always share the orchestra's enthusiasm. In fact, they are confused and more than a little frustrated. This guy had the opportunity to kiss a willing Olive on the lips and he settled for her forehead?!?!? What's up with that? Maybe the creators just meant it as a joke, but maybe there's more to it than that. Throughout the cartoon the sheik shows himself to be very knowledgeable in affairs of the heart. It could be, therefore, that he knows that getting physical is all the more sweet when it's not rushed. So, the sheik takes his time, giving he and Olive a tantalizing taste of what's to come later. And the fact that they will both have to wait heightens their eager anticipation. Maybe the sheik's not such a fool after all!

He certainly has the desired effect on Ms. Oyl. The cartoon cuts to a close-up of the upper portion of Olive's head. The sheik's lips are definitely stuck there, but seem to be stuck in a tender fashion. Suddenly, we get a cut-away view of the inner workings of Olive's brain. Revealed is a Rube Goldberg-like machine with turning gears, a mechanical hand, a bell, a horn, and a mechanical mouth. As it operates, the machine matches the sucking sound of the sheik's lips, letting us know that he is the one that set it in motion. The machine and its noisier parts make their own rhythm. The sheik is reaching Olive at her deepest levels. He is ringing Olive's bell. He literally gets her gears turning. He's causing a horn, like a bicycle horn or a party horn, to be sounded in her mind, signifying either warning or celebration. The sheik is definitely communicating with Olive and getting her excited! The mechanical mouth of the machine acts as if it is totally spent and exhausted, or as if its owner is fainting. The meaning may be that Olive's resistance is completely gone and that she's swooning.

As the sheik gently ends the kiss, his face is drawn realistically, and he's devastatingly handsome and wearing a look of pure delight. Olive's eyes and mouth are now joyfully open and the lower half of her body is shapely.

A WOLF IN SHEIK'S CLOTHING (1948)   107

The orchestra hits a note or two appropriate for introducing a comical moment, then morphs into the romantic theme once more. While the sheik affectionately gazes at her, Olive rises straight off the ground by putting her hands at her sides and flapping them along with her feet. Bird sounds are heard on the soundtrack. Eyes closed in rapture, Olive giddily proclaims, "Look a' me! I'm a lovebird! I'm a lovebird!" and then laughs. As the sheik watches her ascend his facial expressions go from affection to tender delight to wolf reaction lust. He reaches his hand up and snatches her by the boots. He pulls her down into his arms. We see that he has now jumped over the counter to be with Olive. As he holds her off the ground, his left arm/hand is wrapped around her thighs, while his other massive hand covers her torso and chest. Olive is utterly smitten.

The sheik begins in a sexy voice, "Reign…" and the filmmakers cut to a close-up of Olive and the sheik as he pulls her close and snuggles against her, cheek-to-cheek. Cuddly Olive narrows her eyes in a flirty, appealing, "come up and see me sometime" blink. The sheik goes on "…as my Queen and with jewels, I will shower you!" The sheik's eyes morph into jewels. Olive is surprised and then delighted as she realizes that she's being invited to marry a millionaire.

A wide-angle shot then shows us Olive wrapping her arms around the sheik's neck. His one hand is now on her knee. The sheik looks back over to his right, puts two fingers of his free hand to his lips and whistles. "Taxi!" he calls and gestures for it to come forward. The "taxi" is a horse driven by T.L.G.G. The romantic music that had been playing comes to a conclusion as the horse is mounted, then a princely fanfare plays for the sheik and his mate, serving to announce them and prepare us for their journey. The sheik looks at Olive with a happy, righteously possessive expression on his face. He has won his bride! His pose displays his manly glory, and then he turns toward Olive with a look of unadulterated lust as the horse executes a super-speed cartoon take-off, zooming Olive and the sheik out of the picture in order to whisk them away to the sheik's home as quickly as possible. Olive has implicitly accepted a guy's marriage proposal and is now willingly being carried off to his place!

The cartoon cuts back to Popeye (remember him?) who has exited the "washroom" and is walking to his "car." A goofier version of his theme song is playing. "Okay, Olive," he says, "let's go!" Popeye doesn't ask if she's ready, or if she had a chance to refresh herself, or how she's feeling, or anything! He's the stereotypical, selfish man who only cares about his own needs, or he's like the bossy father on vacation who demands that his plans and schedule be adhered to. And he certainly gives no indication that he was going to be the slightest bit romantic with Olive. He just wants to get going. His mounting of the camel causes him to face backwards. Maybe he wouldn't have otherwise even looked where he presumed Olive to be at all. He would have just "started up" the camel and pulled out without even realizing that Olive was gone. As it is, he stutters, "Bu…

wh... where are ya?" Popeye looks around and then spots the departing couple in the distance. The shock hits Popeye. "Huh?!?!" His hat flies off his head, and the orchestra shares his surprise.

Meanwhile the horse is galloping ever further away. Olive enthuses, "Oh boy! Just like in the movies!" She and the sheik are holding each other. The sheik is proud, dashing, in control, and in love. Olive is totally contented. The fanfare/traveling music is playing again, but it morphs into a minor, menacing key, signifying peril — for Popeye, that is! He's lost Olive! And maybe peril for Olive, too. She's given her heart, and is presumably about to give up her virginity as well, to a guy that she only knows as a romantic fantasy figure, as opposed to a fully rounded human being. And what kind of guy is he going to turn out to be, really?

We go back to an angry, determined Popeye, giving pursuit on his camel. Then there's a joke about him having to stop at a traffic light to wait for an Eskimo and a dogsled to cross in front of him.

"Wow!" Popeye follows the crossing with his gaze. "How'd he get in this picture?" Throughout this sequence, Popeye is portrayed as a helpless, slack-jawed, frustrated victim. And because he is delayed, the sheik and Olive get more time alone together.

The scene fades out and we fade in on an oasis. An ornate, tall, but thin tent, with a rich-looking welcoming rug leading into its entrance, is there. The romantic music plays again. The sheik and Olive approach the tent. The classy, sophisticated, exotic sheik gestures humbly and says in a sexy voice, "Entrez-vous, s'il vous plait, Ma Cherie."[2] He's still inviting Olive, not trying to force her to do anything.

And Olive's response to her environment and her future mate is quite endearing. A gloriously overwhelmed Ms. Oyl has a "savoring every moment" look on her face. Her hands are together alongside of her head, then she drops them down and out in front of her. The emotions cascading over her are making her give herself little hugs. As the sheik enters his tent, still looking back at her, Olive executes a coy, flirting, delighted partial turn away, showing off her figure — and she does have a nice one. In fact, throughout this sequence, Olive is drawn with curvy hips, pretty legs, and/or a figure in many frames. She turns back as she answers the sheik with, "Likewise, I'm sure." Sweetly naive Olive didn't know what his French words meant, assuming that the sheik was expressing his feelings for her (which, in a sense, he was.) Olive goes through a cute, humble, elaborate gesture of her own, curtseying and opening her arms wide, bowing her head and body before the sheik. She communicates acceptance of the sheik's offer, submission, respect for him and his culture, and a presentation of her whole self to him. It's an "I'm all yours" move. She comes upright and steps to the tent's opening, looking inside. She then does a cartoony double-take. She's stunned; she elongates, and leans backwards. Her hat flies off her head. One musical instrument expresses surprise along with her, but mostly the orchestra keeps up the romantic mood. As Olive returns to normal, and as the hat lands on her head, she displays one of the shapeliest derrieres she's ever had in any cartoon, and also a curvy figure. She then super-speed whips her head into the entrance for another look.

We see what she sees. The tent is like the British science-fiction character Dr. Who's *Tardis*. It's huge on the inside while being small on the outside. The sheik's probably using the reality manipulating powers that so many cartoon characters have, or he's taking advantage of his knowledge of cartoon universe physics, or enjoying the good fortune that the writers have bestowed on him, or all of the above. In any case, the inside of the tent is palatial with marble columns, rich wood carvings, doorways, stairs, crafted lanterns, food, wine, sumptuous pillows, plush rugs, and beautiful tapestries. Obviously there is much more to the sheik than there even initially appeared to be. The classy sheik once again gestures elaborately and appealingly, indicating that "all of this is mine and now it is also yours," as he says in an ultra-sexy voice, "Welcome to my humble abode." There's a bit of "Magnificent Lady, you honor me" ancient chivalry in his gesture as well, along with an attractive "I'm confident that this will knock your socks off, but I'm not pushing it on you and you can still say, 'No'" attitude. The sheik is still wooing Olive and is very appreciative of her, not taking her for granted.

The scene shifts back to Olive outside of the tent. She pulls back a little from the entrance, while still holding on to its side flaps. She then begins to move her body around the side of the tent, but instead, elongates her neck all the way around its small circumference to peer in the entrance from the other side as only a cartoon character, or a comic book star such as Mr. Fantastic or Plastic Man, can. The romantic music comes to a conclusion and uses a sustained brass chord and violins to depict Olive's stretching. As she returns to normal, she catches her breath and says, in perhaps the sexiest voice actress Mae Questel has ever used for either Olive Oyl or Betty Boop, "I don't believe it!" Those four short words, voiced as they are, depict a young, innocent girl being ravished and wanting more — overwhelmed, yet hopeful and grateful. The scene and the music end with Olive peering into the tent again. The music has done its job. Olive and the sheik will be together.

But, of course, there's Popeye to consider. (Darn it!) We fade-in on Popeye still in pursuit. An even goofier version of his theme is now playing, reinforcing the idea that he can't match the sheik. Suddenly, he and we are surprised by the sound of a tire exploding. Popeye halts the camel and then leans over the edge of the "car" saying, "Well, blow me down! A blow out!" One of the camel's legs is deflating and going flat. The music mocks Popeye's situation, but an ominous tone is lurking in the background.

The musical mocking briefly continues as the scene changes to Popeye, sweating bullets and acting like it's a tremendous effort for him to take every step, trudging doggedly on foot through the sand in the heat of the day. Now the music is totally ominous. Popeye tramps along in time to the beat of his fatal-sounding theme song as the camera pulls back and we see that his shadow

One of the many exotic and appealing outfits the creators had Olive Oyl wear in the Famous Studios cartoons.

is using a shadow umbrella and, as opposed to poor Popeye himself, is doing okay. "Whew!" Popeye manages to get out, "I wish I could find me a nice, cool sewer!" (Let's assume he means just a storm sewer!) At least Popeye is exhibiting some of his more positive character traits here — his determination in the face of adversity and his stick-to-it-iveness even when it causes him hardship and pain. And maybe he actually does love Olive, after all, if he's willing to march through a burning "hell" for her. But it would be nice if he'd put as much effort into an ongoing relationship with her as he does into trying to win her back after she goes off with another guy. Speaking of another, more attentive guy, the last note of the song morphs into romantic music as the scene switches to…

…the inside of the sheik's tent. Olive has changed into a harem girl's outfit that the sheik has provided. Olive has now completely entered the sheik's world, and he has taken the first step of fulfilling his promise to shower her with expensive ornaments. Olive's wearing many gold bracelets that move up and down her arms as she gestures. She's standing in front of an expensive looking full-length mirror. She's on tiptoe, arms wide to the sky, head tilted back, eyes closed, with a look of pure bliss on her face. She's opening herself up to experience every iota of sensation and pleasure her new world offers. Maybe she's even offering some sort of ecstatic prayer of thanks to whatever cartoon gods there be. And she's definitely also swooning over her new outfit. We viewers like it too, because not only does the O.O.O.P.S. kick in, but the outfit also shows off her curvy hips and her hourglass figure in many frames during this scene. As she comes down off her toes, she scrunches into herself with delight for a moment and then checks herself out in the mirror. As she revels in her new clothes and the way she looks in them, she wiggles her hips seductively and strikes revealing and appealing poses. Her facial expressions as she does so range from happiness to those of a lower economic class woman teasingly "putting on airs" as she tries on clothing too costly for her and pretends she's a princess. Her left hand goes up along the side and top of her head as she's overcome with delight and having fun striking her poses. While "strutting her stuff," Olive purrs in a sexy, Mae West voice, "Mmmm! I feel so Cleopatric!" The sheik has been looking on with pride and ownership, saying by his expression, "Look at my beautiful woman, World, and see what I can provide for her!" (Of course, since his eyes stay locked on her curves and derriere, he's probably thinking other things, too!) Olive's last pose leaves her right arm outstretched, with her hand open and palm facing downward in front of the sheik. This snaps him out of revering Olive's form to take advantage of the wooing opportunity which is presenting itself. So, tenderly, gently, and appreciatively (although he does have a brief, mini-wolf reaction), he positions her hand with his left one and then takes hers in his right one, and bows forward to kiss it. His expression shows us that he is caught up in the romance himself, as he looks as if he's kissing royalty and sampling something exquisite. Great animation portrays him as super classy, desirable, and handsome while his lips touch Olive's hand.

Now there's a close-up of Olive's arm and hand and the right portion of her torso and hips. The sheik is on the left of the screen, his eyes closed as he savors the taste of his Olive. His lips are on and around her hand. His own right hand is still seductively holding Olive's using his fingertips. This guy is good! Olive undulates her midriff, belly dancer style, in reaction to the sheik. The camera moves in closer to focus in on Olive's arm — while also showing us more of her right side — as a row of literal goose bumps form on it, start quacking or honking, and travel up her arm to vanish inside her sleeve, presumably to go on to affect and cover all of her. "Oooo, Sheiky, you're making with the goose pimples!" Olive gushes in a voice that's urgently gasping — thrilled by the ride and wanting MORE, yet not sure she can take all the sensations without exploding — and turned on. Male viewers can be forgiven for not focusing on, or caring too much about, the goose pimples joke, as the scene also lets Olive show off her curves. The kissing/suction sound effect continues the whole time the sheik's lips are on Olive's arm. He's obviously in no hurry to detach from Ms. Oyl.

The director now cuts to a shot outside in the oasis. T.L.G.G. is sleeping outside of the tent, resting against circular metal grillwork which is now on top of the dark welcoming carpet, making it look like a manhole. There's a sign on the tent which reads, "Sheik At Work." The visual gag makes us think of tents in city streets, covering summer underground construction projects. Besides being part of the joke, the words "Sheik At Work" lets us know that the sheik is doing what he and sheiks do best, wooing and winning women and adding them to harems. Olive doesn't stand a chance of resisting him! The sign also directs all traffic to go around the sheik's tent because nobody should interrupt the important work going on.

A hot and tired Popeye enters the picture, fanning himself with his hat. He reads the sign and, for a few seconds, doesn't interrupt. He just stands there sweating and looking ugly (Sorry, Popeye!) and out of it. The romantic music continues to play in the background to let us know what is still going on inside the tent. If we needed even more confirmation, we get it as we and Popeye hear Olive letting out a "Ooooo, Sheiky!" in a flirting, "What did you just do to me, you impetuous boy! Whatever it is, I *love it*!" voice. (The creators of the cartoon realized what many modern filmmakers have forgotten — some things are meant to be just between two people. The world doesn't need to see everything, particularly when lovemaking is involved. We don't know what the sheik just did, nor do we need to. Restraint, mystery, and our own imaginations can make the scene just as hot, if not hotter, than more explicit ones.) As Olive begins her "Oooo…" the music changes to a more standard version of the Arabian theme, possibly because Popeye's about to confront an Arabian and end the romance, or because the Arab has the upper hand and is winning, or because Olive, in mating with the sheik, is becoming Arabian herself, or maybe all of the above. Anyhow, Popeye, hearing Olive's ravished voice, does a shocked double-take. Then, angrily and determinedly, he squashes his hat back on his head and leans, stretches, and reaches up to yank the tent away from the grillwork and over to himself, as only a cartoon character can. Vowing, "I'll fix that dirty desert rat!" he rushes through the entrance. But, how and why is the sheik a "dirty desert rat?" Thus far in the film, he hasn't done one villainous or dishonest thing — NOT ONE!!! And what is it that Popeye is going to save Olive from? Becoming the mate of a rich, romantic man? With friends like Popeye, Olive doesn't need any enemies!

Cut to inside the tent. The "triumphant Arab" music is still playing, and well it should because the sheik has Olive in his arms. His one hand is around her hips, the other around her back. Olive is leaning back, her eyes closed, happily surrendered. The sheik is leaning forward, puckered up to continue kissing her "all to pieces." As he pulls her close and moves in, his face is handsome. He tenderly kisses Olive on the chin — probably intending to softly kiss her all around her face until finally joining his lips to hers — as Popeye enters, skids to a stop, and ducks between the two lovers. Popeye leaps up, pushing against the sheik's torso

A WOLF IN SHEIK'S CLOTHING (1948)   113

with his back and using his left elbow to break the sheik's hip-hold on Olive. Then he delivers an uppercut to the sheik, saying, "Leggo me goil, ya phony pharaoh!" (Er, how is anything about the sheik phony?)

Popeye has now burst into another's private home where he wasn't wanted and interrupted two who desired to be alone. He had blown off Olive and so she moved on to another. What right does Popeye have to attack the sheik? Who is really the villain here?

The momentum from Popeye's actions forces a staggering Olive Oyl back and out of the picture. Before she vanishes, in a frame or two as she starts falling backwards, we see that she had puckered up for the sheik. Now Olive is surprised, distressed, and worried. She keeps reaching her arms out as she goes helplessly backward, because she's struggling for balance, to be sure, but also because it seems as though she's trying to hold on to her sheik and her fantasy for as long as possible.

The sheik recoils from the blow, but recovers quickly. Popeye lands, after having put his body behind the uppercut, and his face is sort of scrunched up. The sheik, by contrast, is seen in profile and he is "movie star" handsome. Popeye turns smugly away with an "I showed him" expression on his face. The sheik closes his eyes in anger and frustration, but he's still attractive. Popeye strides away, keeping one eye looking back at the sheik, daring him to try anything. The sheik's expression changes to one of malevolent confidence, anticipating happy victory over his enemy. "Ah, ze little worm makes challenge, uhh?" he asks and reaches out and restrains Popeye by holding on to one of Popeye's hairs. "Popeye in danger" notes sound. Pulling out his sword, the sheik lifts and dangles the now helpless and worried-looking Popeye. The "Arab triumph" music starts again as the sheik takes aim with the sword. Popeye knows that he has bit off more than he can chew and is done for. As the sheik swings his sword, looking as if he is guiding it straight to Popeye's middle, the sailor closes his eyes, recoils in fear, and covers his face with his hands. Our "hero" is very vulnerable. But the sheik was aiming for the hair. He slices it, and Popeye falls to the ground, stunned, defeated — an anxious, helpless victim for whatever will come next. Fixing Popeye with a "pay attention, Hated Enemy, because I could do this to you" stare, the sheik holds the hair up between his fingers and takes aim again. A close-up shows him cleaving it in half, an impressive stunt on its own, but equally so because the sword stops right before it would slice the sheik's fingers. Rather than killing Popeye outright, it seems the sheik will settle for warning him off by displaying skill and the sharpness of his weapon. The sheik is showing some mercy here, even though he wouldn't have to because POPEYE IS AN ILLEGAL INTRUDER!!!

The sheik's lesson isn't lost on Popeye, as he reacts with a stunned, scared, "I'm lost" double-take. He shakes his head, as if in pain, and drops his jaw as waves of animated impact emanate from his head. Either the loss of his one hair hurt, or the idea that the sheik is his superior is hitting his brain like a hammer, or both. He lets out a "Wow!" Arab music is playing, but switches to strains of "The Sailor's Hornpipe" as Popeye clamps his mouth shut, gets a determined look on his face, twirls his pipe in anger, and sticks out his jaw. His tenacity, courage, and lifelong mission never to let himself get bested have all kicked in. It's nice at this point in the cartoon to be reminded that there are some things about Popeye that we like!

Popeye snatches the sheik's sword away, puffs up his chest, and then exhales a huge flame from his pipe below the sword. When the flames and heat that engulf the sword subside, we see that Popeye has reshaped it into a giant safety pin. He moves to the surprised sheik and, pulling the sheik's long cape between the sheik's legs, he lifts his adversary off the ground, twists him in the air, and then bounces him on the ground, all the while making the cape into a giant diaper. He finally pins it. Lifting the sheik upright again by the pin, Popeye says, "Dere ya are, Pinup Boy!" The orchestra briefly plays a bit of *Rock-A-Bye Baby* before the sheik frees himself. The sheik then shoves his index finger under Popeye's nose and lifts the sailor off the ground with it. He brings Popeye in to him, and a close-up shows that they can now see eye-to-eye. The sheik says slowly, with hate-filled and deliberate emphasis, "You…I…do…not…like!" Then he pings Popeye's nose with his thumb. The nose wiggles and Popeye winces.

An ominous note sounds as Popeye squirms off the finger. The sheik assumes a battle stance and he and Popeye charge at each other, intent on doing damage. Furious stringed instruments are heard in the background. But Olive rushes between the antagonists, scolding, "Now, now, boys!" and carrying a water pipe that has two long tubes coming out of it and two mouthpieces. She forces the men apart and plants her one foot on Popeye's stomach and the other on the sheik's shoulder. Her feet move up and down the combatant's upper bodies as she, suspended between them, tries to keep them separated. "Both of you smoke a piece of pipe," she commands, "and make peace!" She shoves each of them backwards and thrusts a mouthpiece into each of their mouths, saying, in a New York accent to remind us that Olive, despite the exotic setting, is one of us, or because Mae Questel, a NYC resident through and through, used her real voice for a change, "They-uh!" ("There!") The boys flop down on their butts. Olive's face was pretty at times during this sequence, and near its end she displays her figure again. And the idea of Olive trying to play peacemaker makes her appealing, too, even though she's taken on an impossible task.

As the boys start to recover from shock, she strides away. Her steps are proud, but a few of them are hesitating, stutter-steps. In fact, Olive "walks like an Egyptian" and looks almost like an hieroglyphic come to life in some frames. This is appropriate because the whole reason for the fight is to resolve the question of whether or not Olive will become an Egyptian by marriage. She acts either like she already has, or really wants to. Olive's body is drawn sort of boxy here, but that unusual look, combined with her weird movements, serve to focus our attention on her, where it's been for most of the film. Then, as she's leaving the picture, she wears a cute expression of satisfied, female accomplishment (and even female superiority) on her face. Clearly, she believes her efforts for peace will bear fruit. And while hope is an appealing character trait, even her most ardent fans must admit that Olive is slow on the uptake here and has inexplicably forgotten how these cartoons always end.

The sheik comes out of "stun mode" first and super-blows into his mouthpiece. We see the tube attached to it bulging as the air travels down it. Then the air goes into the pipe and then up through Popeye's tube to the sailor. Popeye just sits there watching it coming. It enters his cheeks and chest, inflating Popeye and lifting him like a giant balloon as the sheik keeps on blowing. The tube finally pops out of Popeye's mouth and he flops back and forth helplessly like a deflating balloon, as the air leaves him via his gaping maw. He falls to the floor, landing on his head. The momentum sits him upright again. Defiantly, Popeye says, "Oh, yeah?" to the sheik while pulling himself to his feet. He picks up his tube and mouthpiece and starts super-sucking on it. Before the worried sheik can react, he's being sucked into his own mouthpiece. He fights the force of Popeye's suction, but soon he's traveling through the tube, and arriving in the cramped, glass ball of the pipe. The momentum spins the entrapped, scrunched sheik around as Popeye laughs heartily and walks out of the picture toward Olive. Triumphant Popeye music is heard, but the sheik doesn't stay helpless for long because T.L.G.G. enters the scene carrying a large wooden hammer. He smashes the glass and is happy as the liberated sheik springs upright again and looks angrily off after Popeye. The sheik then sticks his neck out in grim determination.

The scene changes to outside the tent. Popeye exits the tent, leading Olive by the hand. "Hmmm…," he says, "that sheik is a freak." Then he giggles. Olive, though, doesn't agree. She doesn't join in on his joke, or share his laugh, or celebrate in any way. In fact, she's expressionless. Olive's more stunned or resigned than she is willingly joining Popeye's side. And she's drawn very Fleischeresque and comic strippy here. So, she's very plain-looking for Popeye, but was a Baby Doll for the sheik when she still had her dreams? Which of the boys, therefore, should we really be rooting for, and who, at this point in the film, do the creators really think is the best man for Olive? She's vital and beautiful when she's with the sheik, but a non-entity when she's with Popeye. Certainly Popeye, in this cartoon, has only treated her as an object to be won and a person to be controlled, not as someone to be cherished, listened to, or even considered in the plan-making process. Is Popeye just as abusive in his own way as the guys who try to force themselves on Olive?

As Popeye and Olive depart, the music strikes a chord as though the cartoon is over.

But inside the tent (where gorgeous, sumptuous backgrounds are on display), the sheik super-speeds to a lever on a wall next to two massive doors. Ominous music plays as he pulls down the lever and the doors open to reveal a giant vulture-like monster/bird. The sheik gives it an order in another language and gestures toward Popeye. The horrible creature takes flight as it wails/calls/crows.[3]

We see Popeye and Olive walking across the sand. They hear the bird-thingy and look back in fearful shock. The bird swoops down and snatches Popeye up in its claws. A stunned Olive looks on as it carries him ever further away, finally dipping below the horizon. Scary flight music building to a disastrous climax plays. We see signs in the distance of a great battle taking place, and then a tornado appears where Popeye and the bird had vanished. The orchestra helps it travel back past Olive and into the tent, where it stops spinning to reveal itself to be Popeye carrying a gargantuan platter of roast fowl. As the revelation is made, a gong sounds. Popeye triumph music plays again as Popeye bows and says, "Here ya are, Sheiky! Your goose is cooked!" Then he laughs. Another thing we like about Popeye, his ability to come back from anything, has been displayed. It's a good thing that we've been reminded that Popeye has admirable traits, or we might not care when he's put into the cartoon's final trap.[4]

Cut to the angry sheik. Danger music sounds as he whips out a whip. It is a solid wooden handle with a super-long stretch of rope, cloth, or bandage attached. The sheik swings it mightily.

The scene shifts to Popeye, suddenly worried and helpless as the end of the whip coils around his feet, pulling them tightly together. Popeye starts being wrapped up as the whip spins him around toward the sheik. We see his arms pinned to his sides as the rope/cloth/bandage rises even higher on him. By the time he reaches the sheik, he's bound like a mummy and can't move. Only his head and neck are free. The sheik gestures as though he were a skilled sportsman bagging a prize, or a demented magician finishing a trick. He grabs the pained, now unconscious Popeye mummy by the neck, turns, and stomps down on another lever on the floor. A trap door opens and a cannon rises from it. An evil version of the Arabian theme plays. Olive enters the picture as the sheik mercilessly thrusts Popeye part way into the cannon and then puts his massive hands on Popeye's head and pushes him in the rest of the way. A shocked Olive advances on the sheik, trying to shove him away from Popeye and pulling on his moustache. "You let go of that mummy, you dummy!" she shouts. (Olive doesn't mind guys competing for her, but draws the line at cruelty and murder.) But the sheik puts his hand on her head and effortlessly pushes her away. He has now become physically abusive to Olive! As the music builds to a climax, the sheik fires the cannon and gleefully watches as Popeye flies away.

Cut to a shot of Popeye helplessly sailing through the air. He's unconscious (or worse). There's a good visual effect of wind resistance against his pipe and head. An ominous note is sustained to accompany "hurtling through the air" music.

We see a sphinx. Maybe it's even The Sphinx. Anyway, it opens its mouth and receives Popeye with a sound that's a cross between a swallowing noise and a trap shutting. The sphinx closes its mouth again. A cut-away shot shows us Popeye as a ball, bouncing down the corridors and chambers inside the sphinx, going lower and lower down, and deeper and deeper in. Electronic sounds and pin ball machine noises are heard as Popeye acts like a small ball in an arcade game, and the orchestra follows him to his fate. When Popeye reaches the bottom, he first is squashed by the momentum into an amorphous mass on the floor of the crypt, but then he rebounds to his normal, but still mummified, shape. There's a corpse in there with him as well! A prize bell rings, mixed with a deadly "that's the end of Popeye" chord. After all, the sphinx and the sheik have won. A close-up of the sphinx's head then shows us that the word "Tilt" is blinking on its forehead, accompanied by an electronic sound and staccato notes, completing the pin ball joke. But the sphinx is now broken. It won't open up again. And since gamers stay away from a machine that has gone "Tilt," nobody will come to the sailor's rescue. How will Popeye get out?

In this cartoon, as in *Tar with a Star*, Popeye is entombed in a grave. This kind of thing made kids watching these cartoons quite uncomfortable. Kids knew that graveyards were where ghosts and evil spirits dwelt. And were we supposed to believe that maybe Popeye was actually dead?!?!? And if he wasn't, what could be creepier than being buried alive? And what must it be like to be totally immobilized? Or to die slowly because your air is running out? Okay, for much of the cartoon we may have wanted the sheik to win Olive, but Popeye was still our buddy and nobody deserves to be buried alive. If indeed Popeye still is alive, which at this point is doubtful.

The scene with the sphinx fades out and the interior of the sheik's tent fades back in. The sheik is hungrily chasing Olive. As they run right up one wall and across the ceiling, Olive pleads/scolds/commands, "You keep yourself to you! You, you, you, wolf in sheik's clothing!" Frantic, perilous chase music is playing, and the sheik is always so close to grabbing her. As Olive starts up the wall a second time, the sheik, gleefully confident, stays on the ground, but using magical abilities or cartoon physics, reaches to the left of the screen and actually pulls the camera's "eye" partway shut! Olive snaps, "I hate you!" but she realizes that the sheik is literally closing the scene around her. She tries to grab the ceiling and hold on, but the sheik is now pulling the other side closed. The sheik brings blackness in upon Olive, so that she's left on an empty screen with nothing to hang on to or stand on. She falls through the inky void, yelling for help. (Olive is obviously frightened, but this journey through Limbo was also pretty scary for kids. Imagine having your world literally pulled out from under you!) Olive lands in another scene, a stone basement beneath the tent. She falls into a recess in a floor of cement, hardened sand, or marble blocks, and onto a steel trap door. There's a human skull and bones lying near the door. The halves of the door spring up and open, propelling Ms. Oyl into the air, and we see a crocodile leaping and swimming in the pool beneath the door. Olive lands, balancing herself with each foot on an opposite edge of the open halves of the door. As the croc's mouth opens wide, so do the halves, effectively lowering Olive to the hungry reptile. She tries to get herself higher, but loses her balance a little, causing her upper body to pitch forward and downward at the crocodile as it snaps its jaws shut. For a microsecond it looks as if Olive's been eaten! But then we see that her body has swung through the jaws and, because she's a cartoon character and isn't like you and me, rotated through her own legs to become upright again. This keeps happening and the croc's jaws keep snapping shut with a sound like a door closing. Olive keeps yelling for help. Her calls sound less shrill, and more sweetly feminine, than usual in this scene, and especially later. The evil version of the Arabian theme continues on the soundtrack.

There's a quick cut to Popeye in the belly of the sphinx. Great scenics are used. There's a mummy lying in the lower right-hand corner of the screen. Hieroglyphics can be seen on the walls. Various shades of purple, blue, and black are used to convey shadows. Popeye is coming to and hears Olive's cries. He shakes away the fog and looks around with determination, saying, "What I needs is some spinach!" There's a metal can with a hieroglyphics label on a ledge near his head.

We get a close-up of the can's label. In one of the coolest, most brilliantly executed, Popeye cartoon sequences ever, the figures on the label move and re-shape themselves into the word, "spinach." A few notes of Popeye's theme are played. Then we see a happy Popeye use his upside-down pipe as a blow torch/can opener while "spinach eating" music plays. As the lid flies open, Popeye sucks up the contents with his mouth. He chews and swallows it and, as the spinach bulge moves down his body, it bursts open his bonds. Popeye then flexes a huge bicep. As the music builds to an explosive climax, a volcano appears within the muscle and erupts. The director cuts to an exterior shot of the sphinx as the eruption blows its head off. Popeye super-leaps out and zooms off to the sheik's tent.

We see that the sheik has obviously offered Olive "help" to escape the croc — a short rope tied to a fishing pole he's holding. But, as Olive hangs on to the rope for dear life and some threatening Arabian strains are heard, he lowers and dangles Olive over the pit. As the croc opens wide and leaps up to chow down, the sheik pulls Olive up, only to lower her again. "And now, my proud beauty," he sneers, "you make between me or ze crocodile, eh?" The cruel playboy is letting Olive know that, in some manner, she will be devoured tonight — either by the croc, after its fashion in the pit, or by the sheik in his own fashion in his chambers. Calling her "proud beauty" shows us that the sheik realizes that now, despite his wealth and looks, Olive has decided she's too good for him. And she's right! Fortunately for her, Popeye comes into the picture and zips the croc's mouth shut. His triumphant theme is played.

But wait! Seeing what happened, the sheik pulls Olive up and out, grabs her leg, and happily runs off with her! The orchestra suddenly doubts whether Popeye has ultimately won. But our hero doggedly skedaddles after the villain, executing a stretchy cartoon exit as he does so.

Cut to the sheik, with an evil grin on his face, carrying a horizontal Olive, his arm around her midsection. Olive is beside herself and is yelling, "Help!" again in the sweeter voice. The sheik glances behind him and is alarmed. He faces forward again as Popeye catches up and stomps down on the sheik's trailing cape. The sheik now just "spins his wheels," unable to move forward. Popeye powerfully and painfully (for the villain) grasps the sheik's shoulder and lifts the villain up and moves him, suspended in the air, to the rear of the group. Olive is released in the process. The sheik is wearing an "out of it" look on his face and Popeye delivers an uppercut which punches him out of his cape and out of the picture.

Cut to a wall of hieroglyphics. Pretty, nubile women are posing before a leering pharaoh who is holding a whip or a ruling staff. The sheik smashes into the wall and is embedded there in place of one of the women. The knocked-silly sheik is even now in the same pose that the woman was. Poetic justice has been served. The sheik suffers the fate he had planned for Olive — he's now the love slave of a rich, powerful Egyptian!

We fade in on Popeye and a hero-worshiping Olive Oyl. They seem to be riding in some sort of open-air conveyance being driven by T.L.G.G. We can see clouds behind them. A part Arabian/part goofy version of the Popeye theme is on the sound track. Popeye gestures and commands, "Home, James!" Olive puts her one arm around Popeye and holds his head in her other hand. She puckers up and pulls the pleased sailor forward for a long, intense, adhesive kiss which sends Popeye into a dreamy state as she keeps pressing herself into him. But suddenly, Popeye realizes that T.L.G.G. has turned his head and is watching them. Popeye and Olive look at him in anger, and then Popeye, showing he understands the needs of lovers for privacy and that he can manipulate reality, too, pulls a screen down from nowhere, blocking them from T.L.G.G.'s vision, and saying, "Hey, you! Keep your eyes on the road!"

The camera pulls back to show us that they are all on a flying carpet (another fantasy we had as kids), as the frustrated Little Gnome Guy returns to his driving,

Olive returns to her kissing, and Popeye to his being caught up in "Olive Oyl bliss."

We hear an antique car horn as they fly away from us and out of the picture. The iris follows them and then closes.

A Wolf in Sheik's Clothing (1948)

Director: I. Sparber
Animation: Tom Johnson and George Rufle
Musical Direction: Winston Sharples
Story: Larry Riley and I. Klein
Scenics: Tom Ford

CHAPTER 11

Snow Place Like Home (1948)

Pierre is another handsome Famous Studios antagonist who isn't Bluto.

Snow Place Like Home has a most unique setting for a Famous Studios romance — the Artic Circle and the North Pole itself! The Title Card features the words "Snow Place Like Home" carved on an igloo. There's a glow coming from somewhere behind the igloo. The glow could be interpreted as centering around the igloo itself, the place of warm shelter in a hostile environment. The igloo has a chimney as a visual gag, but maybe, too, this emphasizes the "Home" of the title.

Viewers may puzzle over the cartoon's opening scene following that title card as there's not a snowflake or iceberg in sight. Instead, Popeye and Olive Oyl are wearing bathing suits and are relaxing in a boat off the coast of a sunny, sandy beach. But, as is the case in many Famous Studios cartoons, though Popeye and Olive are next to each other at the same geographical location, they don't really seem to be together. They aren't even facing one another. Each is engaged in a separate activity. Olive is eating three ice cream cones at once — vanilla, chocolate, and strawberry, of course. (The food stand must have run out of Neapolitan.) And Popeye has a fishing line attached to one of his toes. No sooner does the line hit the water than another fish is hooked, and Popeye, with a minimum of effort, jerks his foot so the fish joins the ever-growing catch in Popeye's bucket. The radio in the boat is playing a romantic song, *June In January*, but there's no romance evident on screen. Popeye and Olive could be a loving couple that's comfortable with each other, but they could also be "just friends," or even brother and sister, according to what the cartoon has shown us so far.

Olive is having a great time with her ice cream cones, her tongue licking each one in sequence and then starting over again. As it rubs across the surface of each scoop, her tongue makes a high-pitched squeaking sound similar to a cloth taking the last of the Windex off a mirror, or a hand running over a head of hair that's just had shampoo rinsed away. Olive Oyl is squeaky clean and innocent, which is part of her appeal in this scene. Olive is totally caught up in the joy of ice cream on a hot day. Her happiness, some frames where she's drawn with a cute face, and the O.O.O.P.S. factor[1] attract us to her. Also, though the creators at this point in the film gave her a Fleischeresque figure, they at least made her bikini top fuller and rounder than Max and Dave would have, and it remains so until Olive covers up with a fur coat later.

Popeye, for his part, is attired in a kind of dorky-looking one-piece suit that covers up much of his torso. It was probably all the rage in the 1890s, but today not so much. It makes Popeye seem old and out of it. The Sailorman is enjoying his pursuit as well, but he has a kind of cocky, smug expression on his face. He gives a backward glance over his shoulder to Olive at one point as if to say, "Ain't I something?"

The camera gives us a close-up of the radio by Olive's foot. Olive, being a cartoon exaggeration of femininity, wears slightly high-heeled sandals. Her foot is drawn here to resemble a real human foot. Because of her choice of footwear and the fact that she looks "real," the impression is again given that Olive is attractive. A voice on the radio warns that, for "Miami and vicinity, a slight blow is forecast." It repeats, "A slight blow."

We're now back to viewing Popeye and Olive as Popeye laughs, "Guess we could use a little breeze around here, huh, Olive?" The two remain cheerfully oblivious to the hurricane/tornado/tropical storm that's coming until it's practically on top of them. It sucks them into its vortex and carries them north, and as the orchestra portrays the ominous, uncontrollable nature of the storm, it transports them over a topographical map of the North American continent, finishing its journey and its fury over the frozen region at the top of the world.

We then see Popeye and Olive, freed from the storm but still spinning, suspended in the air. As their spinning slows and then ceases, they drop like rocks below the screen. Olive's face is drawn to resemble the expression that stuffed animals which came to life in children's picture books always had when something bad was happening, making the viewers want to go, "Awwww!" and protect her. Poor Popeye just looks like a goofy cartoon character who has been battered silly and is insensate.

The camera itself drops down to find Popeye and Olive. They've landed at the North Pole and their radio is now perched on top of it. The Pole itself is a barber's pole. The glow of the Northern Lights pulsates through the sky. The radio is trying in vain to finish singing *June*, but it keeps shivering, sneezing, and stuttering because of the cold.

Popeye has landed face-first on snow-covered ice. He looks unconscious or stunned, as his tongue is hanging out. Olive has plunged feet-first through the ice. Her head (with a lovely face in a frame or two before it reverts back to a plainer design) and shoulders are bobbing up through the hole. Futilely hugging herself, Olive manages to yell, "Ooowoooo! Help, Popeye! Ooooo! I'm freezing!" as the water re-solidifies around her and the music on the soundtrack plays desperate chords. Popeye comes out of his stupor, exclaiming, "Wow!" and tries to pull Olive free by grasping her head and yanking. Ouch!

The scene dissolves into Popeye, with ice tongs, carrying Olive Oyl, encased in a huge block of ice, on his back. As he trudges across the arctic waste, the soundtrack plays mystical sounding chords made up of the notes in *June*. The music conveys a sense of foreboding, a feeling of being in an otherworldly place, and even a hint of romance. The only romance on screen, though, is Popeye making a remark that, depending how you look at it, could be an attempt to flirt with Miss Oyl, or a tasteless, unfeeling pun in light of Olive's situation, or an expression of Popeye's optimism, or proof that Popeye is self-centered as he laughs at his own joke. Popeye says, "Oooo! What beautiful ice you got, Olive!"[2] Olive is too stunned to respond. A penguin then appears with a sign flashing on his belly, "Pierre's Trading Post. Furs Bought and Sold." He leads Popeye the ice man and Olive the ice block princess to what could be their salvation.

Hopeful, "introducing a beautiful sight," royal presentation music starts swelling as the scene now shifts to the exterior of the Trading Post. It's a giant igloo with an ice chimney. There's a mailbox out in front and a huge sign on top of the igloo which has changing, colored neon lights — the glow from it extending to the sky. The suggestion is given that maybe this is what the Northern Lights actually are.

The camera goes inside while "business as usual is being conducted" music plays.[3] We see the handsome, but bored and disgusted, Pierre behind the counter bilking an Eskimo out of a stack of pelts by paying the "best price" for them, namely a fan and an ice cream cone. The Eskimo goes away happy, though. This joke might be considered offensive in today's politically correct, sensitive world, but it doesn't have to be interpreted as a slam against all Eskimos, just this particular cartoon one.

Speaking of Pierre, though he is revealed right away as being a selfish swindler, the expression on his face tells us that he doesn't enjoy the cheating, and he's not congratulating himself. It's just what he needs to do in order to survive. In fact, Pierre looks lifeless, joyless, and lonely. He's living all by himself at the Post, after all. So while we begin to fear for what will happen when Popeye and Olive encounter the crook, we feel a little sorry for him as well.

But Pierre is about to be pleasantly jolted back to life! A goofy version of the Popeye theme starts playing on the soundtrack as Popeye waddles into the picture. Pierre is still disgusted and disinterested as Popeye says he needs a couple of fur coats and a sleigh. Then Pierre glances over the top of Popeye and spots Olive Oyl. Instantly, his hand scrunches Popeye's face into the countertop with a sound effect like a door slamming shut and locking, emphasizing both face meeting wood and the fact that Popeye's been effectively done away with for the next sequence. Pierre's body leans toward Olive. His neck stretches forward and his eyes pop out. His mouth hangs open in an expression of amazed, rapturous delight. Life has re-engaged Pierre by enthralling him with one of its most potent forces. As testosterone and desire course through his veins, the music on the soundtrack strikes an excited chord and then begins mixing the mystic version of *June* with the sounds of a fire alarm bell. The bell and the sounds of a fire gain dominance as a close-up of his face shows us that Olive Oyl has inflamed Pierre, literally! His eyeballs turn into flames as the musicians strike a chord that lets us know that a fire has begun, in more ways than one.

The camera pulls back as we see Olive innocently shifting her eyes to look around the Trading Post, unaware that Pierre is gazing at her. Beams of heat come out of his combustible eyes and start to work on Olive's icy prison. The musical score joins Pierre in giving Olive a slow once-over, his eyes melting her ice block as they travel from her top down to her toes. When she first feels the heat, she turns, with a cute face and an appealing ponytail, in openmouthed surprise, to see Pierre. As she understands what's happening, her face becomes cartoonier. She follows Pierre's liberating gaze down, and she gets a look of delight on her face. Delighted that she's being freed, yes, but the impression is given that she's also delighted that she has this kind of effect on Pierre. She *wants* this guy to give her the once-over.

Even though he's using our hero's head as a surface to lean against while he appreciates Olive, sympathy for, and empathy with, Pierre are built up during this scene. Discovering Olive Oyl gives Pierre joy, hope, and meaning. It's easy to start to root for him to win Ms. Oyl because he needs, and craves, her so much. Popeye, though, it seems, would probably be happy enough off doing something alone, telling himself jokes under his breath to keep amused. After all, it wasn't

Popeye who literally melted Olive. In fact, there doesn't seem to be any sparks at all between he and Ms. Oyl!

Speaking of Popeye, he removes his face from the countertop after Pierre, with a look of pure lust and then an expression of happy determination, speeds off toward the back of the store. Popeye must have had extra doses of his "mild mannered" or "stupid" pills that morning because he, not realizing that Pierre is gone, smiles as if nothing happened and begins again, "As I was sayin'...eh, huh?!?" Popeye notices that Pierre, with a great look of eager love on his face and carrying several fur coats in his arms, has rocketed past the sailor toward Olive Oyl. Popeye's expression is one of sad shock as he does a double-take. The fact that Pierre is now with Olive sinks in. As he sees the couple, he has a despairing, giving up look on his face. Here, the film makers build up sympathy for our hero. Popeye knows he has been out-classed and he knows Olive. She has a sweet spirit, but is still a 1940s version of The Material Girl. Could she fall for a handsome, amorous Frenchman who is presenting her with the gift of a fur coat? You bet!

And that's exactly what's happening. We see that Pierre is eagerly and expectantly, yet tenderly, helping Olive slip into a fur. In an enraptured voice, she declares, "It's just gorgeous!" She then closes her eyes in delight and gets caught up in the fantasy come true of a fur coat and a romance. She adopts a fashion model's walk as she either pretends that she's on the runway, or starts using body language to flirt with Pierre, or both. Romantic music starts playing. But unknown to Olive, Pierre's expression has now changed to a very animalistic one.

Then Pierre makes a move to grab Olive Oyl. But, of course, by now, Popeye has rushed over to them. He taps Pierre on the shoulder, abruptly interrupting the Frenchman's plans. The smiling, naive Popeye (seemingly suddenly all over his consternation in seeing a guy making a play for Olive) asks where *his* fur coat is. Catching himself, Pierre answers in a smooth, common voice, "Of course!" He clears his throat and puts his arm around his "good buddy" Popeye. "Just step this way to ze men's department."

The scene shifts to Popeye standing outside of the trading post at the entrance to an ice cave with a sign on it, "Furs Cold Storage." Pierre comes out of it, dragging a fur. Pierre ties what looks like the arms of a polar bear around Popeye. "Zair!" Pierre declares. "A genuine bearskin coat." Snoring sounds are heard. As Pierre is leaving, Popeye checks out his new wrap in an ice mound mirror and says, "Thanks, Pierrey!" Playing with the coat, he jokes, "Nothing like a bearskin to cover your bare skin!"[4] and he laughs. Then the live polar bear which is Popeye's "coat" wakes up and begins mauling the sailor. Desperate, "in danger" music starts up as a furious fistfight (which is great to watch in slow motion) begins. Popeye and the bear rumble and tumble their way into the cave where the battle continues off camera. The end result is that Popeye, with a sophisticated air, strolls leisurely out of the cave wearing a stylish bearskin coat and hat, and twirling an icicle he's using as a walking stick. After he ambles off, the newly-skinned bear comes out wearing only Popeye's bathing suit. "Brrrr!" he shivers.

Back in the trading post, a cute-faced and curvy Olive Oyl wearing a beautiful fur coat is happily, confidently, and expectantly powdering her face in preparation for a date with Pierre. A romantic version of *June* is playing on the soundtrack. The camera pans over a few feet to show us Pierre shaving before a mirror and using a large iron file to do it! Aside from being a good joke, this also lets us know how tough Pierre is. And how tender, as well. He wants a REALLY close shave in order to get close to Olive. This idea of two people getting all spruced up for their time together is very romantic. Pierre, taking one last look in the mirror, strolls off toward Olive with his eyes happily closed as he dreams of love. But with a kettle drum's "boing" on the soundtrack, he bumps into shrimpy Popeye!

A slightly dopier version of Popeye's strolling music begins as Popeye nonchalantly says, "The coat fits swell, Pierre-y! Now, uh, how about me sleigh?" Popeye, here still adopting the sophisticated air that Pierre has naturally, is either supremely confident that he can handle whatever Pierre will throw at him to the point of not even bringing up the polar bear incident, or incredibly easygoing and forgiving, or unbelievably shortsighted and stupid. Take your pick.

While Popeye smugly stands there, Pierre snarls, "Sleigh, eh? Uhhh!" Or maybe in context it's the punny "Slay, eh? Uhhh!" He rolls up his sleeve and gives Popeye such a powerful punch that Popeye flies all the way across the store to land in a barrel of grease. If the scene is played in slow motion, Popeye is seen to be unconscious and totally helpless as he goes into the barrel. The impact and the unspent kinetic energy and momentum from the punch tip the barrel over and send it rolling out the door and off of an overhang to burst into pieces on the frozen ground below. A combination of the grease and the collision has apparently ripped Popeye's garment asunder because he now has the slick, black grease as his only covering! "Danger" music was used as Popeye was flying and rolling, then a "death knell" sounded as he landed on the ice. As Popeye comes to and tries to pull himself together, he's spotted by a female seal. Mistaking the darkened Popeye for a potential mate of her own species, she falls for him while a mocking version of *Love In Bloom* plays in the background. As she tries to snuggle and kiss him, Popeye finds that he can't maneuver on the ice with his coating. He can't escape the amorous seal and finally has to propel himself away by running/skipping on all fours, with the female right behind him. The goofy music continues and some funny "chase notes" wrap up the scene.

Although the cartoon has awakened sympathy for Pierre and got us hoping that he and Olive have a great date, our hearts really go out to Popeye here. This is about as humiliated as the poor guy has ever been! He's been outclassed by his rival and cast out into the dark and the cold. He's been de-robed and covered in grease. The comparison with a person being tarred and feathered and run out of town is obvious. And though the bit with the seal is cute, it conveys the idea that Popeye's love affairs are nothing but jokes. He can only find romance when he's not being himself, and then only with an animal, not a human! And while Popeye's assuming of the usual Olive Oyl role — the helpless, pursued object of desire — is humorous, it also has the effect of feminizing him. The rough, tough, masculine sailor, he ain't in this scene!

The music and the scene change at the same time. The orchestra is now playing the romantic version of *June* as we look in on the dating duo of Pierre and Olive. The camera first centers in on a box of bubblegum on top of a barrel and then pulls back to reveal Olive Oyl and Pierre standing on opposite sides of the box, each chewing gum. Chewing bubblegum on a date?!?! Well, it does focus attention on puckering lips, as Olive and Pierre use the gum to flirt. Pierre goes first, blowing a heart-shaped bubble (as only a cartoon character can do) toward Olive. He's expressing what's going on inside of him and bringing it out for Olive to see. She responds by giving him a flirty, sexy, "I'm yours," inviting laugh. Popeye has now crawled in the door, but is still away from the couple. He spots them as the camera returns to them. Olive has her lips puckered and is blowing a huge, ever-growing bubble at Pierre. Pierre puckers up in response and anticipation. Then, grinning and confident, Pierre pulls out a pin. Olive's bubble hits the pin and POP! After the bubble's explosion clears away from the screen, we see that Olive has landed in Pierre's arms. His left hand is around her legs and his right is holding the curve of her figure. He goes to kiss her as the music sweeps to a romantic conclusion.

The orchestra wants Pierre to kiss her. We viewers want Pierre to kiss her. After all, that's what this entire romantic scene has been leading up to. And Olive wants him to kiss her. She puckers up, half closes her eyes, then opens her mouth in an "O" shape in preparation for the kiss. But Popeye quickly snatches her out of Pierre's arms and puts her aside out of the picture as he growls, "Hey! Let go me goil, ya fur flusher!" Olive, as Popeye came into the scene, had started to turn away from Pierre with a serious look on her face. (Incidentally, as Olive turns and becomes concerned, her face and her hairstyle are among the prettiest they have ever been in a Famous Studios' cartoon. And that's saying something!)

Why did Olive turn away from Pierre? Why is she looking so concerned? Some have interpreted this to mean that she didn't want to kiss the Frenchman after all. But it could be because she spotted Popeye coming and didn't want to kiss Pierre in front of him, eschewing public displays of affection and wanting her smooching done in private. Or perhaps, her reaction is, "Oh no! Two guys competing for me are both here at the same time! Now what do I do? Is there going to be a fight?" These interpretations could have some merit, because, aside from a very brief, fleeting half-smile acknowledging Popeye's presence, and discernable only when the cartoon is viewed in slow motion, Olive's face keeps wearing her concern even after Popeye has taken her out of Pierre's arms and is setting her down. But there is another option. Popeye, though covered in grease, and not showing anything he shouldn't be, has no clothes on! Maybe Olive, being the sweet, innocent miss, is turning aside from what is a potentially startling and immodest sight.

In any case, the sexual/romantic tension that the cartoon was building up goes unresolved, as Pierre and Olive never again woo by mutual consent for the remainder of the film, and Popeye and Olive never so much as throw a kiss toward each other. The audience members, along with Pierre, remain frustrated.

The soundtrack of *Snow Place* now plays a little Popeye ditty and a fight begins. Amid metallic machinery sounds and industrial music, Pierre and Popeye go through a robot-like, violent, repeating cycle, as though they themselves are now parts of some "Perpetual Battle" device. Pierre scrunches Popeye down toward the floor with a punch. Then Popeye springs back up and delivers an uppercut to his foe. And so it continues, with neither antagonist able to overcome the other. Pierre is every bit Popeye's equal!

Fortunately for Popeye, he receives some help, not from spinach, as we can see that he hasn't any on him, but from the seal. The love-struck animal had entered the Post happily searching for her honey, Popeye. Seeing the rhythmic battle, she becomes angry. She quickly positions herself under Pierre and balances him like a ball, spinning him around on her nose. Circus music plays in the background. Coming out of his battle stupor, Popeye races off screen. Popeye takes a quick shower in a water barrel to rid himself of the grease. He grabs a fur coat hanging nearby and covers his bare skin.

Then he positions shovels around the barrel so that their handles are touching over its opening. Popeye whistles for the seal. The seal throws Pierre into the barrel and the shovel heads are propelled upward and inward to hit him repeatedly.

"As I was sayin', Pierre-y, eh, how about me sleigh?"

Seemingly defeated and breathing hard, Pierre answers, "Ho-kay! You win. Zair she is! (points) Ze best what I have." Triumphant Popeye music is heard. But wait! Doesn't the orchestra remember that Popeye can't trust Pierre?

Evidently Popeye doesn't remember either, because he naively goes over to a big contraption that's recessed into the wall, like a hideaway bed. A tentative ditty is heard on the soundtrack. He pries the first layer of the contraption out and down to the floor. It seems indeed to be a sled. Popeye happily jumps onto it. This causes the door holding back the next layers to open. A thick metal bar falls upon the sailor, pinning his arms at his sides and knocking him, stomach first, down onto the "sled." Popeye's eyes are now closed and he's wearing a pained expression. Next a solid, heavy looking, metal lid ringed by steel teeth comes down on Popeye. Other teeth seem to rise up out of the bottom section Popeye is lying on to meet and greet them. Popeye's head and neck are now poking out through a narrow space between the teeth. Popeye is seemingly unconscious, or at least in shock again. A sign reveals what the device really is — "Super Bear Trap $98.50." We see that there's a big eyelet on top of the lid with a rope attached to it. Pierre grabs the other end of the rope with an evil expression on his face and hurriedly exits with it as Olive comes on screen, horrified. Angrily, she races toward Pierre. Desperate, final, jeopardy music is playing.

"Stop it, you igloo icky! You might hurt my Popeye!" she screams. In some frames of this and the following scenes, Olive's coat clings appealingly to parts of her figure. This is in keeping with the Famous Studios' practice of prettying Olive up when it looks as if the villain has won, probably in order to increase the suspense. Villains aren't supposed to have their way with pretty girls, you know.

But Pierre is attaching his end of the rope to a huge metal harpoon and stuffing the harpoon into a cannon. A smug, evil, and determined look is on his face. Olive beats on him, but her blows have no effect. Not only is Popeye clearly doomed, but it is evident that Ms. Oyl will be unable to defend herself against this villain. Pierre pulls the cannon's firing mechanism and forces/knocks Olive backward with the same motion. Olive is stunned and then throws her arms up in front of her face as blast protection, and perhaps to blot out the terrible thing that's happening, as the cannon fires. The rope sails past her as she puts her hands outward as if to ward off, or undo, Popeye's peril, and her own. Her expression tells us that she's expecting the worst. The Popeye trap/missile breaks through the igloo. The sound effects, music, and the visuals convey to us that it is traveling a great distance out over the ocean. A whale spots the projectile and happily leaps up to swallow it whole, grateful for fresh meat. As the whale snaps his mouth shut contentedly, the music comes to a conclusion, conveying a sense of finality as if to say, "That's all folks! Popeye is gone!"

But the scene switches to Popeye, entrapped, floating on water inside of the whale. It's dark and scary. Pieces of a wrecked ship drift past him. We know he has no spinach. And so, evidently, does the orchestra as a flutist plays a soft, mournful, minor-keyed, dirge version of the Popeye theme. Popeye, sounding weak and desperate (though still having the presence of mind to make a pun — what a guy!) moans, "Oooohhh, what a whale of a spot I'm in!"

The danger of Popeye being eaten is one that is used again and again in the Famous Studios cartoons. And it is quite effectively creepy most of those times because being eaten would totally obliterate any trace of our hero. Popeye would disintegrate and become a part of the very thing that ended his existence, whether it be animal, monstrous giant, or cannibal. So, Popeye's body would be used to give fuel to an engine of destruction! There ARE fates worse than just death![5]

Meanwhile, since Popeye seems irrevocably gone, back at the Trading Post Pierre is doing what any Famous Studios male cast member would do in his shoes. He's chasing a frantic Olive all over the place, reaching out with his hands and arms while making kissing motions with his lips. His happy facial expression reveals that he believes that lovemaking is inevitable. And he appears to be right because he always seems just about to reach her. A futilely fleeing Olive Oyl yells at him to keep away from her. Intense, quick, jeopardy music is playing. Pouring on a burst of speed, Olive plunges into a potbellied stove and closes the door behind her, so that a diving Pierre ends up with a face full of iron, rather than a smooch. But the angry, determined Pierre won't give up. He tries to open the door to no avail, so he picks up a sledge hammer and begins rhythmically pounding away on the stove. The music starts building as the stove vibrates violently. Inside, Olive looks sad, worried, and even sort of hypnotized, as what Pierre is doing is shaking her to her core. She's helplessly moving back and forth at sickening speed and her eyes are literally rattling around in her head.

Finally, one of Pierre's blows shatters the stove. Pierre wears a look of malicious triumph. A stove pipe comes down with Olive's feet sticking out from one end of it. The feet start jumping and wiggling as they try to start running away again. As they gain locomotion, which is tough because the legs attached to them inside the pipe are so restricted, Olive's soot-covered head pops out of the other end. Olive is practically immobilized in the presence of a male. And this male is a wolf! Pierre is almost on top of her making kissing and grabbing motions again. And this time there is absolutely no way she can put on a burst of speed to get away. She yells, "Help, Popeye! Oh where are you?"

The camera goes back to the possible savior in question, but he's still in the belly of the whale. The orchestra is playing an "all is about to be lost" version of a Popeye ditty. Will Popeye be digested? Will Pierre have his way with Olive? Popeye looks around helplessly. BUT, a spinach can floats by in the debris as Popeye hears Olive's muffled voice pleading, "Help, Popeye! Save me!" Popeye spies the can and suddenly a look of joy and hope plays across his face. He turns his pipe upside-down in his mouth and uses it to produce a flame ray to get the can open. He inhales the green stuff as the spinach music is heard. He swallows his spinach and, invigorated, he pries the bear trap open. Then he makes a potent muscle. On his bicep, we see hands pushing a plunger down into a box labeled "TNT."

The scene shifts to an outside shot of the whale who suddenly explodes! The whale's skeleton lands on an iceberg and tons of fish fall out of the sky, landing on top of it. (Either they were in the whale's belly, or blown out of the water by the explosion, or the blast turned the giant whale into a heap of little fish!) Popeye leaps onto the pile and firmly plants a "Fresh Fish Today" sign, then zooms off at cartoony superspeed without a second's hesitation.

The Popeye triumph music is playing now, even though back at the Trading Post things have gone from bad to worse. Olive's screams are more desperate. Pierre has caught her and is applying a can opener to the pipe while wearing a ravenously hungry, triumphantly in charge, male look of pure lust on his face. An expression of joyful, very eager anticipation also plays across his countenance. He is working right along with the can opener and soon Olive will be liberated from her metal prison, but exposed to the hot-blooded Pierre.

But, in the nick of time our hero arrives, grabs Olive's ankles and yanks her through the pipe. Popeye plants the freed Olive's feet on the ground (and this time it's she who is covered with black gunk). In a sequence with great timing, Pierre turns and sees what's happening, as an angry Popeye pulls his fist back to hit Pierre, while Olive is busy straightening all the way up. Popeye delivers a powerful uppercut that sends Pierre flying out through the wall of the Post and into the bear's cave. We hear fighting sounds. The bear then comes strolling out dressed in Pierre's clothes. (Score 1 for PETA!) A surprised Pierre emerges, clad only in Popeye's swimsuit. The music mocks him as he shivers and turns blue. Turnabout is fair play! Now it's the rogue's turn to find something to cover his bare skin.

But what a physique he has! He is the total bodybuilding, muscular hunk. With his charm, romantic spirit, sexy voice, attentiveness, and looks, he could have made an excellent match with Olive Oyl! While we're cheering as he receives his just desserts, there's still a sense of tragedy here. Olive could have been his if only he was able to control himself! As Maxwell Smart might put it, "If only he had used his maleness for niceness, instead of evil!"

And speaking of just desserts, Pierre's punishment seems relatively minor compared to what Popeye sometimes dishes out. Of course, though, Pierre lost Olive and will have to go back to his life of ennui and futility. But as far as the immediate physical consequences that we see on the screen go, it seems as if it will be an easy enough thing for Pierre to race back into the Post, cover up, and get warm (after repairing the holes in the igloo, of course). Popeye may be showing mercy. He got Pierre to desist, caused him discomfort, turned the tables, and maybe that's enough.

The beefcake shot of Pierre dissolves into Popeye holding on to the back of a dogsled commanding, "Mush! Mush!" We see that Olive is happily riding in the sled. Popeye jumps onto its runners as the camera reveals that the sled is being pulled by three happy seals — presumably one is Popeye's former pursuer along with some more suitable potential beaus, or two other girlfriends — and the smiling penguin whose flashing signs now reads "Miami Or Bust." Has he switched sides, or is Pierre now out of business for some reason? (Actually, it makes sense he's going south, as penguins only reside in Antarctica. Just a fun science fact, Kiddies!) A happy, cute variation of *June* plays as the camera irises out.

Snow Place Like Home (1948)

Director: Seymour Kneited
Animation: Dave Tendlar, Martin Taras
Musical Direction: Winston Sharples
Story: Carl Meyer, Jack Mercer
Scenics: Anton Loeb

CHAPTER 12

Symphony in Spinach (1948)

In this cartoon, Olive, perhaps inexplicably, rejects Bluto when they are finally alone and in the mood at the piano.

The title makes it obvious that this is going to be a musical cartoon. And indeed it is, as many of the gags are timed to, and involve, the playing of musical instruments. What isn't so obvious from the title is that this cartoon is also about sex and romance, and that the seductions in the film will center around music.

And in this film, characters often talk without moving their mouths, calling to mind the days when Fleischer voice artists would often throw ad-libs into their performances. Whether *Symphony in Spinach* was the result of Jack Mercer, Mae Questel, and Jackson Beck ad-libbing like crazy, or of extra dialog being added to the script after the animation was completed, or of a series of bloopers, we will never know. But the finished product is very entertaining and contains lots of witty lines.

The cartoon begins with Bluto and Popeye reading *Variety* in the park, looking for work in the entertainment industry. Bluto is wearing a suit and tie. Popeye, though, is in his typical white sailor's outfit. Nobody even taught him how to dress for success. Suddenly, they come to life because of an ad they're seeing. We see it, too. It features a picture of Olive Oyl in an evening gown, so the O.O.O.P.S. factor kicks in for us.[1] Bluto and Popeye exclaim, "Oh boy!" Then they read the text of the ad out loud. "Miss Olive desires a good musician for her band. Must have class and double in brass." Then Bluto turns to say to Popeye, "Now dat's what I call a swell…Huh?" But Popeye is already racing to the rehearsal hall to audition. "Bein' a gob, I can play boat instruments," Popeye laughs.

The rehearsal hall is evidently one of the top floors of a classy older downtown skyscraper. Bluto catches up with Popeye as The Sailorman is in the elevator on the ground floor. Forcing the door open, Bluto grabs Popeye by the shirt and throws him out of the car saying, "I'm taking that job, Wise Guy!" The elevator ascends with Bluto. But Popeye super-speeds up flight after flight of stairs. A piano tinkling on the soundtrack accompanies him.

When Bluto exits the elevator in the rehearsal hall, Popeye is already there! He's leaning across an open grand piano talking to Olive, who is seated on the bench. "I used to play with the sympathy orchestra once." Way to make yourself sound like a total incompetent, Popeye! An angry Bluto yanks the prop for the piano lid away, and the lid crashes down on Popeye. Then Bluto leans on the lid right at the spot where it has trapped Popeye by his neck. Popeye's body struggles in vain to free the neck and head, while Bluto comes on to Olive. "We could make beautiful music together, Babe!" And he's not just talking about a "sympathy" or symphony orchestra, either!

The orchestra on the sound track gives Bluto a sexy introduction as he says, "Get an earful of dis!" He scoops up a violin and begins playing *I'm in the Mood for Love*. Olive swoons and enthuses, "The way you fiddle with the fiddle tickles my librato!" (This cartoon is full of double-entendres!) That gives Bluto an idea. He actually does tickle Olive under the chin with his bow while he plays, staring at her all the while with a look of pleased desire on his face. Olive gives a sweet, turned-on giggle.

Popeye lifts the piano lid and frees himself, sort of. (Not that we care. Bluto and Olive are more fun and more titillating to watch!) But his head is still entangled in piano wire which actually seems to be denting, or cutting, his skull! "Hey! Whuh happen'? Who toined out the lights?" He twirls his pipe in anger when he sees Bluto with Olive.

Bluto is continuing to tickle the giggling Olive. Then he uses the bow to gently stroke, and guide, her face toward his. Olive knows what he has in mind and she goes right along with it. As they draw tantalizingly ever closer, they close their eyes and pucker up. Though their necks are stretched in a cartoony fashion, the anticipation and the looks of dreamy desire on their faces make this a hot scene. They come closer, and closer. A piece of paper could barely squeeze between their lips. But suddenly a loud version of *The Sailor's Hornpipe* is heard. Jarred out of their romantic reveries, they separate. Bluto glares over at Popeye, but Olive is delighted.

Popeye is playing the harmonica with his hands and mouth, and the guitar with his feet! Olive comes over saying, "Hmm, harmonicas make me feel sooo groovy!" She leans on the back of Popeye's chair and sways her curvy backside to the music. Bluto, meanwhile, is using his violin as a bow and arrow. "I'll fix that longhair lowbrow!" He lets fly the violin's bow. It hits Popeye in the rear, knocking him off his perch, and causing him to swallow the harmonica. We see that it's stuck in his throat, as a pathetic looking Popeye tries to explain while his windpipe makes harmonica sounds, "I don't know how it happened, Olive! I was just…" Then his speech degenerates into incomprehensibility.

A trombone starts laughing. Bluto is playing one and he's going to use it for another one of his creative seductions. Of course, it helps that he's seducing a cartoon character, because he hooks the cutey's neck in the slide and pulls her close as he starts up *I'm in the Mood for Love* again. Olive coos, "Oooo, your toodlin' just trills me!" The two enjoy a moment of cheek-to-cheek rapture. But they are startled again by the notes of a bass fiddle.

It's Popeye playing sailor music once again. It's interesting to note that, throughout the cartoon, Popeye plays sea music, while Bluto plays romantic tunes. This gives a clue as to what each of the two gent's passions actually are. And it makes us root for Bluto and Olive to get together all the more.

But for now, a happy Olive dances over to Popeye. "C'mon, Jackson, dish out with the jive!" she playfully urges. As Popeye lays down a jazzy riff, she bends over, displaying an hourglass figure, and moves one of the most spectacularly rendered derrieres Famous Studios has ever given her in time to the beat. Bluto, reaching around the corner secretly substitutes a saw for Popeye's bow. When The Sailorman picks it up and uses it, he saws the bass in half. The instrument collapses, sending Popeye to the ground and tangling him up in its strings.

Bluto laughs. And we see a close-up of him playing an accordion. "Now here's some music accordion to Hoyle." He laughs again and puts the accordion up on his outstretched arm where he uses his massive muscles to manipulate it. He sends it stretching impossibly out, and it wraps itself around Olive's waist, snatching her back to Bluto as Popeye is extricating himself from his predicament. Popeye never seems to blame his rival for the troubles he's having. Instead, Popeye acts as if he genuinely can't fathom what's going on. Earth to Popeye: Bluto's in the room and he wants to make out with Olive!

Now Bluto has Olive cradled in his arm and leaning against his chest, as he's playing the accordion with his two hands in front of her, effectively trapping her. Not that she minds being the prey! She makes goo-goo eyes at him and exclaims, "Oooo, you're so vigoroso!" Olive, you only know the half of it! Bluto makes kissing motions with his lips while tightening his arm around Olive's middle. A happy, contented Olive leans back on his arm. They both come forward again, give each other teasing, but encouraging, looks, and start the process all over again. This time a curvy Olive dreamily closes her eyes and awaits the kiss. As their lower lips just barely touch, and before they can press their mouths passionately together, Popeye starts playing music again. This time he's got a tuba. An impressed Olive ducks away from Bluto and, once again, dances over to Popeye. She displays her figure, along with a shapely bustline, and even some cleavage, as she bends in her off-the-shoulder gown.

"Hooba, hooba, I just love that tuba!" she declares.

An angry Bluto tears the skin off of a drum. "Horn in on me goil, will he?" Bluto slips the skin over the tuba's bell so that, as Popeye blows, it inflates like a balloon. As Popeye is finishing his tune, the huge bubble/balloon lifts him into the air and then bursts on a sharp light fixture in the ceiling. Popeye and the tuba fall floorward. The tuba lands right on top of Olive, engulfing her. She sticks her head out of the mouthpiece, as only a cartoon character can, and lays into Popeye. "Why, you, you offbeat baboon!" Snubbing him, she sticks her high heels out from the bell and waddles away, as an embarrassed version of *The Sailor's Hornpipe* plays on the soundtrack, signifying that this is the end for the humiliated Popeye. He follows her. "But, but, but, but, I was just tryin' to send ya!" Bluto comes up from behind him, grabs him by the shoulder, and plunges him to the floor. Then he lifts the stunned sailor and whisks him away. The orchestra's notes of alarm let us know this is the final trap for Popeye.

Bluto has stuffed Popeye into an outgoing mail chute, and he's holding him in a tight grip around the neck. Popeye's tongue lolls out of his mouth. Bluto smiles at us and says to Popeye, "This'll send ya!" He licks a postage stamp and slams it across Popeye's face, painfully gluing The Sailorman's eyes shut. As Popeye futilely uses his facial muscles in an attempt to free himself, he looks truly pathetic — and completely old, worn out, and ugly. The first few notes of a mocking, "all is lost" version of *I'm In The Mood* play. Popeye's chance for love is gone. Bluto gleefully bops him down the chute. The orchestra follows Popeye's rapid descent into the basement, where his journey comes to an abrupt and painful-sounding end as he's trapped in a small mail box. The orchestra plays some spectral music. Popeye is either unconscious or dead. And, yeah, Popeye's been a nuisance so far in the cartoon, but did he deserve to be treated like this?

Back up in the rehearsal hall, Bluto and Olive are happily sitting together at the piano. Bluto is confidently playing *Welcome, Sweet Springtime*. An admiring Olive swoons and turns coyly away. As she does so, for a few frames her baby doll face is stunningly cute. She seems to give him a quick "come ahead" look. Bluto, seeing the enraptured state she's in, moves closer. He puts his arm around her and slides her over to him saying, "Now that we're alone, Cookie, how about gettin' amoroso with this virtuoso with a kissamum?" A shocked Olive ducks out from under his arm and resumes her seat a little farther from him on the bench. She turns up her nose at him and looks away, snubbing him. And Olive is gorgeous when she's haughty! In fact, in some frames of this sequence, the creators have given her one of the prettiest faces she has ever had, or ever will have. And that's saying a lot! Bluto comes over and kisses her bare shoulder. He comes away wearing a look that's pleased, satisfied, and at the same time ravenous for more. Olive hauls off and slaps him hard. But it doesn't have the effect the worried miss was hoping for. Bluto just laughs it off. Olive is powerless!

But why is Olive resisting Bluto at this point when she was ready to be intimate with him earlier? I could be cynical and say it's because the creators realized that she's alone with a guy she likes, Popeye has been done away with, l'amour was in the offing, and they couldn't let that happen because convention and tradition say that Olive has to end up with The Sailorman. So they needed to make her turn against Bluto. But, I can also say that Bluto didn't show as much finesse this time and seemed to be more demanding. And flirting with one guy while another is still there in the room is much safer than getting physical when there's just the two of you. However, in Bluto's defense, it sure seemed as though Olive was giving him the "full speed ahead" sign at the piano. And actually, Bluto's been a gentleman up to this point in the cartoon. He had tentatively tried seductions, and if Olive was eating it up, he'd continue.[2]

He's a gentleman no longer, though. His face and head take on a wolfish appearance. "C'mon, Babe," he says, "don't B-Flat, B-Natural!" (Yes, this is yet another one of those double-entendres.) He snatches her and pulls her to himself, so that she's now basically on his lap, or between his legs, facing him as he sits on the bench. Olive struggles and squirms and moves and ineffectually punches him in the chest a few times. But he never releases his hold on her waist. "You, you, keep your hands to you! That's what you are," Olive desperately protests. But as she forms some of her words, it looks for all the world like she's starting to kiss Bluto a few times! And that's not all! As her struggles make her shift positions and she rubs against Bluto, he experiences paroxysms of pleasure! His face registers male rapture and satisfaction. When you view this scene at regular speed, you can tell that something more than the obvious is going on, but you might not be able to determine exactly what. However, when the scene is viewed frame-by-frame, it's obvious that the creators pulled a fast one on the censors because, though they are fully clothed, Bluto and Olive look like they are getting VERY intimate with each other!!!

Meanwhile, inside the mailbox — like anybody still cares — Popeye is conscious and mutters, "What am I — a male or a mouse?" The background music is all doom and gloom. Popeye puffs and gets his pipe to spark up and give him light. He sees an envelope that the Samson Spinach Company is mailing to Famous Studios (!!!), containing a free sample. (What happened to the can Popeye usually carries?) Popeye rips the envelope open and downs its contents. On his forming and expanding bicep, a picture of a symphony orchestra appears and the opening notes of Beethoven's Fifth, the "V For Victory" music, is heard. Popeye then super-leaps back up the chute, saying as he travels upward, "I gotta special delivery for that tin horn!"

Back in the hall, Bluto and Olive are still at it. Olive's hair is pleasingly mussed up. Her dress is coming dangerously close to falling off as she struggles. Her blows and shoves still are having no effect. "Lemme out of here, you, you, you hepcat! Lemme go!" But Bluto just keeps playing both the piano and Miss Oyl.

Popeye zooms out of the mail slot and into the scene, uppercutting Bluto away and taking his place at the piano. The Sailorman immediately begins playing a jazzy, improvisational version of *Welcome, Sweet Springtime*. Evidently the spinach has put him in a romantic mood at last. Olive responds with delight and gives Popeye the same flirty looks she was giving Bluto earlier. "Oh," Olive laughs and gushes, "a piano maniac!" Popeye is overjoyed.

Bluto, though, has landed on a xylophone. He scoops up its broken keys and says, "I'll take the sharps out of that flathead!" He hurls them one-by-one at Popeye. But The Sailorman turns, while now playing the piano with his feet, and belts each away in turn, making a little tune as he does so. They go flying into, and then out of, Bluto's mouth. Now the big guy grabs a trombone and races to Popeye grumbling, "He can't soft pedal me!" Bluto swings the instrument at Popeye like a club a few times, but without missing a beat, Popeye easily dodges. Popeye then grabs the trombone and begins playing it, poking Bluto in the stomach and the face a few times with the slide, before using it to knock Bluto into an empty bass fiddle case. Bluto emerges, now temporarily shaped like a bass. Getting himself back to normal, he mutters, "That windbag needs mutin'!" He then picks up a bass, runs over to Popeye and bops him over the head with it. But Popeye instantly jumps up, his head now sticking through the bass, hits Bluto away with its neck, and begins playing it as though it were a violin. Olive, caught up in Popeye's music, is dancing around, showing off some curvy hips. Now Bluto has lifted a grand piano and is carrying it over his head to Popeye. He smashes it down on top of The Sailorman and then rubs his hands together and licks his lips over his opponent's demise. But the broken piano opens up to reveal that the unaffected Popeye is using its interior as a harp. Popeye finishes the song and uppercuts Bluto so that the big guy bounces helplessly down a row of kettle drums. Bluto then crashes into, and demolishes, shelves of instruments which go flying. Popeye zooms over and catches them all, transforming himself into a one-man band. The stunned Bluto sits on the floor wearing a cymbal on his head. Popeye begins a ragtime version of his theme song, hitting Bluto's stomach with a drum pedal and clanging the cymbal on Bluto's head. Bluto now looks painfully unconscious.

Olive, oblivious to the pain being administered to another human being and to the fact that some of her instruments and parts of her hall have been destroyed, comes into the picture, hugs, and snuggles with, Popeye, then pulls the pipe out of his pocket and toots it to end the tune and the cartoon.

Symphony in Spinach (1948)

Director: Seymour Kneitel
Animation: Tom Johnson, John Gentilella
Story: Bill Turner, Larry Riley
Scenics: Robert Connavale
Music: Winston Sharples[3]

CHAPTER 13
Beach Peach (1950)

Popeye performs his "dying swan" dive, oblivious to the fact that the water in the pool has been drained. In the Famous Studios cartoons, Popeye is often unaware of what his enemies have done until it's too late.

The beach is a romantic place. Or so we've been told in countless books, TV shows, and in many movies that run the gamut from *From Here to Eternity* to *How to Stuff a Wild Bikini*. Not to mention songs like *Surfer Girl* or *Surf City*, which were on the radio around the same time that Baby Boomers were watching Popeye cartoons on TV.

The books, TV shows, movies, and songs are right. Leaving aside such things as sunburns, sand fleas, and the kid that drips his melting snow cone onto your blanket, the beach has many enchantments with which to put one in the mood for love, not the least of which is the fact that people at the beach aren't usually wearing much of anything. In *Beach Peach*, Mr. Lifeguard (not Bluto, but another character who shares the spirit and build of Bluto) shows off his muscles, while Olive spends the entire cartoon in a bikini, causing the O.O.O.P.S. factor to kick in big time.[1]

The title of the cartoon itself helps to enhance Ms. Oyl's sex appeal, as she is the *Beach Peach* referred to. On the title card the words are written in appealing cursive letters, and we see the ocean, the sky, and a beach umbrella propped up on the sand.

An opening note on the soundtrack leads into an, appropriately enough, happy version of *It's A Hap, Hap, Happy Day* as we see the shoreline of a crowded beach where people of various shapes and sizes are enjoying the afternoon. There's a realistically drawn bathing beauty in the foreground. A wave comes ashore and washes them all away out to sea. But then a second wave comes in and re-deposits them just as they were.

Cut to Olive Oyl walking. She's cartoony looking and skinny, particularly in humorous contrast to the bathing beauty of the previous scene. But then we notice that her walk emphasizes a shapely derriere, and that she has a cute, and even very pretty, face in some frames, along with a curvier figure. Her eyes are closed at first as she breathes in the invigorating sea air. Her hands are clasped together in front of her in delight. Then she throws her arms wide open to welcome, and take in, the beach experience. Then she hugs herself. She talks to Popeye, who is following her, though all we see of him is the huge bundle of beach recreation equipment and supplies he's carrying. As Olive walks out of the picture in a feminine way and attention is called to her rear once again and to her beautiful legs, she says, "Oh, Popeye, the beach just sands me!" Clearly the ocean front has worked its magic, as Olive is in the mood for romance.

The camera now focuses on Popeye as we hear Olive continuing, "Now if we could only find an excluded spot to set up our..." Then she lets out a sexy, "Hmm?" as we see that Popeye has tripped over a board and has unintentionally flung his burden up in the air.

Popeye, frankly, is dressed as a dork from another century. He's wearing a long, red, short-sleeved shirt, which completely covers up his torso, tucked into a pair of black shorts/swimming trunks. He tops it all off with an old-fashioned straw hat. And his body will never look anything other than cartoony and unappealing throughout the whole cartoon.

We see Popeye landing on the sand and then looking up to the sky in horror. He tries to duck and cover as the equipment lands around him, perfectly setting itself up as it does so. The radio is the last thing to land, and it turns on and begins playing a singer singing the love song, *June In January*.[2] Even in the middle of a slapsticky scene, the creators make us think about love. Popeye looks around, sees what has happened, and makes the most of it, gesturing with his arms and tipping his hat. "Uh, dere ya are, Olive! A poifect spot to squat!" He laughs and is quite cute in doing so. He's a male taking advantage of a fortuitous accident to impress his date.

Olive knows this and delightfully plays along, satisfied with what Popeye has done. She's a fun date! She enters the picture from the right and, in some frames during this scene, has an hourglass figure. She gives Popeye some feminine, coy, flirty signs of pleasure, such as squeezing her shoulders around her head. And when she straightens up at the close of the scene, she's unconsciously showing a great figure, pretty legs, and that shapely rear again. "Ooo, ooo, ooh," she swoons in a sexy vibrato and then gasps, "it's just ducky!"

The scene fades out and then fades in on a sign and sign post in the water. A naval bell rings, heralding the full reveal of the words on the sign, "When You're Pooped." The camera quickly pans to subsequent signs, Burma Shave style. Other bells are heard but they are crescendoing, leading up to something. "From Swimming Hard," "It's Time to Holler," then there's a quick camera pan to a sign on the legs of a wooden tower, "LIFEGUARD."

The camera and the music travel up the tower to reveal what they had been waiting for. We see a handsome, blonde, unbelievably muscled, male lifeguard wearing a muscle shirt, which shows off his great pecs and arms, and short trunks. He's sitting on a chair on a platform under a canopy. There's an elevator shaft behind him. He's facing away from Popeye and Olive watching a ballgame on TV. There's a fan on top of the TV set and a beer tap built into the railing by his left hand. He's one of Famous Studios' most handsome men, and he joyfully gets himself a mug of beer while showing off even more of his award-winning physique. Why isn't he diligently scanning the beach? Is he being lazy or selfish? Are we being alerted to the fact that he's not all he's cracked up to be? Or is he just a guy who enjoys life and grabs moments of pleasure when he can? And he's about to get the supreme pleasure of meeting Olive Oyl. Since he's not scanning the waterfront, he must have no interest in the gorgeous beach bunnies who are lounging there. It will take a special girl to capture his attention.

He's about to drink his beer when he hears Olive's pretty voice let out a cute, musical giggle and say, "All right now, Popeye, let's have our lunch." He turns to see the source and collapses in on himself doing a double-take. He throws his mug away. His body goes out of control. Olive is deeply affecting him. Then he springs forward. A "Boing" sound is heard as his body stiffens, and his neck stretches forward toward Olive. In fact, he launches himself toward her off the tower, only catching himself by his feet on the railing. It looks as though he lost some of his clothing, or his belt, in the process, as there is a string trailing something hanging from him. Is he starting to get undressed for Olive, or is this a blooper of some sort?[3] He clasps his head in his hands with delight. His eyes enlarge and stretch out. "Hubba, hubba!" he enthuses. His eyeballs go back in, but then pop completely out of his head, leaving him in an enraptured state.

The eyeballs travel quickly over to Olive and, starting at the top of her hair bob, they work their way down every luscious inch of her, tracing an hourglass figure and shapely legs. The lifeguard wolf whistles as the eyeballs are doing their thing. We viewers see an Olive Oyl who, at first glance seems very thin, but if we take a second and third look, we can tell that her body actually does curve the way the eyeballs have indicated. But the curves aren't what makes Olive so sexy in this scene. It's her mannerisms and attitude. Olive is facing away from the lifeguard and has settled into a feminine stance with her left leg bent, and is up on the toes of its foot, in back of her. She's delicately holding a compact and a powder puff, applying make-up. Does she want to look good for Popeye? She definitely wants a beach romance with someone! As for her face, it starts out in the scene looking cartoony, but cute, then changes to be very pretty and actually realistic. Then it goes cartoony again, but wears a cute, exotic, mysterious, intriguing expression promising that the guy who wins Olive will be confronted with the wonderfully complex enigma that is Woman. She smiles a confident, pleased grin. She is looking forward to some loving. And has she heard the wolf whistle? Could she be subconsciously aware that she's being ogled? Did she sense the eyeballs and then decide to give them something beautifully intriguing to look at? She maintains an air of innocence, though, while being given the once-over. At this point, we viewers are with Popeye and the lifeguard. Olive Oyl is definitely the hottest girl on the beach, and there's no sense in wasting time with the others.

The music had traveled with the eyeballs, and a triumphant note is sounded when they complete their thorough, close quarter's examination of Olive. Then the eyeballs pop back into the lifeguard's head, and the orchestra lets us know a decision has been made. The music begins a fast "going places/making progress" tune. The lifeguard is now standing on the platform, leaning over the rail. With a show of massive muscles, while still looking at Olive, he launches himself into the air and propels himself into the open elevator. His lower half has to scramble to keep up. He can't wait to get to Olive! The elevator speedily descends while contorting. Physics can't keep up with male desire. Quickly the elevator reaches the sand. The doors open, and out comes the lifeguard riding a motor scooter. The force of the scooter's acceleration has pushed the lifeguard back, but he pulls himself forward. (What a guy!) His feet are perched on the seat. He didn't even take the time to sit down. Besides, he wants to be able to leap off the second he reaches Olive. Leaning forward on the handlebars in amazed, rapturous delight, focusing on Olive, he speeds across the sand. Then he turns and brakes the scooter using only his super-strength. The scooter skids and sends up a stream of sand. The lifeguard uses his strength to make the tires dig into the sand even more.

Cut to Popeye and Olive Oyl. Olive is under the umbrella getting out the picnic lunch, facing away from the lifeguard. Popeye, however, is facing the stream of sand and is ineffectually trying to keep himself from being buried by it. He's clearly helpless and there's a look of terror, and then unconsciousness, on his face as he goes under the ever-forming mound. He lets out a "Wha? (choke) Hey!" before he succumbs. The music as Popeye is buried tells us that plans are coming to fruition. The orchestra sort of feels for Popeye, but also sort of is looking forward to what will happen when Olive and the lifeguard meet, too. Olive hasn't seen what has happened to Popeye. For all she knows, he has walked off somewhere and left her. (As we've observed in other cartoons, he tends to do that.)

The lifeguard super-speeds into the picture with the grace of an athletic dancer. He stands on the sand that used to be Popeye, thoroughly supplanting The Sailorman. Bowing to Olive and removing his hat, the lifeguard rubs his hand against Olive's face and playfully balances her chin on his finger as he says, "Hi ya, Dollface!" A soft, smooth, sexy version of a traveling theme is heard on the soundtrack. And Olive is very happy to meet this handsome guy.

He puts his hat back on and goes into a muscle man pose. He's drawn great! He flexes while looking at Olive and smiling and saying, "If you're ever drownin', dese muscles will save ya." He then puts on a demonstration in which he makes a bowling ball out of one bicep (as only a cartoon character could do) and uses it to bowl over the pins he's made out of the bicep on his other arm.

He has unwittingly just played into Olive's love of strong men and her desire to be watched over and protected. He's out-Popeyed Popeye! There's no question that he will win Ms. Oyl.

The lifeguard is posing and looking pleased with himself. Olive scrunches her head into her shoulders with delight. Then she leans forward toward him. Throughout the scene, Olive hugs herself, rests her head on her hands, and acts like she's having a dream come true. And she never takes her eyes off the lifeguard and his body. "Oooo," she coos, looking like she's blowing him a kiss. "What a unique physique!" She's giving him a close once-over of her own, and he's happy that he's turning her on. The camera begins to pan while Olive is overcome with amazed, rapturous delight.

It pans over to an empty stretch of sand. Popeye struggles to come up out from under the sand and then emerges. He couldn't come up under the lifeguard but had to tunnel elsewhere. The lifeguard is too much for him. Popeye angrily glares in the lifeguard's direction. "Why, that...!"

Cut back to the lifeguard and Olive for one of Famous Studios' hottest scenes, which uses the enjoyment of food as a metaphor to let us know that the lifeguard intends to savor and devour Olive Oyl, and that she can't wait to be consumed by him. The lifeguard and Olive are setting next to each other, and their legs are touching. He has reached his arm around her, supposedly to get a sandwich, but it will soon be clear what he really wants for lunch. Olive is beside herself with feminine delight. He has an appealing, cocky, "I'm about to be satisfied" look on his face. As he brings the sandwich to his mouth, he's actually closing his arm around a curvy Olive, while showing off his own magnificent body. Olive now has her hands out in front of her in a welcoming gesture. She laughs and hugs herself as he's pulling her closer and closer, not looking at the sandwich at all, only at her. He takes a bite — of the sandwich I mean — all the while giving Olive a look filled with male desire and anticipation. Olive, in her best Betty Boop mode gives him a flirty, "anytime anyplace" look, and then a coy, flattered, innocent one. The lifeguard takes a healthy bite of his sandwich as Olive lowers her arms to let him get closer. As the lifeguard chews deliberately, letting her know he takes his time with his pleasures, she is completely enveloped by him. Her right shoulder is against his chest, her left against his massive arm. Her hands are now around his foot. She invitingly turns her head partly away and swoons in words, sounds, and expressions impossible to capture on paper, "Oooo, uh, ih, ih, ha, ha, mm, hmm, hmmm… Mr. Lifeguard!" It's sexy, flirty, melodic, and slightly trembling. Olive's pleasantly shocked at what the lifeguard is doing to her, both protecting her innocence, yet wanting to encourage him to go further. She conveys, "Oh, you mad, impetuous Boy, you! I know exactly what's on your mind! You really shouldn't be doing this, but keep it up! I'm loving it! I'm probably not supposed to, but I do! You're making me totally yours!" And her swoon is also filled with expectation. She turns her face back toward him. Both wear expressions of a man and woman enjoying making out and wanting more. He then gets a sly, lustful look on his face, pulling her even closer. Olive's hands are unclasped and her arms are open now. She leans her cute face against his shoulder, then she's turned right toward him. Her hands appear to be on his leg. As he chews, their mouth move in sync and their faces flirt with each other. Olive turns slightly away again, while making inviting eyes at him. He swallows with a deliberate, "next, I'll savor you" motion. Then he goes for the second bite which will basically put Olive totally up against him. She opens her arms to put them around him. They both want what's coming next. So does the orchestra. So do we.

But Popeye comes hurtling in from the left of the screen, waving his left arm menacingly. As the camera pans to focus on Popeye and the lifeguard, The Sailorman rears back and then snatches the sandwich out of the lifeguard's hand. "Hey," Popeye shouts, "dat's me lunch and dat's me goil!" Frustration lines emanate from the lifeguard. Popeye and Mr. Lifeguard both contract in on themselves, preparing for a battle. Then they begin to expand. We get a close-up of the muscular lifeguard REALLY expanding his chest and upper body. We see a tattoo of a battleship, emerging from his muscle shirt, on the center of his chest. It swells to gigantic proportions. Cut to Popeye and the lifeguard. Popeye's not swelled out any more. Instead he looks puny and worried. Mr. Lifeguard has more weapons in his personal arsenal than Popeye does, in more ways than one! The lifeguard is still livid at Popeye. The cannons and missile launchers on the side of the tattoo nearest Popeye fire in The Sailorman's face, as the soundtrack begins playing *Rule Brittania*, heralding the lifeguard's triumph. Fire and smoke obliterate our view of Popeye's face. The force of the explosion lifts Popeye off the ground. The guns fire again and propel Popeye right out of the picture. Just Mr. Lifeguard's swelling and flexing was enough to defeat Popeye!

Cut to a man sleeping under an umbrella some distance away. A helpless, shocked Popeye flies into the picture and into the umbrella, uprooting it and taking it through the air with him. The umbrella closes around Popeye like a shroud. The Popeye umbrella keeps hurtling over the beach, flipping end over end as it passes people. Finally it lands and plants itself in the sand next to a bathing beauty. The cessation of forward momentum shakes up the still-enshrouded Popeye. He then opens the umbrella while wrapped around it, glares in the direction of the lifeguard and Olive, and says, "'N' dat settles it!" Popeye is fearless, even though outmatched. The orchestra, though, is apprehensive. Are they worried for Popeye? Concerned that Olive is giving herself to the "wrong guy?" Or upset that Popeye is going to interrupt the lovers again?

Speaking of whom, they are still together. Mr. Lifeguard's left arm is still around Olive and his massive left hand is around her middle, with his one finger pointing straight down at, er, her lower female part, as if we didn't already know what his intentions were! (Where were those censors?) He's giving her a toothy, "I'm in love" smile. She, slightly turned away, responds with an "I'm surrendering" look. He's gently holding her left wrist with his right hand. Her right hand, bent in a delighted, "Oh, you man, you!" pose, is down near her legs. As he gently brings Olive closer and she's acquiescing, Popeye once again enters the picture from the left. The lifeguard's and Olive's bodies are touching each other, as Popeye raises his arm to snatch the lifeguard away. Unaware, Mr. Lifeguard stretches his muscular neck out toward Olive and closes his eyes and gets his mouth ready for a kiss. Olive is dreamily closing her eyes, too. Then the lifeguard notices Popeye, as Olive still happily awaits the kiss. The lifeguard is surprised as Popeye, using super-strength of his own, grabs Mr. Lifeguard by the muscle shirt, and yanks him out of the picture while challenging, "Get up and fight…" Olive opens her eyes in alarm. She does a shocked/worried/concerned double-take and nervously bites her nails while she leans forward to see what's happening. We hear Popeye finish "…like a man!" Mr. Lifeguard answers, "Why, you little…" Olive quickly and determinedly gets up and runs toward them.

As Popeye and Mr. Lifeguard are squaring off, Olive places herself between them. As the boys try to mix it up, she gets one hand on Popeye's chest and the other on Mr. Lifeguard's shoulder. She pushes them apart. In a comic sequence, Olive's arms keep shortening and lengthening, as need be, while the boys push against her. The orchestra joins the tug-of-war. Distracting male viewers from the laughs is Olive's incredibly shapely rear which keeps thrusting out. And in some frames she has pretty legs, a nice figure, and a really cute face. "Now, Boys,

Boys," she amiably scolds, "fighting ain't friendly like! Let's play some games!" Now that Olive is totally aware that Popeye has returned from wherever he went, she graciously wants to give both men a chance with her. She's sweetly playing peacemaker, wants to enjoy being together with both guys, and innocently and naively believes that they can all be friends.[4]

And maybe they can be at that, because the lifeguard cheerfully and sincerely responds, "Okay! I'll get me medicine ball!" He heads off.

It's A Hap, Hap, Happy Day begins again on the soundtrack as the camera fades in, signifying the passage of time, on poor Olive trying hard to lift the heavy medicine ball. Her rear is toward us and her bikini bottom highlights her shapely derriere. "I hadda go and…open my…big mouth!" she mutters while straining. She manages to lift the sphere a little and give it a roll over to Popeye.

The camera has pulled back and revealed a triangle (appropriately enough) of Olive, Popeye, and the lifeguard on the beach. There's a sound effect to imply tremendous weight as the ball goes to Popeye. He then pitches it underhand to the lifeguard. We're treated to a close-up of Mr. Lifeguard catching the ball easily and managing it with a firm grip. He brings the ball into himself and then lifts it over his head, showing off his physique the whole time. He's not consciously posing, though. He's just honestly enjoying the game. He happily looks at Olive *and* Popeye! He's willing to include The Sailorman in the day's activities! Besides, he is no doubt confident that he can get a date alone with Olive later. He prepares to throw the ball back to Popeye, knowing that Olive can't catch it. All of this makes him a very appealing romantic lead.

But then there's Popeye. We get a close-up of the shrimpy guy trying to flex, pose, and show-off, but failing. Maybe this is supposed to be cute and funny, but he is deliberately calling attention to himself. Popeye can't ever just happily take part in a group activity. He always has to be Number One! "Ah," he brags, "there's nothin' like exkercise and vitaliky, Olive!" He's got to be kidding! Aside from his bloated forearm, he shows no signs of ever exercising! And he gets his vitality out of a can of spinach!

We see the lifeguard still looking happy, but his expression subtly changes. He's as annoyed with the self-centered, self-deluded, game-wrecking, lecturing Popeye as we are. He winds up for the toss and, putting all his muscle mass and super-strength into it, lets go with an overhand throw. He still looks happy, not evil. Maybe he's happy that the bragging phony Popeye is about to get what's coming to him.

Cut to Popeye standing smugly like a proud peacock with his EYES CLOSED! Er, Popeye, when medicine balls are being tossed around, shouldn't you pay attention? The ball flies into the picture and hits Popeye in the stomach, chest, and pelvic region. His hat flies off, his jaw drops, and his tongue hangs out in pain. The ball carries him through the air and out of the picture.

Cut to a lamppost on the boardwalk with a trash receptacle marked "Refuse" in front of it. A helpless and pained Popeye and the ball fly into the picture and collide with it. Popeye is now embedded in the lamppost. The ball drops away. Popeye is "out of it." He slides down the lamppost to be deposited feet first in the receptacle. Its lid twirls around from the impact. The lid comes to a stop with the words "Jack Pot" now on it. The receptacle's bottom door opens and trash begins pouring out. We get a close-up of the mound of rotting trash. Popeye's head and shoulders poke out, and his hat blows into the scene. He still looks pained and unconscious. The happy music had kept playing until the ball hit Popeye, then it traveled through the air with him, and was embarrassed by him. It humiliated him further as he slid down the lamppost. As Popeye comes to, a chagrined version of his theme begins. After all, he's in a trash heap! We hear Olive's voice protesting, "I'm af…f…fraid…"

The scene shifts to Olive with her right arm and leg wrapped around a docking post. The Lifeguard is in the water, pulling on her outstretched left arm and hand. But he's doing it in a playful and encouraging way and is obviously not using his full strength. He is insistent, though! "…of the water!" Olive finishes. Romantic music plays as they engage in a tug-of-war of sorts. "C'mon, Babe, I'll learn ya to swim like a mermaid!" Mr. Lifeguard says. Olive shows off some cleavage and curves in certain frames, but she also wears a concerned expression. The lifeguard's features go from happy, to tender, to handsome, to "in love." Both he and a curvy Olive are surprised as Popeye enters the picture carrying a huge, blown-up, inflatable, pool toy horse. The orchestra, probably feeling for Olive, is glad he showed up.

Popeye enters the water as Mr. Lifeguard lets go of Olive. She leans against the post using a very feminine stance. She's suddenly happy. Her legs are more shapely than usual, and the bottoms of her bikini briefs are flaring out. Though she is drawn skinny and has a cartoony face here, she is still very appealing. "Here ya are, Olive! Ya can ride the waves safe-like on this!" Popeye presents the horse. The lifeguard is getting angrier and angrier. Popeye hops on the horse and gallantly offers his hand to Olive to help her aboard. Olive accepts it with more very feminine movements, "Oh, Popeye, (gasp) you're smart like anything!" Olive reminds us, and perhaps herself, that she still likes Popeye, too. As Olive is lowering herself onto the horse and makes contact with it, she's drawn with a *Sports Illustrated Swimsuit Edition* cover girl's body for a frame or two. Olive's hands are on Popeye's shoulders, and Popeye begins to propel the horse forward, using his legs as oars. The rowing motion makes Olive bounce up and down and moves her midriff in and out, showing off some curves. The angry and determined lifeguard watches them go out of the picture. There's a close-up of the lifeguard saying, "Why that double-crossin' little sandworm!" He tenses his muscles in frustration and to prepare for action.

We see Popeye and Olive close together and happy. But Olive warns, while putting her cheek next to his and shaking her head in an appealing way, "Now, Popeye, remember, no aquabatics!"

The camera pans down to show us below the waterline. The lifeguard is swimming up to them underwater. We can only now see Olive's lower half, but it's enough. She is undulating like a belly dancer. Is she still being controlled by Popeye's motions? But she looks like she's doing it deliberately. Is she turned on? At any rate, she's doing just what the lifeguard hopes she'll do for him later. And she reminds us once again that the best Famous Studios cartoons are about love and sex.

With an evil grin, the lifeguard undoes the air valve at the back of the horse. *It's A Hap, Hap, Happy Day* comes to an end as the horse, leaking air, turns into an out-of-control jet. Popeye and Olive are bounced and rocked. Popeye urges, "Steady, Seabisket, steady!" (Doesn't he realize that he's talking to a rubber toy?) As the horse and Popeye, who is clinging to its neck for some reason, fly up and out of the picture, Olive falls off into the water. She sinks beneath it. Her bare shoulders, appealing head, soaking hair, and arms and hands emerge. Olive flounders to stay afloat, but to no avail. The jeopardy music which had been playing gets more frantic and desperate. "Help, save me!"

Cut to Popeye and the horse going up in the air, and back down into the water again. The horse is now spewing dark smoke like a wounded aircraft. "Whoa, Boy, Whoa!" Popeye urges as they continue their manic flight and their dunkings. Why doesn't Popeye let go, drop off, and go save the drowning Olive? Is it really so important for him to stay with his toy?

Cut to a still struggling Olive, her mouth full of water. She inevitably sinks completely beneath the sea. Her hand breaks the surface with one finger pointing up. A funeral bell tolls, as the low brass on the soundtrack tells us her time is almost up. The hand comes up again with two fingers raised. Then a third time with three. Olive and the music are sinking down for the last time. Before that can happen, though, Mr. Lifeguard's arm comes into the picture and pulls a water-logged, helpless, and bedraggled Olive out of the water and out of the picture. The music travels with her.

The camera pans over and we see that the lifeguard has made a raft of his body, as only a cartoon character can. A curvy, feminine, happy Olive, who has gotten herself together quickly, is sitting on him and striking a seductive pose. Her legs are bent in front of her and are resting on the lifeguard's chest. And as the scene progresses, they are very shapely. The happy, confident lifeguard, floating on his back, never takes his eyes off of her. Olive is overcome with emotion and presses her hands against her chest. (The creators even drew one of her breasts.) She tips her head slightly and closes her eyes. Then she bends and moves forward toward the lifeguard. She lets out a sexy gasp. "You saved my life, (another gasp) you great big hunk of hero!" And there's no question that Olive's going to reward him! In fact, she gets almost close enough for a kiss. A very romantic version of the lifeguard's theme has been playing. Olive gives him an encouraging "do with me whatever you will" expression and the scene ends with the two of them gazing into each other's eyes, enraptured by love, as they head for shore. The lifeguard has completely won Olive the way Popeye always does — he saved her life. True, he was the one who endangered her in the first place, but she doesn't know that. She probably thinks it was Popeye's fault and that he was doing those dreaded aquabatics. And the lifeguard was near and watchful the whole time. And he did actually save her life. Popeye did nothing, choosing instead to try and save his rubber horse.[5]

Speaking of which, Popeye and his mount are continuing their wild ride, going toward an ocean liner. "Whoa! Whoa! Steady, Boy!" They hit it hard while submerged. When the waves, splashes, and impact lines subside, we see there is now a big hole in the ship. But there's no sign of Popeye. The horse has taken him through the hull and into the bowels of the ship.

The scene changes to a long shot of a swimming pool by the ocean. Mr. Lifeguard is on a diving board at the top of a very tall ladder. Olive remains on the ground, looking up at him. He points down to her. A sexy version of his theme is playing as he expertly shows off for his beloved. "And now, Cutie, me sharpest dive is…"

Cut to the ocean. "…the jackknife!" Popeye's head, sticking through a massive propeller weighing tons, surfaces. He's all done in. He slowly walks up to the shore. An embarrassed, mocking, humiliating version of the lifeguard theme plays, signifying that the handsome hunk has thoroughly defeated Popeye. And the orchestra is glad of it! Popeye stumbles and trudges wearily forward. The music sounds an alarm as Popeye worriedly double-takes when he spots the lifeguard and Olive. He lets out a "Huh?" then gets a beaten look on his face. The alarm was because he has lost Olive.

We see the top of the diving board as the lifeguard is going off of it, in perfect form, naturally. We hear Olive give a long, sexy, flirtatious, overwhelmed, ravished, "I'm yours" laugh, gasp, and say, "Ain't you the gay blade!" The lifeguard morphs into a real jackknife and then back to normal again as he cleaves the air. A peppy version of *It's A Hap, Hap, Happy Day* plays as the orchestra helps Mr. Lifeguard displays his form. He enters the water, as Olive, acting like an umpire, makes the "safe" sign. The lifeguard swims toward the ladder as we see Popeye run toward it, reach it, and begin to climb up.

There's a rear close-up shot of the impossibly cartoony and dorky and thoroughly unappealing Popeye going up the ladder. "Phooey on that phony! I'll shows ya some real diving, Olive!" (Er, how is what the lifeguard did phony diving?) But there's a button at the base of the tower with a sign near it that says,

"To Raise Tower Push Button." Of course that's just what the happy, confident lifeguard does as the music sounds a sinister chord. A dark, dangerous, "someone's about to die" version of *It's A Hap, Hap, Happy Day* begins as the motor and belt system noisily raise the tower.

Popeye doesn't notice, though. What is wrong with this guy? He has reached the board. Olive yells, "Popeye, you better be careful!" Ah, Olive, you're a sweetheart! Popeye travels up through the clouds. He yells, "Now I calls this dive, 'The Dyin' Swan!'" being unwittingly prophetic. He dives off the board, striking a graceful, birdlike pose as he plummets through the air. The orchestra had been progressing toward a disastrous end, and, as Popeye dives, it gives us a "he's finished" fanfare.

The music switches to a "final deathtrap" theme as we cut to an Olive with shapely legs, and the lifeguard near the tower. Mr. Lifeguard is watching Popeye's descent while cheerfully pulling with his super-strength on a rope attached to something under water. Olive is looking up worried. She doesn't at first realize what the lifeguard is doing. Then she notices that something's up. She covers her eyes and displays some curves. She leans forward to yell at the lifeguard, "What are you doing?" Mr. Lifeguard gives a mighty, triumphant yank, and the large drain plug that is attached to the other end of the rope comes out of the water. The water level in the pool is rapidly dropping. Olive jumps around in alarm and looks back up at Popeye, expressing an impossible wish as she yells, "Turn back, Popeye!"

Cut to Popeye in flight as he hears, "Turn back!" He double-takes, "Uh, oh!" He's slack-jawed with worry and fear, and the music begins a run that will drop him into the pool. We see the empty pool, from Popeye's perspective, coming up fast.

Cut to a long shot of the pool area. Olive has her arms and hands up imploring Popeye, or even the gods. Popeye drops into the picture and on into the empty pool as the brass section of the orchestra lets us know that he's done for. There's a loud crash like a thunderclap which makes the whole scene shake. Olive bends over to see what's happened. There is now a Popeye-shaped deep hole in the bottom of the pool's cement floor with cracks all around it. A funereal version of the Popeye theme plays. Olive turns on the lifeguard. "You, you sea monster!"

Okay, Mr. Lifeguard has gotten rid of Popeye, but why did he have to do it in this drastic fashion right in front of Olive Oyl? If he had just tolerated The Sailorman awhile longer, he and Olive could have gone off together for a date later. Or maybe another stealthy way to dispose of his rival would have presented itself. Fans love to imagine new endings for this cartoon, because Mr. Lifeguard had won Olive Oyl. But now he's lost her.

Speaking of the devil, Mr. Lifeguard is waving, "Bye, bye" to Popeye, while looking triumphant and like he's trying to be cute. Olive's face and upper body enter the picture. "What have you done to my Popeye?" she demands. Mr. Lifeguard, though, lustfully and hungrily buries his nose and mouth into the side of her head. The camera pulls back as he and Olive move away from each other a little. An upset Olive points down to the Popeye hole. Mr. Lifeguard is concerned now. With a mighty, swift grab, he takes both her wrists in his gigantic, powerful hand. Olive is once again immobilized by a male. But he doesn't need rope or a straitjacket to do it. All he needs is himself. Olive's face is cute as he begins to pull her forward, saying, "C'mon, Quail, let's go for a sail!" Mr. Lifeguard and Olive engage in a not-so-friendly tug-of-war. Olive is cartoony and contorting, but her legs and face are often beautiful. She's worried because she knows resistance is futile, and the lifeguard is confident. As he finally strides out of the picture, Olive is pulled off of her feet and unwillingly goes with him.

The scene changes to a dock with a boat in the water tied to it. The jeopardy music keeps playing. Mr. Lifeguard enters the picture carrying Olive and running to the boat. He has a determined, hungry grin of anticipation on his face. Olive is cradled in his massive left arm. Her own arms and hands flail helplessly. The lifeguard's hand is around her midriff, but as he stops and prepares to jump into the boat, the hand moves down lower. As Olive shows us a figure and a pretty face again, he's touching her where he shouldn't. As he leaps like a graceful Greek god through the air, he has an angry, "I'm getting what I want or else" look on his face, and his hand slides up to caress Olive's stomach. No wonder Olive is saying, "Keep all your hands to you, you you octopus you!" He joyfully lands in the boat and his thumb is now covering a strategic spot on her bikini top. His hand goes back to her tummy as he attempts to lay her down on the boat's seat. But quick-moving Olive gets her feet under her and stands next to him instead, looking forlornly over the side. Mr. Lifeguard gets behind the wheel and accelerates the boat in a flash, so that the G-forces temporarily flatten he and Olive. He just can't wait to get her all alone at sea where, because she can't swim, she'll have no chance to escape him. The music also is hurrying the boat along.

As the craft speeds through the water, Olive is standing in the back of the boat holding a towing rope. The lifeguard keeps attempting to grab Olive and pull her close. "Now make with the kiss, Sis!" She keeps managing to hold him off and slip out of his grip, often displaying great legs and a bathing beauty figure as she does. But he stretches out his lips toward her with a romantic expression on his face when he gets his hands on her middle. She tells him, "Not on your life, Guard!" Olive pushes him away and hauls off and gives him an uppercut, putting all of her strength behind it. He's actually knocked back momentarily. But then he grins. She's shocked. She's given it her best shot and failed. Mr. Lifeguard grimaces and waves an accusatory finger at her. "Get out your water wings, Angel! You're walkin'!" He angrily grabs her entire face in his hand, pulls her forward as if she were an arrow, then pushes her back and out of the boat. Fortunately for Olive, she's still holding on to the rope. Unfortunately, she doesn't have any water wings. The line deploys as the now joyful lifeguard is behind the wheel and accelerating again.

Does he want revenge on her for rejecting him? Maybe. Does he want to kill her? Doubtful. The explanation which makes the most sense, given what we know about him, is that he's wearing Olive down, knowing that eventually she'll beg to get back in the boat and he will finally be able to have his way with her. Every foot the boat travels brings him closer to his ultimate goal.

The camera follows the line back to where Olive is struggling to stand upright and water ski on her feet. The orchestra is anxious for her. She helplessly flails around and is lifted in the air and comes back to the water again. "Help, Popeye, save me! Help!" She looks behind her and cutely pouts. Then she looks ahead of her and does a leaping, stretching, cartoon double-take, her eyes popping out in alarm. The boat is speeding toward a buoy which she will hit. Shouting "Woo…ooo…ooo…ooo!" in a sexy tremolo, she stretches her legs way up and out like Mr. Fantastic, so that she passes over the buoy. As she goes back to normal, her right hand is against the side of her face in resignation and worry.

But now the boat is approaching a lighthouse on a small island. Olive is heading right for it. "Woo…ooo…ooo…ooo!" She tries to stretch her legs wide apart, but the amount of flexibility required is beyond even her. Her legs end up straddling the lighthouse as it hits her right in her lower female region. The lighthouse bends and shatters. There is a pipe running up the whole height of the former lighthouse. There's a bathtub and a male bather on top of it. The pipe is now bent and Olive is skimming along it as it rubs her body where it shouldn't. Her mouth is wide open. Her body passes over the bathtub and the male bather and travels on and out of the picture. The pipe springs upright again, shaking the bathtub and the bather. The shaking stops and we see that the bather looks sort of like an older version of Popeye, or Popeye with a bubblebath beard. He continues to wash his back with a brush as though nothing happened.

The bit with the lighthouse is a good gag and is certainly sexually charged. Because the bather looks somewhat like Popeye, it also helps to remind us that The Sailorman is out of action.

An exhausted, half-dead Olive is now off her feet, being dragged through the water. She tries to call for help nonetheless, burbling, "(drowning noises) Help! (drowning noises) Whu-Popeye! (drowning noises)."

"Do something!" she finishes and makes more drowning noises, "…ave me! (drowning noises)." We see the Popeye-shaped depression in the bottom of the empty pool. Popeye's head, hands, neck, and shoulders, all two-dimensionally flattened like a piece of cardboard, come up and out of the hole. He hears Olive, does a double-take, and gets a determined look on his face as he sees what's going on in the distance. But then he is puzzled, weary, and defeated as though he can't think of a way to help Olive in his current condition. But he climbs the rest of his flattened body up out of the hole as a triumphant version of the Popeye theme begins playing. He reaches into his shirt and pulls out an equally flattened can of spinach. We hear the spinach-eating music. Popeye rips the top off the can as though it was paper, pours the contents into his mouth, and consumes the green stuff. It first reinflates him, then morphs him into a torpedo. The Popeye torpedo dives into the drain pipe which leads to the sea.

The boat and Olive are on the horizon. The Popeye torpedo enters the picture and speeds on a collision course with the boat. It hits the boat and we see a force/explosion cloud, and the lifeguard sails into the air. The tow rope goes slack and Olive sinks. The helpless, pained lifeguard tumbles head-over-heels through the air to crash into his tower, landing awkwardly on his rear on the floor. He convulses and falls into unconsciousness. His shirt has been ripped, his tongue is hanging out, and his eyeballs are each unfocused and moving in opposite directions. The camera moves in for a close-up of the tattoo on his chest. The battleship is upended and it sinks beneath the tattooed waves, causing a waterspout which then, too, disappears. Exit Mr. Lifeguard.

Fade in on a happy Popeye pumping Olive's right leg while she lies on her stomach. Her legs and rear are shapely. *It's A Hap, Hap, Happy Day* is on the soundtrack, then it changes into Popeye's theme. "Artificial perspiration is me speckulty, Olive," he laughs. The camera pans up Olive's body. She's got her elbows on the sand and she's holding her head up in the interlocking fingers of her hands. As Popeye is pumping, water comes pouring out of her mouth and ears as if she was a fountain. It stops, she smiles, then the process starts over again.

Red-blooded American Baby Boomer males wondered why Popeye didn't take the opportunity to do some mouth-to-mouth with her. But then again, Popeye doesn't think the way normal people do.

Beach Peach (1950)

Director: Seymour Kneitel
Animation: Tom Johnson, Frank Endres
Story: Larz Bourne, Larry Riley
Scenics: Tom Ford
Music: Winston Sharples

CHAPTER 14
Jitterbug Jive (1950)

A clean-shaven Bluto appears in this cartoon.

Each generation has its own music that takes its members on flights of romance, frenzy, fantasy, dancing, and danger. And the older generation just doesn't get what the younger people are into and wants to ban it. *Jitterbug Jive* is all about how jazzy swing music can move people to their souls and about how old-fashioned folks just don't get it and want to stop it. In this cartoon, the younger generation is represented by Olive and Bluto who swing, and sway, and rock away their day, jive talking all the way! The old fuddy-duddies are represented, unfortunately for him, by Popeye. It's just one of the reasons he's such an unsympathetic character in this film.

The title card has a modern art/stained glass mosaic background, looking like the front of a juke box, and perhaps representing the beauty, complexity, craftsmanship, and yet utter wildness of jazz. The title itself, *Jitterbug Jive*, lets us know that the cartoon will be about dancing to modern music and having fun, but also about the flirting, teasing, and coming on to each other that couples do while caught up in the rhythms of their tunes.

The opening scene is in Olive's dining room. The music is bold and jazzy from the start. She's setting the table to a rhythmic beat. "Well dig me, Jackson, with a mellow jive! Popeye and Bluto will soon arrive! This here party's gonna be reet neat, we're gonna make-a with the fun and make-a with the feet!"

She saunters over to answer the doorbell. She smiles to see Popeye. He's carrying a stack of boxes. "Howdy doody, Olive," Popeye says, sounding like an uncool hick. "I brung ya parlor games for a real old fashion party." A bucolic theme plays on the soundtrack.

Olive's shocked. "Who said 'old fashion'?" Then she smiles in anticipation, sways with a feminine motion, and does some sliding dance steps as she explains, "We're gonna boing and bop and blow our top!" She tips her head back with her eyes closed. This will be good news for Bluto, because boinging and bopping and blowing her top is what most guys in the Famous Studios universe want to make Olive do. As for Popeye, he's already proved that he isn't on the same page as Olive, and that he's trying to take over a party she's planned.

He's at Olive's record player, holding a disc. "Foist for your enjoyment, a surprise novelky." Popeye puts the record on. A classical waltz plays. Olive's not amused. Bowing, Popeye asks, "Uh, shall we dance?" Olive puts her hands up in surprise, and Popeye takes the opportunity to move in on her, grab her, and start to dance. Or at least he attempts to dance by clomping around on heavy feet and pushing a resistant Olive, who is thin but curvy, back and forth on the floor. Popeye moves like a penguin, and he's forcing Olive to do something she doesn't want to do. When Bluto forces Olive, he's labeled the villain! Anyway, Olive finally pushes Popeye away. "Oh, Popeye! You and your antique antics!"

We get a close-up of Olive continuing to tell Popeye off. "You're a square for fair! You're so old fashioned!" She goes into a classic "cute female snubbing a male and letting him know he'll never have her" pose.

Popeye is cheerfully undeterred, though, because he just doesn't get it. He reaches into a box that says "Taffy" and pulls out a big, sticky glob. "C'mon, Olive! This may be old fashing, but it's tricky."

Olive protests, "Ahh, don't be an icky! Pulling taffy is sticky!" Disappointed, Olive nonetheless still gamely grabs ahold of one end, and Popeye stretches two thick strands out and begins to twist them into a rope. The bucolic music is still playing.

But then, the doorbell rings. In breathless eager anticipation, Olive says, "Hold everything! There's a mortal at the portal!" Olive is looking to Bluto to save her from this unhip drudgery. She lets go of her end of the taffy, which then goes whipping and turning and flying to wrap itself around Popeye's head like a turban and around his hands and arms, binding them. A brass instrument mocks Popeye. Then, instantly, a jazz intro begins because Bluto is here and the mood is about to change! As a stunned, weakened Popeye looks on, Olive opens the door.

A clean-shaven Bluto in a zoot suit is there, striking a "cool guy" pose. He propels himself through the doorway with a dance move. The suit emphasizes his broad shoulders and muscular physique. He says in a fun-loving masculine voice, "Greetings, Gate!"

"Welcome, Skate!" Olive responds in a sweet voice.

Bluto does another cool move and sticks out his hand, palm up. "Slip us some skin, Dreamboat!" Olive happily slides her open palm across his. Their hands seem to stick and merge together, so that Bluto and Olive are like one person, or two who have willed themselves to become permanently joined. Each hand is reluctant to let go of the other, so, as the slide is complete, they stretch way out, keeping contact until the very last possible second. Bluto, breaking the fourth wall, flashes looks of pleasure, triumph and "how about this" to the audience. Then, as he's watching the hands and fingers stretch and hold on, expressions of pure pleasurable satisfaction and lust for more play across his features. As the hands finally let go, we hear the suction and pop sounds usually reserved for kisses in Popeye cartoons. Did the two of them just symbolically kiss or symbolically have sex in front of us? At any rate, it's a very romantic and hot sequence.

The music switches to a saucy, sexy jazz. Bluto and Olive hop into dance steps perfectly in sync with each other as Bluto says, "Let's get this joint jumpin'!" They prance into the house. Olive's face is very beautiful in several frames.

Throughout the cartoon, Olive and Bluto not only are perfectly on each other's wavelengths, but they have obviously been dancing together many times before. So, Olive and Bluto regularly date, and they must love it when Popeye's not around!

Speaking of Popeye, he angrily stomps toward the couple as the brass sounds a note of alarm. Is the orchestra concerned that a fight is brewing? That Popeye is losing Olive? That Popeye is going to threaten to tear apart the real romantic couple we're already rooting for?

Cut to Olive and Bluto at a piano. Olive is leaning dreamily on the back of it, while Bluto plays a boogie-woogie piece with skill and joyful abandon. Olive lets out a sexy gasp and swoons, "Your technique leaves me weak!" She closes her eyes in ecstasy and rests her head on her hands. Her curvy lower half is constantly dancing to Bluto's music.

We hear Popeye's voice. "Hey, ya male booby-soxer!" The camera pans over and we see him enter the picture next to Bluto. "Who invited you?" Popeye demands. Note that Popeye has insulted Bluto first and wants to dictate to Olive who she can and can't invite to her own party! Bluto finishes his riff. He spins around on the piano stool and uses it to propel him forward. Everything is a dance prop to Bluto. He lifts his jacket above his head in a move showing off his muscles and killer physique. He says, "Well rip my suit zoot! The old cornball himself!" Bluto grabs the taffy, still stuck to Popeye's hands and arms, and, as his massive muscles bulge, he stretches it way out like a giant rubber band and then lets it go. It hits Popeye in the face, knocking him off his feet and sending him flying into a square-shaped alcove in Olive's wall. Popeye becomes embedded in the alcove, scrunched into the shape of a square himself. Then he falls out of the alcove and onto the floor, totally stunned and still in the shape of a square. The music mocks him, then strikes a mournful chord. We hear Bluto's voice, "Ha! Ha! Ha! What a square!" As Popeye's limbs pop back into place and he regains his original shape, a fanfare accompanies him. He jumps to his feet, seething.

The happy couple is still at the piano. A smitten Olive is still resting her head in her hands, but her eyes are open. Bluto is balancing on his fingertips which are touching the keyboard on the end away from Olive, as only a cartoon character can. He trills a couple of keys, then begins "walking" down the keyboard to Olive, playing a "descending note ditty" as he goes. He closes his eyes in anticipation, rapture, and delight as he begins kissing the air. Because his lips are on a level with Olive's, in a few moments he will be kissing her. And she happily awaits him, not moving an inch. So, of course, Popeye comes zooming in behind the piano and, at super-speed, snatches Olive away before she can react or resist. When she realizes what's happening, she's shocked. At this point in the film, it is still our supposed "hero" Popeye who is forcing Olive to do things she doesn't want to do. She wanted a kiss from Bluto. Bluto, unaware of what is transpiring, continues his finger walk right off the end of the piano and out of an open window. We hear a metallic crash and see dust and trash flying. An angry Bluto appears in the window with his head through the hole it made in a still-vibrating trashcan lid. But as he hears Popeye say, "Here's a game with a pernt to it," his expression changes to one of gleeful cunning, as he realizes that Popeye himself is unwittingly providing the means to get rid of The Sailorman, and that Olive doesn't like what Popeye is doing and wants to be rescued from the boorish lout.

Cut to Popeye and Olive at the other end of the house. There's a donkey poster that Popeye has mounted on a door. He's blindfolded and has a tail in his hand with a nail in it. He's facing the door while the bucolic music is playing again. As for Olive Oyl, she is incredibly sexy in this scene. She says in a scolding, but sweetly whimsical voice, "Awww, this donkey game isn't lively. Let's do something jivey!" She sways her hips to an imaginary, hoped-for, beat, moves her hands with feminine dancing motions, closes her eyes, and purses/puckers her lips in a dreamy, inviting way. And she is unconsciously showing off a 36-24-36 figure! Luckily for the dreaming lass, the man of her dreams, Bluto, zooms into the picture. Motioning for her to be quiet, he slides to the door and opens it. Bluto and Olive watch smiling, as an oblivious Popeye exits into the outdoor saying, "Pinups is me favorite specialtky (laughs)." Uh, no, Popeye, you didn't see the real pinup because you were blindfolded, and Bluto is the one with her now!

Bluto closes the door. "C'mon, Date, let's exhilerate!" They exit back to the center of the house using some cool dance moves. Each leans way back, but balances, then each has a rhythmic step while throwing in some hand jive. Cool, happy expressions are on their faces. Olive is almost, but not quite, up against Bluto. His massive muscles are on display again.

Meanwhile, outside, Popeye is about to jab a police horse in the rear, saying, "This game sure gives me a big kick!"

Cut to the inside of the door. We hear the horse's distressed whinny and then a kick. Popeye comes crashing through the door, causing the donkey poster to raise up in the breeze, so it isn't damaged. Popeye lands on the floor and the poster flops back down into place, covering the hole Popeye made on reentry. Popeye has a huge horseshoe stake-sized bump on his head with, sure enough, a horseshoe on it. He looks at the horseshoe and at the poster and mutters, "I don't believe it." Then he reacts in shock as he turns and sees…

…Bluto and Olive dancing a perfect jitterbug together to upbeat, jazzy music. Some moves they do are realistically human, some are pure animated cartoon, but the whole sequence conveys their joy in being together, throwing themselves into the music, and using the dance as a flirtatious come-on. The two make quite the dance team and, once again, it's obvious that they've done this many times before. Bluto is reveling in his skills, his partner, her skills, and the fact that he's won her. Olive gives him cute, coy, and encouraging looks. Bluto is very handsome in some frames and Olive has curves and a bustline. Some of her poses and moves really show off her figure to Bluto — and to us.

Popeye angrily looks away from the couple, expressing his helpless frustration. But he sees Olive's dress form, which is displaying a perfect figure. He gets an idea.

After Bluto spins Olive away during their dance, Popeye quickly substitutes the dress form for Ms. Oyl, so that Bluto, with his eyes now closed in delight, is holding onto the sleeves of a sweater on the form. He dances with it for a few seconds until one of his moves removes the sweater from the form, sending the form flying up into the air. As Bluto sees that he's holding empty clothing, the form crashes down onto him, trapping him inside of it as the song ends. He hears Popeye laughing outside and makes his way to the window. Popeye and Olive are out on the lawn. "Hey, Olive, how about a game of croquet?" The Sailorman says, but he isn't really asking.

Cut to a close-up of Popeye and Olive on the croquet court. That bucolic music begins yet again. Olive, though, is still in motion, swinging to the rhythm she hears in her mind and feels in her bones. "Croquet?!? Huh! You got rocks in your head! Who wants to play that?" But, Popeye, choosing to ignore her, demonstrates by knocking the ball away from them. He says, "See, there's nuttin' to it!"

The ball rolls over to a short stone wall surrounding Olive's property. Bluto pops up from behind it. He snatches the ball and tosses it away. Then he lifts a gatepost that has a ball on top of it up out of the ground and replants it where Popeye's ball was. Only the ball on top of the post is showing. Bluto ducks behind the wall again. Popeye and Olive enter the picture. He's lecturing, of course. "You gives the ball a whack tru' the wicket." Olive, bored, exasperated, and unenthusiastic, nonetheless gamely hangs in there. She's a sweetheart. "Okay, I'll try it." She executes a swing but when the mallet hits the planted ball, the mallet rebounds up and hits Olive in the face. It keeps bouncing between the pseudo-ball and Olive's head. The vibrations and the whackings work the post up out of the earth. Olive falls back over a wicket. She spies the post and thinks Popeye has played a prank on her. She's not amused. "Popeye! You and your corny capers!" The music mutters ominously in the background. Bluto pops up. Instantly a jazz intro to the jitterbug music begins. He takes Olive's arm. "C'mon, Plume! Let's resume!" He leads her away and Olive gives Popeye the "brush off" gesture. She's through with him, and he's flabbergasted and dumbfounded.

There's a dissolve to Bluto and Olive doing their seductive, sassy, but sweet jitterbug again, this time outside on the lawn. Some of the same footage of the characters from earlier in the cartoon is recycled, but we don't mind because Bluto and Olive are so much fun to watch together. The camera pans right as the dance is ending, showing us Olive Oyl and the empty yard. Olive's last dance move ends with an alluring pose in which she presents herself to Bluto, curvy figure and all. But, unseen by her, Popeye comes walking into the yard carrying a wooden tub filled with water and apples. The first few notes of the Popeye theme sound. Popeye sets the tub down and says, "Let's have some fun and dunk for apples, huh?" Olive is utterly disgusted. Bluto quickly slides between Olive and The Sailorman, holding his arm out in front of Olive to protect, and separate, her from this foolishness. Bucolic music is heard again. Suddenly, Bluto gets an idea.

He breaks the fourth wall, and in a close-up says to us, "I'll gag that Gee but good!" He winks at us. Then with ultra-cool, quick motions, he enthusiastically goes to Popeye, putting his one arm around him and motioning to the tub with his other. "Reet! How do ya dig it, Jackson?"

"Now you do like this. Ya glob-a glob-o-(babbling and gurgling)," Popeye tries to talk while demonstrating bobbing for apples. This guy just can't shut up! Bluto reaches off camera to grab a bag of "Quick Drying Cement." The bucolic music turns ominous and dangerous. Bluto pours the bag's contents on top of Popeye. Olive is horrified! The cement hardens instantly. Popeye tries to pull his head free to no avail. As the staves of the wooden tub burst open because of the expansion, Popeye becomes stiff as a board and springs up to the center of the now tub-shaped, big, cement plug. His head is buried inside of it.

Olive chastises Bluto, "Hey, You! What have you done to Popeye?" The background music is scared. Olive tries to get Popeye out of the cement, but she can't, and he doesn't budge, respond, or even twitch. Could he already be dead? Bluto grabs Olive's wrists and pulls the struggling miss with him as they go off camera.

"C'mon, Bait! We've got a date!" In calling Olive, "Bait," does Bluto mean she's jailbait, or wolf whistle bait? He certainly is making his intentions clear. He's going to devour her after a fashion! And why did he have to resort to attempted murder in front of Olive? He had already won her. She wanted Popeye to get lost. She was approving of the less drastic methods Bluto was using. But not this!

We now see Bluto and Olive in Bluto's convertible jalopy. Olive is protesting, but he has his hand around her waist. The car begins sputtering, contorting, bouncing, stretching, and jumping, as goofy sound effects tell us it is starting up. Bluto and Olive have no choice but to move along with it. The sequence is funny, but it also suggests that Bluto is unleashing something that can't be controlled, and that the two of them are in for a wild time. The car finally starts and the two zoom off. Now their ride is nice and smooth, but the jazzy theme in the background sounds dangerously sexy, fast, and furious.

The car is traveling on a country road. Bluto turns to Olive. His one track mind doesn't worry about steering. He says in a sexy voice, "Slip us some lip, Chick!" He goes to grab her. But Olive pushes him back while standing up. She warns him, "Stop, or I'll jump!" Bluto doesn't believe that her virtue is so important to her that she would leap from a moving car, so he gives an evil "I'm the one in control" laugh. Bluto and Olive don't realize that the car is now crossing a bridge over a ravine. He grabs at her again, and she does jump — unfortunately for her, over the side of the bridge to her doom, and screams, "Yeooww!" A shocked Bluto quickly leans over and grabs her reaching arms. Then, as he is pulling the utterly helpless lass back up to the car, he suddenly smiles with an idea. He lifts her face to his for a kiss, and there's absolutely nothing Olive can do about it. But, just as their lips are about to touch, a beam of the bridge comes between them, causing Bluto to temporarily drop her. He grabs her again and goes for the kiss. "Stop! Help!" she pleads. Another beam. Another drop. Another save. Another almost kiss, but this time it's not a beam. This time it is a very wide post. "Stop! Heellppp!" Olive drops completely out of the picture, to Bluto's horror. We see Olive falling. Just as she's about to hit the mountain road below, Bluto drives the car underneath and she lands safely in the seat. (If any girl can be safe in a car with Bluto!) The two motor away.

The music turns to a mournful version of the Popeye theme as we see he now has his feet on the ground and is trying to stand. He finally manages to yank his cement head up off the ground, but the momentum works against him. He tries to keep his balance, but trips over a rock. He falls and his cement head lands on a sloping stone wall. Popeye helplessly rolls along its top. At the bottom, he continues on and rolls across a highway where he's almost hit by a truck! And how long can he hold his breath? He rolls out of the picture.

Back to Bluto, Olive, and the saucy music. Olive is now riding on the trunk of the car, facing forward, her legs hanging over the backseat and straddling

Bluto! Bluto is standing in the front seat, facing backwards and leaning/lying to get to her. He has her in his arms, his massive hands around her waist, going for the kiss. Olive is struggling, pushing, and slapping, but Bluto is unaffected and undeterred. Bluto's hands move up and down a little. Olive shouts, "You...you keep your paws to you! You...you hep wildcat!"

The car speeds into a barn, and we hear a bump sound. It exits the other side with a mound of hay on it, so we can't see the couple. We hear a kissing sound. Has Bluto gotten what he wanted? The hay starts to blow away from Bluto's side first, prolonging the suspense. But finally it is revealed that Bluto is kissing a red cow. Bluto is very tender as he ends the kiss and adopts an "I pledge my heart" stance. Maybe he's not a total animal after all and really does love Olive! He and the cow suddenly realize the mistake that has been made. Spitting and wiping off its mouth, the cow jumps out of the car. (Presumably no animals were harmed in the making of this cartoon.) Immediately Olive springs up from the hidden rumble seat, livid at Bluto.

The scene switches to Popeye rolling through the doorway of "Joe's Vegetables." We hear a crash and see clouds of dust. In the interior of the store, the dirge-like version of Popeye's theme plays. Popeye has come to rest in front of a knocked-over basket of spinach. And his pipe is protruding out of the cement. So that's how he kept breathing! Maybe there's hope now! But the pipe is bent and the swirling lines emanating from the cement tells us that Popeye's in no condition just yet to realize there's spinach at hand.

We go back to Olive and Bluto and the racy music. Olive is kicking Bluto in the face while yelling, "Save me, Popeye!" And she's actually managing to fend him off! But then the car crashes into a stand that sells, according to the sign, "Red Hot Franks" and "Soda." When the dust and smoke clear, we see that the stand has been destroyed.

Cut to Olive suspended in the air behind the moving car like a kite, lassoed around her neck by a string of red hots. The camera follows the string back to Bluto, facing back toward Olive, in the racing car. He's calmly resting his head on one hand while using the other to pour mustard on the franks as he ingests them one-by-one, each bite bringing Olive inexorably closer. Bluto is now lying completely down, like a Caesar being fed grapes by a pretty girl. But in this case, he's about to be fed the pretty girl, too. Bluto is now Olive's lifeline. They are connected and she needs to stay connected to survive. But he's also Olive's biggest threat! It's a dangerous scene and a, pardon the pun, red hot one. And the music suddenly changes to a cheerful ditty to accompany Bluto as he eats his way to bliss with Olive. Bluto's having fun and evidently the orchestra is, and wants us to, as well.

Back at Joe's, Popeye's pipe suddenly comes to life and looks around as Olive's voice in sweet, desperate, "all is lost," "I'm about to lose my virginity," "hopelessly giving in to the inevitable" tones reaches him, "Help, Popeye, help!" The "Popeye in danger" music turns into the spinach-eating music. Popeye's eyeball comes out of the pipe and sees the spinach. The eyeball returns and Popeye uses the pipe to suck in the green stuff. Popeye leaps to his feet as spinach gives him the power to totally recover, crack the cement, and be transformed into a costumed hepcat.

Spinach often gave Popeye new duds, like this zoot suit, along with new abilities.

But instead of a watch chain, this swinger has a heavy anchor chain. Popeye does a little dance and says, "Well, horreet!" (I have no idea what this means.) Celebratory, fast, transitional music plays as Popeye grabs the chain and pulls a huge anchor out of his pocket. He begins twirling it around, leaves the store, and, once outside, gives the anchor a mighty toss.

Cut to Olive and Bluto with only about a frank and a fourth now separating them. Bluto keeps consuming, but he's slowed down — not because he's full, but because he wants to tease Olive and to assure her that he's going to take his time savoring her, too. His expression combines smugness, confidence, male expectancy, and gloating. And he never takes his eyes off Olive as he chews with a very deliberate rhythm. Finally, he's halfway through the last frank. One more bite and Olive will be his. This scene, too, is red hot.

But the anchor comes crashing into the picture and hooks the back of the car. The impact sends Olive and Bluto into the air. They land in the car and Olive is now in Bluto's arms! But just momentarily. Momentum starts propelling her from the car as Bluto grabs her arm and the entire car is pulled off camera.

Popeye is pulling the chain. The car comes sailing past him. He grabs Olive out of it and begins to dance with her. The transitional jazz that had been playing becomes an introduction for a fast, joyous, version of an earlier musical cue. Popeye starts "scatting." Both Popeye and Olive are overjoyed. But though

Olive shows a glimpse of her underwear as her skirt swirls, and does some figure-emphasizing moves, she was drawn much prettier and sexier when she was dancing with Bluto. Why is that? Is it because now she's stuck with a spinach-spawned copy, rather than the original?

Speaking of Bluto, he enters the picture and draws his arm back to punch Popeye. The Sailorman is too quick for the big guy, though. As part of his dance, he kicks Bluto in the stomach twice, then once in the chest and once in the head. As a dazed Bluto totters forward, Popeye gives him an uppercut that sends him flying. Bluto plunges face down into the pavement, furrowing over to a fire hydrant where a metallic "klong" lets us know that his journey has stopped. The hydrant swells up, its valve pops, and out comes a gigantic drop of water, containing Bluto. In a voice-over, Popeye laughs and says, "That drip's all wet!"

Popeye and Olive continue to dance, doing a jazzy "buck-and-wing," facing us and smiling. Popeye's scatting becomes more frantic and furious. Does he know the cartoon's about to end, or is he "blowing his top," finally caught up in the music?

Still, Popeye and Olive spend most of their time looking at us, instead of each other. When Bluto and Olive danced, they were totally entranced by one another. Hmm, maybe this isn't such a happy ending after all. If only Bluto had been more patient!

Jitterbug Jive (1950)

Director: Bill Tytla
Animation: George Germanetti, Harvey Patterson
Story: Carl Meyer, Jack Mercer
Scenics: Lloyd Hallock, Jr.
Music: Winston Sharples

CHAPTER 15

Vacation with Play (1951)

An example of how the Famous Studios artists would enhance portions of Olive's anatomy. Here, her calves are quite shapely.

Vacations are romantic, at least in theory. While "on holiday," you are freed from being occupied with your daily responsibilities, are in a different location (and thus mentally in a different world), are on the lookout for fun and adventure, and are encountering new members of the opposite sex. All of which can lead to the infamous "Summer Love" which is warned about in the golden-oldie, *See You In September*, and celebrated in the song, *Summer Days, Summer Nights*, from the movie, *Grease*. The creators of this cartoon knew all about "Summer Love."

The film's title card is nothing special, but the title itself is. Aside from obviously being a pun on the phrase, "Vacation with Pay," *Vacation with Play* points toward what will happen in the cartoon. Olive Oyl and the Instructor will enjoy playing sports and exercising together. And the word, "Play," is used by some couples as a euphemism for "making love" or "making out" or "sex." Olive and Mr. Instructor will certainly enjoy this other pleasurable way of getting physical, and will share a cute and hot romance, as the plot unfolds. I can hardly wait to see it, can you?

The camera irises in on a cute-faced Olive Oyl driving what looks like an oversized Model T that is laden with luggage, sports equipment, and gifts. She turns her pretty head and says, "Oh, Popeye, soon we'll be in Lake Narrowhead and our vacation begins!" as the camera pulls back to reveal The Sailorman running beside the car, holding up the passenger side's rear axle. He has an old tire around his shoulder and looks put upon and very tired.

"Used car!" Popeye spits out in disgust. "Wait 'til I gets me hands on that smilin' Dutchman!" Any sympathy we may have been building up toward Popeye the Human Fourth Wheel evaporates. He actually bought this clunker of a car from a used car salesman who couldn't be trusted? What a chump! The orchestra, which had been playing a happy, expectant traveling song at the cartoon's beginning, now switches to an embarrassed version of Popeye's theme as he speaks. The musicians share our disdain of Popeye.

The scene fades out, and then we fade in on a hotel, tennis court, and patio tables with umbrellas in a mountainous, rustic, but classy, setting. The camera pans toward Olive as we hear her enthuse, "Popeye, we're here!" She's looking at the hotel, and the music shares her excitement and anticipation. "(gasp!) I can't wait 'til we partake in the athletics!" She gestures enthusiastically, but when she turns to Popeye, she does a shocked double-take.

The music begins an old-fashioned lullaby/sleep theme with a slightly embarrassed, or belittling, or humiliating tone to it, as the camera goes over to Popeye who has his eyes closed and is stretched out on a hammock suspended between two trees. He mutters, "I'm so tired, I could sleep on a picket fence. Ahhh… mbblmbbzzz (snoring)."

A still joyful and hopeful Olive walks into the scene. As she enters she has a very pretty face, nice legs, and a decidedly and deliciously feminine walk. Also, since she is wearing a sports top and short shorts (which will get even shorter depending on the needs of the creators in any given scene/frame of this cartoon) and high heels, the O.O.O.P.S. kicks in.[1] She playfully motions for Popeye to get up. "C'mon, Popeye! Let's play tennis! Let's swim! Let's live!" ("Let's live!" could be the motto of the Famous Studios Olive Oyl.) As she exhorts, "Let's live!" she throws her arms skyward in an exuberant gesture. Her shirt goes up a little, and we get a glimpse of her midriff. Because of her personality and cuteness, Olive Oyl exudes pure sex appeal in this scene, and indeed throughout the entire cartoon.

Popeye cracks open his eyes halfway and answers her disinterestedly and dismissively, "Let's don't and say we did!" He rudely turns his back on her with a "you bore me so get lost" expression on his face. Then a look of smug, self-centered contentment comes over him as he closes his eyes once again. He's not just glad he's going to sleep; he's glad that he sure told off that silly female, Olive Oyl, as well.

At this point, viewers have sympathy for Olive. She doesn't deserve to be treated like this. Popeye could have said something like, "Just lets me have some quick shuteye and then I'm all yours!" But maybe we should also feel sorry for Popeye? After all, he has just borne the weight of a car traveling downhill. However, we, and Olive, have seen Popeye do lots of stupendous super-stunts without needing to take naps afterward. And later in the film, when Olive's with a new guy, Popeye will suddenly have plenty of energy again. Then, after The Sailorman has won her at the end of the cartoon, he will ignore her and blow her off all over again. Popeye really is a jerk in this film.

But we're getting ahead of ourselves. Let's pick up where we left off.

Olive is understandably upset. But suddenly her attention goes to a loudspeaker mounted on the tree. A strong, smooth, flirty male voice is announcing, "Attention all guests! Attention all guests! Will all you lovely girls desiring athletic instruction report to the little old swimming pool immediately." During the announcement, the camera travels to the pool where a well-built instructor in a tight muscle shirt (Bluto playing a role) is speaking into a microphone.

Back to Olive. She angrily says to a happily snoring Popeye, "Aw right, Grandpa! Go ahead and sleep! I'm gonna join that class!" Olive is determined not to let Popeye ruin her vacation and is hopeful that some fun can be salvaged. As she strides off, she once again exhibits an appealing feminine walk and displays spectacular legs. Popeye sleeps on, and two squirrels, one from each of the hammock's supporting trees, descend cautiously down to join him. Woodwinds playing descending notes accompany them, but the music also seems to portray that Popeye is sinking deeper and deeper into slumber. Finally the music concludes as if to say, "We're done with Popeye."

The scene switches to the handsome instructor poolside looking over his "recruits." The soundtrack begins a "things are moving forward on a fun, sunny day" theme. He claps his hands and says, in a voice once again smooth and masculine with just a hint of playful lasciviousness thrown in, "All right, Girls, line up!" Unlike Popeye, he *really* wants to pay attention to girls and enjoy being with them.

A parade of beauties in skimpy two-piece outfits and bikinis begins. They move in feminine ways, are drawn as pinup girls, and flirt with the instructor. The Famous Studios artists outdid themselves on this scene! The camera assumes the instructor's point of view as he is scanning the line of babes. Olive, with a made-up face and shapelier legs than usual, confidently strides into his line of sight. At first it might seem as though the cartoon's creators mean for the skinny Olive among the buxom beauties to be a joke. But Olive has a dreamy, aloof, and appealing look on her face, as though she knows the instructor will want her and that she can turn him on. She puts her hands on her hips, then swings them to the right, making her shorts swirl around her legs and showing off a shapely derriere. Then Olive brings her left hand up alongside of her head as she strikes a traditional mating/flirting/modeling pose and thrusts out her hips to the right. Mr. Instructor's eyes continue to pan past her to the next girl, but then they zip back to Olive and zoom in on her. She deserves a second, and closer, look. Music and sound effects help Mr. Instructor zero in on Olive. A "zoinging" sound is heard on the soundtrack because the lovely Ms. Oyl has had quite an effect on him. Olive then coyly, but skillfully and playfully, goes from being aloof to projecting that she's REALLY available as she opens her eyes and gazes at him. The artists give her one of the prettiest, sexiest dollfaces that Olive has ever had in any cartoon as she tilts her head in a gesture that is both submissive and "come hither." She has pretty, luscious red lips, a cute nose, and gorgeous long-lashed eyes that she knows how to use as she blinks them ultra-seductively at Mr. Instructor. Olive is using body language and a demure, yet enticing, coy, yet purposeful, innocent, yet romantically wise facial expression to convey her desirability, availability, and interest to Mr. Instructor. No matter what the intent of the creators was at the beginning of this scene, by its end they have convinced themselves, the viewers, and Mr. Instructor that Olive Oyl is indeed the sexiest, most alluring woman at the resort.

Speaking of the instructor, a close-up shot shows us that his mouth is hanging open in amazed, rapturous delight, and he's wearing an expression of healthy male desire (not wolfish lust). He does another double-take. Olive Oyl rates two. His baseball cap flies off and his eyeballs pop out of his head, rolling down ramps formed by his elongated lower eyelids, to get the best, and a closer, look at Olive. Then his eyeballs go back in, his cap returns to its perch, and he's left with a love-struck expression on his face. The orchestra wraps up the piece they have been playing with a satisfying and expectant fanfare-like chord. The members of the orchestra, and we viewers, believe that things are now as they should be. The instructor and Olive Oyl will be together. And we can't wait to see what they will do next!

But unfortunately, we have to quickly check in on Popeye and the squirrels. They are just happily snoring away. Square, boring, sleepy music is playing. We hope he'll stay unconscious for the rest of the cartoon, and maybe he actually will because he is totally unaware that Olive and the instructor are seducing each other.

Cut to a happy Olive Oyl, holding a bow, and the instructor standing near a quiver. He says in a smooth, masculine, gentle but strong, seductive voice, "Now, uh, first, Angel, we'll have instruction in archery." He steps over to her, holding an arrow. It's pointing straight out at Olive and her, er, lower region. Does this represent Cupid's arrow? And, although as Freud said, "Sometimes a cigar is just a cigar," does the arrow represent something else? At any rate, Mr. Instructor reaches his right hand around Olive to grab the top of the bow. His left hand fits the arrow to the bow, as Olive's hand joins his. Olive is now inside of his arms. She looks at him and he can't take his eyes off of her. They are enjoying more than the lesson. "Having fun and making progress" music plays again.

But the cartoon takes us back to Popeye and the squirrels sleeping. Off camera, Olive, in a gushing, flirty voice, declares, "Oh, Mr. Instructor! You're so strong and muscular thing!" Her last word may not be "thing" but "zwing," "ring" (like a bell), or maybe a slang term of endearment. It's hard to hear. But the squirrels have heard it, have awakened, and are alarmed. Popeye still peacefully slumbers. If it wasn't for those darned squirrels, Popeye wouldn't have to be in the remainder of the cartoon at all! But one squirrel pokes Popeye in the nose twice to rouse him, as Olive gives the instructor a trilling giggle. Popeye is still half out of it until the squirrel points over to where the instructor and Olive are. He's pretty groggy as he tries to look. Then he does a shocked double-take, "Huh?!"

We go back to the smitten couple. Mr. Instructor continues his sexy vocal, "You just pull the bow back slowwwwly..." He does so, bringing Olive's head and body close to him at the same time. They let fly the arrow with matched expressions of delight on their faces, and they move their heads and bodies perfectly in sync with each other to watch it go. They were made to be together!

Cut to an apple hanging on a tree. The arrow pierces, and sticks in, it and the momentum swings the apple up over the branch, breaking its stem, and sending it back toward Olive and Mr. Instructor. A surprised Olive ducks, letting out a sexy, "Oh!" Mr. Instructor, though, is muscular, confident, and unworried. He leans forward, catches the arrow in flight and says in a calming and sweetly teasing voice, "There you are, Sugar! An apple on a stick!" The music strikes a note of triumph as he presents it to Olive. The apple now looks just like a cartoon heart. Is Mr. Instructor presenting his heart to Olive? Does the apple/arrow signify that Cupid has struck?

There's a close-up of Olive, with pretty eyes, receiving the gift. She hugs it close to her chest. Now it looks almost like a real human heart. She looks adoringly at Mr. Instructor. "Ooohhh, how utterly, utterly!" She's not just talking about the gift.

Mr. Instructor strikes a manly "it was nothing — even though I know I'm really so cool" pose. Olive looks the apple/arrow up and down and then turns her attention again to her new boyfriend. But her old one zooms into the picture.

"Hey...Hey, Olive," Popeye says, "archkery is my spec'alty! Watch this!" Olive, though, is annoyed. Mr. Instructor is neutral, then mocking. He doesn't believe anyone can show him up. Popeye walks over to a patio table, bends three arrows into U shapes, then stretches one of the few hairs on the top of his head to act as his bow (yuck!), and lets the arrows fly. They hit, and collect, a variety of foods set out on a circular lunch counter and then boomerang back to Popeye. The Sailorman lifts the table to catch them, then displays his makeshift "shish kebobs." "Luchkon now being soived in the Dining Car!" Popeye announces and then stands there laughing over and over again like a dork.

An ominous note sounds as Olive and Mr. Instructor, again with matching expressions and movements, are furious with him. Popeye has butted in where he wasn't wanted. And remember that he had his chance earlier with Olive and blew it. She has moved on. Popeye is trying to horn in on someone else's date. Popeye has also cheapened the instructor's cute, from the heart, gift by trying to top it. And throughout this cartoon, Popeye will never actually include Olive in his activities. He just wants to show off. The orchestra, Olive, Mr. Instructor, and the viewers are outraged.

Olive dismisses the showboat sailor, "Hmmph! Very funny, Popeye!" Then an Olive Oyl, in microshorts, whose long, shapely legs go on forever, turns to stride away from him in a feminine manner. Popeye, caught up in himself, doesn't even notice that she's mad and she's leaving. Mr. Instructor happily notices her reaction, her spectacular legs, and the means at hand to keep Popeye at bay. As the instructor leaves with Olive, he pulls down on an arrow that has skewered a pie, bends it back, and lets it go. The pie is shot onto Popeye's head and into his face. Popeye is now covered with pie filling, blind, and stumbling around. His head appears to have been squashed flat inside the pie plate, too. The music concludes by playing embarrassed opening notes of his theme. He's been humiliated and taken care of.

Fade in on Mr. Instructor and Olive at the first hole of a golf course, obviously still happy to be together. Mr. Instructor positions a ball and picks up a club. He's in back of Olive and both are facing the ball. He helps her grip the club, with the result being that she's now in his arms. Olive's eager to learn, and for other things. The two give each other "lovey-dovey" eyes during this whole sequence and snuggle cheek-to-cheek. They take a few truncated practice swings, Mr. Instructor essentially totally guiding and controlling Olive's compliant body. She's completely in his power and his massive muscles surround the happy miss. Sometimes he nuzzles the back of her neck. Finally, when they pull back for a full swing, Olive's face is dreamily buried in his muscular arms. He has a look of healthy desire and lust on his face. He's saying, "Now in golf, Toots, ya relax yer sacroiliacs and then swing. Fore!" They launch the ball and the force of the swing is sweeping Olive off her feet in more ways than one.

The camera follows the ball into the hole, then goes back to Mr. Instructor, who still has his arms around a delighted Olive. He and Olive are making no move to break the hold. He announces, "There ya are! A hole-in-one!" The music concludes triumphantly. It's not only happy about the hole-in-one, but also that the couple is in love. Olive gazes at Mr. Instructor in hero worship, then turns demurely, but encouragingly, away slightly, as if to say she knows what comes next. Mr. Instructor certainly does. As she dreamily closes her eyes, he cuddles cheek-to-cheek with her and gets ready to move in for a kiss. Olive turns away, but in a flirty manner, coyly encouraging the kiss. Mr. Instructor relaxes his grip on her and lets her pull away slightly. They are both enjoying their amorous teasing and the prolonging of the magic moment. But Mr. Instructor notices Popeye approaching to his left. Olive is still shrugging and then snuggling into herself in ecstasy. She turns back to Mr. Instructor happily and expectantly. But upon noticing Popeye, she joins Mr. Instructor in putting an enraged "go away" expression on her face. Olive is gorgeous when she's angry.

Popeye insults and demeans what has just happened. "Why, that's just putterin' around!" We get a close-up of him. He makes his bicep into a tee and places a ball on it. "Keep your eye on the ball, Olive!" He yells, "Fore!" and stretches his neck, twisting it around and around. He unwinds, using his pipe for a club and whacks the ball out of the picture. Why he thinks any female would find a tiny, strangely shaped bicep, and a guy who can whirl his neck around like he's demon-possessed, attractive is beyond me.

We see the ball going into one hole, springing out of it, and then going into the next one, and so on. Popeye is now casually leaning against the flag at the 18th hole. As the ball approaches, he picks up the flag, and the ball drops into the hole. Popeye gestures dramatically. "There ya are! 18 holes-in-one!" His eyes are shut in smug delight. But suddenly, he hears a tennis volley. Bright, fast-moving, "having fun" music starts again. In shock, Popeye leans toward the direction of the sound and opens his eyes wide. "Huh?!?!?" Olive and Mr. Instructor didn't watch him or wait for him. (Good for them!) They are off having fun together again. Twice now Popeye has interrupted, however Mr. Instructor hasn't gotten lethal with him yet, but has been pretty benign. This makes us respect Mr. Instructor.

Cut to one of the sexiest scenes in any Famous Studios cartoon. It's impossible to fully describe, but I'll do my best. It really ought to be watched, and then rewatched, in frame-advance or slow motion modes. Essentially in this scene, a game of tennis represents the playful give-and-take between a man and a woman, and the dynamic forces that draw and bind them together. Olive and Mr. Instructor engage in a long volley, and each time the ball hits the court, it is nearer to the net, drawing each player closer, ever closer, to mid-court, and to each other. Olive's pretty legs, shapely rear, and luscious lips are emphasized in some frames, along with Mr. Instructor's hunky build. Though they are flirting with each other, they are both truly enjoying the game and even move in sync with wild, joyous abandon after a return. This makes them seem even more perfect for each other because they both get swept away by the same things. Finally, as the ball hovers over the net, their rackets come together as they both hit it at the same time. The sound that's made by the joining is like that of two objects becoming one permanently by being glued, or stapled, symbolizing Olive and Mr. Instructor being joined in love forever. As the couple rushes the net, Mr. Instructor doesn't even look at the ball. He's totally zeroed in on Olive, overcome with desire. He moves his face closer to hers and puckers up. A close-up of the two of them shows that a curvy Olive realizes what's going on and is happily waiting for the kiss. The soundtrack music has been progressively, and playfully, building up to the rackets coming together. Then it follows Mister Instructor in for the kiss.

As Mister Instructor and Olive were volleying, they each called out a score when they hit the ball. It went like this:

> *Mr. Instructor: (firmly, as though putting himself out there for Olive)* Ten!
> *Olive: (in an answering tone with a bit of flirting in it)* Twenty!
> *Mr. Instructor: (with a hint of expectation)* Thirty!
> *Olive: (answering with playful and flirty excitement and anticipation)* Forty!
> [Smack! The rackets come together.]
> *Mr. Instructor: (puckering up and proclaiming an emotional truth in a tender tone)* Love!

But Popeye appears and shoves his racket between the couple, so that Mr. Instructor's lips get pressed against it. Popeye, once again judgmental, know-it-all, self-centered, and interrupting, scolds, "That's no way to play tennisk!" Mr. Instructor turns and glares at him, but Olive keep the same smile on her face. She was mesmerized by the instructor and is still in "here comes the kiss" mode.

The camera pulls back to show us a long shot of all three of them. The couple comes apart and the ball drops onto Popeye's racket. "Your soive is all wrong!" The music starts cheerfully speeding ahead again. Popeye walks past Olive, intending to take her place and play opposite Mr. Instructor. "Let me shows ya the right way!" Mr. Instructor is livid and frustrated. Olive is cute and seems willing to let Popeye join in on the fun, or maybe she's just confident Mr. Instructor can handle him. Either way, it makes her appealing to the viewers, as do her shorts which cling to her curvy hips.

A fit-to-be-tied Mr. Instructor says to Popeye, "Okay, Wise Guy, go ahead, serve!" Popeye does. Mr. Instructor uses quite a backhand to try and return the ball, but, to his helpless shock, the ball stretches out the strings of his racket, and then orbits around him with such power and speed that it spins him around like a top, drilling him into the court. He snaps out of his stupor and glares as we hear Popeye laughing.

There's a close-up of The Sailorman as he says, "Love that soive!"

Then the camera switches to Mr. Instructor as he strides to the net. Evil, ominous, plotting music is heard. But, frankly, it's about time Mr. Instructor plotted to get rid of Popeye for good. At this point in the cartoon, audience members wanted to punch the sailor's lights out! After all, Mr. Instructor is protecting his new girlfriend and new relationship from an interloper. Mr. Instructor mutters, "That runt is crampin' me style!" He then twists a metal ball of the top of a net post. He calls to Popeye, "Let's see if you can return me cannon ball!" The music is happy again. Either it thinks Popeye can handle it, or is glad Popeye's about to get what's coming to him. Popeye answers, "Go ahead! Fire away!"

Mr. Instructor leaps off the ground and hits the metal ball with such superforce that a large "Boom" sound effect is heard and the word appears on the screen, along with the colors and smoke of an explosion. It's as though a real cannon has been fired.

We hear the ball whistling through the air. Popeye raises his racket to intercept it, but it stretches his racket out and lifts him off the ground and away with it as it flies over the court's fence. The music soars with it. The ball smashes into the top of a tree. Popeye is already looking helpless and out of it when the ball rebounds and collides with the top of his head. There's another mini-explosion effect. Popeye's neck, back, and head are driven into his body. His body scrunches into a misshapen form, then seems to flatten out, and then a huge bump grows out of Popeye's head and pushes the ball off. His eyes are closed and his tongue is hanging out. He is either unconscious, or dead! Popeye's body comes back into shape as he falls helplessly out of the picture.

Cut to the hammock. Popeye lands in it, head first. He stretches the hammock all the way to the ground where his head hits terra firma accompanied by yet another "painful impact" effect. The hammock rebounds Popeye to a "sleeping on his back" position. His eyes remain closed. There are several large bumps on his head, and his arms hang limply at his sides, but he's wearing the same blissful expression he had while sleeping at the beginning of the film. The background music wraps things up as though it, too, is disposing of Popeye. Then a piano does the equivalent of an aural wink at us, suggesting romance and hanky panky, as Mr. Instructor and Olive stroll into the scene and on past Popeye.

In his best, "let's go somewhere we can be all alone, Gorgeous," tones, Mr. Instructor says, "While your boyfriend's sleepin', Chicken, I'll give you a canoeing lesson." Clearly he's going to give her more than that, and clearly she won't mind at all. She never looks at Popeye once. She has eyes only for Mr. Instructor. Her walk is very feminine, emphasizing in some frames her shapely derriere. Mr. Instructor has unknowingly played into Olive's disappointment with Popeye from the beginning of the cartoon. She probably thinks Popeye is snubbing her for a nap again. Mr. Instructor is carrying a guitar.

The sleepy music begins again, but with a slightly more ominous tone. The squirrels climb on Popeye again, but this time they are fearful for their napping buddy. The squirrel on top of Popeye's head reaches down and pulls open Popeye's eyelid. The white of his eye is all bloodshot, and there's no pupil. Instead, the words "Out Cold" appear there. Brass on the soundtrack lets us know that Mr. Instructor's plan has worked and that Popeye is now out of the way for hours, or days — maybe forever. The other side of Popeye's face appears to be in pain.

The scene changes to Olive and Mr. Instructor in a canoe. Olive is laying back on a huge, comfy pillow[2] in the bow of the craft, facing Mr. Instructor with an enraptured look on her face. A happy, eager Mr. Instructor is serenading her, while accompanying himself on the guitar. He sings, "I'm in the mood for love…" And in a sexy voice counts the beat, "two…three…four…simply because you're near me…"

The camera goes in for a close-up of Olive Oyl. She stretches comfortably out in a welcoming position. Then she lets out an emotionally ravished, and totally sexy, swoon which is a cross between "Ohhhhhh!" and "Ahhhhhh!" and she starts to turn into the pillow, burying her face in it. Experiencing paroxysms of delight over Mr. Instructor, his musical skills, the setting, and the theme of the song, she puts her arms over her head, as if she's doing a swimming stroke, and completes her turnover. She peeks her face cutely out of the pillow, looks back at Mr. Instructor, and gives him a flirty, teasing, satisfied look. Then with her face turned toward the camera, she dreamily closes her eyes, totally contented and totally under the spell of Mr. Instructor. Now, her top half is in the pillow, her knees are on the floor of the canoe, and her derriere is sticking up at Mr. Instructor!

He continues to sing, "Funny, but when you're near me…" He drops his guitar in the water to use it as an oar, as the orchestra quickly finishes his song for him. Mr. Instructor paddles furiously, and his face takes on a wolfish appearance as he zeroes in on Ms. Oyl's shapely behind. And Olive's feet move up and down in time with his strokes as though she is moving things right along, too, and as though Mr. Instructor is controlling her and moving her to her core. The orchestra joins the couple in their frantic furiousness. It, like the couple, wants their relationship to go full-speed ahead and can't wait until they get where they are going next.

Cut to a log cabin on a small island. The front door is open. The canoe speeds across the water, and Mr. Instructor paddles it up on to, and through, the land (leaving a rut). He paddles it into the cabin as the music swirls to its finish, which coincides with the cabin's door slamming shut and locking. This is the moment the whole cartoon has been building toward.

It's at this instant that many fans turn off their TVs or stop their VCRs. Mr. Instructor and Olive Oyl are all alone and in the mood behind closed doors.

Popeye isn't present and isn't even a factor. This ending is so much more satisfying than the one the film gives us later.

We still see the exterior of the cabin as Mr. Instructor says, "How about a little kiss, Babe?" "Olive in danger" music begins, letting us know that Mr. Instructor has stopped the wooing and begun the forcing. Olive comes out of a window yelling, "Help, Popeye!" But Mr. Instructor reaches out, grabs her, and pulls her back in. A trombone on the soundtrack emphasizes Olive's hopeless situation. She quickly appears again, jumping out of an upstairs window. "Popeye, where are you?" Mr. Instructor snatches her back inside again. We hear three kissing sounds. Was Mr. Instructor just kissing the air, or did he manage to steal some from a struggling Olive? I believe he actually got those kisses, because of what the squirrels will act out in the next scene. For now, though, Olive pops out of the cabin's chimney. She gives a hailing whistle, and shouts, "Taxi!" But, sure enough, she's grabbed again.

Olive is rejecting Mr. Instructor! Looked at one way, this is pretty inexplicable. She's wanted to get intimately physical with him and has given him all the signals. And one can hardly blame Mr. Instructor for thinking he had a green light. Looked at another way, though, there's a big difference between being wooed on a lake and maybe sharing kisses and cuddling with a guy in a canoe, and letting a guy rush you into his cabin and lock you in! Especially without asking! So, once again, the impatience of Ms. Oyl's lover will prove to be his undoing.

The scene changes to the two squirrels on either side of Popeye, watching what's happening with concern. A funereal "all is lost" version of Popeye's theme plays with a frantic strain, underscoring what's happening to Olive. One squirrel scampers down to Popeye's tie, the other to the top of his head. Pulling and pushing respectively, they manage to get Popeye's head up off the pillow. Popeye dully half-opens his eyes. The squirrels position themselves on his torso and start chattering desperately in squirrel talk. They jump up and down and point over toward the direction of the cabin. But Popeye's eyes close again, then open uncomprehendingly. When he seems finally to sort of focus on the squirrels, they act out lovemaking to convey to Popeye what's going on between Mr. Instructor and Olive. A romantic and light version of *I'm in the Mood for Love* plays on the soundtrack. Is this because the squirrels are having fun, or because the orchestra doesn't think that what's happening to Olive is so bad? The one squirrel, happily and male-like, leaps at the startled other one, taking it in his arms and leaning it way back for kisses. The facial expressions on the aggressor squirrel are like Mr. Instructor's wooing faces. The other squirrel looks helpless. But as the first squirrel administers rapturous kisses to the second's cheek, the "female" squirrel suddenly gets a look of dreamy, submissive delight on its face. Are the squirrels just enjoying themselves, or is part of Popeye's jeopardy that Olive will start to enjoy what Mr. Instructor is doing to her and give in? After all, we haven't heard any cries for help lately. Maybe Olive is not just trying to get away from a guy who wants to have his way with her, but she's also trying to escape because she knows she will want the guy to have his way with her, and she knows the relationship really isn't at that point yet.

At any rate, Popeye moves his head forward as though he's starting to get what's going on, but then his eyes quickly cross, glaze over, and close again. His head flops down on the pillow, not with a pleasant expression like he's asleep this time, but like he's in a coma, or even dead, or at some unconscious level aware that he is helpless. So Olive is being ravished and there's absolutely nothing Popeye is able to do about it! He's probably completely unaware it is even happening! He's dead to the world! The music, which had briefly seemed to believe that Popeye could shake off his stupor, ends with brass notes that express in no uncertain terms that Popeye is finished and that the worst is coming to pass.

Cut to a shot of the back of the cabin and the dock which leads out from it. We hear thunderous pounding on the door, which suddenly bursts out of its frame as a fleeing Olive pushes it before her. She runs off the dock and into the air, as Mr. Instructor comes through the doorway. He runs to the end of the dock, frustrated. But not for long, because there's a boat tied there.

Olive warns, "You keep your hands to you! You, you, you…that's what you are!" using a sweet innocent, "in trouble" voice. She runs through the air as long as she can, but real-life physics take over in this cartoon universe. The door drops down, hitting the water, taking Olive with it. She has a cute face, and we get glimpses of her bare midriff throughout this scene.

Olive's body impacts the door hard, smashing her upper third right through it. She's now kind of on a crazy raft with her head and arms upside-down under the water. But she keeps trying to propel herself away from Mr. Instructor by kicking the water with her feminine legs.

Mr. Instructor, in all his muscular glory, is now in the boat holding a fishing pole. Wow! What a body! He determinedly, smugly, and sneeringly casts his line toward Olive. It hooks the top of her shorts, and then the line goes taut as he starts reeling her in. Though Olive is being pulled and contorted out of the hole in a cartoony manner, she has a shapely rear and pretty legs in many frames. Finally Olive is pulled free of the raft, let's out another sexy "Oh!" and goes flying backward to Mr. Instructor. As she skims the surface of the water, she reaches in and pulls out a large fish. As the instructor hauls her up into the boat, she swings the fish and smacks him in the face with it, saying, "You octopus!" (Just what was he doing to her in that cabin?!?!?) Olive's swing gives us a glimpse of her still-hooked, and suspended, feminine underwear. As Mr. Instructor is reeling from the blow, Olive drops into the water again. A give-and-take now occurs between she and Mr. Instructor, as though she is a fish he is trying to land. The boat is propelled forward in the struggle. Olive keeps breaking the water's surface and leaping and flopping in the air at the end of the fishing line while yelling a vibratory "Heellpp!!" The orchestra expresses her desperation, helpless state, and the inevitable outcome.

The scene transitions to Popeye and the squirrels. The orchestra begins a helpful theme as the squirrels, using tremendous effort, manage to prop up Popeye's head with a slingshot-shaped broken-off branch, and prop his mouth open with his pipe. The squirrels pull the spinach can out of his shirt, open the can (with one squirrel using the other's head and teeth as a makeshift can opener), and kick the spinach into his open mouth. Popeye's mouth closes, and he chews and swallows the green stuff automatically as the appropriate music plays. Even so, he still seems to be blissfully unconscious. But suddenly the spinach has an explosive effect on him, empowering him as it travels through his body. The hammock becomes a giant rubber band, launching Popeye into the lake.[3]

Cut to Mr. Instructor scooping Olive out of the water into a fishing net. Her hands and arms are immobilized by her sides and her shapely legs protrude from the bottom of the net. She's now really, completely helpless. The camera moves in on the two of them. Mr. Instructor puckers up and pulls her into him. His lips are massive, as though he's going to devour her. He will, at the very least, overwhelm her. He has a delighted expression on his face. A worried Olive, sweetly trying to change the subject, asks, "Di…di…did you read any good books lately?" Mr. Instructor's lips get less than a micron from Olive. She turns her head away and screams, "Help, Popeye!" Mr. Instructor makes kissing motions and sounds with his lips.

We see Popeye's pipe knifing through the water like a periscope. His arm and fist are also out of the water, winding up for a super-powered punch. The triumphant Popeye theme is playing.

The scene switches back to the boat. The Popeye torpedo enters the picture as Mr. Instructor is toying with Olive in a scene that could be incredibly sexy if Olive were playing along. He keeps pulling her close and stretching his neck and lips toward her, making kissing motions, and then backing off and starting all over again. He's enjoying prolonging the lead-up to the kiss, or teasing her, or reveling in his power over her. Popeye comes up under the boat, using his fist as a ram. The boat flies up in the air and breaks in two. Popeye continues to rise up out of the lake like a missile. Mr. Instructor has flown up and out of the picture and has let go of the net. Popeye grabs it on his way back down and plants his feet on the half of the boat that is still there. Then he pulls Olive over to him as she struggles to get free of the net.

Cut to Mr. Instructor in the half of the boat which is in midair. He looks beneath him, stunned that there's nothing else there. He double-takes when he spots the angry Popeye and starts using the oars to attempt to row away from him in the air as his half-boat falls. But he comes down in front of Popeye and

Olive. The Sailorman delivers a strong punch that sounds like a thunderclap to the bottom of Mr. Instructor's half-boat, and it and Mr. Instructor go flying out of the picture again.

Cut to the water wheel of a mill. Mr. Instructor collides with it, becoming embedded in one of the spaces between its slats. The momentum of the collision speeds the wheel up. Mr. Instructor goes round and round, all washed up, as the orchestra follows the rotation of the wheel while finishing its take on Popeye's theme song.

The scene dissolves into the two squirrels on a ping pong table, holding its net up. Happy music is playing. We see and hear the ball going back and forth. The camera pulls back to reveal a leggy Olive on one side of the table, paddle in hand. She's volleying as she says, "Oh, Popeye, isn't this fun?" The camera follows the ball as she hits it over the net to Popeye who is on the other side, reclining in the hammock with his eyes closed. His right leg is resting on his left, and he hits the ball with the sole of his shoe. The camera moves in on the comfortable Popeye. "Yeah, ya can't beat exkercise, Olive." He yawns, mumbles, and makes snoring/going-to-sleep sounds, as notes from his theme song play.

So Popeye has learned nothing from all of this! He's back to putting as little effort into his relationship with Olive as possible! Instead of the passionate, vital, attentive, and creative Mr. Instructor, Olive winds up with this slugabed! And this is supposed to be our happy ending!

Vacation with Play (1951)

Direction: Seymour Kneitel
Animation: Tom Johnson, John Gentilella
Story: Carl Meyer, Jack Mercer
Scenics: Tom Ford
Musical Direction: Winston Sharples

CHAPTER 16

Beaus Will Be Beaus (1955)

Olive's beautiful when angry. The Famous Studios Olive Oyl, much like all incarnations of the character, knew what she wanted out of life and wasn't afraid to demand it.

Here's a cartoon which zeroes right in on a love triangle. "So what?" you may ask. "All the romantic Famous Studios cartoons feature a love triangle." Yes, but this one is different. Olive doesn't catch the eye of a guy (and vice versa) who then proceeds to try to steal her away from Popeye, nor is Bluto disguising himself in order to trick Ms. Oyl into falling for him. In *Beaus*, Olive obviously has ongoing, satisfying relationships with both Popeye AND Bluto, enjoys being with each of them when they are just being themselves, and has feelings for each of the two sailors. The question of who she will eventually wind up with is very much up in the air.

This cartoon takes an "All's Fair in Love and War" attitude toward courtship. Its punny title plays off the idea that "boys will be boys," so whatever Bluto and Popeye do can be forgiven because they're just behaving like males trying to win a girl. And Olive Oyl has an interesting point of view, which seems to be that her suitors can play whatever underhanded tricks on each other that they want to, as long as said tricks don't entail them boxing or wrestling with their rivals, or breaking their word to Olive Oyl. In fact, Popeye triumphs at the end of *Beaus* not by out-fighting Bluto, but because he finally uses his head and out-tricks the trickster.

Beaus Will Be Beaus was originally going to be named *Popeye's Promise*. However, *Beaus Will Be Beaus* captures more of the spirit of the film. The title card features hearts bordered by a ribbon. Each capital B in the title is in a heart. If the title alone wasn't enough to clue us in that we're about to see a romantic cartoon, these graphics would be.

The cartoon opens with a shot of a street in a suburban neighborhood. The orchestra plays an energetic intro leading to Popeye pulling up to the curb in his convertible. Then the soundtrack music is one of the film's "happy, everything's great" themes. Popeye jumps out of the car and goes up Olive's sidewalk as he says, "Oh, boy! Me and Olive's gonna have a good time at the beach today!"

The director makes a hard cut to Bluto walking in the same neighborhood. His eyes are closed in delight. He takes a breath and says, "Mmmmm, Mmmmm! What a day for the beach with Olive!" This is an example of why, the older I get, the more I can relate to Bluto in the cartoons. Popeye, like a little kid, can't wait to get to the fun place. Bluto is savoring the journey and the feel of the air. Besides, adults are interested in affairs of the heart and know that the atmosphere itself, on certain days, can put you in the mood for love. In *Beaus Will Be Beaus*, the erotic spell of the days of Summer has entranced Bluto, and his "Mmmm Mmmm!" is not only an appreciation of the forecast, but an anticipation of Ms. Oyl and the time he will spend wooing her.

But it wouldn't be a story, and certainly not a cartoon, if Bluto didn't then spot Popeye.

As Popeye arrives at Olive's door, Bluto lifts him up from behind and throws him backwards. Popeye then returns the favor to prevent Bluto from getting to the door. As Popeye rings the doorbell, Bluto gets him in a wrestling hold around the waist and pulls. Popeye grabs onto the doorframe to stand his ground, but it comes right out of the wall, bringing the door with it, and lands on top of the two rivals who are now on the ground fighting. Olive comes to answer the bell and sees the hole in her wall. Shocked, she bends down and turns the doorknob. As the door opens, the boys spring upright again through the doorway and continue with their frantic, violent fistfight.

Disgusted, Olive gasps and yells, "Boys! Boys! *Break it up*!!!"

They snap out of their mating combat frenzy and say in unison, "Olive, I came to takes ya to da beach."

We're treated to a close-up of a long-lashed Olive as she solemnly declares, "Oh, no! I won't go out with either of you roughnecks unless you promise to stop fighting!"

The camera then switches to a shot of Popeye from behind as he's looking at Olive. He holds up his right hand and swears, "I promises, Olive."

A similar shot of Bluto as he says, "Me, too, Olive! I won't fight with Popeye no more and dat's a promise," shows us that he has the fingers on his left hand, hidden from Olive behind his back, crossed. The music, which had been soft and hopeful, now plays an ominous strain, but this is one of the few times in the entire cartoon when the orchestra, even briefly, considers Bluto to be a villain. After all, "boys will be boys" and "all is fair." Actually, although Bluto may have intended to break his promise later, he really doesn't at any point in the film. He tricks Popeye, hampers Popeye, and gets Popeye out of the way, but he doesn't start boxing or wrestling with him again. And Olive doesn't seem to mind all the maneuverings, outwittings, nor even the dirty tricks. All of which makes it easy to say, "So if Bluto wins, well, more power to him!"

Anyway, a pretty-faced Olive whose attempt at playing peacemaker endears her to us even if she is rather naive, now agrees to the day's plans, using a cute voice. "All right, you both promised. Now, let's go to the beach!"

Popeye, Olive and Bluto walk to Popeye's car. Bluto goes to the rear of the car as Popeye says in an "I'm putting on airs for fun and because you are special" voice, "Uh, this way, Madam!" and opens the door for Olive. If Popeye had remained this jovial and flirty throughout the rest of the cartoon, it would have been easy to start to root for him, but, as it is, Bluto will soon take over as the one who is sporting with, and coming on to, Olive. For now, though, Olive enjoys what Popeye's doing. She gets into the car with a demure, happy, "I'm with my boyfriend" look on her face. "Everything is moving along nicely and is just swell" music begins playing.

The scene changes to the rear of the car. Bluto, with an evil look on his face, is tying a thick rope around the bumper. The other end is secured to a hydrant.

Popeye no sooner gets behind the wheel and closes his own door than Bluto comes around the car to him. Olive has her eyes closed in delight and anticipation. Bluto lifts Popeye up and deposits him in the backseat saying, "Reeelax, Pal! I'll drive!" He hops over the closed door into the driver's seat. Popeye is understandably angry. Olive opens her eyes warily, and her mouth in surprise. She keeps giving Bluto a wary (and pretty) look as he, with an air, and the look, of a person getting what he wants, puts the car in gear and begins driving off. An open-mouthed Popeye is still in the backseat — for the moment, that is, because we see the rope growing taut, and the car and the orchestra play a brief "tug-of-war" with the hydrant. A helpless, consternated, perplexed, (and, let's face it, wimpy) Popeye just sits there. Finally, the back of the car, including Popeye's seat, rips loose from the chassis and crashes to the ground in front of the hydrant. The sound effects not only convey what's happening, but are also similar to effects used for "Popeye is in the trash" or "our hero has been done away with" moments in other cartoons. We get the feeling that Bluto has won and Popeye is a goner.

The creators must not want us to be too upset about the situation, though, because delighted music continues playing, and we see Bluto and Olive happily motoring along as each second moves them farther away from Popeye and closer to a date alone on the beach. Maybe at this point we should feel concern for Popeye, but Bluto and Olive seem so comfortable together that it's hard to root against them as a couple. (Even though Bluto has just wrecked the sailor's personal property and committed Grand Theft Auto!!!)

Popeye sees what's happening and exclaims, "Well, blow me down!" The music ends as the scene fades out, further conveying the idea that Popeye is out of place.

The screen now shows us the beach's parking lot. Fast, thrilled, transitional music is heard as the car drives up. Then the happy, "things are going along just as they should be on a perfect day" theme plays again. Bluto and Olive seem to think that this IS a perfect day, as they are grinning and enjoying each others' company. Bluto jumps out of the car and comes around in back of it, as a smitten Olive watches him approach her. He does a little hop dance of joy and anticipation, then comes to her car door all smiles, muscles, and male determination. He very tenderly, gentlemanly, and romantically opens her door with his left hand and takes Olive's hand in his right one to help her out of the car. Olive is eating it up. Feminine and alluringly demure, she exits the car. She shows off a curvy figure as Popeye races into the picture. Olive and Bluto are gazing into each others' eyes. Olive doesn't take her hand away from his, but instead steps toward him to offer him even more of her — a kiss, a hug, and/or her heart. Bluto gets ready to put his arm around her waist.

But, of course, Popeye now scrunches himself in between the two love birds. The music seemed to have been building up to something — Bluto and Olive's intimate moment or maybe Popeye's interruption. Olive never mentions, or seems to notice, that the back half of the car is missing. Either she's too besotted by Bluto or has deemed that Bluto has played by the rules in his disposal of Popeye.[1] Popeye shoves Bluto away.

There's a close-up of Popeye and Bluto as Popeye completes his shove and pulls back his left fist to pound Bluto. His rival just stands there with his palms raised at his sides and a peaceful expression on his face as if to say, "I'm not fighting." Popeye verbalizes, "Why you good for nuttin'…"

Cut to a close-up of Olive Oyl with gorgeous, wide, Famous Studios eyes and full lashes. She points the finger and says in her best Betty Boopish, "I'm cute and innocent, yet sexy" voice, "Popeye! Remember your promise!"[2]

Popeye stops his punch as it's about to connect. The sound effect is of a brake catching hold. Bluto has his hands behind his back with a beatific smile on his face, demonstrating to Olive that he doesn't intend to fight. Chagrined, Popeye looks back at Miss Oyl as the music conveys that he's blown it and that his plans will be hopelessly inadequate to thwart Bluto under the new rules.

There's a close-up of Bluto raising what Olive could perceive as a friendly, but admonishing, finger as he says in a voice that's part sincere, part mocking, and part "dark side," "Yeah, Popeye, remember your promise! (Laughs)"

Olive, characteristically and appealingly forgiving and life-affirming and willing to put the past behind her, happily walks toward a three-stalled changing area/bathhouse. "C'mon, Boys!" she giggles, "Let's go swimming!" She enters the middle stall and closes the door. Bluto goes into the one on the right, Popeye the one to the left. The music starts up again.

No sooner does Popeye's door shut than Bluto emerges from his own area, fully changed and carrying a hammer. Bluto obviously takes advantage here of being a cartoon character and uses super-speed and the power to materialize objects he needs out of thin air. The orchestra is surprised, but helps Bluto sneak over to Popeye's stall. We then see a close-up of him starting to nail Popeye's door shut. The music briefly treats him as a villain again, but starts a trepidatious version of the cartoon's main theme as the scene shifts to inside Popeye's shed. Popeye, adjusting the swimming outfit he has put on, notices nails coming through, and encircling, the door frame. The music then conveys that Popeye is locked in, as does the sound effect, as Popeye fruitlessly tries the doorknob. The noise he makes as he yanks on it actually falls into, and completes, the rhythm that was started by the nails, giving us the impression of finality as regards Popeye's plight. Our hero grumbles, "Why that no good so-and-so!"

Back outside, Bluto has hopped in front of Miss Oyl's now open door. "C'mon, Olive," he says, "We'll meet that slowpoke Popeye on the beach." The happy, "things are going along just swell" music is playing again. Certainly things are going swell for Bluto as Olive emerges wearing a two-piece bathing suit consisting of a bikini top and a skirt which makes the O.O.O.P.S. factor[3] kick in, and lets him slip his arm in hers. They walk totally in step and in sync down the boardwalk, past Popeye's prison, and out of the picture, Olive's face growing happier by the second. The camera stays behind, though, and we hear sliding, stretching, tearing, sandpaper sounds as the board on the walk in front of Popeye's stall lifts up, and a bump in the sand moves under and away from it. It's Popeye tunneling beneath the surface. He seems to be floundering a bit, trying to find his way. This, combined with the sound effect of sandpaper which calls to mind a bloodhound sniffing a scent, makes it seem as though Popeye is lost and may not find his way in time to stop Bluto's amorous plans.

Speaking of which, Olive and Bluto are now sitting under an umbrella on the sand, giving each other the eye. Olive's face is very cute as Bluto takes her right hand in his left. He lifts it as Olive gets a very appealing, "smitten young woman" look on her face. She flirts by turning her head coyly away and closes her eyes dreamily. Bluto, recognizing the invitation, begins to encircle her right shoulder with his right arm. She turns back toward him as he completes the action. Bluto draws the "in heaven" miss to him and she doesn't resist — in fact, she helps! Olive snuggles into his chest. Bluto, in an unbelievably romantic, tender, wistful, but confident, voice asks, "Isn't the beach romantic, Olive?" He looks like he's in love and contented and joyful, and not like the animal about to eat Ms. Oyl he is in some cartoons. In fact, though Bluto is definitely turned on in this film, he is never portrayed as an out-of-control wolf, which makes him all the more appealing.[4]

The moving sand bump has entered the scene. Popeye pops upright out of it. Olive and Bluto, perfectly in sync with their timing and facial expressions, notice him. As they stare at the sailor in disbelief, Olive's face is very lovely. The music had stopped when Olive and Bluto were fully into their clinch, but maybe it ceased because Popeye was appearing. It sure was building up to something, though it's impossible to determine just what. The orchestra did seem surprised, though, when Popeye emerged. Speaking of the indignant Popeye, he winds his arm up for a punch as Olive and Bluto separate in shock. "Why, ya chizzler! I'm gonna..." Popeye begins.

Cut to one of the most beautiful close-ups of a gorgeous, but angry, Olive Oyl that Famous Studios has ever given us. Sweet, pretty, and angelic chimes sound as Olive scolds, "Remember, Popeye! No fighting!" They convey that Olive is the innocent who wants peace, and/or even that keeping one's word should be a heavenly virtue.

The chimes continue as we see that an utterly confounded Popeye has now dropped his arms to his sides. He stands there helplessly while we're thinking, "Stop resorting to boxing, Popeye, and start playing by the rules or you'll lose Olive!" And maybe he already has lost her, because Bluto says to her, "C'mon, Sunshine, let's get away from dis ruffian." The music starts again. Bluto takes Olive's hand, helps her up, and starts to lead her away. She gazes at him with a hero-worshiping "my boyfriend will take care of everything — I'm so attracted to you" look. She walks across, and out of, the picture with an exaggerated cartoon female walk which is attractive in some weird way. Bluto stays behind for a second and kicks a disgusted Popeye into the umbrella which collapses and envelops the hapless sailor. Bluto has an air of confidence, finesse, righteousness, and innocence about him as he completes the action and exits. An orchestra that's embarrassed for, and by, Popeye helps him as he struggles to open the umbrella from within. After doing so, he hangs upside-down underneath it, glaring in the direction Bluto and Olive went. He whirls his pipe in anger.

We hear happy transition music as Bluto and Olive enthusiastically and joyfully scamper up the ladder of a high-diving board of a swimming pool. One of the "things are going swell and building up to something" themes begins to play as we get a close-up of Olive swan diving through the air. When she hits the water, her body leaves an impression, which then fills in.[5] The cute-faced miss surfaces and happily swims for the side. The scene is romantic in its own right, as it shows us two people sharing an activity they enjoy.

Cut to the top of the diving board as the music concludes and a newly arrived Popeye advances on Bluto. "Ya double crossin'…" But both the music and Bluto bid Popeye to halt. Bluto puts his left arm and hand up in front of Popeye's fist and he puts his right hand under Popeye's chin. "Take it easy, Pal!" Bluto smoothly urges. Then he magnanimously gestures for Popeye to dive first. "After you!"

The orchestra trusts him (nobody said an orchestra has to be bright), or maybe it wants him to win Olive. So, the happy music starts again as Bluto races down the ladder, while Popeye gets ready to dive at the edge of the board. We see that the ladder, diving platform, and board are on wheels. Bluto uses his super-strength to move it away from the pool. Bluto happily places a child's sand bucket down on the cement and Popeye, of course, dives headlong into it. The impact bounces him back on his rear. A close-up shows us Popeye, with the bucket covering his head, trying to pull it off and offering up cries of anger, surprise, and desperation. When the bucket finally comes off, his head retains the bucket's shape, as an embarrassed, humiliated "our hero's in trouble" version of Popeye's theme plays on the soundtrack. Popeye shakes himself back to normal, as the orchestra helps him and then shares his frustration, while he looks off in the direction Bluto went, makes a fist, and says, "Why that sneaky snake!"

Musical notes suggesting Popeye's dilemma turn into tender, dreamy, romantic ones that give the impression that things are pleasantly heating up, as the scene changes to Bluto and Olive in some sort of narrow boating channel. Bluto is holding Olive while she is also suspended in the water. Olive is positioned as if she's doing the Breast Stroke or the Australian Crawl, but she's not really going anywhere, nor does she want to. Her up and down motions emphasize her shapely rear. Bluto's own hunky physique is also emphasized. His hands are around Olive's waist and hips and touch her derriere. As Olive bobs in the water, the motion causes Bluto's one hand to massage up and down her midriff. (Or is Bluto just using the bobbing as an excuse?) Olive is extremely pleased, and Bluto's facial expression is "turned on" but tender, expressing legitimate longing and the hope of coming satisfaction, with a hint of girl-watching thrown in — very male, but not animalistic. It's more "I love my girlfriend and can't believe I'm finally alone with her and this is just the beginning of good things to come" than the "I'm about to pour steak sauce on you and eat you" expression that he has in other cartoons. In a tender, yet romantic and sexy "invitation" voice, he says, "I'll show ya how to improve your stroke, Baby Face." As Bluto speaks to Olive he bends closer to her and sticks his neck out so that his face winds up near hers.

But suddenly, whirling musical notes are heard as Olive rockets out of Bluto's arms as though she was a speed boat. One of the "happy times" themes starts playing again, even though Bluto is startled to find his romantic interlude interrupted and Olive gone.

We see Olive skimming across the water, leaving a huge wake, at a speed that can't be explained by her strokes. She comes to a stop as Popeye surfaces from beneath her, laughing. He now assumes Bluto's former position. Olive's still happy, though. Has she forgiven Popeye and is glad to be with him? Or is she approving of the male competition now that Popeye has finally wised up and is using subterfuge instead of fisticuffs? Does she not realize Popeye has replaced Bluto?

The music seems to be, at least temporarily, on Popeye's side, yet it is also building up to his eventual removal from the scene. Because of this, it could be argued that the orchestra is happy because their buddy, Bluto, is about to get the upper hand again. The scene changes to Bluto grabbing some sort of rubbery rope used for mooring boats or blocking off areas of beaches and waterways that are unsafe or restricted. It's suspended between two posts embedded in concrete on either side of the channel. He stretches it out to bring it along with him as he angrily strides through the water. An exaggerated sound of straining/expanding elastic is heard.

Bluto comes up behind Popeye as The Sailorman is saying, "Keep it up, Olive! You're doing fine!" The music on the soundtrack is startled as Bluto slips the stretched, rubbery rope around Popeye's neck. Bluto's improvised giant slingshot yanks Popeye up, up, and away. As he leaves the scene, his facial expression tells us he's done for. And Bluto's changes from angry to a greedy, pleased, "at last" expression. Piano notes help convey Popeye's flight and inevitable crash, as we see him soaring helplessly through the air across the beach and then "smash landing" into a section of the boardwalk. The impact lifts the section up and deposits it, and Popeye, upright onto the sand, such that Popeye is tightly wedged in, imprisoned stock-like with his hands, feet, neck, and head protruding from the cracks between the planks. Just a couple "Popeye in jeopardy" notes are heard. But as Popeye shakes off being stunned and looks off camera, shocked and dismayed by what he sees, revelatory, transitional, "Popeye is embarrassed" music plays and then changes into one of the "happy, things are going along as they should" themes. This is quite surprising to hear, as the "stocks" are the final Popeye trap of this cartoon, and we would expect dire tones or the funeral version of Popeye's song, or even "Olive in trouble" music, on the soundtrack. But no, the orchestra wouldn't mind at all if Bluto and Olive ended up together while Popeye was left behind.

And neither would we viewers. Because the director now cuts to one of the most romantic, laced with the hopes and promises of a life together, crackling with healthy sexual tension scenes in all the Famous Studios cartoons. It involves two "normal" people, obviously in love, having spent an enjoyable day having fun and flirting together at the beach, now getting ready to go out for an evening together because they don't want their time together, or their relationship, to end. It's a scene that anyone who has seriously dated someone, or wanted to, can relate to. We're shown the bathing houses/changing booths again. Bluto and Olive walk into the shot. They are holding hands and look happy. Olive's eyes keep growing wide with pleasure as she can't keep them off Bluto. Her once again exaggerated feminine steps emphasize her shapely derriere. Bluto exudes confidence. Dropping Olive off at her booth, he asks, as he goes on to his changing area, in his flirting male voice that anticipates a night full of all sorts of fun, "How about a shore dinner, Gorgeous?" As she listens, she stands with her hands on her hips, not in an indifferent way, but expressing, "here I am ready to be with you." She verbally replies with a cute, endearing pun while leaning towards him, "Why, shore!" A look of total delight and anticipation is on her face. They enter their booths and the doors go swiftly shut, one after the other, demonstrating that Bluto and Olive are still in sync and are in a hurry to go off together, and that Popeye has been locked out of the picture.

All of this causes a delicious dilemma for us viewers. The creators have made us long for Bluto and Olive to get together.[6] Yet what about our old pal, Popeye, the funny, resilient, basically nice guy superhero we all wanted to be when we were younger? He's now in one of his most desperate situations, not because he's in any real physical danger, but because it's near the end of the cartoon, Olive's not rejecting Bluto, she doesn't want to be rescued, and she and Bluto are eagerly getting ready to spend a romantic evening together. Do we really want things to end this way? Do we really want to keep Popeye in the "stocks"? Yes, we certainly do! But, no, we certainly don't! Yes, we do! No, we don't! The internal debate rages on. And what can Popeye really do to change the situation anyway? Wait and see.

The scene changes back to Popeye vowing, "That's all I can stands 'cause I can't stands no more!" He stretches his cartoony arm, hand, and finger around the "stocks" and pulls a can of spinach out from under the back of his swimsuit. The first few measures of his theme song modulate and build. Popeye brings the can forward and squeezes it open. A generous portion of its contents land in his open mouth. The "spinach-eating" music plays on the soundtrack. Popeye chows down and his limbs expand to mammoth proportions, bursting free of the "stocks," accompanied by the sound effect of a prize bell ringing. The Sailor-man, now free, stands in super-powered glory, holding the scrunched can that still contains some of the wonder veggie. He runs in place in the air, as only a cartoon character can, and then zips out of the picture.

But even at this point, our anxiety for Popeye isn't quite gone. In other cartoons after he eats his spinach, he punches his rival, but in this cartoon, he can't! So what exactly CAN he do? Again, wait and see.

A hurried, modified version of *The Sailor's Hornpipe* plays as Popeye rushes over to the booths and leaps onto the roof of Bluto's. He leans down and knocks on the door. Bluto exits happily looking toward where he expects Olive to be. Popeye grabs Bluto's nose with his left hand and pulls Bluto toward him, while tilting Bluto's head back and pulling his mouth open. A determined Popeye then feeds Bluto the remaining spinach. "Down the hatch" music plays and then strains of the Popeye theme mixed with the "eating spinach" music are heard. Another bell rings on the soundtrack when Bluto swallows. The orchestra is briefly shocked, perhaps sharing Bluto's surprise, or wondering why Popeye would do such a thing. But there's a method to Popeye's madness. As Popeye smiles, a mound of power travels down Bluto's left arm, causing it to begin punching. Then, likewise the right arm. A sound like thunder or a bowling ball rolling down an alley is heard on the soundtrack, portraying power being released. Fast "machinery at work" music plays, as Bluto becomes machine-like himself, falling into a spinach-induced robotic trance. Bluto begins shadowboxing. A delighted Popeye jumps down in front of him, knocks on Olive's door, and then walks right into the flailing fists and takes a terrific beating. Watch it in slow motion! What Popeye endures for love!

Olive emerges from her door with a smile on her face, thinking she's meeting Bluto for their date. Her smile turns into an expression of shock when she registers what's going on. She lets out a feminine, "Ohhh!" Now the sound effects accompanying the pounding are of metal against metal and machinery breaking down. With a final bopping noise, Bluto appears to lay Popeye cold. The music conveys an ominous ending. Is it Bluto's powers that are ending? The Bluto/Olive romance? Popeye's consciousness? Popeye's plan to doom Bluto? All of the above?

An Olive with a figure turns angry. She strides over to Bluto and yells, "You broke your promise, you brute!" She pulls Bluto's hat down over his eyes and nose, declaring, "I'm through with you!" Then an adrenalized Olive, proving that Hell hath no fury like a woman who feels betrayed and lied to, delivers an uppercut that sends him flying out of the picture and across the beach. The "humiliated" version of Popeye's theme plays, but it's not Popeye who has been humiliated this time. The orchestra hits some final-sounding notes as Bluto travels through the air and lands in a trash can which overturns, scrunching and trapping him inside, making it look as if he's in prison. In fact, the sound effect is of a prison door shutting. Bluto comes out of his stupor, looks around, and helplessly asks, "Wha' happen'?"

Cut to Olive Oyl kneeling next to, and supporting, a barely conscious Popeye. Like any animated character just injured, Popeye is now magically wearing bandages. Soft, romantic music briefly plays. Sympathetically, Olive says, "Ohh, Popeye!" She puts her right hand around Popeye's left shoulder and her left hand on his head and starts kissing his cheek repeatedly. Olive's "Hmm, Mmm, Mmm, Mmm!" is mixed with kissing sounds. Her kissing starts out as sympathy and as a healing balm, but quickly turns romantic. Popeye is finally getting some intimate time alone with Olive. But, of course, he did have to let himself be beaten to a pulp first!

A close-up of Popeye and Olive shows us that the sailor has fully come to, and is enjoying the kissing. His theme song is playing. Olive's expression shows that she's getting a lot of pleasure out of the smooching, too. She gets all flirty and sexy using her pretty eyes and, coquettishly while still giving Popeye a "come on' signal, withdraws from the picture. Maybe Olive has more cleverness than she often is given credit for. Maybe she has realized that Popeye played a trick and won the competition. Maybe she's rewarding him. Popeye "breaks the fourth wall," looks right at us and says, "Love that spinach!" Then he laughs.

FADE OUT!

Beaus Will Be Beaus (1955)

Director: I. Sparber
Animation: Tom Johnson, John Gentilella
Musical Direction: Winston Sharples
Story: I. Klein
Scenes: Robert Little

CHAPTER 17
Mister and Mistletoe (1955)

This is the type of violence and injury Famous was infamous for. Here, Popeye is electrocuted while setting up a toy train.

This film is a near-perfect example of how to make a Christmas cartoon as part of an ongoing series. It is first and foremost a Famous Studios Popeye cartoon with a Famous Studios plot — a guy tries to take Olive Oyl away from Popeye using unusual methods of seduction. This time, the methods relate to the holiday, as do the traps, jokes, and situations. And there's absolutely no contrived sentimentally forcibly injected into the Popeye hijinks. No tearful orphans get adopted. Bluto doesn't see the light and reform. Popeye isn't merciful to the villain. Olive doesn't decide that Bluto is welcome to stay because, after all, it's Christmas. Yes, it is Christmas, but this is also a Popeye cartoon, and the creators never forgot that.

And this cartoon is one of the most romantic of all the Famous Studios cartoons — and that's saying something. This cartoon believes that Christmas Eve is the most romantic night of the year. It's the night on which Olive gets her wish that Santa Claus is real. And it turns out that he's handsome and *very* interested in her!

So, let's delve into the cartoon itself, shall we?

First, there's the title card with the words "Mister and Mistletoe" in red letters on a piece of white wrapping paper or a Christmas card. A sprig of mistletoe is present, too. *Mister And Mistletoe* is a great title for the cartoon as it promises romance to come and, of course, is a seasonal pun on the phrase, "Mister And Missus," which helps convey the idea that the important thing is not just getting to kiss Olive Oyl, but winning her and establishing a long-term committed relationship with her. The "Mister And Missus" connection also reminds us that the warm, family-centered, fantasy-laden holiday season gets people in the mood to mate. Bluto and Olive will certainly get caught up in this tender atmospheric trap as the cartoon progresses.

But as the establishing shot comes on screen and the first scene unfolds, there's no romance to be found. Instead we are outside of Olive Oyl's house in the wintertime. The camera moves toward the house as a wreath in a window and a celebratory version of *Deck The Halls* playing on the soundtrack lets us know that "'Tis the season to be jolly!" Specifically, it's the night before Christmas. The stars shine brightly in the cold, clear winter sky, and we long for the cozy warmth that the light coming from Olive's window promises.

The scene dissolves into the interior of the home. Popeye's three nephews[1] are addressing The Sailorman and Olive. They want the adults to tell Santa Claus to bring them lots of toys because they have been very good boys. A joyful, enthusiastic Olive agrees to do this, and Popeye says that he will even speak to Santa "poiskonally." (If he only knew what was coming!)

Expressing their thanks, the nephews zoom over to the fireplace and quickly hang their stockings. The boys speed away to bed before the stockings unravel, each stocking longer than the one preceding it.[2] The nephews rush into a bedroom and swoop into bed. Instantly, they are asleep and snoring with each snore divided between the three of them.

It's scenes like this one that contribute to the confusion some people experience over Popeye and Olive Oyl's marital status. Some believe that they are husband and wife and have a family, or even that they are single but have kids out of wedlock! It's easy to understand why these misconceptions exist. Consider that, in this cartoon, not only are Popeye's nephews staying overnight at Olive's house, but also that they aren't in a guest room. It's one that seems designed specifically for young boys. The curtains have sailboats on them, there's a picture of a clown on the wall, and the bed is large enough to accommodate all three nephews. Just how often do they stay with Olive, anyway? And why does single female Olive Oyl need such a huge house? And why, oh why, does Popeye have three nephews who look, sound, and dress just like him? Well, let me set the record straight.

MISTER AND MISTLETOE (1955)

In the Popeye animated cartoon universe, our hero and his "goil" are single, live separately, and the nephews are really nephews. They were added to the Popeye cast by the Fleischers to compete with the popularity over at Disney of Donald Duck's nephews, Huey, Dewy, and Louie. Their presence in this particular film is a plot device to introduce the idea of Santa Claus. As for the unanswered questions, just remember that, while watching cartoons, you often just have to accept everything and go with the flow.

Now let's go back to the cartoon.

Popeye and a cute-faced and happily sighing Olive Oyl are busily decorating the house. There's holiday music on the soundtrack. Olive is hanging paper bells and crepe paper streamers from the ceiling while her feet are perched on Popeye's hand. (It pays to have a boyfriend with super-strength!) Popeye's other hand is holding a box of decorations.

The camera spies an open window. Bluto comes up to it from the outside, wearing his white sailor's hat and a black (?) shirt. Looking in, he's surprised and then angry. "That rat Popeye got here ahead of me," he says, reminding us that Olive isn't committed to Popeye. She's also interested in Bluto, and it's just a matter of which suitor arrives, or asks her out, first that determines who she has a date with.

Cutting back to Popeye and Olive, we find the feminine object of so much affection caught up in the season, nostalgia, and wistful longing. "Oh, Popeye, it's wonderful to be a child and believe in Santa Claus!"

"Yeah, Olive," Popeye replies. "It's too bad there ain't no Santa Claus for us grown-ups."

At the window, Bluto is listening and stroking his beard. He spots a Santa Claus suit and a bag of toys inside the room by the window. As he reaches through and snatches them, he happily and expectantly says, "Dat gives me an idea how to get rid of that runt!" (Not to mention how to seduce Olive Oyl!)

The scene changes to the rooftop. An ominous fanfare heralds that Bluto is there, dressed in the Santa suit. We see him for a few frames basking in his male, muscular, handsome glory, then he calls down the chimney in a disguised voice, "Merry Christmas! Huh, huh, ho!" Jackson Beck, the voice of Bluto, does a great job in this cartoon. His Santa voice certainly sounds like the Bluto voice modulated and modified, yet it sounds enough unlike Bluto to fool Popeye and Olive.

Speaking of Popeye, he's curiously looking up the fireplace and saying that it sounds like Santa on the roof.

And on the roof, Bluto rips off the top of the chimney and hurtles the masonry down into the fireplace. Popeye is now buried under a pile of bricks! The soundtrack music and "Santa" both slide down the chimney next. Unconsciously showing off his muscular physique, "Santa" cheerfully says, "Merry Christmas!" and laughs again as he walks out of the picture toward Olive.

Popeye pokes his head out of the bricks and happily rubs his peepers. "I can't believe me eyes! It IS Santy Claus!" Er, Popeye, shouldn't you maybe wonder why Santa just literally hit you with a ton of bricks? This is yet another Famous Studios cartoon where Popeye comes off at best as being naive and maybe too trusting, and at worst as being just plain stupid.

An utterly amazed, excited, and delighted Olive Oyl lets out a squeal, "Ooooohhhh! It's Santy Claus!" as Bluto approaches her with a look of unbridled desire on his face, puts his arm around her, and says, "Merry Christmas, Babe...(coughs) uh, Miss." His voice is very male, fun-loving, romantic, and actually kind of innocent and pure sounding. Olive doesn't seem to mind that "Santa" first called her "Babe." She's enjoying the attention. And, since all males in the Famous Studios universe find her irresistible, it only makes sense that a mythological figure come to life would, too! But before the potential lovers can do or say anything else, Popeye eagerly runs up between them, takes "Santa's" arm from Olive, and begins shaking his hand, pleased to meet him.

The camera gives us a close-up of Olive as she departs saying, "I'll get Santa a hot chocolate." As she moves to, and starts past, the right of the screen, the artists briefly give her a bustline. Perhaps the subtle message is being sent that, although Olive thinks she is getting a sweet treat for Santa, she's actually the sweet treat he wants. Then the bustline dissolves into wrinkles in Olive's blouse. The creators have had their little joke and now they are moving on.

Meanwhile, Santa is under a ceiling light and proclaims, "Ho! Ho! Ho! This is a good spot for the mistletoe." He hangs a sprig. Popeye, with a goofy look on his face, comes over, thanks Santa and calls, "Look, Olive, mistletoe!" Bucolic music begins playing, reinforcing the idea that Popeye is a backward bumbler and that, if he finds love, it will only be by accident. After all, the mistletoe was Santa's idea, not his! Olive responds by coming over and giving Popeye an appealing, feminine, coy but not too coy, expectant laugh. They close their eyes and pucker up. Popeye is standing on an area rug while Olive is on the hardwood floor. But the rug and Popeye are moving out of the picture. We see Bluto on the other end of the rug hauling away on it and then throwing it and Popeye down an open doorway into the cellar. With evil glee, he firmly closes the door and races over to the still-puckered Olive. Closing his eyes, he goes all tender as he moves in on her. But a puzzled Popeye has popped up out of a heating grate in the floor in front of Olive. Santa ends up kissing the back of Popeye's head instead of the lips of his intended. Bluto still acts tender until he sees what happened, and then he and Olive react with shock. Popeye gets all shy and says, "Oh, Santa, this is embarassking," and then laughs.

My childhood memory of this cartoon was that Olive Oyl was mad at Popeye for coming between she and Santa as they were about to kiss. But when I saw it decades later, I wondered where I had gotten that impression. My VCR's slow motion mode answered that question. When viewing the scene at a slower speed, and also going frame-by-frame, you can see that Olive's first reaction is indeed anger. It passes quickly. Then she joins Santa in being shocked. Was she angry that her kiss with Popeye had been interrupted, or had she quickly taken stock of the situation and become upset that Popeye had spoiled her kiss with Santa? Ah, the deep mysteries of the Famous Studios cartoons!

Speaking of anger, an obviously hate-filled Bluto quickly gets control of himself, clears his throat as though correcting an error or starting again, and asks Popeye, "How would you like to fetch me some toys?"

An enthusiastic, exuberant Popeye replies, "Okay, Santa!" and rushes over to the bag by the window. Cheerful Christmas music plays in the background until Bluto sneaks up behind Popeye, lifts him up, and stuffs him into the bag. The music then accentuates Popeye's plight. Santa super-tosses the bag out the window and far away through the air. Unfortunately for Santa, though, the rope around the top of the bag catches on the top of a tree, which bends forward because of the bag's weight and momentum, and then springs upright again, hurling the bag back the way it came.

In the house, Santa and Olive are seated together, facing each other on a stylish couch/lounger. A soft, but rather speedy version of *Jingle Bells* is playing on the soundtrack. It's as though the orchestra is saying, "Hurry up and start the wooing! Popeye's on his way back!" Santa has taken Olive's hands in his hand and his other arm is around her. Olive has her eyes closed with a dreamy expression on her face. Santa's expression is pleased and tender and romantic. He slowly guides the happily acquiescent Olive Oyl even closer to him as he begins reciting in a gentle, yet definitely masculine and sexy voice, "'Twas the night before Christmas..." The two snuggle and, as the bag is re-entering the picture and coming through the window, Olive lowers her head slightly in a flirty, feminine, submissive, yet choosing her own destiny manner which conveys, "I'm yours." The look on Santa's face is one of PURE romantic joy. Here Bluto isn't the wolfish playboy just wanting to devour Olive. He's in love. And so is she.

But the bag hits the end of the couch, surprising the orchestra, and tipping the couch and its occupants into the air. On their way up, Santa and Olive still only have eyes for each other and remain in lovey-dovey mode for a few frames. Their shocked reactions when they are forced out of their own world, where there's only room for two, are in perfect sync with each other.

Popeye struggles to get out of the tied bag as Olive lands to the right of him and Bluto to the left. Once again, Popeye has managed by accident to come between them. As Santa and Olive react, respond, and recover from their landing, they once again are in perfect sync. These two seem made for each other! Bluto shakes off the effects of the fall, as Popeye pops out of the bag and glares at him. Has Popeye finally figured out what's going on and that Santa can't be trusted? No way! Santa quickly pats Popeye on the head, which instantly mollifies him. Santa clears his throat again and tells Popeye to "Be a good boy, My Lad, and set up the electric trains." Notice that Popeye is called "boy" and "My Lad," conveying the impression that he's the uncomprehending, inexperienced kid who's told to go play with his toys, or who is given fifty cents to watch TV in the next room, so that the adults can kiss.

And Popeye does go off to play with a toy that always meant Christmas to me — a Lionel electric train set. Popeye throws himself into setting it up. "Oh, boy! Disk is fun!" he proclaims to nobody and then laughs. A version of *Jingle Bells* plays merrily away on the soundtrack, even as Bluto secretly plugs in the train while the transformer is on. A trombone plays mocking notes as the electrical current travels through the tracks and hits Popeye, engulfing him in a bluish arc light. He screams, "Owwww!" Red and yellow sparks and flames leap high around his body in the ultimate object lesson of what happens when you ignore holiday safety warnings. The shock propels Popeye into the air, taking the train set with him. He thuds back on the ground, flat on his stomach, with the tracks now protruding from his mouth, which serves as a dark tunnel. We see the toy engine coming out of the "tunnel," riding the rails from inside Popeye, whistling and making those treasured electric train sounds. Some bright traveling music plays as we watch the train coming forth from Popeye. The idea seems to be that the train is moving right along on schedule, that things are good and normal, and that the orchestra is glad that Popeye is now part of a train exhibit. The orchestra definitely seems to want Popeye out of the way. Why? Because that's when the real fun starts!

The scene dissolves into what is one of the most romantic and sexy sequences from the Famous Studios era. We see Santa and Olive decorating a Christmas tree together, or maybe I should say that they are using the tree decorating as an excuse to be close to each other. Santa has one arm permanently around Olive, and her positioning in the scene indicates that she has one of her arms around him, too. With his free hand, Santa places candles on empty branches, and with her free hand and the help of an ever-burning match, Olive lights them. Santa and Olive are both figuratively and literally playing with fire. The music transitions to a soft, romantic version of *Deck The Halls*. Santa, with facial expressions that start out lustful, but then turn tenderly cherishing, and then into the pure joy of a groom in love, says in an ultra-sexy voice, "Ah, My Dear, too bad Christmas comes but once a year." Olive gives him her own soft, ultra-sexy giggle and an "overwhelmed with emotion" gasp, then replies in a voice that's part Mae West, part Olive Oyl, part sophisticate, and part young woman giving her heart away, "Drop in any time at all, Santa." Bluto has done it — he's won Olive Oyl! The expressions on her pretty face in the scene range from flirty, to swooning, to warm contentment as she snuggles, to sexy, and finally to the rapture of a dream come true.

MISTER AND MISTLETOE (1955)

Popeye's calling voice, "Oh, Santa!" pulls the couple out of their dream world. In sync, Bluto and Olive register annoyance, then shock, as they look over toward where the voice came from.

We get a close-up of Popeye standing and gesturing in a dorky, big kid way. "Can I help to lights the candles?" If we were Popeye, we'd probably be asking,

Though a holiday cartoon, this film is very much a Famous Studios Popeye cartoon, right down to the romance between Olive Oyl and another guy.

"How come you two are wrapped around, and wrapped up in, each other?" or "What's the big idea of sabotaging the train?" But, no, "little boy" Popeye is easily distracted, doesn't seem to know or care about sex, and only wants in on decorating the tree. No wonder the orchestra wanted Bluto and Olive to wind up together!

The camera goes back to Bluto and Olive. They *still* haven't broken apart and have their arms around each other, totally shameless and proud of their feelings, even in front of Popeye. Bluto, feigning delight at being able to include Popeye in the holiday preparations, says, "Of course, My Lad! It gives me great pleasure to have you light the top candle."[3] Olive, who is sincerely and sweetly happy that Popeye is being included (making her all the more appealing), looks at her "nice" Santa Claus with admiration and then, for a frame or two, snuggles into his beard as though it were a pillow or a soft bed, overcome with hero worship and sexual attraction, and wearing an enraptured, "this is where I belong," flirty countenance. She's definitely Santa's girl now. And forever?

But no, Santa/Bluto has to mess up his good thing, of course. He has placed a stick of dynamite on the top of the tree. Popeye, like an idiot, climbs a ladder saying, "Oh, thank you, Santa!" Using a lighter from his pocket, he ignites the fuse and lets out a "Merry Chriskmask!" while bending over the TNT. The music, which had been getting faster and seemingly building to a conclusion — maybe of the song, or Bluto's plot, or possibly even of Popeye's life — is surprised when the dynamite explodes. Popeye is blown out of the roof of Olive's house and across the neighborhood to helplessly smash through the ice of a frozen pond. A column of water splashes up from the hole, forming a mini-waterspout which sucks Popeye up into its center. It instantly freezes solid. The music swells to conclusive chords, and chimes are used to convey a winter fairyland, the process of freezing, and even that maybe Popeye has now passed into the spirit realm. The background scenery during Popeye's flight and plight is simply beautiful, and the night lighting effect captures the wonder, clarity, beauty, and danger of being outdoors after dark on a crisp winter evening.

Back inside, Olive and Bluto are now apart. She stares in shock at the hole in her ceiling, and the ruined treetop, while Bluto further messes up by beginning the most evil, uproarious laugh in Popeye cartoon history. A scowling Olive transfers her stare to him. She looks like she's getting ready to slug him.

There's a close-up of Bluto continuing his satanic, celebratory laughter (a superb and scary job by Jackson Beck), but he's bending way too close to a candle still on the tree and his fake white beard catches fire. His laugh suddenly transforms into a "Huh-Wha-uu-ooo-ppp!" as he's taken by surprise and he realizes the jig is now up and he's lost Olive's affection. His voice isn't just shocked and stuttering. It also conveys disappointment and desperation. The white beard quickly burns completely away, revealing his black beard and true face.

A quick close-up of Olive Oyl then switches to a shot from behind her looking toward Bluto. Olive accuses, "Why, you're not Santa Claus! You're Bluto!" in a voice of injured and stolen innocence, dreams dashed, helpless desperation, sweet young thing vulnerability, righteous indignation, and feminine shock. People of both sexes have told me that, to them, this is one of Olive Oyl's most endearing and memorable lines. I agree. It makes us simultaneously want to protect, comfort, and avenge Olive Oyl. Voice actress Mae Questel did a fantastic job!

Bluto, now with an evil look on his face, tips his Santa hat to Ms. Oyl and says, "You're sooo right, Olive!" with the sneer of male dominance in his voice. He moves to her, her face taking on the characteristics of a ravenous wolf and a ruthless, utterly determined man. He asks (but it's not really a question) "Howzabout a kiss for Christmas?" The background music is all now naughty, saucy woodwinds, portraying not romance, but a cheap, dangerous affair. This is not love any longer, but lust, and solely "Hanky Panky" with no lasting emotion or commitment propelling it. Bluto snatches Olive into his arms and pulls her close into him as she keeps struggling to get away. He now has her up against him and goes for the kiss using a variety of positions and maneuvers that would be very romantic and sexy if Olive was a willing participant, and not a violated victim. Bluto manages to get his lips on her forehead and the side of her face as Olive tries to command, "D...D...D...Don't you touch me!" and breaks free, running off camera.

The scene shifts to the room Olive is fleeing into. There's a bag of Christmas toys and a tricycle on the floor. Olive leaps on it and starts pedaling away. She's now drawn with very childlike features because the cartoon is continuing its transition from fantasy to horrifying nightmare. Olive is now the child faced with the fears felt by many boys and girls. Plenty of kids are afraid that the strange-looking, huge, boisterous man in the red suit that they are expected to talk to, confide in, request their desires from, hug, and be willing to sit on is really secretly evil. He may have the adults fooled, but the kids know he will turn on them in an instant and scare, harm, or maybe even devour them. Olive is living out the bad dream of being chased by a dangerous Santa Claus.[4] And Bluto is definitely dangerous. He's out to harm Olive. The look on his face as he's closing in on her is now one of pure anger. There's no hint of tenderness, or even of lust. He's just a male, angry that he didn't get his own way, who is determined to punish and dominate the one who thwarted him. And Bluto *will* catch her. He is right behind her. Either Olive better wake up from her bad dream or Popeye better intervene quickly! Motorcycle sound effects start. Olive and Bluto now travel up onto the walls of the room and race around them in circles. Olive is still frantically pedaling away, and Bluto must have been bitten by a radioactive spider at some point in his life, as he is sticking to the wall while running!

The film cuts back to Popeye. His eyes and mouth are now open, but he's still not moving. Hearing Olive's cry for help, he does a double-take, as if he's just now becoming fully conscious, or just now finally realizing what's been going on. Using his pipe as a blowtorch, he melts his icy prison and races to Olive's house. (Again the backgrounds as he does so are "Christmas card" beautiful.) Popeye stops at Olive's window and looks in. Why is he hesitating? Doesn't he usually zoom to Olive's side when she's in trouble? Maybe Popeye has persevering faith and still wants to give Santa the benefit of the doubt. Or maybe he's just slow on the uptake. He spots the racing pair. "It's Bluto!" Ah, now we see why the hesitation was necessary! The kids in the audience had to be assured that Popeye knew his nemesis was Bluto, otherwise it would be out of character for their hero to belt Santa Claus. But the hesitation still makes Popeye look stupid. However, stupid or not, we and Olive need him and we need him *now*!

Popeye rushes into the house and goes over to a bag of presents. He pulls out a gold-plated (???) spinach can. The tag on it says, "To: Me Nephews From: Uncle Popeye." The background music is still suspenseful, yet is also hopeful as it builds up to the familiar "spinach-eating" tune. So, Popeye downs the green veggie, and one of his arms then morphs into a sledge hammer. Racing between Olive and Bluto, he uses the sledge hammer to belt Bluto clear out of the Santa suit (the brute now wears gray flannel long underwear), into unconsciousness, and across the room. Bluto lands on his head, bounces, and ends up dazedly sitting by an undecorated Christmas tree. Stars form around Bluto's head and begin orbiting it. Then they break away and become the ornaments for the tree. As the last star tops the tree, Bluto looks over toward Popeye, his tongue hanging out of his mouth. Bluto is wiped out.[5]

The cartoon should have ended with Bluto's defeat. Instead, we're "treated" to a pointless denouement. After the emotional, psychological, spiritual, and even sexual roller coaster we've just been on, do we adults care any more about whether the nephews will get to meet Santa Claus? But Popeye puts on the suit and another white beard and calls out, "Ho! Ho! Ho! Merry Christmas everybody!" The nephews hear him and hurry down. Popeye announces himself with, "It's Santa Claus!" But his nephews excitedly ask, "What did you bring us, Uncle Popeye?" and begin climbing into the bag searching for various types of toys and questioning "Uncle Popeye" about where this-and-that are. Popeye turns to us and says, "Oh my garshk! They recognized me!" He laughs heartily. Evidently, the kids in this cartoon are wiser than the adults, in that they aren't fooled by a fake Santa, a fact which endeared the cartoon to real-life kids everywhere.

Iris out.

Mister and Mistletoe (1955)

Director: I. Sparber
Animation: Al Eugster, Wm. B. Pattengill
Musical Direction: Winston Sharples
Story: Jack Mercer
Scenics: Joseph Dommerque

CHAPTER 18
Parlez Vous Woo (1956)

Olive Oyl is gorgeous in this cartoon from the first frame to the last.

In order not to sound like a broken record throughout this chapter, let me say from the outset that Olive Oyl is drop-dead gorgeous in this cartoon from start to finish. She has a beautiful face, a 36-24-36 figure, full and shapely breasts, and a curvy derriere. The O.O.O.P.S. factor[1] is also present, as she's wearing a strapless and backless red evening gown. Famous Studios' makeover of Olive Oyl reaches its pinnacle here. And though the animation is slightly more limited in this film than in the films of the 1940s, the creators do quite a lot with what they have, and Girl-Watchers won't be disappointed. Having said all of this, I will only note in what follows the scenes in which an already exceptionally attractive Olive is even more exceptionally attractive.

The title card features a top hat, like the one Bluto will be wearing in the cartoon, a pair of white gloves like Olive Oyl will have on, and a decorative cane like Bluto will use. These, along with the title itself, let us know that the characters will be dabbling in sophistication, classy lovemaking, and dressing up. And the fact that all of the items have been discarded may symbolize that the plot of the cartoon will revolve around who Olive will want to slip into something more comfortable for later on.

The cartoon begins with Popeye sitting on one of three chairs which could form a comfy couch if they were pushed together. But they aren't. Instead Popeye is in the foreground of the shot, disgustedly resting his head on his hand and crossing his legs while facing away from Olive. Miss Oyl herself is on another of the chairs in the background, glued to her television set. Once again a cartoon has begun with Popeye and Olive being physically together, but spiritually and emotionally apart.

We hear the character on the TV speaking in a seductive voice with a romantic French accent, "Good evening, Dear Ladies! I am Ze International."[2] Olive gives out a pleased sigh. "Come a little closer..." Olive leans in toward the set, her hands together beside her head in dreamy rapture, "...and I will make ze great love to you! Ah, your eyes are like ze limpid pools, sparkling in ze sunshine!" Olive blinks her pretty eyes and they temporarily turn into — you guessed it — limpid pools sparkling in the sunshine. "And your lips, they are so red like the ruby!" Olive leans forward, unconsciously showing off her bustline, and reaches for a red ink pad that actually contains lipstick. She stamps the lipstick on her mouth and, as she does so, her face is cute and kissable. "Ze flowers that bloom in ze Spring do not compare with your exquisite beauty!" A soft version of *Cocktails for Two* plays in the background.

"But, Olive..." Popeye protests.

"Shush, Popeye!" an annoyed Olive scolds while placing her hands on her hips and giving off "go away" signals with her body language. "Don't interrupt The International!"

"But, but, Olive! What about our date? You and me is supposed to go to the movies!"

Bluto, strolling up outside, hears the tail end of this from an open window. He complains to himself, "Why that runt Popeye got here ahead of me!"

Note that the guy who shows up first at Olive's winds up with a date. She's equally willing to go out with either Popeye or Bluto. But here, she seems to be canceling a date with Popeye in favor of watching a fantasy figure on television. Maybe Olive is heartless and shallow. But maybe going out with Popeye just isn't very appealing to her and she's changed her mind. After all, Popeye and Olive demonstrate their incompatibility in this cartoon. Olive's all dolled up for a night on the town, while Popeye is just in his usual sailor duds. You wonder how much communication really took place about this "date." In other cartoons, Popeye has mistakenly believed that Olive has made some sort of commitment to him when she hasn't. Maybe he's done that here, too. Maybe in Olive's mind there was no date. And maybe she got dressed to kill just to watch The International on TV. This either makes her an uber-geek, or endears her to us because she's always willing to throw herself totally into her fantasies and live out her dreams. At any rate, why couldn't Popeye get onboard at least a little? Why couldn't he say something like, "I tells ya what Olive, after the movie we'll stop at a classy joint for a drink. And you can pick the movie! It can be one of them lovey-dovey things instead of a cowboy pitcher. Whaddya say, Beautiful?" Instead, he makes no move toward her. It will be Bluto who will be willing to enter Olive's world, and he will reap the rewards of doing so.

Back to the cartoon. The International is saying, "And now I have a surprise for you lovely ladies. One of you shall be selected to have a date with me tonight. So, stay at home! For who can tell? You may be ze lucky one! Good night! See you later!" Olive swoons. Bluto listens.

An angry Popeye stands up and says, "C'mon, Olive, let's go out!"

"No, Popeye!" Olive replies in a close-up which focuses on her beautiful face and gorgeous torso, as she smiles, puts her hands on her waist, and leans forward and back. "I may have a date with The International!" Then Olive gives a super-appealing laugh which combines school girl innocence, sexual desire, anticipation, rapture, and hope. (Great job by voice artist Mae Questel!)

Outside, Bluto snaps his fingers as he gets an idea. The music plays an ominous version of *Cocktails*. His hair morphs into devil's horns, and he gives an evil laugh.

A stringed instrument acts as a ticking second hand on a clock to let us know time has passed. And if the clock on Olive's wall is to be believed, it's now 12:20 AM. Popeye is still sitting there seething and tapping his foot impatiently. Olive is still enraptured. If I was Popeye, I think I would have headed to the docks to shoot some pool or something by now, instead of hanging around while the girl I was interested in waited to go on a date with someone else!

Suddenly, the doorbell rings. Olive leaps up, and while Popeye stands in her way, ineffectually gaping at the door, a delighted Olive runs in place in the air for a second or two to gain momentum, as cartoon characters can. Then she races right over Popeye, flattening him into the rug.

In a sequence that displays her fantastic body, Olive opens the door. A handsome mustached man in a tuxedo and a top hat is there. "Good evening," he says in a sophisticated voice. When he tips his hat to Olive, a white sailor's cap falls out of it and lands on his head. He quickly snatches it away and stuffs it in a pocket. He's Bluto disguised as The International, of course. "Is this the residence of Mademoiselle Olive Oyl?"

Popeye has now recovered and reacts in shock and helpless resignation to the presence of this rival.

We get a close-up of Olive, also reacting to "The International." Enraptured, she says in a sexy, breathy voice, "(gasp) Wh-uh-oh! It's The International!" Her pupils roll around and groups of her hair stand straight up or go straight out from the sides of her head. She quickly composes herself, but still wiggles with unsurpassed delight. "Oh, oh, ha, ha, do come in!" The International enters, twirling his hat on his hand with supreme male confidence. He takes Olive's hand and gives it a long kiss. As his lips adhere to Olive, we see a volt of thrills and love traveling up Olive's arm to her shoulder, through her neck, up to her head. Her hair all stands on end, her eyes turn into hearts, and those hearts and her ears pulse along with the magnified beat of her real heart.

So, Bluto looks just like Olive's favorite dashing TV star, he can act just like the star, and he sounds just like the star.[3] And he can turn Olive completely on like a light switch. Why on earth does she ever bother hanging around with Popeye?!?!?

Speaking of whom, he angrily twirls his pipe and strides toward the couple saying, "I'll show Olive I can be romantical, too!" Well, Popeye, you had your chance earlier in the evening and you didn't take it. Now Olive is with another guy and wants you to go away. It's interesting to note that Popeye only thinks to get romantic when he is competing with another guy.

The International is still attached to Olive, and she's still under his spell as Popeye enters the picture. The Sailorman says, "Pardon me, Olive!" The International lets go of Olive's one hand while Popeye takes her other one. But Popeye's kiss displeases her and leaves her totally cold — literally transforming her into a block of ice! The music is embarrassed for Popeye, and then it shares his shock when he realizes he doesn't move Olive at all.

Meanwhile, The International has pushed all of the pieces of the couch together. (Something Popeye never thought to do.) "Mademoiselle Olive, sittez vous!" he invites.[4] Olive sashays over, holding onto her skirt and wearing a smitten expression that appealingly combines coyness with delight that the guy she loves is looking her over and liking what he's seeing. Olive is putting on a show for him. And he checks her out from head-to-toe, especially focusing on her well-formed derriere, while his mouth hangs open in amazed, rapturous delight. They both sit and The International moves close to her. But Popeye butts in between them starting to insist, "Lisken, Olive, you…" But The International and the orchestra hardly miss a beat of *Cocktails For Two* as The International shoves the part of the couch Popeye is on out of the picture and then uses his cane to bring Olive's seat over, reconnecting it to his own.

"Ah, My Cherry, nothing shall ever separate us again!" They both close their eyes in delightful anticipation. The International reaches out his arm to put it around her. "Now dat we are alone, I shall give you ze magnificent kiss!" He tries, but Popeye has been pulling on the rug his part of the couch is resting on, and now The International is far from Olive.

Popeye rushes over to her and, finally taking his cue from The International, puts his piece of the couch together with Olive's. Popeye's not romantic at all, though. Instead, he is insistent. And he can't take, "No," for an answer. Not very endearing traits! "Olive, don't ya remember? You and me has a date tonight!" As we see The International use a knife to secretly cut away at Popeye's perch, an annoyed Olive responds, "Humph! You've got some nerve butting in on The International!" A giant spring from the weakened seat suddenly emerges and launches Popeye up to the ceiling. His head goes through to the next floor, and he hangs there stuck by his neck.

As he's trying to pull himself free, The International and Olive are engaged in a romantic, sexy, and realistic-looking waltz. They are caught up in each other and, at times, a mote of dust couldn't be squeezed in between their bodies. And if you watch the scene in slow motion, you'll see that they actually share a quick kiss on the lips! The cartoon's creators definitely are showing their bias here. Maybe convention dictates that Olive will have to end up with Popeye eventually, but the creators are actually rooting for Bluto, and they allow he and Olive at least one moment of pure, heart-sealing bliss.

But Popeye hurries into the scene and interrupts this musical seduction by snatching an unwilling Olive away and placing a broom in The International's arms. Caught up in the dream-like moment, The International at first doesn't realize what's happened. But when he does, he's once again seething mad.

Popeye, meanwhile, is trying to force an unwilling Olive to dance to a jazzy tune with him. He uses his strength to manipulate and jerk and spin and propel her around the floor. (If Bluto did something like this, we'd say he was a villain! So what does this make Popeye?) Olive is helpless and isn't enjoying it one bit. And Popeye can't even get on her wavelength about what kind of music she's in the mood for! Fortunately for Olive, The International comes to her rescue, frees her from Popeye's tyranny, and tricks the sailor into pushing around a dress frame for a few moments. When Popeye realizes what's happened, it's his turn to seethe.

The International, top hat back on, with a smitten and expectant Olive on his arm, is heading for the door. "And now, we shall take a stroll in de moonlight." But Popeye runs up and blocks their exit. Olive throws her hands up in shocked dismay.

"Just a minick! I got a date with Olive," one-note Popeye says again, being oblivious to the obvious.

"Ah, you wish to fight ze duel for Mademoiselle Olive?" The International challenges.

"Okay, you asked for it!"

We see a close-up of the curvy and voluptuous Olive saying, "Oooo, a duel over me? How perfectly romantical!" She's still caught up in her fantasy and doesn't yet realize what a duel will entail. Notice that it's The International's suggestion that Olive finds romantic. She hasn't swooned over any of Popeye's ideas.

The International opens his coat and we see two swords hanging inside it. Obviously, Bluto came prepared for this eventuality. But he only used the swords as a last resort, so he gets some credit. "Have one!" he says to Popeye. "Oh, thank you!" The Sailorman replies. They each take a weapon and the orchestra signals impending doom. "En garde!" The International begins. Right from the start, it's obvious that Popeye hasn't a clue about fencing, and The International is outclassing and outfighting him, and is making him give ground. The orchestra is terrified. Popeye tries to push the point of his sword against The International's. Popeye's blade splinters in two and peels back like a banana.

The International gives out a hearty, evil, triumphant laugh. Then he angrily backs Popeye up against the wall. He continually tries to stab The Sailorman, as Popeye dodges by moving his torso and his neck as only a cartoon character can. But the orchestra doesn't think Popeye can keep it up and is making each sword thrust by The International sound like a death knell.

Finally, The International rears back for the final, life-ending thrust, and we then see him spear Popeye through the heart! "Oooowww!" Popeye moans and his eyes close.

Olive gives out a horrified shriek!

We're pretty horrified, too! Granted that Popeye was a jerk and we wanted him out of the way so the romance could continue, but…murder?!?! Once again, Bluto goes too far as he gives in to his emotions. But, on the other hand, Popeye did accept the challenge, and Popeye lost fair and square. Still, Bluto could have been merciful, and just bopped Popeye into unconsciousness.

But as The International withdraws the sword, we see that he's actually impaled Popeye's spinach can, rather than The Sailorman himself. As The International is momentarily stunned, Popeye positions his mouth under the hole in the can and consumes the spinach. His sword gets repaired and straightens out, and suddenly Popeye is a master fencer. He knocks The International's sword away, backs the big guy against a wall, and then methodically removes pieces of The International's tux to reveal the sailor suit underneath.

Olive gasps in alarm. "He's a fake! It's Bluto!" Olive doesn't like to be lied to. Of course, she did love everything Bluto was doing, and he won the duel for her hand!

Even though he's been found out, Bluto's not finished yet. He runs over to Olive's TV, lifts it up, and is going to smash Popeye with it. But Popeye gives him a thunderous uppercut first. Bluto ends up knocked silly inside the broken TV which has crashed into a wall.

Olive approaches Popeye gushing, "Oh, Popeye, you're wonderful!" Yeah, but only because of spinach. Popeye pulls out another can (How many does he carry?) and chows down again. This time it transforms him into a classy, tuxedoed gentleman. "Aw, Mademoiselle Olive, you have ze date wiz me!" This time his kiss on the hand heats Olive up. She turns red, and steam explodes out her ears as a sprightly, concluding version of *Cocktails* is heard. Then Olive melts down to a literal pool of butter on the floor as she says, appropriately enough, "Oooo, I'm just like butter in your hands!" Popeye is shocked at first, but then laughs, evidently trusting that cartoon universe physics will enable the flowing-away pool of buttery goodness that is now Olive to pull herself back together again.

Kids watching this cartoon weren't so sure, though, and the ending left them disquieted. As they grew up, they remained disquieted, but for another reason. Yes, Popeye is able to woo and win Olive, but only after spinach transforms him into what Bluto is naturally, and gives him the power to turn her on. So, who really is the better man for Olive? Does this cartoon really have a happy, satisfying ending?

Parlez Vous Woo (1956)

Director: I. Sparber
Animation: Al Eugster, Wm. B. Pattengill
Story: I. Klein
Scenics: Anton Loeb
Music: Winston Sharples

CHAPTER 19

The Rest of the Cartoons

Now we'll take a whirlwind tour through the other Famous Studios Popeye cartoons. Some cartoons we'll pass through quickly. When we come to others we'll linger awhile. We'll be concentrating on those "magic" elements that make the Famous Studios Popeye cartoons unique: the way the characters of Popeye, Olive Oyl, and Bluto are portrayed; the violence and suspense; the emphasis on sex and/or romance; the way that the plots, situations, and characters aren't all black-and-white and clear-cut.

In general, the best Famous Studios Popeye cartoons are the ones that contain all of these elements perfectly blended together. Also, in general, the quality of the cartoons began to go downhill in the 1950s. Aside from decreased budgets and company mandates to cut costs, this was because some "magic" elements were skimped on, or ignored completely, in some of the films from this period.

And the cartoons from the World War II era, while containing lots of wild, completely over-the-top violence, didn't really generate much suspense. Everyone knew that American Navy Man Popeye would, of course, eventually triumph over our nation's enemies. And the enemies were freakish, unpleasant, stereotypical, exaggerated caricatures of Japanese and Germans, who were more often buffoons than threats in these films. If you can dehumanize the enemy, it makes it easier to kill and hate them, I guess.

Some cartoons are laugh riots and highly recommended, even if they may not truly seem like Famous Studios Popeye cartoons because they don't feature the "magic" elements.

Okay, so much for the introduction. Fasten your seat belts! The tour begins!

The cartoons are listed in chronological order according to their release dates. The titles are spelled and punctuated the way they are on the title cards of the copies of the films I viewed. Capitalization was more problematic, though. Title cards can be stylized for effect, and checking various sources yielded various ways to capitalize the titles.

You're A Sap, Mr. Jap (1942)

Director: Dan Gordon. *Animation:* Jim Tyer, George Germanetti. *Story:* Jim Tyer, Carl Mercer. *Scenics:* Uncredited. *Music:* Uncredited.

Popeye has a very close encounter with a stereotypical Japanese commander.

A cheerful, off screen male chorus is singing the title song, as Popeye, on patrol in the ocean, joins in. He spots a broken-down Japanese fishing boat. When he goes to board it, two foreign sailors hand him a phony peace treaty. While Popeye tries to sign it, they hit him over the head with a giant mallet and stick a firecracker in his shoe. (Who's the sap, now? Although the fact that Popeye is excited about peace endears him to us.) They give him a bouquet of flowers, but it has an angry snapping lobster in it, so Popeye gives it back. The broken-down ship is actually disguising a huge destroyer. The Japanese sink Popeye's ship, but Popeye eats spinach, turns his bicep into a huge "V" for Victory, and raises his ship by blowing air into it. He then boards the Japanese craft and makes short work of the artillery, the crew, and the ship itself — because it was made in Japan, after all. Then, in a strange scene, the enemy commander, to save face, drinks gasoline and swallows a string of firecrackers. As he starts banging around, he gets tangled up with Popeye. Popeye drops a lit match down the commander's throat. Hastily making his way to his own ship, Popeye watches as the destroyer blows up and sinks to the sound effect of a toilet flushing. Subtle, this film is not! The male chorus ends this wartime propaganda cartoon.

Alona on the Sarong Seas (1942)

Director: I. Sparber. *Animation:* Dave Tendlar, Abner Kneitel. *Story:* Jack Ward, Jack Mercer.

Popeye and Bluto are stationed in the South Pacific when the sarong-clad island princess, Alona — a dark-skinned, Fleischeresque Olive Oyl with a curvy rear — surfs by their ship. They follow her to her island where she enjoys being a "nature girl" and singing, *Too Romantic,* while being mostly oblivious to the fact that she's driving the boys crazy with desire. This fact isn't lost on her parrot, though, who warns the sailors that Alona's under the protection of the volcano god, who probably wants the virgin for himself, as volcano gods usually do. The whole thing is played for laughs, not romance, even when all three temporarily lose their clothes after diving into water, and when Alona teasingly throws coconuts down on the boys. Things get a little more serious and ominous when Bluto knocks Popeye out and into a pool of hungry, approaching crocodiles, and then almost grabs the princess as the volcano begins to erupt. The parrot feeds Popeye spinach, though, and The Sailorman torpedoes the reptiles into luggage and uses Bluto to plug the volcano. As he's about to kiss Princess Alona, we realize that this was all a dream Popeye's been having. He kisses Bluto in the hammock next to his, and Bluto responds by bashing him over the head with a guitar.

If Bluto is a villain even in Popeye's dreams, why does The Sailorman hang out with him and call him, "Pal," in other cartoons?

A Hull of a Mess (1942)

Director: I. Sparber. *Animation:* Al Eugster, Joe Oriolo. *Story:* Jack Ward, Jack Mercer. *Scenics:* Uncredited. *Music:* Uncredited.

Bluto, looking handsome and fit in a suit, and Popeye compete for a contract to build ships for Uncle Sam. The two are working in shipyards side-by-side, of course. A bunch of construction gags follow. For once, Bluto is actually more incompetent than Popeye and keeps getting injured. Popeye finishes first, so Bluto fills a bottle with nitroglycerin and comes over to "christen" Popeye's ship. It blows everything to bits, leaving Popeye buried under a pile of rubble. Bluto takes a hearty swig from a real bottle of champagne, christens his own ship, and begins to sail off to win the contract. But Popeye eats spinach and instantly constructs ship after ship to beat Bluto.

One has to wonder why Popeye didn't eat spinach earlier in the cartoon if he really was so eager to help build up the United States Navy and win the war?

In this cartoon, Bluto is portrayed as a real evil menace, not a prankster, or a slacker, or a friend who sometimes walks a little on the dark side. This foreshadows other cartoons yet to come.

Scrap The Japs (1942)

Director: Seymour Kneitel. *Animation:* Tom Johnson, Ben Solomon. *Story:* Carl Meyer. *Scenics:* Uncredited. *Music:* Uncredited.

Serving on board an aircraft carrier, an incompetent Popeye has K.P. duty, but he finds inventive and cartoony ways to get his jobs done. When the Japanese attack, his bumbling is evident again as he almost drops the bomb he's carrying, and then, at first, he takes off without his plane. A Japanese pilot fires at the indestructible sailor, but gets the worst of it. Popeye finally wises up to what's happening and blows him out of the sky. Popeye then lands on a Japanese destroyer and is getting beat up by the crew until he eats his spinach. Transforming into The Statue of Liberty, he opens up the ship with a can opener. Then he tows away a cage full of Japanese sailors, who turn into squealing rats. This is a typical World War II propaganda cartoon with an ending that's unpleasant and disturbing when viewed with today's sensibilities.

Me Musical Nephews (1942)

Director: Seymour Kneitel. *Animation:* Tom Johnson, George Germanetti. *Story:* Jack Ward, Jack Mercer. *Scenics:* Uncredited. *Music:* Uncredited.

A clever and funny cartoon! Popeye wants to get to sleep, so he tells his nephews to quit practicing their instruments and go to bed. The tykes get ready, and Popeye then comically smashes several bedtime stories and nursery rhymes into one. The nephews say their prayers, asking God to bless the cast of the Popeye cartoons — including Bluto! The nephews can't nod off, though, and soon they discover they are making a cool rhythm as they turn pages in a book, swat a fly, etc. Then they start blowing and banging on toys, bottles, trash cans, etc., using everything as musical instruments — even an insecticide gun! In an expertly timed scene, Popeye keeps coming into their room to catch them in the act, and the nephews keep diving under the covers, pretending to be sleeping. Desperate for some shut-eye, Popeye finally closes the iris of the movie camera that is filming the cartoon, after moving his bed outside of it. But the music keeps playing. Cracking up, Popeye jumps out of the movie screen and runs through the theater. The nephews appear on screen as they play the closing notes of the cartoon.

Spinach fer Britain (1943)

Director: I. Sparber. *Animation:* Jim Tyer, Abner Kneitel. *Story:* Carl Meyer. *Scenics:* Uncredited. *Music:* Uncredited.

Incompetent, constantly "Heil"-ing Germans in a sub attack Popeye's ship as he's trying to export spinach to our allies. They accidentally back their sub into Popeye's craft and begin machine-gunning it. Popeye, as slow on the uptake as ever, thinks he has woodpeckers. Popeye's ship comes apart. Popeye ends up in a rowboat filled with spinach cans. When the sub tries to shoot him again, he turns it upside-down. Then, Popeye gets two mines tangled on his oars, and his rowboat blows up. Yes, Popeye sinks his own boat! The sub then sinks Popeye himself and accidentally catches the spinach in its open hatch. But, underwater, Popeye has one can left for himself. He eats it, morphs his arm into a depth charge, blows a hole in the sub, and punches the members of its crew up into the mines which are floating on the surface. Popeye then begins rowing the sub to shore. He goes into a fog bank and keeps rowing. When the fog clears, we see he has rowed the sub all the way to No. 10 Downing St. Popeye got the job done, but in a goofy, bumbling way.

Seein' Red, White, 'N' Blue (1943)

Director: Don Gordon. *Animation:* Jim Tyer. *Story:* Joe Stultz. *Scenics:* Uncredited . *Music:* Uncredited.

A wild cartoon that throws everything but the kitchen sink at the audience in order to get laughs. Slacker Bluto receives his draft notice and tries to convince Draft Board official Popeye that he's too ill to serve. But Popeye calls in his secretary, a gorgeous woman, who makes Bluto forget all about his so-called infirmities. As Bluto takes her in his arms, Popeye removes her disguise. It turns out "she's" really a thousand pound weight! Bluto isn't as weak as he pretends to be! Then Bluto tries several times to injure himself to get an exemption, but fails. At one point, he leaps from a window, but Popeye races downstairs to catch him, and they both crash through the pavement into Hell. A devil kicks them back upstairs, and then an angel appears to kick the devil back down into the pit. Finally, a frustrated Bluto throws Popeye into an "orphanage," which is really a Japanese spy center. The "orphans" reveal their true identities and begin beating up on Popeye. A bandaged Bluto, stopping by to say he got his exemption, sees what's happening, and his patriotism comes to the fore. He takes off his bandages, saying, "They can't do that to the Navy!" Popeye feeds both he and Bluto spinach and they wade into the spies in a furious fight sequence. Popeye then sends a long-distance punch to Emperor Hirohito and Adolf Hitler. The cartoon ends with Bluto enlisting willingly and the captured spies helping him spell his name by singing, "B-L-U-T-O" in a spoof of Jell-O radio commercials.

Too Weak To Work (1943)

Director: I. Sparber. *Animation:* Jim Tyer, Abner Kneitel. *Story:* Joe Stultz. *Scenics:* Uncredited. *Music:* Uncredited.

Slacker Bluto feigns illness to be able to relax in the hospital. But Popeye tumbles to the scheme and disguises himself as a nurse to give Bluto the treatment. Popeye sets Bluto's throat on fire, nearly drowns him in a pool, shrinks him in a steam room, and inflates him like a Macy's balloon with oxygen. Bluto soars up to the sky and is hit by lightning. Utterly deflated, literally, he comes back to Earth. Popeye hangs this limp piece of shipmate on a hook and pumps spinach into him. It restores Bluto — and how! He becomes a boat-painting machine. This is a fast-paced, surreal, gag-filled cartoon.

A Jolly Good Furlough (1943)

Director: Dan Gordon. *Animation:* Joe Oriolo, John Walworth. *Story:* Joseph Stultz. *Scenics:* Uncredited. *Music:* Uncredited.

Popeye blows up a Japanese island fortress, which sinks beneath the sea to the sound effect of a toilet flushing. Then he goes home on leave to get some rest. But, upon his arrival, Olive accidentally runs him over twice with her car, and his nephews, thinking at first that he's a spy, bind him up and nearly chop off his head with axes! Popeye and the nephews then assure themselves, and the audience, that everyone is doing their part for the war effort. The nephews demonstrate their Home Defense techniques and, in the process, repeatedly injure and confound Popeye. Then Olive runs him over again! Popeye decides to get some rest — by returning to the war!

Ration fer the Duration (1943)

Director: Seymour Kneitel. *Animation:* Dave Tendlar, Tom Golden. *Story:* Jack Mercer, Jack Ward. *Scenics:* Uncredited. *Music:* Uncredited.

As his nephews plant a victory garden, Popeye dreams that he goes up a beanstalk to confront a giant who's hoarding supplies that Uncle Sam needs. The giant is more goofy than scary, although when he takes a meat cleaver to Popeye, some suspense is generated. Then, in a scene guaranteed to send children under their chairs, the giant makes a sandwich out of Popeye as the sailor is struggling to eat his spinach. The giant chews and swallows Popeye, but our hero has ingested the spinach and the giant is soon sorry. Popeye wakes up to see his nephews' garden growing pots, cans, rubber baby nipples, plungers, tires, and shoes. If everyone had such a garden, Uncle Sam would be all set!

The Hungry Goat (1943)

Director: Dan Gordon. *Animation:* Joe Oriolo, John Walworth. *Story:* Carl Meyer. *Scenics:* Uncredited. *Music:* Uncredited.

A prime example of Famous Studios not quite knowing what to do with Popeye in the early years, this cartoon makes him the fall guy for a goat that is trying to eat his battleship. The goat is one of those goofy little pranksters that populated so many theatrical shorts, and the cartoon spends more time with him than with Popeye. Popeye is cast in an "Elmer Fudd" role. The cartoon has fast-paced, imaginative gags, but it's just not a Popeye cartoon. It also plays fast and loose with movie-going conventions. The goat asks for the film to be reversed so he can read the title. We see members of a theater audience supposedly watching the cartoon, including a little boy who asks, "Aw, why don't Popeye eat his spinach and sock him one?" Why don't he, indeed?

Happy Birthdaze (1943)

Director: Dan Gordon. *Animation:* Graham Place, Abner Kneitel. *Story:* Carl Meyer. *Scenics:* Uncredited. *Music:* Uncredited.

Popeye prevents his lonely depressed pal, Shorty, from shooting himself. Instead, Popeye invites Shorty to come along with him to Olive's. It seems that it's Popeye's birthday. When the sailors arrive, Olive gives Shorty a welcoming kiss that leaves him floating on air — despite the fact that it is the Fleisheresque Olive Oyl in this cartoon. The enthusiastic Shorty keeps inadvertently sabotaging everything — washing Popeye out to the sewer a couple of times, playing golf using Popeye's mouth for a hole, causing destruction in the kitchen so that Olive mistakenly hits Popeye over the head with an iron, etc. Finally, Popeye and Shorty wind up in the boiler of Olive's building. As the scene goes dark and Shorty is singing "Happy Birthday to my pal," Popeye shoots him! The words, "The Bitter End," appear on the screen. The cartoon is finished. And apparently so is Shorty! Popeye commits murder for the sake of the cartoon's final joke! And nobody eats spinach to bring him to justice!

Wood-Peckin' (1943)

Director: I. Sparber. *Animation:* Nick Tafuri, Tom Golden. *Story:* Joe Stultz. *Scenics:* Uncredited. *Music:* Uncredited.

Our big, strong, he-man hero Popeye gets continually foiled by a small woodpecker as he tries to cut down its tree to use as a mast! Lots of jokes with axes and saws mean that Popeye suffers a lot of unkind cuts, and near cuts, in this cartoon. And the woodpecker even matches Popeye in a tug-of-war, holding up the weight of the massive tree! At the end of the cartoon, Popeye and the woodpecker are friends. The bird now lives atop Popeye's new mast. They don't make 'em like this anymore. And I'm glad!

Cartoons Ain't Human (1943)

Director: Seymour Kneitel. *Animation:* Oresto Calpini, Otto Feuer. *Story:* Jack Mercer, Jack Ward. *Scenics:* Uncredited. *Music:* Uncredited.

Normal categories don't apply to this wildly hilarious and infinitely creative film, because Popeye makes his own animated cartoon with stick figures that spoofs old-fashioned melodramas and some of the conventions of the Popeye mythos. Then, as he shows the cartoon to Olive Oyl and his nephews, the projector travels all over the room, projecting the film on just about every available surface. A frantic Popeye provides all the sound effects, music, and voices, too.

Her Honor the Mare (1943)

Director: I. Sparber. *Animation:* Jim Tyer, Ben Solomon. *Story:* Jack Mercer, Jack Ward. *Scenics:* Uncredited. *Music:* Uncredited.

Popeye's nephews want to keep a reject from the glue factory as a pet, but Popeye doesn't want a horse in the house. So the boys smuggle the horse in by disguising its rear as a house painter — Adolf Hitler! (Get it?) Then, of course, they have to keep hiding the beast from Uncle Popeye. They feed it while Popeye is snoring and wolf whistling in his chair. (He fell asleep reading a girly magazine.) But unfortunately, they feed it horse radish and the horse starts galloping all over the house in a panic. But finally, Popeye realizes he can't throw the horse out. The horse is a she and has just given birth to quadruplets.

The Marry-Go-Round (1943)

Director: Seymour Kneitel. *Animation:* Graham Place, Abner Kneitel. *Story:* Joe Stultz. *Scenics:* Uncredited. *Music:* Uncredited.

Popeye doesn't have the nerve to propose to Olive Oyl, so his pal, Shorty, eggs him on. Unfortunately, Olive is busily doing the daily chores at her boarding house and can't be bothered with The Sailorman. Popeye accidentally goes through Olive's washing machine, is hung out to dry, gets pressed and ironed, and folded into the shape of a small handkerchief. Shorty then does literally what the creators were doing figuratively — Shorty blows his nose on Popeye! Next, Popeye inadvertently destroys all of Olive's dishes. Needless to say, this doesn't endear him to her.

Disgusted with Popeye, Shorty tells him, "Lemme show ya how it's done in the movies!" Shorty then makes like a French lover and, whispering sweet nothings to Olive, takes her in his arms and gives her a passionate kiss. The result is that now Olive is in love with Shorty! She gussies herself up and chases him. (Olive is still drawn according to the Fleischer model at this point in the Famous Studios era.) She keeps catching and kissing him, while Popeye advances on them wielding a baseball bat. Shorty ducks and Olive kisses Popeye instead. His kiss does absolutely nothing for her, though, and she grabs the bat and clubs him. Finally, Popeye throws Olive into the washing machine and carries Shorty off.

Back aboard their ship, Popeye hangs the pictures Shorty had of Dorothy Lamour up on the wall by The Sailorman's own bunk. A tied-up Shorty is forced to look at pictures of Olive Oyl instead.

We're On Our Way To Rio (1944)

Director: I. Sparber. *Animation:* James Tyer, Ben Solomon. *Story:* Jack Mercer, Jack Ward. *Scenics:* Uncredited. *Music:* Winston Sharples.

(Actually, the title card contains a misspelling — W'ere for We're.)
Sailors on leave, Popeye and Bluto, sing the title song as they make their way into the city. At a nightclub, they fall for Latin entertainer Olive Oyl. Even though she's drawn in the Fleischer style — but has a prettier face, curvier hips, and a shapelier rear in some frames — the boys have some of the most extreme, out-of-control wolf reactions to her that ever appeared in a Famous Studios cartoon. She prefers Popeye, so Bluto tries to humiliate him by telling her that Popeye is a champion Samba dancer. An embarrassed Popeye hides from the spotlight and attempts to conceal his lack of talent. But eventually, he makes a fool of himself trying to dance. Hearing Bluto laugh, Popeye eats spinach and

then dances a great Samba, while punishing Bluto with some of his moves. At the end of the film, Popeye and Olive Oyl go into such an intense spin that they wind up wearing each other's clothes! This is an extremely well-animated and well-timed cartoon.

The Anvil Chorus Girl (1944)

Director: I. Sparber. *Animation:* Dave Tendlar, Morey Reden. *Story:* Bill Turner, Jack Ward. *Scenics:* Uncredited. *Music:* Winston Sharples.

Fleischeresque blacksmith Olive Oyl gets a wolf reaction out of Popeye and Bluto, particularly as the glow from her forge enables them to see through her dress! Bluto says, "She can park her horseshoes next to mine any time!" (Where were the censors?)

Olive needs a hired man, so the boys compete for the position. Bluto bends pieces of iron on an anvil to make a pair of horseshoes. Popeye takes a red hot iron rod out of the fire and repeatedly presses it against his chin to fashion eight pairs. And so on. Popeye keeps outdoing the big guy. Olive swoons over Popeye, and soon the guys are brawling. Bluto finally super-punches Popeye into the forge, turning both it, and seemingly Popeye, into a glowing and smoking pile of rubble in the process. Bluto grabs a worried Olive and says, "Okay, Beautiful, I'm all yours!" Then he morphs into a wolf and howls.

Back at the rubble pile, Popeye is cooking spinach in its can. He eats it and his biceps turn into anvils. Bluto has trussed Olive Oyl up on a pole as though she were a side of beef and is swaggering away with her to some place where he can enjoy being a wolf with his helpless prey. Popeye frees Olive and knocks Bluto into a wall. The boys then shoot nails and horseshoes at each other.

After Bluto has been pinned to a wall, Olive, with a slightly cuter face, comes up to him and comes on to him! She wants him to have the job! Has the world turned upside-down? No, she wants to go on a date with Popeye and just needs Bluto to mind the shop while she's gone.

Bluto places his head on an anvil and begins hitting it with hammers. Ouch!

Spinach-Packin' Popeye (1944)

Director: I. Sparber. *Animation:* Dave Tendlar, Joe Oriolo. *Story:* Bill Turner. *Scenics:* Uncredited. *Music:* Uncredited.

Popeye has just given a gallon of blood to the local blood bank. As he's resting, he dreams that he was knocked out by a muscular Bluto in a prize fight and that, therefore, Olive is leaving him. To convince her he's still strong, he shows her clips from the Fleischer films, *Popeye the Sailor Meets Sindbad the Sailor* and *Popeye the Sailor Meets Ali Baba's Forty Thieves*. Upon awakening, Popeye rushes over to the real Olive's house and lifts it to impress her.

Puppet Love (1944)

Director: Seymour Kneitel. *Animation:* Jim Tyer, William Henning. *Story:* Joe Stultz. *Scenics:* Uncredited. *Music:* Winston Sharples.

The cartoon opens with Bluto putting the finishing touches on a life-size Popeye marionette he's made while they have been at sea. (The Navy lets Bluto have way too much time on his hands!) Popeye himself is getting ready for a date with Olive by shining up the red nail polish he's put on his toenails. (The boys really *have* been at sea too long!)

Bluto beats Popeye to the park where a Fleischer version of Olive Oyl is waiting. He fools her into thinking the marionette is the real deal. Puppet Popeye tickles Olive's arm, giving her goose pimples. She puckers up, closes her eyes, and goes for a kiss. Bluto, in the tree above her, hangs down to receive it, and the two share an upside-down smooch long before Spider-Man and Mary Jane ever did in the movies. It's a long, slow, face merging, "lips reluctant to let go" one, which has Olive saying, "Mmmm" and being completely turned on, and leaves Bluto wearing a look of delighted satisfaction. Olive and Bluto are good kissers, and good kissers together! But then Bluto has Puppet Popeye knock Olive off the bench, pull it out from under her as she's about to sit down, lift her up by her nose, snap a mousetrap — hidden in flowers — on her face, and deposit her in a trash can that the puppet rolls into a pond. Then Bluto pulls Puppet Popeye up into the tree, so the real arriving Sailorman can experience Olive's wrath.

Olive belts Popeye with a brick she's carrying in her purse, and Bluto arrives to save her and take her away from all that. But Puppet Popeye falls out of the tree, so real Popeye sees it. As Olive is touching up her face, Popeye knocks Bluto out and attaches strings to him. Now Popeye has his own "Puppet Bluto." He makes Bluto tromp on Olive's foot, catapult her through the air, and request a locket of her hair by putting a huge knife to her neck and saying he's going to cut the hair off just below her chin! So then Popeye arrives to save the damsel.

But Bluto comes to and punches Popeye into a lamp post. Then he walks away as Popeye is being electrocuted. Popeye eats spinach, frees himself, and beats Bluto up. In the process, Puppet Popeye falls out of the tree and Olive thinks the real one has been injured. She begins covering the puppet with kisses. The real Sailorman didn't get one the entire cartoon!

Pitchin' Woo at the Zoo (1944)

Director: I. Sparber. *Animation:* Nick Tafuri, Tom Golden. *Story:* Bill Turner, Jack Ward. *Scenics:* Uncredited. *Music:* Winston Sharples.

Popeye takes a Fleischeresque Olive Oyl to the zoo, where she nevertheless draws an appropriate reaction from zookeeper Bluto who is standing under a "Wolf" sign. He comes on to Olive, touches her gently under the chin, and rubs noses with her. Maybe he's part Eskimo? Anyway, Popeye drags her off, so the keeper feeds him to a tiger. The tiger closes its mouth on Popeye, but the sailor battles his way out.

Meanwhile, Olive is watching Bluto supposedly wrestle a crocodile and put it to sleep by rubbing its stomach. He's really put a bear trap over its mouth. As Olive swoons, Popeye jumps into the pit to prove he's the better man. Bluto removes the trap and kicks the croc awake in order to get it to "croak that corny sailor." Popeye tries to wrestle the crocodile, but it pulls a reversal and Popeye's the one on his back being rubbed to sleep by the beast. The croc takes a bow as Bluto and Olive laugh. Then Bluto, putting his hand around her waist, leads a willing Olive Oyl away. Popeye tries to wake up, but the crocodile lying next to him keeps rubbing him back to dreamland.

So, Popeye is permanently sedated, Olive and Bluto are strolling off together, and the orchestra is happy about this. Bluto is telling her to leave Popeye and stick with him. He promises to give her the moon and, reflecting the times, "a pair of nylon stockings." But Olive has inadvertently walked right into the cage of two ferocious leopards. She screams for help! Bluto begins donning a suit of armor to rescue her.

Popeye gets fortified by something else. His snoring sucks spinach out of a can and into his mouth. Now wide awake and energized, Popeye knocks the croc out, turns the leopards into a pair of dice, causes Bluto to shoot himself, and hurls an elephant up against a wall as though its trunk were a suction dart. Bluto releases a horde of dangerous animals to stop Popeye, but The Sailorman re-cages them and then throws the cage onto Bluto, turning the keeper and the animals into a merry-go-round. Popeye and Olive hug as the sailor uses his pipe to provide the calliope music.

Moving Aweigh (1944)

Director: Uncredited. *Animation:* Jim Tyer, Bill Solomon. *Story:* Carl Meyer. *Scenics:* Uncredited. *Music:* Uncredited.

Popeye's annoying little "pal" Shorty tries to help him move Olive's furniture, with predictable results. Although Shorty is the one who keeps messing up, Popeye's the one who keeps getting blamed by a cop and Olive — not to mention injured. Finally, Popeye, Olive, and Shorty are enjoying their new home — a jail cell!

Seeing Popeye as the butt of endless jokes isn't my idea of a good time. Thankfully, this is Shorty's last appearance in a Famous Studios cartoon.

She-Sick Sailors (1944)

Director: Seymour Kneitel. *Animation:* Jim Tyer, Bill Soloman. *Story:* Bill Turner, Otto Messmer. *Scenics:* Uncredited. *Music:* Winston Sharples.

Paying homage to another popular character, the Famous Studios creators have Superman (Bluto) stop a train.

A Fleischeresque Olive Oyl, who has a cuter face than normal in some frames of this cartoon, is reading a *Superman* comic book. (See, Guys, she's one of us!) She has posters of The Man Of Steel up on her wall and says he's her dream man. Popeye shows up for a date, but she'd rather stay in and read comics. (See my last parenthetical comment.) She claims that the only man who makes her heart jitterbug is Superman. Bluto overhears this and gets an idea.

As Popeye is taking Olive's comic book away and teasing her (the jerk!), Bluto, clean-shaven and dressed as Superman, bursts through her window to save her. And Bluto has the physique to pull this masquerade off. Olive says in a breathy, sexy, "I'm yours" voice, "Superman!" He puts one arm around Olive and punches Popeye out of the picture. Superman tells Olive, "Babe, I'll stick to ya like glue!" Olive giggles while responding, "Ohhh, the feeling is muscilage!" Popeye, who pokes his head out of the ruined chair he's now a part of, sees what's going on, frees himself, and rushes over. He says that Superman has to prove to him that Superman is a better man than he is.

So, Superman (Bluto) saves Olive from falling from a building. He uses an umbrella for a parachute and floats to Earth with the snuggling, giggling, smitten Olive. Popeye just ties himself up in knots. Superman and Olive stroll away together. Popeye runs in front of them and makes another challenge. Superman pretends to halt a train. Actually, he knew when it was scheduled to stop and placed himself in front of it. Popeye tries to do the same, but can't, of course, so he passes right through the train, being hit by every interior wall along the way. He's frozen in position and tips over. Superman laughs, but now Olive is getting worried. A weak, injured, half-dead Popeye staggers over and says he still ain't convinced. So Superman hands Popeye a machine gun and commands, "Pepper me chest with this!" "But that'd be moider!" Popeye protests. "Yeah," Bluto agrees, "when it's your toin!" The anxious orchestra thinks so, too. Superman secretly slides a metal plate into his costume. A shaking Popeye doesn't look, but shoots anyway. The bullets bounce off Superman, but funeral music plays because now it's Popeye's turn. Popeye tries to be brave, but is practically melting with fear. Sweet Olive desperately tries to stop Superman. He shoves her aside and lets Popeye have it. Yes, Folks, Bluto guns Popeye down in cold blood! We hear Popeye cry out in pain. Bluto grabs a struggling Olive and makes off with her, while children watching the cartoon cried out for their mothers.

Popeye is on the ground, but he's alive! His spinach can absorbed all the bullets! Bluto has tied Olive to the railroad tracks to change her mind. "Never!" yells Olive. Bluto's sailor's hat falls out of his costume and Olive realizes who he really is. Popeye eats the spinach, and gains a red cape and a "P" on his chest. He rockets through the air, prompting this dialog:

> *Olive:* Look! Up in the sky!
> *Bluto:* It's an eagle!
> *Olive:* It's a rocket!
> *Bluto:* It's a meteor!
> *Popeye:* (pushing through a forest) It's Popeye The Sailor!

Bluto tries to roll a boulder down on Popeye, but the spinach-powered superhero uses his superbreath to blow it back to Bluto, knocking him and a group of trees down like tenpins. Then Popeye rockets to Olive and demolishes the oncoming train with just one punch.

Pop-Pie A La Mode (1945)

Director: I. Sparber. *Animation:* Joe Oriolo. *Story:* Morey Reden. *Scenics:* Uncredited. *Music:* Uncredited.

Shipwrecked Popeye comes to Joe's Always Inn on an island inhabited by cannibals. The chief views Popeye as if he were a leg of lamb and says, "Ah, dere's a man to my taste. And I think he'll agree with me." Years before the classic *Twilight Zone* episode, the chief consults a cookbook, *How To Serve Your Fellow Man*, and his tribe fattens Popeye up by force-feeding him mounds of mashed, French fried, boiled, and baked potatoes, starch, and cake in scenes that are nauseating. But the worst is yet to come.

The chief tells Popeye he is going to be initiated into a secret order. As drums ominously beat out their rhythms, Popeye, wearing a lady's sarong (!) gets into a public bathtub. It turns out he's really in a cooking pot, and as the music becomes more frantic and frightening, a bonfire is lit under it. A small cannibal tries to make a sandwich out of Popeye's arm. Popeye winces in pain and realizes he's among cannibals. The tribe approaches him, clucking their teeth together and licking their lips. The small cannibal holds up a sign that says, "I get the neck." A dinner triangle is rung and the call goes out to "Come and get it!" Popeye puts up a fierce battle, but is overwhelmed as the tribe gangs up on him.

When the smoke clears, a bound Popeye is standing on a stump. A sickened orchestra follows the action as two cannibals pound Popeye down until he is flattened into a raw steak. Then they toss the steak into a frying pan over a fire, where two cooks sing, "O you take the high ribs and I'll take the low ribs and I'll get the white meat afore ya!" They flip the steak, and a flattened spinach can comes out of it and the green stuff pours into the side of Popeye's mouth. He eats it as he lands in the pan again. Either the spinach starts affecting him, or he's starting to bubble and sizzle (being cooked by the heat), or both! Finally he springs back up into a better, more muscular shape than he had before. He pounds his chest and gives a Tarzan yell. We look down his throat as he does so.

Popeye beats up the tribe, turning them into spears, and bests the chief. The chief then fires cannons out of every window in the hotel. Popeye catches the rounds and turns them into a huge bomb. He hurtles it back from whence it came. The chief is blown into the ocean, where he chases sharks because he's hungrier and scarier than they are.

Popeye is now king of the cannibals. But the little cannibal takes another bite of the sandwich he's made of Popeye's leg saying, "I love dat man!"

This is a nightmare-inducing cartoon for children and a sickening one for adults. And Popeye is feminized in this film, not just because he wears the sarong, but also because he is cast in the traditional Olive Oyl role as the one who is taken in by a big strong man who is really a ravenous wolf. (Though in Olive's case, the wolves are trying to satiate a different kind of appetite.) It's not by accident that Popeye only gains a masculine physique after he eats the spinach.

The cannibals in the cartoon are offensive — not because they are Black. There are such things as tribes of cannibals who happen to be Black, after all. But the problem is that the cannibals here are drawn according to the stereotypical caricatures of American Southern Blacks that were prevalent in society when this film was made. The "secret society" reminds one of *Amos 'n Andy*. And the cannibals even talk with drawls, especially the chief. Were the creators trying to say that Blacks in our country are dangerous, liars, and no-good? Were Whites being called on to be men and oppose them?!?!?

Let's just move on, if the image of Popeye looking exactly like a raw, red steak can ever be forgotten!

Tops in the Big Top (1945)

Director: I. Sparber. *Animation:* Nick Tafuri, Tom Golden, John Walworth. *Story:* Joe Stultz, Carl Meyer. *Scenics:* Robert Little. *Music:* Winston Sharples.

Olive Oyl is drawn in the Fleischer style in this cartoon, though she's wearing a circus performer's minidress so the O.O.O.P.S. factor kicks in. She also has a figure of sorts, and is drawn with a cuter face than she had in the Fleischer days.

She and Popeye are circus stars and, at the beginning of the film, she's encouraging him as he puts his head in a lion's mouth. Olive is unaware that handsome ringmaster Bluto is giving her an extremely close, hungry once-over. He morphs into a real wolf and lasciviously says, "Mmm! What a feature attraction I'd make with Olive Oyl." In order to bring this about, he places a steak on Popeye's head as the orchestra gets worried. Sure enough, the lion chomps down on Popeye's neck and The Sailorman can't pull himself free. He fills the lion's ever-expanding head with smoke from his pipe. The lion turns green and essentially spits Popeye out off camera. Viewers are feeling a little green at this point themselves. The circus audience and the orchestra mock Popeye, and Olive thinks he's purposely trying to ruin the act.

Next Popeye balances blindfolded on a high-wire while carrying Olive and her piano! Bluto tosses a banana peel upon the wire. After trying to save themselves, Popeye's puffing on his pipe makes Olive let go of the wire in pain when the flames burn her feet. Now she has yet another reason to be angry at Popeye. And there's more to come. Bluto cuts the net below, so that the two performers crash down into the hole the piano made in the ground. Popeye emerges first, but Bluto knocks him cold by hitting him twice with a swinging block and tackle.

This makes the sailor drop Olive into the hole again. Then Bluto pretends to fan Popeye, while secretly dousing him with whiskey, saying, "All you need is a little air." As Olive climbs back up to ground level, she sniffs Popeye and declares in a shocked voice, "He's drunk!" The orchestra is ashamed of Popeye, and the crowd boos and yells, "Throw that drunk out!" In the voice of an appealing young woman needing to be rescued, a cute-faced Olive sadly mourns, "Now the show can't go on!" Bluto grabs her, pulls her close, and assures her, "Babe, the show will go on!" He whips off his ringmaster's suit to reveal an acrobatic costume on underneath — and his unbelievably muscular and chiseled physique. Olive is taken with her savior and his looks. "Bluto," she swoons and leans into him, "you're such a handsome monstrosity!" Bluto picks up the inert Popeye and, while showing off his muscles, tosses Popeye away snarling, "Hit the road, ya Bum!" This has got to be one of Bluto's greatest plots ever, as he's won Olive's heart, and her approval in disposing of the shamed Popeye!

Speaking of whom, he lands on top of a cage. A strong finger reaches up through a hole, and pulls Popeye's leg down through the hole. We see the finger belongs to a gorilla who is now pulling and stretching Popeye's leg, which is making a sickening sound effect.

Meanwhile a Bluto whose lust, impatience, and need to dominate and control has taken over once again, is now dangling from a trapeze and has tied Olive up and is using her as a kissing yo-yo. Why did he have to do this? He had already won her! Why not do the act with her and celebrate their new contract as partners later with wine in his wagon? A traumatized Olive cries out for help, but she is forced to keep kissing Bluto on the lips. And their lips really stick together and then stretch way out to stay together until the last possible second. Maybe this is just a cartoony effect, or maybe it's supposed to symbolize Olive's helplessness, or Bluto's power and his lust. At any rate, one can wonder why Olive isn't twisting her neck or shaking her head to try and break the supposedly unwanted liplocks. Could it be that at some level, deep down inside, a teeny tiny part of her is enjoying this? The orchestra and sound effects person seem to be!

Meanwhile, three gorillas are now pulling on all four of Popeye's limbs, enjoying their new toy and seemingly trying to tear him apart! The gross sound effects are back. As Popeye's head is about to go down the hole and join the rest of him so all will be lost, his spinach can is squeezed out of his shirt. He downs the magic vegetable and boxes the gorillas into statues of "Hear No Evil, See No Evil, Speak No Evil." Then he launches himself into the air, knocking Olive aside and right out of her dress. After Bluto mistakenly kisses him, he and Bluto have a midair fight. Popeye punches Bluto through some circus equipment and into a cannon. Popeye makes him into a human cannonball and then tries to catch him in an empty water tank usually used with diving acts. Olive is busily sawing away on the tent pole she's wrapped around. Unfortunately, it's the tent's main support! Everything comes crashing down as Popeye catches Bluto, bottling him in a water cooler. Popeye and Olive then share a hug.

Olive goes through that whole frantic finale in her underwear, but she's Fleischeresque, so don't get too excited. Popeye closes the cartoon still wearing Olive's dress!

Shape Ahoy (1945)

Director: I. Sparber. *Animation:* James Tyer, Ben Solomon. *Story:* Jack Ward, Irving Dressler. *Scenics:* Uncredited. *Music:* Uncredited.

Popeye and Bluto have sworn off women and are happily living on an island until castaway Olive comes ashore on a raft which uses her underwear for a sail. The boys each try to woo her without the other knowing. Each gets a kiss from her on the nose, which drives them crazy with desire — Popeye twists up and barks like a dog, Bluto turns into a rocket and skywrites, "Wow!" Then a skinny-dipping Olive, singing, *I'm in the Mood for Love*, gets the boys' attention and causes Bluto to dive in after her as she swims underwater. We see hearts rising from the place where they submerged and romantic music plays. But Popeye and Bluto surface, unwittingly holding each other. Bluto then tries to trap Popeye in a pit, but The Sailorman escapes in one of those unexplained ways cartoon characters do. They each propose to Olive, then begin a furious fistfight over her that shakes the island. They stop when they hear Olive let out quite a scream. She's not in trouble, though. She's swooning as she's sailing off on a raft with Frank Sinatra, who is singing *Let's Get Lost*. Angry, Popeye and Bluto say in unison, "Well, I'll be a..." But human hands cover their mouths with labels that read, "Censored."

Olive is Fleischeresque through the entire cartoon. She does have breasts when she poses on the title card, though. An entertaining cartoon, even though the romance and sexual aspects are played almost exclusively for laughs, and there isn't any suspense.

For Better or Nurse (1945)

Director: I. Sparber. *Animation:* Dave Tendlar, John Gentilella. *Story:* Joe Stultz, Irving Dressler. *Scenics:* Uncredited. *Music:* Winston Sharples.

Sailors Popeye and Bluto are smitten by hospital nurse Olive Oyl (O.O.O.P.S. alert — Olive is wearing a nurse's uniform!), as she strolls by the docks where they are working. So, they determine to seriously injure themselves in order to be near her. If they had stopped to think, they could have made dates with her for when her shift was over. But, of course, if cartoon characters ever stopped to think, cartoons would never be any fun. Still, one wonders how they hope to get intimate with Ms. Oyl if they are wearing body casts or are on life support. We can admire their devotion to her. Surely winning a girl at the corner coffee shop would be an easier, and less dangerous, thing to do! But once Famous Studios males see Olive Oyl, no other woman even comes close. And we can admire the fact that the boys will do absolutely anything to win Olive. But at the same time, the desire to have an accident in order to make time with nurse Olive seems a little sick (pardon the pun). It does demonstrate, though, that Bluto, contrary to popular perception, isn't looking just for a quick and easy affair, but for an ongoing relationship that requires sacrifice. In this cartoon he even says, "...for better or worse, I'm falling for a beautiful nurse."

The bulk of the cartoon is taken up with the creators' clever and funny ways to foil Popeye and Bluto's attempts to get hospitalized. For example, a bull charges Bluto, but then stops as it falls for the image of Fifi the Cow (a spoof of Elsie) on a billboard. Popeye crashes a plane and the ambulance shows up — and carts away the plane. Finally an angry and frustrated Popeye force-feeds Bluto spinach, so that the muscular guy will be compelled to beat up The Sailorman.

But it turns out that Olive actually works at a Cat And Dog Hospital, a fact that was ingeniously concealed from us viewers. (Go back and listen to Olive's exact line of dialog earlier in the film.) Popeye and Bluto immediately get down on all fours and begin acting like a cat and a dog, but whether they are still trying to get into the hospital or have just gone crazy after all they have been through is open to debate. I vote for the latter because, as they are hauled off to an asylum to end the cartoon, they haven't dropped the act yet.

Olive Oyl is Fleischeresque in this cartoon, though she has a cuter face than she did in the early days, and a shapely rear as she rounds the corner. She also has a feminine walk, and she sweetly ducks as the boys try to kiss her, causing them to lip-lock with each other.

Mess Production (1945)

Director: Seymour Kneitel. *Animation:* Graham Place, Lou Zukor. *Story:* Bill Turner, Otto Messmer. *Scenics:* Uncredited. *Music:* Winston Sharples.

This cartoon features the first appearance of the Famous Studios' glamour girl version of Olive Oyl, and she elicits wolf reactions from Bluto, Popeye, and, appropriately enough, a factory's whistle come to life, when she shows up for work. Olive enjoys the attention of the men, but she sweetly and innocently is really at the factory just to do her job.

When Popeye liberates her after she's welded herself into a metal container, she goes to reward him with a kiss. But Bluto accidentally hits her with a block and tackle meant for Popeye, and she begins sleepwalking through the factory, making kissing motions with her beautiful face. Supposedly, she's always about to be killed by all the dangerous equipment, and the excellent, threatening, machine-like musical score does its best to convince us this is so. But the characters are so cartoony throughout the film, and the situations so outrageous, that it's hard to take anything seriously. However, you might have a moment's pause when Bluto pours hot metal over Popeye, and The Sailorman slowly becomes a hardening statue, or when Bluto is about to net Olive.

Finally, after spinach, Popeye frees himself and vanquishes Bluto. Then he positions himself in front of Olive, sliding up the length of her body with a happy look on his face in the process, and gets the kiss. The smooch brings Olive out of her trance, but puts Popeye in a love-induced one. He then blissfully sleepwalks through the factory, destroying the equipment instead of being destroyed by it, either because the spinach hasn't worn off yet, or because Olive's kisses are powerful and magical. The romantic in me believes the latter.

This film contains one of Bluto's most memorable lines to Olive: "Why, you're a most delicious dish for a guy what's starvin' for a date!" I don't recommend that you use it to try and pick up girls, though.

House Tricks? (1946)

Director: Seymour Kneitel. *Animation:* Graham Place, Martin Taras. *Story:* Jack Ward, Carl Meyer. *Scenics:* Uncredited. *Music:* Winston Sharples.

Fleischeresque Olive Oyl is building her house. Her slightly cuter face than she had in earlier Popeye films, and her gorgeous legs, turn Popeye and Bluto on. However, the legs are just coatings of the cement Olive was working in, and they drop off. (Not to worry, Guys, Famous Studios will one day give Olive Betty Grable legs for real.) Bluto and Popeye begin competing in slapsticky, exaggerated ways that rely on cartoon universe physics to see who's the best man to build a home for Olive. They are each going to work on separate halves of the new house. Even though Bluto keeps cheating and accidents keep happening, and Olive keeps winding up in pipes, there's no sense of menace generated because everything is played for laughs. Finally Popeye eats spinach and finds ways to use his vanquishing of Bluto to complete the building. It's a great looking home, but when Popeye gently closes the front door as he and Olive kiss, it all comes tumbling and crashing down around them. Evidently spinach makes you strong and fast, but not necessarily competent.

Service With A Guile (1946)

Director: Bill Tytla. *Animation:* James Tyer, Ben Solomon. *Story:* Jack Ward, Carl Meyer. *Scenics:* Uncredited. *Music:* Uncredited.

At Olive Oyl's service station, the Admiral wants air in his tire. Popeye and Bluto arrive to take Olive rowing. Evidently they are both going to date her simultaneously?!?!? But any feelings of cooperation quickly vanish as they compete to fill the tire, not realizing that they are dangerously over-inflating it. The valve pops open and hurricane force winds blow out of the tire. Bluto hits the valve with a sledge hammer. The wind stops and the tire looks like it's going back to normal.

A grateful Olive puts her arms around him and starts to give him a kiss on the lips. A turned-on Bluto knows what's coming. (When Olive and Bluto are alone or on a date, they must get physical. Olive doesn't mind at all. Here, she initiates it!) But Popeye has realized that the huge tire is merely snaking under the car to the other side. The tire explodes, blowing Popeye, Bluto, and Olive across town. They return, and this time Olive wants Popeye to fix the damaged car. But Bluto plays havoc with the grease rack while the car is up on it. The whole thing comes out of the ground, and Popeye has to grab, balance, and carry it, even through a construction site! Finally, the car is wrecked, and the Admiral is coming! Popeye eats spinach and becomes Super Mechanic. He quickly puts the car back together. But Bluto bumps him out of the way as the Admiral arrives, so that Bluto can take credit for everything. Has Popeye lost even after eating the spinach? No, because as the Admiral drives away, the car falls apart. The cartoon ends with Popeye and Olive rowing while Bluto has to scrape the rust off of Navy ships.

How did the spinach know what Bluto was going to do? Or is the spinach not able to impart automobile repair knowledge? Well, whatever the reason, Popeye won through losing.

Klondike Casanova (1946)

Director: I. Sparber. *Animation:* Dave Tendlar, John Gentilella. *Story:* I. Klein, George Hill. *Scenics:* Uncredited. *Music:* Winston Sharples.

WARNING: This is perhaps Famous Studio's raciest cartoon. The censors must have been half-asleep when they passed this one! Don't read on if you will be offended!

In the Klondike, Popeye and Olive own "The Polar Bar And Grill." He plays piano for the customers, while she does a song-and-dance routine performing *I Don't Want to Walk Without You*, and ending with a sexy, provocative striptease! She actually does have another dress on under her showgirl costume, but she teasingly exits the stage before the customers can see it. The men go wild for Olive. And, in this cartoon, she has a pretty and expressive face, a curvy body, and breasts. But she's wearing a Fleischer hairstyle. During their act, both Popeye and Olive have to keep putting everything on pause in order

Olive as a stripper is just one of the shocking things in this cartoon.

to make, and serve, the food and drinks, and wash the dishes. They work hard for their money.

Suddenly Dangerous Dan McBluto comes into their establishment, causing the clientele to run away in panic. But Dan has something other than mayhem on his mind. He strolls to the stage singing a romantic version of *Louise*, and gallantly introduces himself to Olive. A jealous Popeye just sits at the piano and stews. Dan helps Olive down off the stage while giving her a lustful once-over and saying hungrily, "Mmmm, mmmm!"

Then Olive and Dan are on a date in the bar, sharing an ice cream soda that has a cherry on top by using two straws. They make goo-goo eyes at each other. The orchestra helps them fall in love, and even more assistance arrives. The gigantic heart which has appeared in the air between them pops, and there's the god Cupid sitting on a cloud. He, too, briefly ogles Olive Oyl, who seems to be falling out of her dress a little. Then Cupid looks over at Popeye and rejects him as Olive's mate. He chooses Dan instead and bops both Dan and Olive over their heads with a mallet, causing their eyes to turn into hearts, giddy expressions to appear on their faces, and hearts to appear and burst all around them. Their eye hearts come on to one another, then they put their foreheads together, and end up gazing into each other's eyes. Even the gods don't want Popeye and Olive to end up together! And, truth be told, other than being jealous and coming to her rescue, Popeye doesn't act romantically toward Olive at all in this cartoon.

Speaking of being jealous, Popeye is grinding a chair into sawdust and muttering, "If I didn't have no self-control, I'd turn green with envy!" He promptly literally does. But why is Popeye just standing around and watching the date!

The creators, perhaps expressing their true feelings about the eternal love triangle, have Olive and Dan fall for each other. And the artists let Olive show off her attributes.

Why isn't he trying to interfere? And presumably he made the soda that Olive and Dan are sharing!

Next follows a scene between the couple that Cupid has chosen as mates that needs no commentary from me as to what, if anything, it symbolizes. I'll just describe it and your mind can do the rest, or not, as you so choose. The orchestra now gets sexy and the bass seems to be counting down to something. Olive and Dan, foreheads still together, have drained the soda and begin playfully fighting over the cherry at the bottom of the glass, their foreheads and noses rubbing as they do so. Finally, they each suck a side of the cherry into their respective straws. Using the straws, they lift it out of the glass and begin stretching and pulling it, moving closer together or further apart, but always being joined together by the straws and the stretching cherry. Looks of temporary pain, and extreme joy, love, satisfaction, and pleasure alternately play across their faces. Neither wants to stop. Finally, as Olive actually pops out of her dress in a wardrobe malfunction, the straws and the cherry reach a climactic arc above them. They pull and pull, and the cherry stretches and stretches, keeping them attached until the impossibly last second. Their eyes are closed in pure ecstasy. Finally, the cherry comes loose with a pop and slides down Olive's straw to her mouth. Bluto's straw, after the climax, is bent and unusable. Olive balances the cherry on her lips, gives Bluto a look, and stretches out her neck and puckered up lips toward him, offering him her cherry. Bluto does a double-take and is re-energized again. Glorious lust is on his face as he claps his hands together. Olive now suddenly gives him the look of a virgin wondering if she's gone too far and offered too much. As Bluto closes his eyes and puts his massive lips forward to get the cherry and the kiss, Olive ducks, and he ends up kissing Popeye, who has walked into the scene, instead. Actually, he takes Popeye's whole head in his mouth and then spits it out again. Popeye, though, doesn't say anything like, "Hey, quit making out with Olive!" Instead, he just walks away! Though he seethes on the sidelines and calls Olive, "Me goil," in this cartoon, Popeye seems to realize what he hasn't tumbled to in other cartoons — Olive really hasn't committed to him, however much he may wish she would. So, in this film, he doesn't intrude on her date with another guy until she's physically in danger and needs help. It's as though he understands that he doesn't have the right.

Olive is now playfully lying on the railing of the balcony, balancing the cherry on her nose. She wants to prolong the flirting, courting, and magic moment, and doesn't want to be rushed. Dan snatches her down, traps her in his arms, and flashes a message to her with words that appear on his teeth, "Start Sizzling Sister." Olive desperately and sweetly suddenly "remembers" a mah jong appointment. But Dan doesn't buy it and begins strangling her to get her to give into him, thereby blowing the chance he had with her. I wonder what Cupid would say to this?

Popeye, finally appearing again in his own cartoon, tells Dan to let go of her and the two of them briefly battle, using the stretching Olive as a kind of bungee cord. Then Dan uses Olive's legs as a slingshot and shoots Popeye through the beams and wall of the bar and out into the cold to land in a hole in the ice. Instantly frozen solid in an ice block, Popeye is lifted out of the hole by a seal, which then feeds itself a fish as a reward. As spooky, "otherworldly death" music plays, an evilly laughing Dan strolls by the inert Popeye while carrying Olive — tied and trussed up in a sack over her head which covers most of her body — over his shoulder on the way to his place.

Popeye uses his pipe as a blowtorch to make a door in the iceblock. He scurries after Dan, but Dan delays him by dropping a gigantic icicle on him. Olive struggles to get out of the bag at Dan's place. Some fans feel that the shapes the bag takes on make it seem as though Olive has been captured by a male. I'll say no more. Olive stumbles over to caged bears who snatch the bag off of her. After singing a commercial about how McBluto's furs charm girls, they start snarling and growling at the frightened miss. Dan grabs her again and causes Popeye to fall from the cliff in front of his cabin. We see Popeye headed for a sharp peak as the orchestra worries. But he manages to down his spinach, stop himself in midair before being impaled, and use his pipe as a propeller to fly back up the mountain.

In Dan's cabin, a tremendous struggle is taking place, and Olive is yelling. Popeye zooms in and punches Dan out of the chimney. Dan releases the bears, but Popeye's punches take the furs right off of them, providing a delighted Olive with new coats.

In the last scene of the cartoon, Popeye and Olive are dogsledding back to the bar. Only instead of dogs, it's Dan pulling the sleigh, being spurred along by Popeye's whip (!) and by The Little Gnome Guy, who jabs him in the rear with a large, sharp pin.

Peep in the Deep (1946)

Director: Seymour Kneitel. *Animation:* Jim Tyer, William Henning. *Story:* Bill Turner, Otto Mesmer. *Scenics:* Uncredited. *Music:* Uncredited.

Bluto shows no romantic interest at all in the Fleischeresque Olive Oyl in this cartoon. Instead, he wants the treasure she and Popeye are attempting to salvage. Bluto and Popeye go deep sea diving. Bluto makes sure Popeye lands inside a giant clam which had stripped a literal loan shark down to the skeleton in seconds. We see it chewing away on Popeye! But it can't stand the smoke from Popeye's pipe, and frees him. Thinking fast, Bluto covers a swordfish's head with the mannequin of a beautiful blonde mermaid. Popeye falls for it and keeps chasing and kissing "her." So much for Popeye being loyal to Olive! The swordfish finally breaks free and attacks Popeye, but a right hook finishes the matter. Then Bluto blows Popeye to the surface with a cannon. Returning below, The Sailorman and Bluto take the sunken boat's safe from each other, until Bluto makes Popeye fall onto a scary giant octopus. Then Bluto makes off with Olive's ship and the safe containing the treasure. Meanwhile, the octopus is squeezing the life out of Popeye, but our hero consumes spinach and leaves the multi-limbed horror tied up in knots. Popeye catches up to Bluto and metes out justice. Olive then opens the safe to find that the treasure is a picture of Frank Sinatra. She swoons and faints over it. So much for Olive being loyal to Popeye! In this scene and the one where she's painting her toenails Olive has a cute face. Popeye isn't concerned that another man has such an effect on her. He laughs! So much for Popeye being loyal to Olive! Oh, wait...I said that already.

Rocket to Mars (1946)

Director: Bill Tytla. *Animation:* Jim Tyer, John Gentilella. *Story:* Bill Turner, Otto Messmer. *Scenics:* Anton Loeb. *Music:* Winston Sharples.

Olive accidentally launches a rocket she and Popeye are touring. She gets sucked out of the hatch and grabs a flagpole to save herself, but Popeye travels on into outer space as scary, suspenseful music plays.

After Popeye's face and neck get grossly contorted by gravity and the rocket's escape velocity, a smoke ring comes out of his pipe and he thinks he's dead. But there's humor mixed in with the horror. His ship bowls over the bottles that make up The Milky Way and turn it into a cheese wheel. Popeye wolf whistles at Venus. A Japanese soldier peeks out from behind a planet that looks like a giant 8-ball.

And then there's the planet Mars where engines of War literally grow out of the ground. Ominous, relentless, "marching to battle" music is heard. The Martians bring Popeye's ship down with a giant magnet. Their leader is an extraterrestrial version of Bluto with a misshapen nose and a spooky, echo chamber voice.

The scene changes to a weak, beat up, helpless, and hopeless Popeye chained by his hands and feet to a wall. The Martian leader tells him that the Martians are going to invade Earth. Popeye says, "Let me outta here!" The leader pulls a ray gun and replies, "Let you out? Why, I'll wipe you out!" A struggling Popeye is bathed in the ray. He vanishes and the chains fall limply away. Popeye is gone! (And kids watching the cartoon were guaranteed to have bad dreams!)

The Martians load up and prepare for war. The leader sticks a huge sword through a picture of Earth. Back at the chains, one of the shackles suddenly moves and pulls a spinach can from out of the nowhere that used to be Popeye's shirted chest area. Then the disintegrated, or extra-dimensional, or invisible Popeye eats it and reappears. Not only that, but he's loaded for bear! He beats up the Martians and overcomes their weapons of war, turning the whole planet into one big amusement park.

As Popeye flies his rocket back home, he sings, "Now they're peaceful and happy, no more to be scrappy, says Popeye the Sailorman!"

Rodeo Romeo (1946)

Director: I. Sparber. *Animation:* Dave Tendlar, Martin Taras. *Story:* I. Klein, Joe Stultz. *Scenics:* Shane Miller. *Music:* Winston Sharples.

Olive goes crazy over rodeo star, Badlands Bluto, but Popeye is unimpressed. Badlands does some trick riding and ends up tickling Olive under her chin and snuggling cheek-to-cheek. Sweet Olive, though smitten, doesn't want to rush things and slides out of his embrace while giggling. Olive gets so into cheering his next stunt that she jumps high in the air and almost lands on a cactus. Popeye catches her by her nose.

Badlands grabs Popeye and squeezes him so that his pipe embers glow. Then Badlands uses Popeye to light a cigarette. Popeye's humiliation continues when Badlands trick-shoots a bunch of eggs directly above The Sailorman's head. Popeye wants to show Badlands up, so he takes out a huge can of spinach and eats some.

Notice that Popeye needs spinach in order to compete with Badlands. Also, notice that Popeye waited an awful long time to take any action against his rival. And why does Popeye ever take Olive to any shows if the point of the date is always to prove that Popeye is better than the performers he has paid to see? Popeye hated what Badlands was doing even before the rodeo star came on to Olive, so more than jealousy is at work here. There are some massive ego problems involved. So why doesn't Popeye just stay at home, eat spinach, and do tricks all night to impress Olive, if it's all gotta be about Popeye in the end?

Popeye subdues a bucking bronco and then does his own trick shot and some rope tricks. He even lassoes a bullet he fired before it can hit Badlands. Olive, the equal opportunity cheerer, gives Popeye his due.

As the orchestra worries for Popeye, Badlands takes his spinach can and secretly fills it with locoweed. After Olive kisses Popeye on the forehead, Badlands pretends to congratulate him, too, and hands him his spinach can saying, "Now let's see ya throw the bull!" Popeye downs the locoweed, and we see the internal works of his head break down. A tipsy, semiconscious Popeye lets the bull run him over. Now he's seeing the bull as a large woman. He tries to dance with it. It beats him up instead and begins throwing him against the stands where the can is perched. The bouncing can of locoweed goes right into a laughing Badlands Bluto's mouth. We see him go crazy, and he starts to view Olive as a calf that needs branding. In this scene, Olive has a very cute face. Bluto grabs her by the neck, ties her up to a post, and tries to brand her wiggling and dodging rear. The look of hunger, pleasure, and lust he has on his face makes it possible that this branding suggests other things as well.

Meanwhile, the bull has pinned Popeye and is twisting his legs together. Olive's cries snap Popeye out of his stupor, and he pulls another spinach can out of his shirt. I guess he carries a spare. Soon the bull is turned into fresh meat, and Badlands is interrupted just as an exhausted Olive is done struggling and he's about to nail her and put his mark on her. Bluto is the one who ends up getting branded on his hindquarters with the words "The End." And it is.

The Fistic Mystic (1946)

Director: Seymour Kneitel. *Animation:* Graham Place, Nick Tafuri. *Story:* I. Klein, Jack Ward. *Scenics:* Robert Little. *Music:* Winston Sharples.

Popeye and Olive travel to the ancient, exotic, magical city of Badgag. (Too bad we don't use those adjectives to describe the Middle East any more.) Olive and a mystic — Bluto playing a role — fall for each other. The mystic charms her with his magic flute/horn/musical thingy, and switches into a sexy version of the haunting tune he's playing as he makes her literally wrap herself around him in his belt area. This sequence is so fast and so over-the-top that it must have flown by the censors, and the moviegoing audiences didn't have a chance to dwell on it. We do. And the whole idea is pretty sexy.

After the mystic tells Olive, "Stick with me! Riches and love, I'll give to thee," and magically puts her in a harem girl outfit, she responds, "Well, when do we start?" He hungrily replies, "Right now!" He grabs her off her feet and lays her back in his arms and does something hardly any Famous Studios cartoon male ever got to do on camera — he gives her a long, passionate kiss on the lips. After all, they did just pledge commitment to one another, or come as near to doing so as characters in a six minute cartoon can. The kiss melts Olive like butter and she flows down the stairs to re-form, totally ravished, at the bottom. As she is in her liquid state, her face is gorgeous. In fact, she has a cute face and some curves in various scenes/frames throughout the entire cartoon.

Popeye by now has finally realized that Olive is no longer traveling beside him, and he arrives on the scene to challenge the mystic. The sheik first temporarily transforms Popeye into a donkey, then tries to impress Olive and best Popeye by doing a couple of stunts. But Popeye can match him. So, in a sequence that causes children to squirm, he puts Popeye under a spell, gets The Sailorman to drop the spinach, and transforms Popeye into a parrot — permanently. The mystic then cages the Popeye parrot.

A horrified Olive protests, so the mystic locks her in a basket and begins sticking swords in it, spearing her underwear in the process. He thrusts a giant sword under her legs which have popped out of the basket. Freud might say sometimes swords are just swords. I'll leave it to you to decide if that's the case here.

Olive yells for help, but Popeye is now just a parrot and acts like a parrot. He's insensate to Olive's plight. That idea is creepy in itself. But, fortunately, as a chased Olive runs by, she sticks the spinach can in the feeder on the side of the bird cage. The green stuff does its work, and Popeye is restored. The mystic tries to escape with Olive on a flying carpet, prompting an aerial battle. The mystic attempts to turn Popeye into a canary, but the spinach-powered sailor punches the magic bolts right back at him. The transformed villain flies away. So, if you ever see a bearded canary, you'll know who it is!

Popeye and Olive cruise to America on the flying carpet, and Popeye acts like he's going to kiss a pretty-faced Olive, but he walks past her and kisses the Statue Of Liberty instead, proclaiming, "I just loves that woman!" Maybe this went over big with post-World War II audiences, but today it makes Popeye look like a dork compared to the virile mystic. So, once again, the romantic Olive Oyl is stuck with the unromantic boyfriend. Happy ending?

Abusement Park (1947)

Director: I. Sparber. *Animation:* Dave Tendlar, Tom Golden. *Story:* Joe Stultz, Carl Meyer. *Scenics:* Anton Loeb. *Music:* Winston Sharples.

Popeye and Olive are at an amusement park when "Popeye's pal" Bluto introduces himself to Miss Oyl and begins coming on to her. Bluto and Popeye engage in tests of strength to impress Olive. Popeye even blows a lighthouse apart using superlung power. (Who pays for all of the destruction the boys cause in these cartoons?)

Popeye places Olive in a Tunnel of Love boat, and the two begin smooching and cuddling, not realizing that Bluto is in the back of their boat. As they go through the tunnel and are hidden from our view, somebody is doing something to Olive, which causes her to giggle and say, "Popeye, you're so romantic!" But when the boat comes into view again, we see that it was Bluto who was making with the love, having thrown Popeye overboard. The Sailorman is swimming from behind to catch up to them. They are all hidden from our sight again, and when they emerge from behind a wall of rocks, it's Popeye getting the kisses because he's switched places with Bluto once again. The boat goes behind another wall. When it comes out this time, Bluto is mistakenly kissing Popeye! He quickly realizes what's up, knocks The Sailorman out, and plants a blonde mermaid mannequin from one of the tunnel's exhibits in the boat. Then Bluto saves Olive, who is floundering and drowning in the water. "Look," he tells her, as an unconscious Popeye seems to be snuggling with a new girl, "nice guy! He threw ya overboard for a blonde!" Olive declares that this is the last time Popeye will ever two-time her! Bluto has framed Popeye, become Olive's savior, and is now her new boyfriend. So, of course, he'll have to blow everything by being impatient.

The two of them are now posing in a convertible at a photo stand, where The Little Gnome Guy is taking their picture. Bluto wants the picture to be "hot" and goes for a kiss. Olive fends him off, so he grabs her saying, "Aw, stop actin' and let's have some action!" She begins pummeling him, but he, unaffected and waiting for her to tire out, just smiles. Popeye hears her cries for help and enters the scene as Bluto is warning Olive, "I got ways of handlin' dames like you!" Talk about a brutish male power trip! Popeye responds, "Oh, yeah?" But Bluto runs him over with the convertible.

Bluto drives the car up onto the roller coaster tracks and has Olive terrified. He then demands a kiss again, but she sweetly protects her virtue with, "No, no, a thousand times, no!" So Bluto kicks her out of the moving car with a rope tied around her one ankle. She's now trailing behind the convertible like a kite. As the car makes a turn, she swings wide and crashes into a factory's smokestack, the result being that she now has a gigantic smoking chimney between her legs. (Symbolism, anyone?)

Popeye ski jumps on the tracks and lands on Bluto, crashing them both out of the bottom of the car. They fight furiously for a few minutes before they realize a train is coming right at them. Popeye, hero that he is, saves them both by hanging from a rail tie by one hand, while holding Bluto with the other. As they are climbing up on the tracks again, Bluto thanks Popeye for saving his life, then kicks him in the face and jumps up and down on his fingers to get him to fall to his doom. With friends like Bluto, who needs enemies? He'll try to kill you and force himself on your girl!

Speaking of whom, Olive has now ripped through a circus tent and is holding on to a string of elephants. Olive and the convertible must be more powerful than they look!

Popeye eats his spinach, of course, and he and Bluto land on one of the elephants. They have a battle which even takes them on top of Olive Oyl! Popeye finally puts Bluto's head in the car's gas tank, then lights it with his pipe, and sends Bluto soaring like a rocket into the sky. They all end up back at the photo booth. Popeye has his one arm around Olive, and with his other he holds up a pile of elephants, Bluto, and the mannequin.

I'll Be Skiing Ya (1947)

Director: I. Sparber. *Animation:* Tom Johnson, George Germanetti. *Story:* Larry Riley, Bill Turner. *Scenics:* Uncredited. *Music:* Winston Sharples.

Popeye is trying to teach Olive to ice skate when she attracts the attention of official Skating Instructor Bluto. He has a wolf reaction, which inadvertently calls a real, furry female wolf to his side. He swats it away, gives Olive the once-over and muses, "Mmmm, I'd like to teach that figure a figure or two." He volunteers because incompetent Popeye keeps endangering Olive. Finally, she's had enough, and Bluto kicks a shrunken and humiliated Popeye into a hole in the ice. Bluto doesn't have to make Popeye look bad in this cartoon. The Sailorman accomplishes this all by himself!

Then Bluto is behind Olive, holding her around her waist, teaching her to skate backward. She leans into him, swooning and saying she feels as if she's skating on air. Actually, she is, because Bluto has maneuvered them onto a ski lift. When Olive realizes what's happening, she yells for help. Popeye emerges from the hole, looking like a walrus made of snow. He shakes off the covering. Now at the top of the ski run, Bluto has grabbed Olive and is going for the kiss. Olive holds him off with her fists and feet. Popeye reaches the top, and he and Bluto have a furious battle which causes a nervous Olive to chew her fingernails. She gets knocked into a pile of skies, becomes attached to a pair, and goes off a ski jump. As Bluto is about to chop Popeye's head off with an ax (!), the boys see Olive is in trouble and freeze in surprise. Lucky for Popeye, huh? They then race to get to Olive first.

Olive cartoonily contorts and avoids many dangers, but then she's being followed by a boulder which is turning into a giant snowball. Popeye ends up unconscious and dangling from the top of a deep crevasse. His skis are slowly slipping into the void. The orchestra thinks both Popeye and Olive are doomed. But a Saint Bernard rescue dog feeds Popeye spinach. The sailor turns his skis into a helicopter and saves Olive. Then he punches Bluto all the way from upstate New York to a beach in Florida. The bathing beauties there cause Bluto to have another reaction, and the female wolf comes running up to kiss him again.

Popeye and the Pirates (1947)

Director: Seymour Kneitel. *Animation:* Dave Tendlar, Martin Taras. *Story:* I. Klein, Jack Ward. *Scenics:* Robert Connavale. *Music:* Winston Sharples.

This cartoon seems almost like a throwback to earlier films as its emphasis seems to be on fast-paced, wild and wacky humor, and not so much on suspense and romance, though it does have its intriguing moments. Plus, all the characters are drawn very cartoony throughout. Olive Oyl is, however, often drawn with full, shapely breasts.

Once again demonstrating their fundamental incompatibility, Olive Oyl, caught up in the romance and adventure of being on the high seas, wishes she could meet pirates, but Popeye tells her there aren't any such things. Suddenly a pirate ship eerily materializes from out of nowhere. Have Olive's desires called forth a ship from the past into the present? Have the cartoon gods heard Olive's prayer?

The pirate captain, Pierre, spots Olive and has a wolf reaction. He hooks Popeye's boat with an anchor and reels it in, as Olive waves and calls out to him while Popeye is trying to speed his own craft away. Pierre greets Olive warmly, but throws Popeye back as being too little and inconsequential to keep. The captain holds Olive's hand while kissing his way up her arm. When he reaches her neck, he practically ingests it like spaghetti. When Popeye interrupts, Pierre squashes him into an accordion shape. Next, Pierre literally showers Olive with jewels while giving her a marriage proposal that she implicitly accepts! And Pierre is totally unaffected when Popeye hits him over the head with a cannon. The same can't be said for Popeye when Pierre then turns the cannon into a bell with Popeye as the clapper. Next, Popeye tries to give Pierre a super-powered punch in the face, but all that happens is that Popeye's injured hand now has been mashed into the shape of the pirate's face. The great Popeye is totally outclassed and helpless when faced (excuse the pun) with Pierre.

Saying, "When Pierre is making love, he does not wish to be disturbed," Pierre makes Popeye walk the plank at sword point. Fortunately Popeye, like all cartoon characters, can also walk along the bottom of the plank. Pierre has crowned Olive as Queen of the Spanish Main, when Popeye reappears on deck, dressed in drag. Evidently if he can't defeat Pierre as a man, he'll do so as a woman?!?!? Popeye is an ugly female, and it's obvious who he is. Still, the pirates react to her/him. They must have had too much rum!

Pierre takes a curvy and acquiescent Olive into his arms, lays her back — her breasts are really pronounced here — and tenderly says, "And now ze kiss, Cherie ... Yeow!" He sees Popeye and has a wolf reaction. Ditching Olive, he pursues Popeye! The Sailorman tricks Pierre into falling into a treasure chest, which Popeye promptly locks, chains, and throws overboard. But you can't keep Pierre down. As Popeye is discarding his disguise, Pierre comes back aboard and accidentally gets the dumbbells Popeye was using for breasts in his mouth. So Pierre literally gets a bust in the mouth. (This cartoon is certainly fixated on breasts, isn't it?) A scared Popeye (!) then flees from the angry Pierre. Pierre snags and squishes him into a ball and chain, then fires the sailor out of a cannon. Popeye flies through the air and sinks to the bottom of the ocean, unconscious, with his remaining breath escaping in bubbles.

A horrified Olive calls for help as Pierre chases her. But a dying Popeye is oblivious to her plight. A passing swordfish reading a Popeye comic book feeds him spinach, though, and Popeye breaks the chain and sprouts hair on his chest. Has spinach finally, literally, made a man out of Popeye? The Sailorman soon defeats Pierre and his crew, and he and Olive pucker up for a kiss, but this cartoon's version of The Little Gnome Guy pops up between them and gets bussed instead. Poor Popeye! Aside from the swordfish, he just can't catch a break in this film. And it was only after his spinach-induced puberty that he got romantic with Olive at all!

Wotta Knight (1947)

Director: I. Sparber. *Animation:* Tom Johnson, John Gentilella. *Story:* Carl Meyer, I. Klein. *Scenics:* Anton Loeb. *Music:* Winston Sharples.

This cartoon spells out exactly what is at stake in its kissing sweepstakes. Whichever knight awakens Sleeping Beauty (a blonde Olive Oyl with impossibly long braids) with a kiss will wed her. Popeye and Bluto joust for that privilege. Bluto painfully crushes Popeye's hand during the handshake before the match, then trips him up with grease, turns his armor into a stove, knocks him off his horse with an expandable lance, shatters his armor with an axe, and nearly kills him. Popeye, though, dives into Bluto's armor and makes with the fisticuffs. Popeye, therefore, wins the joust (though I had Bluto ahead on points).

But as Popeye is about to kiss Olive, Bluto appears and the two battle, always stopping the other right before the kiss can occur. Bluto looks especially handsome and tender as he tries for his first kiss. Pulling on her braids, the boys engage in a tug-of-war with the still-sleeping Olive and then use her as a kissing yo-yo! Finally, Bluto throws the armored Popeye into the wall of a small room and locks the door. The impact turns the armored Popeye into a radiator. Fortunately, the radiator eats spinach, and Popeye vanquishes Bluto and claims his prize. But Bluto was carrying Olive away when Popeye swooped in and turned the tide. Why didn't Bluto just hurry up and kiss her when he had the chance?

Popeye steps on Olive's toe as he is about to kiss her. This guy can't do anything right! Olive awakens, sees Popeye, and has a she-wolf reaction. (Popeye's lucky she never saw Bluto!) Popeye, the jerk, tries to run away (?!?!?) from the passionate Olive Oyl, but she pulls him back with a magnet and gives him such a kiss on his forehead that he turns into a puddle of molten metal. Imagine what one on his lips would have done!

Safari So Good (1947)

Director: I. Sparber. *Animation:* Tom Johnson, Morey Reden. *Story:* Larz Bourne. *Scenics:* Anton Loeb. *Music:* Winston Sharples.

Popeye and Olive Oyl, whose safari pants show off a shapely rear and pretty legs at points in this cartoon, are on safari in an African jungle. They become separated from each other and don't realize it — Olive because she's caught up in adventure and in the photographs she's taking of a monkey that is leading her away, and Popeye because he's just too dense.

Tarzan (Bluto playing a role) swings in and literally sweeps Olive off her feet. A message flashes out of his head like Morse code, "Wotta Woman!" He dances and bounces around, crazy with desire for her. Olive gives him a wolf whistle and a once-over with her camera, saying, "(sexy gasp) So big and strong! And I adore that sarong!" Then, overcome with emotion and realizing what she's done, she turns coyly away in a flirtatious and encouraging manner, and sweetly giggles.

A guy taking Olive back to his place, either willingly or unwillingly, was a theme in many Famous Studios cartoons.

Popeye, meanwhile, finally realizes she's not with him.

Olive is playing with Tarzan's bicep going, "Mmmmmm," and "Hubba, hubba, hubba!" So, of course, Popeye has to super-speed into the picture and force them apart. Tarzan merely tosses him away, and Popeye ends up wrapped around a tree, humiliated, with his hat now on his rear end.

Olive is snapping pictures as Tarzan shows off his muscles for her. He squeezes a coconut with his arm, and its stream of white milk nearly drowns, and emasculates, Popeye. Then Popeye shoots dozens of coconuts back. Olive, backing up to get a better picture of all of this, nearly has a bite taken out of her derriere by a hungry, and obviously male, crocodile. Tarzan, *not Popeye*, saves her life! Then Tarzan throws the beast at Popeye like a spear. Popeye turns the croc into luggage.

There follows a test of strength and a battle during which Olive Oyl starts, completely inexplicably, to root for Popeye! Tarzan calls on practically every large and dangerous animal in the jungle to surround Popeye. Olive takes pictures of all of this as if she's unconcerned about what will happen to Popeye. Maybe she hasn't completely decided who to root for, and who to end up with, after all. But Tarzan decides for her, swinging by on a vine, snatching her by the hair, and carrying the screaming miss up to his tree house from which there can be no escape and where there will be no interruptions.

Meanwhile, Popeye and the orchestra are scared. He's sweating like crazy as he gingerly pulls out his spinach in front of animals which are poised to attack. They do so before he can eat it, and it flies up in the air to be caught by a monkey on an overhanging branch. Popeye stretches his neck up out of the battle several times to try to get it. As Popeye is going down for the last time, the monkey feeds it to him. Popeye then destroys the animals in ways that would make PETA cringe. Then Popeye takes the time to strike a self-congratulatory pose. Why isn't he racing to save a struggling Olive?

Tarzan has bound Olive's top half up in a sack, and is about to do whatever he wants with her, before Popeye pulls the tree down and saves the day. (Actually, Tarzan had some moments hidden from our eyes to actually do some things we couldn't see before slowpoke Popeye knocked on his door! And Olive went suddenly silent!) Olive takes more pictures of Tarzan, this time as he sits in the makeshift cage Popeye put him in.

All's Fair at the Fair (1947)

Director: Seymour Kneitel. *Animation:* Dave Tendlar, Martin Taras. *Story:* I. Klein, Jack Ward. *Scenics:* Robert Connavale. *Music:* Winston Sharples.

Popeye and Olive may be standing next to each other at the fair, but they are miles apart. He's going on and on about the physical development of a bull, while she's admiring the attributes of "Bluto the Fearless," a daredevil who will leap from the basket beneath a rising balloon later in the day. The curvy, cute-faced miss goes over to him and captures his eyes and his heart as she gives him a coquettish, but encouraging, look, and inadvertently shows off her shapely derriere. The two go off, arm-in-arm and in sync, to enjoy a day at the fair. But, Popeye, continuing his unwanted lecture to nobody, finally realizes Olive isn't there any more. He quickly snatches her away from Bluto.

Bluto follows the couple and frames Popeye for disasters. He knocks Olive into a machine that makes taffy candy kisses, and Olive becomes the world's biggest candy kiss herself. The whole concept is cartoony and funny, of course, but also provocative in some way, as are the machine's mechanical lips and tongue as they move over Olive. Bluto also causes Popeye to make an egg display drop on her. Having had enough, Olive breaks up with Popeye, seemingly for good, and is on her way home when a diamond ring at a ball toss booth causes her to pause and let out a sexy, "Huh?" Popeye tries to win the ring for her, but Bluto once again makes it seem as though Popeye has fouled everything up and hurt Olive. Then Bluto steps in to help Olive win the ring. Olive strolls away with

Bluto, her arms wrapped around his massive one and her delighted, enraptured face buried in his muscles, leaving a dejected Popeye behind.

Bluto invites Olive to see his balloon. After they climb into the basket, Bluto tricks her into looking away as he cuts the mooring lines. A shocked Olive realizes they are ascending, as Bluto pulls a curtain down around them saying, "How 'bout a little privacy, eh, Toots?" Once again, Bluto's impatience and lust-fulfilling power trip prove his undoing. An Olive whom he had won and who was in the palm of his hand is now horrified and trying to escape. Popeye climbs up a line to try and save her, but Bluto drops a sandbag, landing Popeye in a fireworks display. Bluto, having materialized a motorcycle from wherever cartoon characters do that sort of thing, now chases Olive around, and over, the basket and the balloon. As mournful music plays, an unconscious Popeye's pipe lights the fuse of the skyrocket that is caught on his shirt. As Bluto has Olive in his arms and there's no escaping the coming kiss, Popeye's launched rocket crashes into the basket, causing it to catch on fire. Popeye and Bluto hit each other with a materialized lawn mower and iron stove, before Bluto bails out to escape the flames, taking Popeye, who was holding on to Bluto's parachute, with him. Bluto, though the villain, nevertheless acts uncharacteristically here. We've seen him put himself at risk to save Olive before. Why not now?

Olive climbs to the top of the balloon in a vain attempt to avoid the holocaust. The flames keep touching her rear, causing her to say, "Wooo-ooo!" in a sweetly feminine way, which suggests maybe she wouldn't mind something, or someone, else touching her there. On their way to the ground, Bluto uses Popeye as a punching bag. (His head is sticking through the top of the chute.) Finally he knocks the slack, unconscious, maybe dead Popeye through the roof of a spinach canning exhibit. You can guess what comes next.

A revitalized Popeye knocks Bluto into a hay baler, then launches himself into the air and catches Olive as she falls. The two drift to earth on a lawn chair to which Popeye has attached an umbrella.

Olive Oyl for President (1948)

Director: I. Sparber. *Animation:* Tom Johnson, John Gentilella. *Story:* Joe Stultz, Larry Riley. *Scenics:* Tom Ford. *Music:* Winston Sharples.

A great cartoon, even though it doesn't contain violence — unless you count Olive braining Popeye with a frying pan, or Cupid using a machine gun to shoot arrows of love into the Elephants and Donkeys of Congress so that they will agree with each other. There's also no love triangle, though Olive does have a handsome male secretary sit on her lap. Olive is cute at the beginning of the film, and when she appears before Congress, she's utterly gorgeous.

During election season, Popeye — "Mr. Sensitivity and Supporting Boyfriend" as always — mocks out Olive for her idea that America needs a woman President. And he really goes into a laughing fit when she starts to say what she would do if she were President.

Most of the rest of the cartoon shows us what life would be like under Chief Executive Olive Oyl, as she sings *If I Were President* and lays down rhyming stanzas. Most of Olive's campaign promises and proposed legislation have to do with dogs, kids (Little Audrey has a cameo), romance, sex, love, beautifying the world in various ways, nylon stockings, movie stars, getting people married, holidays, women's advancement, and helping everyone to get along. It's all charming and humorous and gives us a good look inside the mind of the character.

Popeye sees the error of his ways and campaigns for her as she rides in a parade dressed as the Statue Of Liberty.

Wigwam Whoopee (1948)

Director: I. Sparber. *Animation:* Tom Johnson, William Henning. *Story:* I. Klein, Jack Mercer. *Scenics:* Robert Connavale. *Music:* Winston Sharples.

Pilgrim Popeye comes to the New World to find a bride. Fortunately for him, curvy and leggy Indian maiden Olive Oyl is taking a shower in a waterfall. When they meet, she first tries to run away and to shoot him with her bow and arrow. Through a series of circumstances that can only happen in an animated cartoon, they wind up kissing instead. Olive decides, "Pale Puss heap hep!"

Meanwhile Big Chief Shmohawk, Olive's current boyfriend, is fantasizing about her, the smoke from his pipe forming a belly-dancing image of the shapely miss. When he spies Popeye and Olive kissing, he tries to do Popeye in, but Olive introduces the pilgrim as her new boyfriend, and Popeye bests the chief in a show of strength. But please note that Popeye is the interloper in this film. He's the guy stealing another's girlfriend. When Bluto does this kind of thing, he's called a villain!

The chief resorts to guile. On the pretense of having a welcoming ceremony for Popeye, the chief has Popeye bound to a stake, and then merrily sprays gasoline around him and lights it. Creepy music is heard. Popeye still doesn't catch onto the fact that he's in trouble! Not very bright, is he? Olive tries to save him, but the chief grabs her and says, "Ah, My Little Sugar, come have tea in my teepee!" Olive breaks away and is pursued by her former paramour all over the village.

It's Olive's cries for help that finally cause a sweating, worried Popeye to take action. (Why was he waiting?) He eats spinach and his toenail becomes a pair of scissors and cut his bonds. (Yuck! Gross! I can't make stuff like this up!)

The flames are afraid of the revitalized Popeye and run away. Popeye then defeats the tribe by hitting all of its members so hard that they turn into Indian

Head Pennies, and the chief so hard that he turns into a Buffalo Nickel. The cartoon closes with Popeye, as the new chief, kissing Olive, while this film's version of The Little Gnome Guy tries to cut off Popeye's hair with a hatchet. The hair breaks the hatchet instead. That Popeye must be murder on barbers and nail clippers!

Pre-Hysterical Man (1948)

Director: Seymour Kneitel. *Animation:* Dave Tendlar, Morey Reden. *Story:* Carl Meyer, Jack Mercer. *Scenics:* Anton Loeb. *Music:* Winston Sharples.

Another non-Bluto antagonist, the Pre-Hysterical Man, is shown here with his pinup girls.

Olive Oyl is drawn plainer and more cartoony throughout most of this cartoon than she usually is in the Famous Studios films. Still, there are fans that feel she's super attractive, and even "hot," in this cartoon. It's because of her personality, movements, and mannerisms. This is good news for anyone who has been "drawn" plainer than other folks by The Creator. You can still have the sex appeal that comes from within.

Anthropologist Popeye (?!?!) and his companion, Olive Oyl, are at the highest point in Yellowstone Park, 24,000 1/4 feet above sea level. Giddy and invigorated by the mountain air, Olive asks Popeye to take her picture. Looking into his camera's viewfinder, Popeye tells her to step back a little, a little bit more, and a little bit more, until he's talked her right off the edge of a cliff! When Olive realizes she's falling, she converts her nylon stockings into parachutes and drifts downward.

We and the orchestra precede her and see that she won't land at ground level, but will fall into a deep crevasse that has a "Land That Time Forgot" at its bottom. Inside a cave there, a muscular man is using a water-powered stone phonograph to play a romantic version of *To Each His Own*, while he carves pinup girls into stone slabs. He drools over one. Hearts burst out of him as he hugs his creation and kisses it, but unfortunately his dream is dashed when the slab turns to rubble. He despairs as his dream girl disintegrates. Our sympathy is with the poor guy who desperately wants a mate.

As if on cue, Olive drops into the valley. She doesn't immediately call for help, but looks for a way out herself. Olive is very resourceful in this cartoon. "Oh, here's a stairway!" she says in a positive, hopeful, sexy voice. But actually, she's climbing the scales up the back of a dinosaur that opens its mouth wide to greet her. She calls for help from Popeye, but he can't hear her and doesn't even yet realize she's missing.

The caveman does heed the call and has a wolf reaction to Ms. Oyl, his eyes turning to hearts and revolving like a slot machine until they come up double peaches. He then saves Ms. Oyl by grabbing the beast's tail and pulling it to straighten out its scales, so Olive can slide down its back. Olive is smitten by her savior and strikes a seductive pose. The caveman bops her over the head with his club, which is how the old joke tells us prehistoric men chose, and proposed to, their mates. A giddy Olive springs up in the air, forming hearts with her arms, hands, legs, and feet. It's as though she herself is a gigantic symbol of love. "Isn't he wonderful?" Then she leans into him. They give each other joyous, expectant looks which leave no doubt about what comes next.

Now Popeye finally notices that Olive's gone. He realizes she fell off the cliff (at his instruction, I might add). He grabs an umbrella and jumps into the void himself saying, "Wow! I hopes Olive ain't overexposed!"

Not yet, Popeye, but she's getting there! She's let down her delicious long hair for the caveman, and he's dragging her by it back to his place. Olive half-sits, half-lays behind him playing "He loves me, he loves me not" with a daisy and acting like she's totally love-besotted. One of her high heels is teasingly part of the way off. Popeye calls out and asks her if she's "hoited." She laughs and replies in a feminine voice, "Of course not, You Silly. A real caveman saved me!" Popeye panics, "A caveman!" He speeds in front of the caveman to stop the "wedding procession." But the caveman simply walks over top of him, still dragging Olive along. Popeye is no match for this guy!

As the couple reaches the cave, Popeye again intervenes. He and the caveman get caught up in an impromptu game of baseball, as only cartoon characters can. By sheer dumb luck, Popeye wins, and so he starts to leave with Olive. But the caveman grabs her, and he and Popeye play tug-of-war with her body and trade blows until the caveman slingshots Popeye away. He then carries Olive into his cave and puts a boulder across its entrance, locking Popeye out.

He's also locking Olive in. As a worried Miss, surrounded by pictures of sexy girls, looks on, he turns a literal skeleton key, made of a dinosaur's bone, in a gigantic lock. She tells him to let her out as she backs away. Then she turns to flee, but he hungrily grabs her hair. He pulls her off her feet and toward him in the air, to be used as a kissing yo-yo. But both he and Olive open their mouths wide as they are coming together and pucker up for openmouthed kisses at a time when such things were routinely censored in films. When Olive's lips hit his, their faces mush together, and then continue in on each other, until man and woman appear to merge into one being. Then, catching Olive's derriere in his hand, the caveman pushes Olive out so that he can pull her in again, and the process is endlessly repeated. Their lips stretch and cling to one another each time by suction, or maybe because they don't really want to let go, before coming apart with a loud pop. We're probably supposed to believe that Olive is stunned and overcome and overpowered and can't resist. But she's not yelling for help, and she seems to even be cooperating! So, at some level, maybe this kissing spree isn't entirely against her wishes, and she must be enjoying it, at least somewhat. The orchestra is positively jolly about it all. Impossible, exaggerated, and slapstick elements notwithstanding, this is still a scene that would have caused movie screens to burst into flames when it was shown in theaters. It's hot!

The music turns more desperate and ominous as Popeye is tunneling his way into the cave. Then it gets even more agitated, as the hungry caveman with enormous lips has grabbed a worried Olive in his massive hands and is about to give her an all-consuming kiss. Popeye comes up under Olive, knocking her out of the way. The caveman kisses Popeye by mistake instead. He then throws Popeye against the bottom of his stone Murphy Bed, which falls out of the wall to crush The Sailorman. The caveman is now happily chasing Olive around his apartment. She runs up onto the bed. (Note to Olive, when being pursued by a wolf, it's probably not a good idea to end up in his bed!) This causes the bed to snap back up into the recess in the wall, just as the caveman reaches it, so that he kisses the flattened, two-dimensional Popeye instead of Olive. Furious, he literally peels the unconscious, or dead, squashed Popeye off the bottom of the bed and then, as funeral music plays, scrunches and crushes and rips and mangles Popeye to the sound effect of dead leaves rustling or paper being wadded up, so that Popeye doesn't even resemble a human any more, but a small amorphous wad of trash. The caveman then stuffs the wad into the spinach can which had been squeezed out of Popeye's shirt. But the orchestra doesn't view this as a sign of hope. Instead, it continues to mourn as the caveman tosses the can over to where a dinosaur is grazing.

A triumphant, but threatening, prehistoric theme plays on the soundtrack as the caveman pulls the bed down again. After all, he finally has Olive literally in bed! Or does he? It turns out she's been knocked through the wall of the cave.

The spinach can now seems to be pathetically struggling. Maybe Popeye is not deceased yet, though the orchestra believes he is. The can's movements attract the attention of the dinosaur. It scoops the can up with its tongue and then begins chowing down, munching away to the sounds of metal being crushed. The Popeye theme stops.

Meanwhile, the caveman has tracked Olive to a waterfall. She lets out an ultra-sexy sneeze, probably one of the sexiest ever recorded, and he realizes she's hiding behind the waterfall. He dives in, and they both begin frantically swimming up the waterfall.

The dinosaur is still chewing away, but Popeye's head sticks out of the side of its mouth. Popeye is eating spinach and his triumph music begins. But as he swallows, so does the dinosaur! However, Popeye springs back to his normal shape partway down the dinosaur's throat. Then he walks back up and pries its mouth open. Popeye zooms over to the waterfall and snaps it like it was a whip, sending the caveman and Olive flying.

Ms. Oyl lands on the nose of the hungry dinosaur, but Popeye super-throws it into a rock wall, making it "Exstink."

The film ends with Popeye and Olive hugging and driving away, towing a cage containing the caveman, who is now carving fruit. He laughs, looks at us, and says, "Women is the cwaziest people!"

Popeye Meets Hercules (1948)

Director: Bill Tytla. *Animation:* George Germanetti, Tom Moore. *Story:* I. Klein. *Scenics:* Robert Connavale. *Music:* Winston Sharples.

Father Time marches backwards to take us to ancient Greece where Popeye and Olive Oyl are in the stadium to watch the first Olympic Games. The Greek gods, in a scene that creeped me out as a kid, are watching from the clouds. Popeye and Olive share a hotdog without using hands, so they end up kissing. They also share a soda pop using two straws. This ends with the bottle inside Olive's mouth and Popeye laughing. Over the PA system — a huge megaphone — the star contestant and champion of champions, Hercules, is introduced. He rides into the stadium in a chariot pulled by teams of magnificent white horses. His attendants remove his boxing robe, revealing his super-muscular physique, as sexy music begins on the sound track. Every pretty young woman in the stadium, including Olive, swoons, shimmies, squeals, faints, and contorts, as they are in the presence of the demigod.

As Hercules displays his biceps, a cute-faced Olive literally sends her heart out to him, flying on angel's wings. Tender music plays as the heart, with a very feminine face, winks at Hercules, giving him the "Come here, Big Boy," signal. He goes over to Olive and tenderly takes her hand. Popeye tries to butt in, but Hercules just kicks him away without a thought. Then Herc goes to town, repeatedly kissing Olive's hand and giving her literal goose pimples. The enraptured Olive's face is very pretty.

Then Hercules issues a challenge for anyone to do the things he can do. A visible yellow streak goes through the crowd. However, Popeye accepts the challenge. Hercules then proceeds to pound Popeye into the ground using only his chest. Herc keeps two elephants from running off by holding onto their tails. Their skins finally come off, and their skeletons flee in panic. Popeye, for his part, punches a pride of lions into the mouth of the last one in line, then he uses the stuffed lion as a basketball. Olive throws him a kiss, which angers Hercules. Next is the discus throw. Hercules does a stratospheric toss and then traps Popeye between two discs as though The Sailorman were a piece of meat on a plate. But Popeye has disappeared, as only cartoon characters can, and pops up inside Hercules' skimpy workout tunic. In a scene that's uncomfortable in more ways than one, Popeye keeps submerging himself inside Hercules' clothing, while the big guy tries to find him.

As a worried version of Popeye's theme plays, Popeye goes to toss a javelin. Hercules catches ahold of it as Popeye lets go though, and it's Popeye himself who flies up into the air. Then Hercules super-throws his own javelin so that it goes through Popeye's tunic, effectively pinning Popeye to it, and soars past the gods like a rocket into outer space, and deposits a hopeless and helpless Popeye on the moon as spooky, doomed, otherworldly music plays. Popeye has no way to get home!

Back on Earth, Herc puts the moves on Olive. "Ah, My Little Goddess, come with me to the Colosseum!" But Olive, appalled at what he's done to Popeye, runs away. She uses the giant megaphone to call to Popeye for help.

On the moon, Popeye prays to the goddess of spinach, Spinachia, who looks like Popeye wearing a wig but has a fantastic female body. (Okay, now the viewers are definitely freaked out!) She feeds Popeye the green stuff, and he morphs into a rocket and blasts back to Earth.

Hercules is carrying Olive away. "Save me, Popeye!" she yells. Hercules replies, "I'll save ya — for myself!" (Great line!) But Popeye arrives and pounds him down to a shrimpy size.

The film ends with Popeye and Olive kissing while riding a centaur, and then putting blinders on him so he can't watch them smooch.

Spinach vs. Hamburgers (1948)

Director: Seymour Kneitel. *Animation:* Al Eugster, Tom Moore. *Story:* Bill Turner, Larz Bourne. *Scenics:* Tom Ford. *Music:* Winston Sharples.

In order to get them to eat spinach at his eatery, Popeye shows his nephews clips from *The Anvil Chorus Girl*, *Pop-Pie A La Mode*, and *She-Sick Sailors*. The boys finally do consume the green veggie, but use their newfound strength to bind Popeye and Olive to a lamppost with a ship's anchor and chain. Then the nephews happily eat hamburgers at Wimpy's restaurant.

Robin Hood-Winked (1948)

Director: Seymour Kneitel. *Animation:* Tom Johnson, Frank Endres. *Story:* Larz Bourne, Tom Golden. *Scenics:* Robert Little. *Music:* Winston Sharples.

Popeye is Robin Hood in this cartoon. He and Little John visit Olive Oyl's pub. Bluto is the Sheriff of Nottingham-like tax collector. We see him literally shake down an old man, even knocking the gold tooth out of the man's head. When Bluto enters Olive's place to collect taxes, she and Popeye are snuggling cheek-to-cheek. Bluto sees the cute Miss, and his heart morphs into a wolf's head, giving out a howl. He comes on to her saying, "For a pretty wench such as thou, ye taxes I'd forgettin'— and how!" Tickling her under her chin, he goes to tenderly kiss her, but of course Popeye interrupts. The two men compete in archery for her hand, and Popeye wins. Bluto offers Popeye a congratulatory drink, but actually he slips him a potent Mickey Finn. We see Popeye's internal mental works get destroyed, and Popeye goes stiff as a board, falling on the brass rail, and denting it, under the bar.

The lustful Bluto carries the curvy, struggling Olive Oyl off to his castle. Little John makes an unconscious Popeye eat spinach, though, and soon Popeye is speeding along in pursuit. In the castle Bluto orders his armored guards to attack Popeye. Popeye turns them into an iron stove. As Bluto carries Olive up a long, spiral staircase, presumably to his bedchamber, Olive cries out a farewell, sounding like she's about to be ravished against her will, and all is lost. But Popeye spins the staircase into the ground, bops Bluto, and forces the collector to be a beast of burden as they return the taxes to the people.

This cartoon contains a major blooper. In one scene, Bluto has no legs!

Popeye's Premiere (1949)

Director: Uncredited. *Animation:* Dave Tendlar, John Gentilella. *Story:* Bill Turner, I. Klein. *Scenics:* Uncredited. *Music:* Winston Sharples.

A cheater cartoon made up mostly of footage from the Fleischer film, *Aladdin and His Wonderful Lamp*.

Popeye and Olive attend the film's premiere, and Popeye drives the audience crazy by overreacting to his own movie. Once again, The Sailorman proves to be a jerk. Olive is attractive in her evening wear and is beautifully coy when wrapped in fur in the limousine, though.

Lumberjack And Jill (1949)

Director: Seymour Kneitel. *Animation:* Tom Johnson, George Rufle. *Story:* Carl Meyer, Jack Mercer. *Scenics:* Tom Ford. *Music:* Winston Sharples.

At Popeye and Bluto's lumber camp, Popeye's eagerly awaiting the arrival of the new cook because he says he's working up an appetite. Bluto replies lasciviously, "Yeah, so am I," but he's talking about a different kind of hunger, as evidenced by the fact that he's carving the face of a pretty girl into a tree. Olive Oyl, the cook, arrives and, after pinning Popeye's neck to a tree with two axes, Bluto is the first to greet her. She's thrilled and smitten by the big guy. But she sweetly and cheerfully greets Popeye, too. Bluto, though, propels all her equipment into Popeye's arms, so The Sailorman has to lug everything to the kitchen, while Bluto escorts Olive arm-in-arm. *Love In Bloom* plays on the soundtrack.

When they get to the kitchen, Bluto claims it's "kind of cozy…just big enough for TWO," and he slams the door shut on Popeye. In a hot scene, Bluto directs Olive's attention to a cabinet, and then, as he hungrily gazes at her body, he puts his arms around her, and his hands on the handles of the drawer she's standing in front of. He pulls out the impossibly long drawer explaining that it's where she can keep her pots, but what he's really doing is drawing her close and laying her back in the drawer as though it was a bed. Of course, Olive is delighted when she realizes what's happening. The music goes all quiet and tender as Bluto moves in for a kiss. At the last possible second, Popeye enters and interrupts. But Olive's pots and pans were all mangled in the crash with the door. She thinks Popeye caused it.

Bluto and Popeye bash each other over the heads with cooking utensils in order to pop the instruments back into shape. Then they compete to bring firewood to Olive. Popeye gets back first, but Bluto pours gas through the chimney as Popeye is lighting the stove. The stove blows apart in the tremendous, resulting explosion. A furious Olive Oyl, who thinks Popeye is the culprit, orders him to fix it. This will be nearly impossible and will keep Popeye busy forever.

In the meantime, Bluto says he will show Olive around the camp. Which means, of course, that in the next scene they are in a canoe, he's serenading her with *Love In Bloom*, and she's swooning into a huge comfy pillow. The two are alone, in the mood, and Popeye definitely won't appear. But the cartoon's creators, continuing their misguided mission to keep the couple apart, have a beaver get angry after being awakened from a nap and gnaw the canoe in two. Olive's half is heading for a waterfall as exciting music plays. She yells for help, and Popeye and Bluto both come to her rescue, riding logs. They each grab one of her stretching arms, and then she's sprung clear of the river by a supple tree. She flies through the air to become embedded in another tree. Popeye works to saw her down, but

Bluto punches him out of the way and catches the slice of tree that contains an immobilized Olive. Saying, "How about a kiss, Babe?" he goes for it. But Popeye has flown back into the scene and accidentally knocks Olive and her wood block out of his hands, so Bluto ends up kissing Popeye by mistake instead!

But Olive is now traveling down a log flume which leads to a giant operating buzz saw, and she needs rescuing again. Bluto smashes Popeye through the flume so that his head is sticking up out of it. A log is heading right for him! Popeye yells in alarm, then eats spinach and turns his head into an axe.

Meanwhile, Bluto makes a grab for Olive, but the bark of the piece of wood she's encased in comes off in his hands instead, and Olive continues her dangerous journey. (Yes, Bluto has peeled off Olive's outer covering, in a sense.) Popeye makes the scene and belts him away and socks the saw off its moorings, just as it's about to make Olive be beside herself. The saw then chases Bluto out of the county, every once in a while cutting up his rear and back. Yeow!

In the cook house, Olive is serving biscuits. Popeye is happy and content. Never once in this cartoon was he romantic toward Olive. He just wanted to get her set up in the kitchen so the food would start coming. When Popeye bites into a biscuit, all of his teeth shatter. He laughs as though the joke's on him. The cook can't cook after all. So what's he going to do with her now? Play *Tiddledewinks*? He has no interest in her as a woman! Where's Bluto when we need him?

Hot Air Aces (1949)

Director: I. Sparber. *Animation:* Al Eugster, Bill Hudson. *Story:* I. Klein. *Scenics:* Robert Connavale. *Music:* Winston Sharples.

Olive Oyl inexplicably has no romantic interest in the handsome Bluto in this cartoon, but loyally roots for Popeye in an around-the-world air race. Olive's kiss energizes The Sailorman. But Bluto gets the chance for some loving, too, as he briefly woos a pretty French miss atop the Eiffel Tower.

Olive helps a stunned Popeye start the race after Bluto sabotages him. After lightning hits Popeye's little plane, it can keep up with Bluto's jet. But Bluto finally removes the engine from Popeye's plane, causing it, and The Sailorman, to crash into a mountain and then sink beneath the sea. Popeye finds a crate of spinach on the ocean floor, transforms himself into a magnet to pull his plane back together, and uses spinach cans for his engine's pistons. He then literally burns by Bluto's jet and wins the race. His cockpit is full of water, though, so when Olive goes to kiss him, she gets a jumping fish instead. Popeye laughs about it. What is wrong with this guy, laughing instead of crying over a missed kiss from Olive?

A Balmy Swami (1949)

Director: I. Sparber. *Animation:* Tom Johnson, George Rufle. *Story:* Carl Meyer, Jack Mercer. *Scenics:* Anton Loeb. *Music:* Winston Sharples.

Popeye and Olive are together at a theater, but they aren't really on the same page. Popeye enjoys a trained seal act, while Olive is bored. Then she goes totally crazy over "The Magical Hypnotist" (Bluto playing a role), while Popeye disdains the act. Olive leaps up into the air, whistling and bringing her legs together and apart, while displaying a great body. Then she cheers and swoons saying, "Love that man!" The magician has a wolf reaction to her, in which his turban springs up and his eyeballs act out for us exactly what he's thinking. He knows he and the buxom and curvy brunette have fallen for each other, and that when he gets her alone, he'll pull the shades down and make love to her.

He conjures up a bouquet of flowers for her. And then he snatches Popeye up as a "volunteer" in his act. The magician humiliates Popeye to the delight of the members of the crowd (and, truth be told, us viewers), who want the handsome hypnotist and Olive to get together. At one point, he chokes Popeye, causing a deck of cards to pour out of The Sailorman's mouth. It's literally a gag-inducing scene.

The magician hypnotizes willing subject Olive Oyl into pretending to be a diving beauty, and she unconsciously shows off her shapely rear in the process. Then he commands the pretty sleepwalker, "Approach me, My Sweet!" She does so with arms wide open. But Popeye speeds over, grabs her, and turns her around. Olive is now headed out the stage door in the wings. After Popeye threatens him, the magician literally shoots daggers out of his eyes to pin Popeye to a board. Again, the crowd goes wild for the magician. But the magician sees Olive has gone out the door and is walking into a dangerous construction site. He speeds off to save her. Please note: Popeye put Olive in harm's way, and the magician is the one who notices her plight and first attempts a rescue. Popeye pulls himself free to follow.

As Olive walks along steel girders at dizzying heights, the boys race to be the one to be her salvation. The magician conjures a brick wall in the path of Popeye. Popeye slams into it. The orchestra congratulates the magician and mocks The Sailorman. Next, Popeye attempts to propel himself upward using a tank of compressed air. He gets himself temporarily knocked out by embedding his head in a girder for his troubles. His eyes spin around like a slot machine and, when they stop, rivets come pouring out of his mouth.

Meanwhile, Olive walks off the end of a girder and begins falling through space. Fortunately, the magician reaches out and grabs her. Then he announces, "And now, I shall awaken the miss with a kiss!" Oh Boy! He's holding a hypnotized Olive, Popeye's nowhere in sign, he's puckering up, and nothing can interrupt the magic moment! So he tenderly kisses her — on the cheek?!?!?! Evidently, the creators chickened out, or maybe they wanted to let the sexual tension continue to build. Olive comes out of her trance, sees where she is, and, not realizing which of the guys endangered her and which just saved her life, tries to get away from him. If Olive only knew, maybe things could have ended differently.

Popeye hooks her with a crane, but obviously can't operate it because, after a series of complications, Olive winds up dangling from the site's highest point by the strap of her shoe. Perhaps wising up, or being desperate, she calls out for help from "somebody." Popeye and the magician have a short, but furious, fist fight that Popeye loses. The magician punches him into an elevator, conjures giant scissors to cut its rope, and sends Popeye plunging speedily to his doom. But Popeye manages to eat his spinach and transform his arms into airbrakes before he splats into the ground. He then rescues Olive, punches the magician, steals his turban, and conjures up the seal act to keep balancing and twirling the magician like a ball. This time Olive loves the act. And Popeye, the man who gained the competence and powers from spinach that the magician had naturally, and who never acted romantically toward Olive once in the entire film other than to be jealous, and who endangered her, takes his bows and gets the girl. Happy ending?

Tar With A Star (1949)

Director: Bill Tytla. *Animation:* George Germanetti, Steve Muffatti. *Story:* Carl Meyer, Jack Mercer. *Scenics:* Uncredited. *Music:* Winston Sharples.

Popeye comes upon a tough old West town that has a spot reserved in its cemetery for the new sheriff. The Sailorman takes the job and is able to keep law and order using his super-strength. He relaxes at the saloon where singer Olive Oyl is performing. But then, Wild Bill Bluto rides in, shooting the place up. When the outlaw spots Olive, he wants more than just a drink.

Popeye proves to be completely ineffectual at stopping him. At one point, Bluto snatches the star off of Popeye's chest, grinds it to powder, blows it onto Popeye, and uses his fist to pile drive Popeye to the floor, turning The Sailorman into a spittoon, and then Bluto kicks the spittoon away. At another, he uses Popeye's mouth as pliers to cut the manacles and chains off that the new sheriff put on him. Bluto has no finesse when it comes to wooing, though. He just wants to grab Olive and have his way with her. She understandably wants none of it.

Bluto finally launches Popeye through the roof of the saloon and into the waiting grave which fills with dirt. A sign over it says, "Sheriff Popeye Retired Saturday – 11th," while a funeral march plays. A creepy scene, especially for young viewers!

Olive locks herself in a safe, while Bluto proceeds to try and demolish it. A buried Popeye's pipe surfaces and enables him to eat his spinach and, of course, the day is saved.

Olive Oyl, inexplicably for a cartoon at this late date, reverts to a more Fleischeresque appearance. And Bluto, while still muscular, has a more generically cartoony face than usual, especially at the end of the film. The romance in the film is practically nil, though there are some provocative lines. Bluto says he wants to make with the close harmony while Olive's hiding in a piano. She screams that he's soft-pedaling her. While in the safe, she begs to be left alone, claiming she has no interest in this bank.

Silly Hillbilly (1949)

Director: I. Sparber. *Animators:* Tom Johnson, Frank Enders. *Story:* I. Klein. *Scenics:* Robert Little. *Music:* Winston Sharples.

Though the creators gave hillbilly Olive a shapely body and pretty legs in this cartoon, they couldn't resist adding in the trademark big feet.

Hillbilly Bluto is sleeping by a picture of his girlfriend Olive. His snoring causes her dress to billow up a la Marilyn Monroe, and she has great legs. Olive, I mean, not Marilyn. But Marilyn did, too, of course. Well, let's move on. The picture comes to life and secures the dress to the wall with a nail, protecting Olive's modesty. The O.O.O.P.S. factor is in full force in this cartoon, as Olive's in the kind of clothes we saw Daisy Mae in the comic strips, and Ellie May Clampett in *The Beverly Hillbillies*, wearing.

We see Olive, singing and prancing as she joyfully hangs up her laundry. She has a cute face, a curvy figure, a shapely derriere, and those knockout legs again.

Popeye the traveling salesman brings his impossibly huge traveling department store to hill country. Bluto begins innocently wrecking the place because he, being a fish out of water, doesn't understand what most of the merchandise is.

But Olive arrives, gets a wolf reaction out of Popeye, and visits his beauty parlor. She calls it a "beautifying saloon." There are a bunch of make-up gags, and then Olive and Popeye wind up tickling each other. Olive tells Bluto she's not his gal any more. Popeye is her new boyfriend. So Popeye is the one stealing another's girlfriend in this film.

Bluto challenges Popeye to some slapstick tests of strength. Popeye keeps besting him, until Bluto takes a huge mallet and smashes Popeye into a flat, circular target on the ground. He then hangs the Popeye target on a tree and calls his kin to target practice. They barrage the target, and we see the bullets hitting Popeye!

Meanwhile Bluto is chasing Olive through the store. At one point, Olive bounces on a bed. Bluto sucks her, and half the store, up in a vacuum cleaner. But, by now, Popeye has eaten his spinach. He saves the day, as Bluto is opening the bag to have his way with the trapped cutie. Popeye leaves Bluto underwater, encased in a washing machine. Olive, wearing a chandelier, kisses Popeye and lights up.

Olive is a living doll throughout this cartoon!

Barking Dogs Don't Fite (1949)

Director: I. Sparber. *Animation:* Tom Johnson, John Gentilella. *Story:* Carl Meyer, Jack Mercer. *Scenics:* Tom Ford. *Music:* Winston Sharples.

A cute and curvy, enthusiastic, singing Olive Oyl gives her poodle Frenchy a bath and then asks Popeye to take him for a walk. Popeye refuses. He doesn't want to be seen with a "sissy dorg." (Note to Popeye: You probably won't win points with a lady by insulting her dog.) But Olive must be pretty persuasive, because we next see Popeye walking Frenchy.

Bluto and his bulldog Killer approach. In this cartoon, Bluto seems to be the town bully, terrorizing and murdering seemingly with impunity. Bluto feeds Frenchy to Killer, but the poodle escapes and the bulldog bites its own tongue. Then begins the sort of cat-and-mouse…er, dog-and-dog chase you'd see in cartoons from other studios. Finally, Frenchy hits the brick wall that is Killer's face, and Killer uses the unconscious poodle as a pogo stick. When Popeye tries to intervene, Bluto wraps him in an iron lamppost and uses him for a punching bag. Killer likewise uses Frenchy. The unconscious Popeye and Frenchy are knocked flat into a hole in the highway and then have the contents of a barrel of tar bury them. Bluto and Killer approach them driving a steamroller. (I guess Killer was aptly named!)

But Popeye and Frenchy both eat spinach and lift the machine as it rolls over the top of them. Popeye punches it, and Bluto, away. The machine turns into a stove, roasting a fleeing Bluto. Killer is also on the run — from Frenchy.

Popeye gleefully feeds more coal into Bluto's fire! Frenchy bites Killer's tail and then smashes him with a manhole cover. Killer squeezes out of one of the holes, having been turned into a string of living sausages!

Popeye and Frenchy now bond as only males who have utterly crushed their enemies can. I think Popeye, Frenchy, Bluto, and Killer would have made good Klingons.

The Fly's Last Flight (1949)

Director: Seymour Kneitel. *Animation:* Tom Johnson, Frank Endres. *Story:* Larz Bourne. *Scenics:* Tom Ford. *Music:* Winston Sharples.

If seeing Popeye go crazy because he can't get any sleep is your idea of a good time, you're welcome to this cartoon. A fly totally bedevils him, then eats spinach in order to beat him up, electrocute him, poison him, and drop a piano on him. The fly forces Popeye to destroy his own house using a shotgun. Then the fly and his buddies square dance on Popeye's noggin as the sailor goes insane. An utterly unpleasant film which may show, once again, that the creators secretly hated Popeye.

How Green Is My Spinach (1950)

Director: Seymour Kneitel. *Animation:* Tom Johnson, William Henning. *Story:* I. Klein. *Scenics:* Lloyd Hallock, Jr.. *Music:* Winston Sharples.

This cartoon begins by supposedly showing us clips from Popeye cartoons in which The Sailorman eats spinach to escape from, and defeat, Bluto. Actually the cartoons don't exist, and the clips were invented for this film.

Bluto cries because every time he is about to "murder" Popeye — and he seems to mean this literally — Popeye eats spinach and clobbers him. This scene helps to reinforce the idea that what happens in cartoons is real to those starring in them. But then Bluto gets an idea. "No more spinach and no more Popeye!" Bluto, along with the viewers, knows that Popeye is completely helpless without the green stuff.

So, Bluto concocts a poisonous spray that destroys all the spinach in the world. He then squashes Popeye into a pancake by flexing his pectoral muscles. A panicked Popeye eats broccoli, but The Sailorman's arm muscles just droop. An evilly laughing Bluto flexes his own arm, and we see that in Bluto's case, even his muscles literally have muscles — and he doesn't need enhancement from any outside source. Popeye eats a sample of every vegetable in the supermarket and then punches the chin Bluto offers him. Popeye's arm folds like an accordion on impact. Bluto then proceeds to beat Popeye to death! He literally sweeps the floor with Popeye and rains blows upon him, and then hits Popeye with the kitchen sink. These visual puns are meant to be funny, but they're just unpleasant. Bluto jumps up and down on Popeye. An announcer wonders if this is truly the end of Popeye and asks, "Is there a can of spinach in the house?"

Sure enough, a young lad in a movie theater watching the cartoon has one in his grocery bag. He tosses it into the movie screen to Popeye. Popeye eats it, turns into multiple Popeyes, knocks Bluto silly, and uses the big guy as a beast of burden on a farm to plant more spinach.

Gym Jam (1950)

Director: I. Sparber. *Animation:* Tom Johnson, John Gentilella. *Story:* Carl Meyer, Jack Mercer. *Scenics:* Anton Loeb. *Music:* Winston Sharples.

There's lots of lust and sex in this cartoon, but precious little romance. Bluto spots Olive Oyl, who has a curvy derriere and shapely legs, out jogging. He has a wolf reaction, then snatches her around her waist demanding, "C'mon, Doll, howzabout a kiss!" Popeye saves the struggling miss, and Bluto tries to follow them into Popeye's gym, but finds out it's Ladies Day.

Not one to be easily deterred, he shaves and disguises himself as a big blonde woman. As he sashays into the gymnasium, Popeye has a wolf reaction to her... er, him, and all but forgets about Olive Oyl. So much for Popeye being loyal to one woman! And, by the way, Popeye either needs glasses or eye surgery.

As Olive gets more and more jealous, Bluto either totally outdoes Popeye at everything The Sailorman tries to demonstrate, or finds ways to injure him. Bluto is the superior athlete to Popeye. Maybe he should be the one who's running a gym! Anyway, every time Olive is about to interrupt Bluto's flirting (!) with Popeye, the punching bag she's working out on thwarts her or tangles her up. It eventually winds up stuffed down the back of her pants! Bluto unhooks an exercise bike that Popeye's riding, and The Sailorman goes crashing through the wall of the gym. As Bluto starts to approach Olive for a kiss, Popeye arrives back at the gym by ambulance, using crutches and wearing a cast. Olive finally becomes trapped in a board that the punching bag was mounted on, and Bluto's wig comes off. He throws a barbell down on Popeye's broken foot, causing the sailor to scream in pain. Then Bluto punches Popeye into a steam cabinet, knocking him out, and knocking his spinach can away from him and onto the floor. As the orchestra convinces us that this is the end of Popeye and that the villain will have his way with Olive, Bluto turns the valve of the cabinet up full blast.

He then unhooks the board containing Olive and goes for the kiss. Judging from the sound effects, maybe he even gets one, as the two are hidden from our sight by the board. Olive's struggles finally free her from the board and Bluto, but she ends up suspended between two hanging rings as she's displaying spectacular legs. Bluto, above her and hanging from another rope, saws away on one of the ropes keeping Olive up. The music has switched to a menacing, saucy jazz number, signifying the sexual threat to Olive Oyl.

Meanwhile at the steam cabinet, an unconscious Popeye is still suffering, and the mournful version of his theme song is playing. The gauge for the cabinet climbs from "Not So Hot" to "Hot" to "Very Hot" to "That's All Brother," as an alarm bell sounds. Popeye has now turned completely red, and sweats, cooks, and shrinks, down to nothingness as he sinks into the cabinet. It certainly seems as though any future cartoons will feature only Bluto and Olive!

Speaking of whom, Bluto scores on Olive — at least in a sense, because he propels her through the rim of a basketball hoop. He then catches her outstretched hands in his as she falls, keeps her balanced in the air, and pulls her down to him and kisses her neck and cheek, raises her up again, pulls her down, and so on. Eventually Olive, not the massive-muscled Bluto, will tire and his lips will find more than just her neck and cheek.

But a mite of a Popeye exits the bottom of the steam cabinet, dives into the spinach can, and is restored. He knocks Bluto into a shelf with a sign above it reading, "DUMB-BELLS." Olive then does to Popeye what Bluto was doing to her, prompting the sailor to echo an old joke — "Don't! Stop! Don't! Stop! Don't! Stop! Don't Stop! Don't Stop! Don't Stop!"

Popeye Makes A Movie (1950)

Director: Seymour Kneitel. *Animation:* Tom Johnson, George Rufle. *Story:* I. Klein. *Scenics:* Robert Little. *Music:* Winston Sharples.

A cheater cartoon made up mostly of footage from the Fleischer film, *Popeye The Sailor Meets Ali Baba's Forty Thieves.* Popeye's nephews come to the studio to watch him make that movie.

Baby Wants Spinach (1950)

Director: Seymour Kneitel. *Animation:* Al Eugster, Wm. B. Pattengill. *Story:* Carl Meyer, Jack Mercer. *Scenics:* Robert Owen. *Music:* Winston Sharples.

While in Popeye's care, Olive's infant cousin Swee'Pea wanders off, so it's up to The Sailorman to save him. Of course, in the process, Popeye gets hit by a streetcar, blasted by a ship's whistle, hung by his neck between the halves of an elevating bridge, and — at the zoo — sat on by an elephant, nearly swallowed by a lion, and chomped down on by an alligator. Finally, Swee'Pea accidentally ingests spinach and saves Popeye from a giant gorilla that is demolishing him and pounding him into the ground. The cartoon ends with Swee'Pea having made friends and playmates out of all the other dangerous animals. A tired, hurt, and disgusted Popeye is on the sidelines. After watching this cartoon, I know just how he feels.

Quick On The Vigor (1950)

Director: Seymour Kneitel. *Animation:* Tom Johnson, John Gentilella. *Story:* Carl Meyer, Jack Mercer. *Scenics:* Robert Owen. *Music:* Winston Sharples.

The creators kept coming up with ways to separate Popeye from his spinach.

Popeye and Olive are walking hand-in-hand at the carnival when a barker calls their attention to one of those "test your strength by propelling a piece of wood upwards to ring a bell" games. Olive says she loves strong men, so Popeye forgoes the mallet and uses his fist to win a box of candy. Then he keeps doing it again and again. Olive watches for awhile, but she has to be getting as bored as the viewers are because, when she hears an announcer say, "Introducing Bluto, The Strongest Man In The World," she lets her weakness guide her and goes over to where he is displaying his magnificent physique and making his muscles vibrate. Olive is smitten, as is Bluto who winks at her and strokes her under her chin saying, "My weakness is a pretty face!" Sexy music starts up on the soundtrack.

Having cleaned out the poor carny, Popeye, laden with candy boxes, finally realizes Olive is gone.

The sexy music continues as Bluto bends a girder into a heart shape and says, "Ya won me heart, Babe!" Laughing with delight, Olive responds, "Likewise, I'm sure!" But Popeye arrives, straightens out the girder, and uses his oddly shaped chin to turn it into multiple hearts. Sure, Popeye is strong, but why is he calling attention to one of his most unattractive, cartoony features? Still, Olive is impressed. The boys have a test of strength, culminating in a scared Popeye allowing Bluto to lock him in a safe in a doomed attempt to push it apart from the

The creators enhanced Olive's appeal whenever they wanted to. In the plane scene, they drew her with pretty legs.

inside. A mournful version of Popeye's theme plays. Bluto gives an evil laugh as he spins the safe's dial several times to mix up the tumblers. Then as Bluto strolls away with Olive, accompanied by more sexy and fun music, we get an interior shot of the safe and see that not even Popeye can do the impossible. At least not when the script says he can't.

Meanwhile, Bluto and Olive are enjoying themselves riding on the Ferris Wheel. When they get to the top, he stops it with his massive leg and says to Olive, "While they're fixing it, Toots, how about fixing me up with a kiss?" He grabs her. Stopping the Ferris Wheel and making Olive think it was broken was a smooth move, but Bluto certainly didn't show much finesse in going for the kiss. Olive rejects him and tries to get away. From her perspective, Bluto trapped her and wolfishly rushed things. From his, she did say the "Likewise, I'm sure" line. But at any rate, he certainly isn't going to respect her wishes, or her personhood, now! He just wants to have his way with her.

Back inside the safe, a defeated Popeye, having literally sweated up a pond, resignedly rests his head on his arm. But, hearing Olive's cries, he uses his pipe as a blowtorch and makes a hole in the wall of the safe. Reaching through it, he manipulates the tumblers and opens the door. His river of sweat comes pouring out. Popeye is free, but the thought of him drenched in sweat is kind of gross. Let's hope Olive has a head cold!

Popeye rips the axle of the Ferris Wheel away from the wheel itself in order to separate Bluto from Olive, but too late he realizes what he's done, as the gigantic wheel, with Olive still on it, rolls through the fairgrounds. Finally, we have been shown one of the consequences of Popeye's super-stunts!

The wheel suddenly stops when it hits a refreshment stand, and Olive goes flying through the air and into a plane ride. Her momentum breaks her plane loose from its moorings, so that she goes sailing over the park in it. Her spectacular legs stick out of the plane's floor and she displays some curves as she fights the wind resistance. Popeye runs to catch her, pulling out his spinach can, but Bluto beans him with a girder, embedding him in it before he can eat the green stuff.

Olive's plane collides with a roller coaster and, as a result, she's balanced on an axle and two wheels, careening along the track. Bluto is right behind her in a roller coaster car, the very picture of macho bravado and male single-mindedness. As she leans back while plunging down a steep incline, he leans forward to go for the kiss. Then they enter a tunnel and kissing sounds are heard. The orchestra seems happy about all of this. And the thought of kissing on a thrill ride is exhilarating, if only both the parties are willing. When Bluto emerges from the tunnel kissing the air, Olive, in a display of cartoon physics, is now behind him. He makes a grab for her as they each temporarily go off on separate tracks. When they come back together again, Bluto is once more behind Olive. Lustily, he pulls out a crosscut saw from between his legs. (Cartoon characters can do that.) And he begins moving it back and forth between Olive's legs, sawing her axle. Whether or not all of this symbolizes anything is open to debate by the fans. Olive's axle breaks in two, and now she's balancing by putting her hands on each half of the sundered axle, and fending Bluto off with her feet.

Popeye uses his pipe to eat his spinach and he rescues Olive just as Bluto is about to grab her for sure. He then punches Bluto up the track and into the test of strength game. Then, while Olive gushes, Popeye uses his flexing bicep to continually hit Bluto's head into the bell by propelling the wooden piece into it. Evidently Popeye believes torture is okay as long as he's the torturer.

Riot In Rhythm (1950)

Director: Seymour Kneitel. *Animation:* Tom Johnson, William Henning. *Story:* Seymour Kneitel. *Scenics:* Tom Ford. *Music:* Winston Sharples.

A remake of *Me Musical Nephews* (1942).

The Farmer and the Belle (1950)

Director: Seymour Kneitel. *Animation:* Tom Johnson, Frank Endres. *Story:* Joe Stultz. *Scenics:* Robert Little. *Music:* Winston Sharples.

Olive Oyl, working hard trying to raise a bucket of water from the well on her farm, says that it would be so nice to have a man around. Cue Popeye and Bluto who are driving by. They have wolf reactions to her — and so does their car! They see her "help wanted" sign, and Popeye says he's going to work. "Work your way outta dis, Buster!" Bluto snarls and stuffs Popeye under the hood of the car and turns on the engine.

Bluto then turns the crank on the well for Olive using only one finger. Then he tickles the impressed and smitten country Miss under her chin and dumps a bucket of water in an empty trough. Popeye, having been spit out of the car's exhaust, lifts the well right out of the ground and uses it to fill the trough. Then the two compete in cartoony, slapstick ways to get Olive to hire them by harvesting apples and shoeing horses. Finally, egg gathering will decide things. Popeye feeds a hen spinach, and she lays a huge mound of eggs. Olive says he's hired, but then sees Bluto trip Popeye up as he carries the mound. All of the eggs land on Bluto.

Popeye and Olive are standing in front of the barn, sharing a laugh at Bluto's expense. But Bluto, up in the loft, throws an anvil down on Popeye's head, embedding him in the ground. Then Bluto hooks Olive with a pulley system, eliciting a sexy, "Huh?" from her, and pulls her up to him. "I'm takin' that job — and you, too, Cutie!" he says. Olive dives into a haystack to escape him. He comes right on in after her. We see movement within the stack that reminds us of the old "a little roll in the hay" jokes, but all Bluto finds is a needle. Olive surfaces in another haystack. Bluto joins her. As he's thrashing around, Olive appears in yet another. He pops up right beside her, and she flees from the haystack with him in hot pursuit. Bluto actually runs over the anvil, pushing it further into the ground. Popeye manages to emerge, but is weakened and still has the anvil literally on his mind. He falls to the ground unconscious.

Olive, meanwhile, is trying to run up a log pile. Her lower half looks like it belongs to a blue jeans model. The logs fly out from under her feet and hit Bluto. But the pile is dwindling.

Luckily, the hen wants to return Popeye's favor and feeds Popeye spinach. The Sailorman runs over just as Bluto has captured Olive and is telling her, "Now I gotcha!" as he goes for the kiss. Popeye punches Bluto into the pigs' mud. But they snub him as Popeye and Olive laugh.

Thrill Of Fair (1951)

Director: Seymour Kneitel. *Animation:* Tom Johnson, John Gentilella. *Story:* Carl Meyer, Jack Mercer. *Scenics:* Tom Ford. *Music:* Winston Sharples.

At the fair, Olive is off to enter her piglet in the Livestock Show while Popeye watches Swee'Pea. The tyke tries to get his helium balloon to stretch like the India Rubber Man in a sideshow, but it sails away from him. Swee'Pea follows it, endangering himself and the pursuing Popeye at an archery range, a bell-ringing test of strength, and a prize bull's pen. When they go to a booth that has kewpie dolls for prizes, Popeye falls on one and thinks he's crushed Swee'Pea. It's a disturbing and sad scene, especially when a horrified Popeye picks up the limp doll, and its sand all runs out while it pathetically tries to say, "Mama." Then Swee'Pea goes on a high-wire and into a hay baler, with Popeye getting the worst of things, as usual. Swee'Pea trades his little balloon for a huge one used to give aerial rides. He undoes the valve and the balloon rockets into the air with him in its basket, and then plunges toward the ground. Eating spinach transforms Popeye into a rocket to save Swee'Pea. When Olive returns, Popeye has tied the gigantic balloon to Swee'Pea's baby carriage. It's the only way to stop the baby from crying.

Alpine For You (1951)

Director: I. Sparber. *Animation:* Steve Muffatti, George Germanetti. *Story:* Carl Meyer, Jack Mercer. *Scenics:* Robert Connavale. *Music:* Winston Sharples.

Popeye is taking Olive Oyl mountain climbing. She's wearing skimpy Alpine duds (O.O.O.P.S. alert!) and is cute, full of life, enthusiastic, and feeling reinvigorated by the scenery, the perfect day, and the mountain air. All of which spells trouble for Popeye, because Bluto the World Famous Mountain Guide spots her with his binoculars, has a wolf reaction, and says, "Ooo, la, la, la, la! Zis I'd like to guide!" Bluto's face is handsome and he looks powerful, but rather inexplicably at this stage in Famous Studios' game, he's drawn with a more Fleischeresque physique.

He speeds to Popeye and Olive, cuts the rope which keeps them in contact with each other and ties a boulder to the end attached to Popeye. Popeye strains to pull it up, thinking he's lifting Olive. The boulder flattens him. Meanwhile Bluto has pulled Olive up to himself and is saying that he's the guy to guide her. The smitten Miss Oyl agrees, telling Popeye who has made the scene, "I'd feel safer with a professional guide." (If she only knew!) Bluto attempts to punch Popeye away saying, "You heard her! She wants a guide!" Bluto and Olive begin strolling away arm-in-arm, with Olive showing off her curves. But Popeye comes swinging back on a rope and snatches her away.

Bluto then begins to sabotage Popeye's efforts to safely climb with Olive. He removes the head of Popeye's pickaxe, and the The Sailorman and Olive go plunging down the mountain until Popeye straps a pair of plungers on his feet. Olive is nearly impaled on a sharp peak! Olive is understandably furious at him. Next Bluto sets fire to a bridge the two are crossing. Then, as Popeye tries to save Olive from an eagle, Bluto puts roller skates on Popeye's feet. Popeye, with Olive attached by a rope, goes rolling down the mountain, and only hitting a warning sign keeps them from going right off the edge of a cliff. Olive declares that she's not moving until they get a guide. Bluto comes into the picture saying, "Ah, you are in safe hands now, My Little Mountain Flower!" She gives a dejected Popeye the brush-off, and she and Bluto happily go off together.

Time passes and we see Bluto leading a naive Olive Oyl into a cave by telling her, "Zis is a shortcut to ze top, Toots!" As they enter it and walk out of our sight, Olive asks in a sweet voice, "Isn't it too dark for sightseeing?" "All the better to make with the kisses!" he replies romantically. And he does! Olive then scrambles out of the cave, but she's still attached to Bluto by rope. He hauls her back to himself and kisses her on the lips again. She breaks away but is pulled back for another, and another, like she's a kissing yo-yo. Olive is helpless, and she's drawn with a shapely backside. The creators have evidently decided to let Bluto have his way with her.

Or have they? Popeye hears her cries, superspeeds to the couple, and he and Bluto engage in such a monumental (excuse the pun) battle that they end up carving Mt. Rushmore's presidents into the side of the mountain. As Popeye stands still and laughs about this, Bluto superpunches him miles away to land in a snowbank and be frozen stiff. Or maybe to be a frozen stiff. Bluto then chases Olive up and down mountains, and down through crevasses. If you can ignore the way Olive's legs stretch to accommodate the terrain, you'll see she has an hourglass figure. And Bluto has his decidedly male, well-developed physique again.

Before these two bodies can come together, a Saint Bernard digs Popeye out of the drift and is about to pour brandy into his pipe, when realization of who he is dawns. The dog whips out a Popeye comic book, then inserts spinach into the pipe instead. Popeye thaws and transforms into Super Mountain Man, complete with an appropriate outfit. He lassoes a peak and pulls it to him, just as Bluto is about to catch Olive. Popeye says, "A trip to the mountings'll cool ya off!" And he punches Bluto into another peak, the stars that appear from the impact go around the mountain to form Paramount's closing logo. Appropriately enough, the cartoon ends.

Double-Cross-Country Race (1951)

Director: Seymour Kneitel. *Animation:* Tom Johnson, Bill Hudson. *Story:* Larz Bourne. *Scenics:* Anton Loeb. *Music:* Winston Sharples.

Popeye, in a jalopy that barely makes it to the starting line with its one-half horsepower engine, versus Count Noah Count, in his powerful, aerodynamic super-car, in a race across America. The Count is handsome and well-built. Popeye is his usual funny-looking self. All of this is supposed to make us root for the underdog, but why on earth would Popeye show up for a race in that heap? The starter blows his own head off with his pistol, and we never see the head pop back into place! The Count cheats from the get-go, so our sympathies should be with Popeye. But The Sailorman is such an unbelievable sap to fall for these tricks. And Popeye, all by himself, gets lost more than once. The racers are also being followed by an aggravated traffic cop.

The Count falls for a sexy Indian lass and stops in her village to pitch some woo. Not only does this give Popeye some needed time to catch up, but it also demonstrates that sex was never far from the cartoon creators' minds in those days.

In a creepy sequence involving a talking cattle's skeletal skull, The Count tricks Popeye into filling his radiator with poison water, and the anthropomorphic car dies. But, as The Count streaks to the finish line, spinach restores Popeye's ride, and our "hero" (?) wins. The traffic cop pops out of the trophy to deluge him with citations. Even when Popeye wins, he loses!

Pilgrim Popeye (1951)

Director: I. Sparber. *Animation:* Al Eugster, George Germanetti. *Story:* Carl Meyer, Jack Mercer. *Scenics:* Anton Loeb. *Music:* Winston Sharples.

Popeye's nephews try to chop the head off of Popeye's pet turkey because they want Thanksgiving dinner. Popeye tells them the story of how a turkey saved his life when he was a Pilgrim (!) in the olden days. Popeye's obviously making the story up because he believes that killing a turkey would be murder. So, is Popeye a member of PETA? Is he lecturing members of the audience, urging them to be vegetarians?

Anyway, it's interesting that, in his story, Popeye paints himself as an incompetent, because the turkey he's hunting in the tale keeps getting the better of him in typical cartoon ways. At one point, though, the turkey heats Popeye's head over an open fire and pops corn in his mouth! Why would Popeye humiliate and injure himself like that in his own story? When Popeye finally corners the bird, the tenderhearted Pilgrim can't pull the trigger. Instead, he gives the skin-and-bones turkey a can of spinach to help it become big and strong. Just then, Indians attack. They capture Popeye and start roasting him at the stake, after continuously pounding him on the head with mallets. The turkey eats the spinach, morphs into an American eagle, and dispatches the Indians by throwing them through a stone outcropping and stacking them into a totem pole. Yes, it's another racist statement from Famous Studios. The symbol of the White Man's nation has humiliated and subdued the Red Man.

Back in the "real world" the nephews decide to feed spinach to Popeye's pet. But the bird complains, "What, no turkey?" Popeye laughs at the thought that the cannibal fowl he raised is safe.

Let's Stalk Spinach (1951)

Director: Seymour Kneitel. *Animation:* Steve Muffatti, George Germanetti. *Story:* I. Klein. *Scenics:* Anton Loeb. *Music:* Winston Sharples.

After all these years, Popeye's nephews still won't eat their spinach. So Popeye tells them the story of when he traded his poor Maw's Tin Lizzy for a can of spinach. But an enormous spinach stalk grows out of it, reaching to the sky. Popeye climbs to the top, and there he finds a giant mistreating a hen that lays golden eggs. The gallant Popeye challenges the giant, who blows him away into a huge can of spinach. Popeye eats some and develops a male physique that bursts out of his childish shirt. Popeye also grows chest hairs. Once again, eating spinach seems to symbolize puberty. Popeye now attacks the giant, eventually tossing him out of the cloud realm down to Earth. The nephews want to know if spinach can really do that. The giant peeks out of a hole in the ground, all bandaged up, and assures them that it's true. The nephews happily chow down on their spinach sandwiches.

Punch and Judo (1951)

Director: I. Sparber. *Animation:* Tom Johnson, Frank Endres. *Story:* Irv Spector. *Scenics:* Robert Connavale. *Music:* Winston Sharples.

Popeye buys orphans a TV set, and they watch his latest boxing match on it. (Popeye had forgotten he was supposed to be at the arena until he heard it announced.) The muscular current champ has a tattoo of a grave with the headstone reading, "Reserved For Popeye," on his arm. Popeye's own biceps are puny little things, and his arms turn to spaghetti and droop when he tries to flex. We're reminded that this is the spinach-dependent Famous Studios Popeye we're watching, and not the naturally strong Segar version. The referee injures both fighters while demonstrating to them what won't be allowed. The champ crushes Popeye's hand in a vise-like grip, then uses him for a punching bag. Popeye turns into a board when the champ knocks him stiff, in a sequence that freaked out children. The champ, fighting fair and square, has done in Popeye! But Popeye's spirit revives him, and he uses cartoony tricks to get the champ on the ropes. So the champ plays tricks of his own, electrocuting The Sailorman, hitting him with a brick, literally tying him up in knots, and finally knocking him cold. Popeye turns into a block of ice, in another sequence guaranteed to scare kids. Before the ref can count Popeye out, the orphans feed him spinach by pouring it into the television set. The rest is history.

Popeye's Pappy (1952)

Director: I. Sparber. *Animation:* Tom Johnson, Frank Endres. *Story:* Larz Bournes. *Scenics:* Robert Little. *Music:* Winston Sharples.

Popeye finds his long lost Pappy, who is now king of an island of incredibly well-built natives and stupefying gorgeous girls. Pappy hates relatives and doesn't want to leave the paradise where he's waited on by the beauties. Popeye tries to forcibly remove him. Pappy responds by trying to feed Popeye to a snake and a crocodile. Then, in a scene that's just plain wrong in so many ways, Popeye dresses in drag to seduce his own father! As Pappy is following him, the disguise comes off, and Popeye ends up swallowing an anchor. The natives save Pappy from another of Popeye's attempts, pinning our hero with spears, and then they cheerfully begin to cook The Sailorman for dinner. The dense Popeye doesn't even realize what's going on! Desperate, voodoo-like music plays. Pappy remembers Popeye as a baby and comes to the rescue by eating spinach. Pappy feeds Popeye some, and the natives end up stacked on spears like they were sides of beef. A sign is hung on them, "Cheaper by the Dozen." Though Popeye and Pappy have a happy ending, there's something very disturbing about watching two white guys beat up, humiliate, and put up for sale, black men that they have deemed "savages."

Lunch with a Punch (1952)

Director: I. Sparber. *Animation:* Al Eugster, George Germanetti. *Story:* Carl Meyer, Jack Mercer. *Scenics:* Tom Ford. *Music:* Winston Sharples.

On a picnic with Olive, Popeye tries to get his nephews to eat spinach by telling them a story about when he was young. We see a flashback to the characters' school days. Little Popeye is dressed like an English fop, complete with a "bowl" haircut. Boy Bluto causes a firecracker to explode under Popeye's desk, sending his inkwell up and all over the teacher. After school, Bluto is showing off for young Olive on a swing. He tries to use the swing to get rid of Popeye, but this backfires and Bluto ends up in a well. Then, Popeye buys Olive an ice cream cone. Bluto, however, puts a frog inside it. Olive, thinking Popeye played a mean trick on her, goes off with Bluto. The frog croaks out to Popeye, "Bluto dunnit! Bluto dunnit!" Popeye takes the frog to Olive and it tells its tale. This time Olive walks off with Popeye. But Bluto catapults Popeye into a basket of spinach outside a grocery. Then Bluto rides off with a screaming Olive on his bike. Popeye eats the spinach, disposes of Bluto, and saves Olive from being hit by a train.

Back in the present, Bluto comes out of hiding and grabs Popeye by the neck saying, "Now I gotcha without yer spinach!" But the nephews eat theirs. Bluto is using Popeye as a punching bag. The nephews return the favor.

Bluto is nothing but an unpleasant bully in this cartoon. The frog is pretty cool, though!

And the cartoon begs questions to be asked. If Popeye, Olive Oyl, and Bluto really knew each other since childhood, why are there so many cartoons in which they meet for the first time? Was a pattern set in childhood that Popeye, Olive, and Bluto are doomed to repeat all of their lives? What about free will?

I need an aspirin. My head hurts.

Swimmer Take All (1952)

Director: Seymour Kneitel. *Animation:* Tom Johnson, John Gentilella. *Story:* Carl Meyer, Jack Mercer. *Scenics:* Robert Little. *Music:* Winston Sharples.

A devastatingly handsome Bluto, with perhaps his best physique of all time, appears in this cartoon wearing a skimpy bathing suit. But he and Olive inexplicably aren't interested in each other, and Popeye is the one the film seems obsessed about when it comes to uncovering a male body.

Bluto and Popeye are having a swimming race across the English Channel. Bluto leaves Popeye hanging from a board on the docks, but Olive saws The Sailorman free. Popeye would even go the wrong way if Olive Oyl didn't turn him around. Then Bluto threads a string from Popeye's dorky old-fashioned bathing suit onto a baited hook. When a fish takes the bait, Popeye begins to rapidly lose his suit. As he's underwater knitting it back on himself, a gigantic fish swallows him. But an internal punch from Popeye frees The Sailorman. Bluto blows Popeye out of the water with a mine, and then finally drops a huge load of wet cement from a barge down on top of him. The cement hardens into a block around a struggling Popeye, until only his pipe shows. The block sinks to the bottom of the Channel. The orchestra believes Popeye is dying. But Olive, in a boat, pumps spinach down to him. Popeye eats it through his pipe, turns into a drill, and frees himself. With a super-powered punch, he turns the cement block into a lighthouse, then speeds past Bluto. Popeye's backwash carries Bluto to the lighthouse, where the big guy becomes trapped, being endlessly speared in the rear by a swordfish.

A string from Popeye's suit catches on a nail on the dock at the finish line, and as Popeye approaches the loving cup, his suit is unraveling. In the closing scene of the film, a presumably nude Popeye is inside the cup while knitting his suit back together. It's a good thing Popeye has this domestic skill!

Friend or Phony (1952)

Director: I. Sparber. *Animation:* Al Eugster, George Germanetti. *Story:* Irving Spector. *Scenics:* Robert Owen. *Music:* Winston Sharples.

Popeye receives a telegram that Bluto is in the hospital dying from the last beating Popeye gave him. This plotline may inject some disturbing reality into Popeye's slapstick world. But no, we see the fault lies with that "killer spinach." To illustrate, Bluto shows Popeye clips from *Tar with a Star* and *I'll Be Skiing Ya*. This reinforced the idea in the minds of children watching the cartoon that the things that happened on screen were real.

Bluto says that his dying request is for Popeye to throw away his spinach. Then Bluto plays a death scene. Weeping, Popeye throws his spinach can out the window. It lands on the back of a truck that's speeding away. The can comes to life and calls out to Popeye, "You'll be sorry!" (Even a spinach can is smarter than The Sailorman!)

A gleeful Bluto, who wasn't actually incapacitated at all, smashes a hospital bed down on Popeye. An injured Popeye's head comes up through the mattress, springs sticking out of his ears. Bluto, laughing like an evil maniac, grabs Popeye by the throat as the orchestra sounds Popeye's death knell. Then Bluto gives Popeye a super-punch which bounces him all the way to a construction site. Bluto uses a gigantic steel piledriver on Popeye's head to push The Sailorman ever lower into the ground. The orchestra plays a grim and desperate theme which seems to be counting down to Popeye's death.

But Popeye sends out a smoke signal "S.O.S." with his pipe. The spinach can comes to life again and responds. It hops its way to the construction zone and feeds its contents to Popeye. Popeye's head transforms into an iron sculpture, which looks really freaky, but which wrecks the pile driver. Popeye punches Bluto back to the hospital. When he visits him, he brings him a spinach plant. Bluto see it, goes nuts, jumps out the window, and runs away, as this time the orchestra plays a mournful tune for Bluto.

What if Bluto hadn't cracked up? What if he had eaten the spinach and trounced Popeye? Is giving your enemy the substance that's the key to your strength really such a good idea? Maybe Popeye was trying to be compassionate. Or maybe he had read the script and knew what would happen.

Tots Of Fun (1952)

Director: Seymour Kneitel. *Animation:* Tom Johnson, Frank Endres. *Story:* Larz Bourne. *Scenics:* Robert Owen. *Music:* Winston Sharples.

Even though Popeye's nephews are not really the main attractions of the Famous Studios era, this cartoon featuring them is pretty entertaining. It's filled with creative gags about construction and house building. Popeye believes he has built his dream house, though it collapses around him when he closes the door. Another example of Popeye's general incompetence! The nephews decide to build him a new one and come up with ways to combine the task with their music practice. A stirring classical score accompanies them as they construct a skyscraper, while inadvertently knocking The Sailorman out a couple of times.

Popalong Popeye (1952)

Director: Seymour Kneitel. *Animation:* Tom Johnson, John Gentilella. *Story:* Carl Meyer, Jack Mercer. *Scenics:* John Zago. *Music:* Winston Sharples.

Popeye tells his nephews the story of how he became a cowboy. Basically he was a prissy, tenderfoot dandy applying for a job on Bluto's ranch. His story is told in flashbacks. When Popeye arrives at the ranch, Bluto squeezes and stretches Popeye's neck to use his pipe as a cigarette lighter. Popeye is dazzled by Bluto's shooting, punctured by a cactus, and abused and punched into a full water barrel by a bull, so that he's drowning. The music emphasizes Popeye's plight. But, of course, spinach saves the day and transforms Popeye into what Bluto already was — Super Cowboy. He does fancy shooting of his own, squeezes the bull into bull-oney, and brands Bluto with hot irons. After the story, the nephews eat spinach to save Popeye from a dangerous bucking bronco.

Why did Popeye even attempt to get a job without first eating spinach? And why aren't all workers in America issued a daily can of spinach? Things would go a lot smoother!

Shuteye Popeye (1952)

Director: Seymour Kneitel. *Animation:* Al Eugster, George Germanetti. *Story:* Irving Spector. *Scenics:* Robert Connavale. *Music:* Winston Sharples.

Popeye's snoring keeps a mouse awake. The mouse attempts to get rid of Popeye, and vice versa, prompting the usual types of cartoon cat-and-mouse shenanigans — though none are as funny as *Tom And Jerry*, or as horrifying as *Herman and Katnap*. Finally, Popeye, dunce that he is, traps the mouse in a spinach can. How stupid can you get! The super-energized mouse then stuffs Popeye into the wall and enjoys Popeye's bed himself. Not the kind of thing I watch a Popeye cartoon to see!

Big Bad Sindbad (1952)

Director: Seymour Kneitel. *Animation:* Tom Johnson, William Henning. *Story:* I. Klein. *Scenics:* Uncredited. *Music:* Winston Sharples.

At a nautical museum, Popeye tells his nephews a story, via clips from the Fleischer film, *Popeye the Sailor Meets Sindbad the Sailor*, in order to prove that he's the greatest sailor of all time. What an ego that Popeye has! And I would rather watch the original cartoon than this one, which is composed of mostly reused footage.

Ancient Fistory (1953)

Director: Seymour Kneitel. *Animation:* Al Eugster, William B. Pattengill. *Story:* Irving Spector. *Scenics:* Robert Connavale. *Music:* Winston Sharples.

In this spin on the Cinderella story, Olive is the Princess holding a ball to find her Prince, and Popeye is the poor abused servant of Bluto who wants to go to the affair. His fairy godfather (Poopdeck Pappy) transforms him to make it possible. Olive only has eyes for Popeye and is soon wooing him on the couch. Bluto blasts Popeye away with a cannon, and to make matters worse, it's midnight and the magic vanishes. The wolfish Bluto then chases Olive through the palace and the Princess narrowly escapes getting kissed a couple of times. Spinach transforms Popeye into a super-knight, complete with a magnificent horse, and he rescues Olive just as Bluto has her securely in his arms and is about to get that kiss.

Child Sockology (1953)

Director: I. Sparber. *Animation:* Tom Johnson, Frank Endres. *Story:* Jack Ward, Carl Meyer. *Scenics:* Robert Little. *Music:* Winston Sharples.

Olive, having invited both Popeye and Bluto over to dinner — won't she ever learn — asks them to play with cousin Swee'Pea while she gets the food ready. Swee'Pea is building with an Erector Set but, when the boys fight over it, he crawls off to the construction site outside. Then follows a series of cartoony near-disasters as Swee'Pea continually almost gets injured or killed, and the boys battle and compete to save him while getting the worst of everything themselves. The exciting music and Popeye's cries of pain and alarm manage to inject some suspense into the wacky proceedings. Finally, in a sick scene, Popeye's head is embedded in a girder, the bump on his head rising up through a hole. Bluto uses a riveter to drive it back down. We see the red swollen bump throbbing, while the unconscious, or dead, Popeye's jaw is slack and his tongue is limply hanging out. It looks like he has just given a death rattle. But soon both Bluto and Swee'Pea are about to fall from a great height and Bluto actually yells for help! Popeye comes to, eats spinach, and rushes to the rescue. Popeye's not entirely altruistic, though, as he leaves an unconscious Bluto precariously rocking in a makeshift chair atop a high vertical girder. Swee'Pea won't leave the site without crying, so the film ends with Popeye, Olive, and Swee'Pea enjoying their dinner high up in the air on a construction platform. (They really need to stop spoiling that child!)

Popeye's Mirthday (1953)

Director: Seymour Kneitel. *Animation:* Tom Johnson, Frank Endres. *Story:* Carl Meyer, Jack Mercer. *Scenics:* Robert Connavale. *Music:* Winston Sharples.

An attractive Olive wants Popeye's nephews to keep him out of her house while she prepares a surprise birthday party for him. They do so by playing sadistic tricks on him, like electrocuting him as he tries to use a key, squashing him with a rolling piano, hitting him with a boxing glove on a spring, taking apart the ladder he's climbing, and launching him into the air with a skyrocket. After Popeye has been flattened by going through a laundry ringer, spinach restores him. He lifts Olive's house and can finally join the party. When he sees what's really going on, the unbelievably easygoing and forgiving Popeye never punishes the boys.

Toreadorable (1953)

Director: Seymour Kneitel. *Animation:* Tom Johnson, John Gentilella. *Story:* Carl Meyer, Jack Mercer. *Scenics:* Anton Loeb. *Music:* Winston Sharples.

Olive and a handsome matador, Señor Bluto from Brooklyn, fall for each other when Popeye takes her to a Spanish arena to see a bullfight. Olive, at the beginning of the cartoon, acts as if she and Popeye are just friends, even commenting to him that Bluto is a dreamboat! And Olive really knows how to use her pretty eyes on Bluto. He dedicates the first bull to her. He defeats it by making it charge into an anvil that's behind his red cape. Then Bluto plays jump rope with the unconscious beast. Olive thinks he's "so toreadorable!"

Popeye pulls out his spinach can and enters the ring. But even after eating some spinach, it's only by dumb luck that Popeye manages to impale the bull by its horns on a flagpole. As Popeye is taking his bows and Olive is cheering while femininely swaying, the bull frees itself and charges Popeye again. The Sailorman pulls out the spinach, but Bluto covers his head with a thrown sombrero, so he can't eat it. Bluto recognizes early on in this cartoon that spinach is a threat. The bull squashes Popeye into the ground and begins doing a victorious hat dance around him. But Popeye sucks up spinach with his pipe, emerges from the ground, and turns the bull into a bass fiddle.

Bluto secretly replaces the spinach in Popeye's can with Mexican Jumping Beans. As the persistent bull charges yet again, Popeye cheerfully empties the can's contents into his mouth and consumes the beans. His body convulses, and he starts uncontrollably leaping around the arena. The bull sharpens its horns with a pencil sharpener and comes in for the kill. It collides with Popeye and tosses him out of the arena, and into a cart filled with spinach. But Popeye is unconscious.

Back in the arena, Bluto moves in on a worried Olive for a kiss. She refuses, so he holds her by her red blouse, using her as his cape to change her mind. But sweet Olive says, "No, no, a thousand times no!" So Bluto keeps on using her to deflect the bull.

Popeye comes to, eats spinach, is transformed into Super Matador, and rockets back into the arena. He punches Bluto into the bull, so that Bluto is wedged between its horns. Then Popeye lifts the side of the arena so that the bull runs out into the countryside, carrying Bluto away and putting as many cacti up Bluto's back as it can.

As the crowd cheers, Popeye and Olive kiss behind a heart-shaped cape. In the context of this cartoon they seem to be falling in love for the first time. It's as though Olive has realized "the boy next door" is the right one for her, as opposed to the muscular hunk who caught her eye.

Baby Wants a Battle (1953)

Director: Seymour Kneitel. *Animation:* Al Eugster, George Germanetti. *Story:* Carl Meyer, Jack Mercer. *Scenics:* Robert Connavale. *Music:* Winston Sharples.

An unpleasant cartoon in which Popeye is telling Olive the story of how he got his first black eye as an infant. Baby Popeye is out in the stroller with his dad — not Poopdeck Pappy in this cartoon, but a sissified version of Popeye — when Bluto's dad and his little bully come along and pick on them for no other reason than that Bluto and his dad can. So, baby Popeye gets hit in the face with a stretched rubber nipple, whacked with a board, and embedded in the metal frame of a swing set, etc. Bluto's dad keeps stopping a panicking Popeye's dad (expertly voiced to get our sympathy by Jack Mercer) from interfering. Finally, baby Popeye purposely drinks a bottle of spinach juice to save himself from being run over by a streetcar, and his father from being a punching bag. Then the tyke disposes of the Blutoes and wheels his dad home.

Back in the present, Bluto smashes a piano down on Popeye, but The Sailorman calmly eats spinach and Bluto winds up wearing women's clothing and crying in a baby carriage.

We never do see Popeye get a black eye, but that's okay. Viewers have seen more than enough child abuse, bullying, and brutality.

Baby Popeye waits as long to eat his spinach as adult Popeye does. The Sailorman didn't learn much over the years, did he?

Fireman's Brawl (1953)

Director: I. Sparber. *Animation:* Tom Johnson, Frank Endres. *Story:* Carl Meyer, Jack Mercer. *Scenics:* Robert Connavale. *Music:* Winston Sharples.

Firemen Bluto and Popeye are at the station playing poker. Bluto cheats so he wins enough money to take Olive Oyl out for a good time. Note that it is assumed Olive will gladly go out with Bluto. But suddenly the alarm rings. Olive's house is on fire! So, of course, the two guys compete with, and sabotage, each other in order to be the first to reach her and save her. Their efforts end up placing Olive back in jeopardy again and again, as anthropomorphic morphing flames do their thing. Attention is called to Olive's rear as a stream of water hits it and she lets out sexy exclamations, and later, as it catches fire and she douses the flames using a shower head. Popeye and Bluto finally get stuck in a boiler about to explode. Popeye pulls out the spinach can, but it's too late. The big bang happens, and everyone is literally up in the air. Olive catches the can, eats the spinach, is transformed into Super Firewoman, and saves herself and the boys.

The film ends with Popeye and Bluto having been kicked out of their station because Olive is using it as her new home. After all, it was the boys' incompetence and rivalry which let the fire totally destroy her old place. And besides, who wants to argue with a spinach-powered Olive?

Popeye, the Ace of Space (1953)

Director: Seymour Kneitel. *Animation:* Al Eugster, George Germanetti, Wm. B. Pattengill. *Story:* Carl Meyer, Jack Mercer. *Scenics:* Robert Little, Anton Loeb. *Music:* Winston Sharples.

The strange aliens who capture Popeye.

In this sci-fi cartoon, originally presented in 3-D, Popeye is abducted by aliens who subject him to tests. The strange, strong, and goonish-looking aliens with their creepy language are guaranteed to give kids nightmares. The eerie score helps, too. First, the aliens make Popeye an old man inside their Cosmic Ager. But spinach reverses the process. Next they stretch him and his neck out on a rack, in order to try out their giant Atom Apple Smasher. But spinach turns Popeye's Adam's apple into the Rock of Gibraltar. Then they use a ray to disintegrate Popeye! More nightmares! The aliens then fight over his spinach can, and it goes flying back over to where the disembodied Popeye is/was. He somehow manages to eat it, emerges back into our dimension, and knocks the aliens so silly that they start dancing around a May Pole. Then Popeye pilots their saucer back to Earth.

Shaving Muggs (1953)

Director: Seymour Kneitel. *Animation:* Tom Johnson, John Gentilella. *Story:* Larz Bourne. *Scenics:* Anton Loeb. *Music:* Winston Sharples.

Because they've been awhile at sea, Olive won't go out with either Popeye or Bluto until they get a shave and a haircut. But the barber is on a lunch break, so Bluto proposes to Popeye, "Look, Chum, suppose you give me a shave and a haircut, then I'll pretty you up?" Popeye, the total sap, agrees to this. What's to prevent Bluto from running off to Olive after he's been made presentable? Or, as we shall see, sabotaging Popeye when The Sailorman gets in the chair?

But first, it's Bluto's turn. Using standard cartoon grooming gags, Popeye gives Bluto a shave and a haircut which leave him looking like Rock Hudson — only with a better build! Once Olive gets a look at him, it'll be all over for Popeye. And the thought of Popeye working to help Bluto look as handsome as he's ever looked for a date with Olive is just plain weird.

Weird definitely describes what happens next, though it's expected by everyone except the gullible Popeye. Under the guise of helping Popeye get spiffed up, Bluto chokes him, uses his tongue to sharpen a razor, scorches his face clear off his head with a hot towel, and puts quick drying cement on him while calling it "shaving cream." Popeye just sits there and takes it, while getting weaker and weaker and more and more hurt. Finally, Bluto pours gasoline and gun powder over him, twists a couple of his hairs together for a fuse, lights it, and runs off to get a date with Olive. The resulting explosion destroys the barbershop and leaves Popeye a wreck. Spinach restores his vitality, if not his looks. Popeye ambushes Bluto and furiously begins to give him the business, but then the two spot Olive Oyl strolling by on a date with Captain Van Dyke, whose long beard she admires. The cartoon ends with Popeye and Bluto taking turns kicking each other.

Aside from providing a good ending for the cartoon, the Captain Van Dyke gag demonstrates that all single males in the Famous Studios universe desire Olive Oyl, and that she's never hurting for a date.

Floor Flusher (1954)

Director: I. Sparber. *Animation:* Tom Golden, Bill Hudson. *Story:* Carl Meyer, Jack Mercer. *Scenics:* Robert Owen. *Music:* Winston Sharples.

Arriving at Olive's house, Popeye and Bluto see she has a major leak in her kitchen plumbing. They each make a stab at fixing it, and Popeye succeeds. Bluto pretends to congratulate him and to leave. It's interesting to note that, at the beginning of this cartoon, Olive likes, and comes on to, both guys equally.

Bluto is actually going into Olive's basement, where he keeps pulling apart pipes and rerouting them so that water gushes up all over Olive's house. Winston Sharples' score is suitably evil, menacing, and relentless. The water comes out of Olive's floor, her player piano, the walls, and even out of Popeye and Olive themselves! Olive gives out a sexy giggle when a stream from Popeye's pipe tickles her derriere. And when she's climbing on the expanding rug which covers a major water bulge, she has beautiful legs. Just as Popeye discovers the culprit and is showing Bluto to Olive, the dam, which is the rug, is about to burst. Bluto punches Popeye into Olive's radiator, and his spinach can goes flying out of his shirt and into a goldfish bowl.

As Bluto is climbing the rug mound to get Olive, it bursts, and Olive's house is flooded. Olive, in a drawer, paddles away from Bluto using a frying pan for an oar. But she won't escape him for long because he's propelling himself along through the water using an electric mixer. Fortunately for Ms. Oyl, the imprisoned Popeye and the fishbowl are now both underwater, so Olive's pet goldfish can swim the spinach over to The Sailorman. It transforms both him and the radiator into a torpedo to scuttle Bluto. Then Popeye lifts Olive's house to pour the water out. As he sings his closing ditty, water spouts out of his pipe.

Popeye's 20th Anniversary (1954)

Director: I. Sparber. *Animation:* Al Eugster, George Germanetti. *Story:* I. Klein. *Scenics:* Joseph Dommerque. *Music:* Winston Sharples.

Most of this cartoon is just footage from *Rodeo Romeo* and *Tops in the Big Top* as, instead of making a speech at his testimonial dinner, Popeye shows two of his old films. This cartoon is notable for its caricatures of real Hollywood stars under contract to Paramount, and for the shot near its beginning which includes a gorgeous, well-endowed Olive Oyl in the strapless gown and white gloves she will wear in *Parlez Vous Woo*.

Taxi-Turvy (1954)

Director: Winston Sharples. *Animation:* Tom Johnson, Frank Endres. *Story:* Irving Spector. *Scenics:* Robert Owen. *Music:* Winston Sharples.

In this cartoon, Popeye and Bluto seem to have no romantic interest in Olive Oyl. They are competing cab drivers out to get her fare, as only cartoon characters can. So they find ways to snatch her from moving vehicles, embed her in a traffic light, deposit her atop a cop, and electrocute her on the wire of a trolley. Finally, Bluto's taxi is wrecked and Olive is riding with Popeye. Bluto tricks

Popeye into stopping at a railroad crossing and then pounds him into the ground with a jackhammer. Bluto then proceeds to drive away with Olive. Popeye almost eats his spinach, but Bluto drives back and grabs it. Bluto finally has wised up, and it seems all is lost for Popeye, but a train hits the cab and everything goes flying, including the spinach can. It lands atop Popeye's head. He eats it, catches Olive, and belts Bluto into the smokestack of the train. The cartoon ends with Popeye carrying Olive to her destination on his shoulders.

Bride and Gloom (1954)

Director: I. Sparber. *Animation:* Tom Johnson, John Gentilella. *Story:* Larz Bourne. *Scenics:* Robert Connavale. *Music:* Winston Sharples.

On the night before their wedding, Olive dreams about what it will be like to be married to Popeye. First, it seems as though Popeye will have to eat spinach in order to say, "I do," during the ceremony. Olive must not think much of Popeye. Then again, knowing what we do about the Famous Studios Popeye, he probably actually will need to down the green stuff to get through his vows! Next, Olive and Popeye will have twins, and the newborn babies will use Popeye's head as a punching bag. This elicits giggles from Olive. But then, when the boys are five, they will begin destroying the house and will torment, injure, and torture their mother — including trying to burn her at the stake when they are playing Indians! A horrified Olive wakes up in the morning and tells an arriving Popeye, "I ain't gonna marry *you*!" Then she drops a dresser on him. Popeye merely makes a joke about females being fickle and laughs. The girl Popeye supposedly loves has broken up with him and canceled their wedding — and Popeye laughs?!?!?!

Greek Mirthology (1954)

Director: Seymour Kneitel. *Animation:* Tom Golden, George Germanetti. *Story:* I. Klein. *Scenics:* Anton Loeb. *Music:* Winston Sharples.

Popeye's nephews want ice cream instead of spinach, so The Sailorman tells them the story of their great, great, great, great, great uncle, Hercules. (I think Popeye left out a couple of "greats" in there.) In flashbacks, we see Hercules (Popeye in a toga) do super-deeds by sniffing strong garlic. Bluto the Hun comes to town and challenges him. They compete in doing super-stunts. Garlic-sniffing Hercules always wins. (Incidentally, garlic seems to give Popeye a better physique than spinach ever did!) Finally, Bluto douses Hercules' garlic with chlorophyll. (I think the creators meant "chloroform." But could it be rather that this is Popeye's mistake and not the creators'? He is telling the story, after all! And he does always have green stuff on his mind....) A groggy Herc has no strength, and Bluto blows him into a spinach patch. Herc discovers that spinach is better than garlic and gives Bluto a super-punch that turns him and his armor into a row of trash cans. But the nephews think this story is just a bunch of spinach, and the cartoon ends with them getting ice cream cones from the ice cream man, Bluto.

What kids in the viewing audience wouldn't relate to the nephews and Bluto, instead of Popeye?

Fright To The Finish (1954)

Director: Seymour Kneitel. *Animation:* Al Eugster, Wm. Pattengil. *Story:* Jack Mercer. *Scenics:* Robert Connavale. *Music:* Winston Sharples.

Olive is reading ghost stories in her house to Popeye and Bluto on Halloween. This gives Bluto an idea how to get rid of The Sailorman. He pretends to go home early, but really hangs around to haunt Olive's home. This includes seemingly blowing off Popeye's head with a firecracker. The music and sound effects convey that maybe Popeye really is now a headless member of the walking dead. He's not, of course, but Bluto frames him as the one who has been spooking Olive. She throws Popeye out of her house and out of her life for good. Then Bluto appears on the scene to protect Olive from all the supernatural Halloween evils. The two begin to get intimate on Olive's couch, proving that Olive isn't averse to being alone and getting physical with the big guy. But Popeye, suddenly wising up — he is pretty stupid for much of the cartoon — uses Olive's vanishing cream to make himself invisible in order to haunt Bluto. At one point, he slams Bluto's neck between two sliding doors. Then Popeye reappears to be with Olive. She rewards him by covering him with kisses. Bluto has quite the muscular body at points in the film, and Olive, likewise, is cute and has some curves. She has fantastic legs in the scene where she jumps out of her nylons. And her face at the end of the cartoon? Wow!

Private Eye Popeye (1954)

Director: Seymour Kneitel. *Animation:* Tom Johnson, Frank Endres. *Story:* I. Klein. *Scenics:* Anton Loeb. *Music:* Winston Sharples.

An entertaining cartoon, although it feels more like a Tex Avery *Droopy* film than a Famous Studios Popeye cartoon. Private detective Popeye is hired by cute heiress Olive Oyl to guard her valuable emerald. But the butler steals it and flees around the world. No matter where he goes, Popeye is there, too. At one point, the butler falls for a gorgeous woman in the Middle East — who turns out to be Popeye in disguise! How did he pull that off??? Finally, the butler punches Popeye into a cart of spinach, and Popeye returns the favor by relay-punching the butler all the way to Alcatraz. Returning the emerald, Popeye receives a kiss, and the red glow of embarrassment and pleasure from his face outshines the glow from the precious gem.

Gopher Spinach (1954)

Director: Seymour Kneitel. *Animation:* Tom Johnson, John Gentilella. *Story:* Carl Meyer. *Scenics:* Robert Connavale. *Music:* Winston Sharples.

Popeye wheels spinach plants out to his garden in a baby carriage! He even diapers them! But a supposedly "cute" little gopher is stealing them and causes Popeye pain. The gopher puts the burning ash from Popeye's pipe on the Sailorman's head, nails Popeye to a wall with shrapnel flung out of a power lawnmower, and floods his garden. Finally Popeye corners the little thief with a shotgun, but can't find it in himself to pull the trigger. Then when a bull endangers Popeye, the gopher eats spinach and saves him. The cartoon ends with Popeye and his new pal working together to plant the garden. If all of this is your idea of a good time, you're welcome to this treacly cartoon.

Cookin' With Gags (1955)

Director: I. Sparber. *Animation:* Tom Johnson, William Henning. *Story:* Carl Meyer. *Scenics:* Anton Loeb. *Music:* Winston Sharples.

A strange, unpleasant cartoon in which Olive Oyl is uncharacteristically cruel and nasty and annoying, and even Bluto is not quite himself when he gets Olive alone.

It's April Fool's Day, and the three members of the love triangle are going on a picnic. This gives Bluto the chance to play a series of harmful, humiliating, and potentially life-threatening pranks on gullible Popeye, while saying in a satanic voice, "April Fool!" Popeye can't do anything about all this because Olive sides with Bluto! She scolds, "Popeye! Can't you take a joke?" So Popeye breathes exhaust, gets pounded into the ground by an ax on a spring, has a barbecue blow up in his face depositing red hot logs in his mouth, and is stung multiple times by bees that also shred his clothing, so it looks like Popeye is wearing a baby's outfit. All of this Bluto — and Olive — laugh uproariously over. In fact, Bluto and Olive seem to be demonically in sync, and totally in love, throughout this cartoon. And both view Popeye as an unnecessary add-on and the butt of practical jokes.

But when Bluto frames Popeye by making it seem that The Sailorman served Olive exploding hot dogs, we learn that Ms. Oyl can't take a joke either. She's finally through with Popeye, causing Bluto to give out another evil guffaw. Popeye pulls out his spinach can, but a paper snake pops out of it. Bluto has replaced Popeye's can with a phony! Why doesn't he do this more often?

While Popeye stands helplessly by and watches, Olive says, "C'mon, Bluto, let's go rowing!" As the two make goo-goo eyes at each other, Bluto puts his arm around her and says, "Okay, Lovergirl!" But when they are alone on the lake and Olive's definitely in the mood, all Bluto does is talk about what a sucker Popeye is for an April Fool's gag. What happened to the passionate guy we've seen in other films? Bluto, get your mind off Popeye! Speaking of Popeye, he swims underwater and inflates a rubber sea monster which terrifies Bluto, chases him, and blows up in his face, depositing him on a nearby tree branch. Popeye and Olive sail by in the boat and laugh at him. Olive declares, "There's no fool like an April Fool!" Evidently she's forgiven Popeye and is willing to join in the "fun" when either of her boyfriends is humiliated.

Though I'd prefer to believe the events in this story never happened, it does show us that Olive has no qualms about being alone, and getting romantic, with Bluto.

Nurse To Meet Ya (1955)

Director: I. Sparber. *Animation:* Al Eugster, Wm. B. Pattengill. *Story:* Jack Mercer. *Scenics:* Robert Connavale. *Music:* Winston Sharples.

This cartoon starts promisingly enough with Popeye and Bluto falling for, and wooing, a pretty-faced Olive Oyl in a nurse/nanny uniform. But then it deteriorates into a typical slapstick contest between the two to get the infant in her charge to stop crying, only with some added Famous Studios unpleasantness. Popeye pulls on his facial features, turning himself into a dog. Just what every girl wants a fella to be able to do, right? But an Olive with lovely legs doesn't seem to mind. Finally Bluto pounds Popeye into the ground with cannon balls. The sailor's spinach squeezes out of his shirt and rolls away. Bluto proceeds then to continually use Popeye's head as a golf ball, hitting it with a club, and making his neck stretch out and snap back. The neck eventually elongates so much that Popeye is able to reach the spinach, which morphs his head into a cement block. Bluto's skeleton shatters into tiny pieces when he next hits it. Then Popeye uses a swingset to turn the boneless Bluto into a puppet. Just another typical day of "fun" cruelty from Famous Studios!

Penny Antics (1955)

Director: Seymour Kneitel. *Animation:* Tom Johnson, Frank Endres. *Story:* I. Klein. *Scenics:* Robert Connavale. *Music:* Winston Sharples.

At an amusement park, rival arcade owners Popeye and Bluto compete for Wimpy's business. They each keep snatching the rotund gent away from the other guy, and cheating one another. Wimpy enjoys seeing clips from *Silly Hillbilly*, *Wotta Knight*, and *The Fistic Mystic* in the movie machines as he borrows pennies from Popeye and Bluto. Finally, the two rivals start a fistfight and a crowd gathers. Wimpy cleans up monetarily by selling admission to the brawl.

Gift of Gag (1955)

Director: Seymour Kneitel. *Animation:* Tom Johnson, Frank Endres. *Story:* I. Klein. *Scenics:* Robert Connavale. *Music:* Winston Sharples.

With nephews like Popeye's, who needs enemies? Here, in an attempt to keep Popeye from discovering his birthday present, they slide a grandfather clock down the stairs to crash into him, saw a hole in his floor, and break all of his dishes by tipping them out of the cabinet on top of him. Then, as Popeye is about to spank them, he sees the gigantic can of spinach they bought for him. He hugs them instead. As long as you feed Popeye spinach, you can nearly kill him and destroy his property and all will be forgiven!

Car-Azy Drivers (1955)

Director: Seymour Kneitel. *Animation:* Tom Johnson, John Gentilella. *Story:* Larz Bourne. *Scenics:* Anton Loeb. *Music:* Winston Sharples.

Popeye humiliates Olive by showing up in a suit of armor to teach her to drive. Some boyfriend! Fortunately, Olive will have none of it. Then Popeye's not very attentive during the lesson, so he's oblivious when Olive literally chokes a dying anthropomorphic engine. Popeye also gets his head embedded in the engine after a quick stop, and becomes some ghoulish-looking part of it. The auto hits a fruit cart and an armored car, and Popeye slaps a policeman. The car then goes out of control in a construction area, and Popeye catches a tree branch in the neck and hangs there, unconscious or dead. After another series of disasters, Olive and the car end up on a railroad track, heading for a collision with a train. But, of course, Popeye eats spinach, turns into a human automobile, and saves the day. But Popeye is so condescending and incompetent in this cartoon that I wish Bluto would have shown up and given the cute Olive Oyl parking lessons!

Cops Is Tops (1955)

Director: I. Sparber. *Animation:* Tom Johnson, Frank Endres. *Story:* Carl Meyer. *Scenics:* Anton Loeb. *Music:* Winston Sharples.

This film features the traffic-stopping version of Olive Oyl.

In this cartoon, Olive Oyl is the perfect combination of the positive, "can do," fun-loving, sweet, innocent Miss, and the sexy siren. She's like the "girl next door" who knows she can turn on her charm when she needs to.

A cute and curvy Olive Oyl has joined the police force and is about to go on her beat. Popeye tries to discourage her from pursuing her dream because, old-fashioned, jerky, male chauvinist that he is, he doesn't think being a cop is a job for a "woming." So he decides to follow her, believing her to be incompetent and needing his help to stay out of trouble. There's nothing like a boyfriend who believes in you, and Popeye is nothing like a boyfriend who believes in you!

As Olive happily sways on the street corner, Popeye disguises himself as a cigar store Indian. Suddenly, a runaway horse careens down the street. Popeye tries to stop it but fails, ending up with a face full of bricks and being shaken around in a cement mixer. Olive stops the horse by spreading fresh tar on the road and by calming it with her pleasing, friendly manner.

Next, there's a bank robbery. Popeye, dressed as a baby (!), pushes Olive aside. The robber then conks him on the head with a giant wrench and drives away. But, as a sexy version of *Frankie and Johnny* plays on the soundtrack, Olive, totally confident in her sex appeal, puts an inviting expression on her gorgeous face, strikes a pose that emphasizes her perfect hourglass figure, and hikes up her skirt, a la

Claudette Colbert in *It Happened One Night*, to show off her shapely legs. The robber turns around to gaze and gape at her, hugs himself, and exclaims, "What a doll!" He promptly smashes his car into a brick wall.

Then, there's a brawl going on in a diner. Popeye wades in to break it up and to teach the "foul balls" a lesson. But Olive attaches the diner to her motorcycle and hauls it down to the jail. She makes everyone inside the diner enter the jail, including Popeye, whom she mistakenly believes to be one of the miscreants.

She then happily strolls through the park. We're happy that she's gotten rid of Popeye, too. But a muscular brute is going for a swim in the lake, despite the "No Swimming Allowed" sign. Olive goes out to him in a canoe and declares he's under arrest. He chuckles and responds, "That's a laugh!" Then he lifts the whole canoe, sliding Olive down toward him, and says, "How 'bout a kiss, Babe?" She hits him with her paddle. "You masher!" He drops the boat and climbs aboard. Olive is soon swimming for her virtue, and yelling for help.

In jail, Popeye hears her, eats his spinach, morphs his arm and fist into a jackhammer, and busts through the wall. He saves Olive and then punches the scofflaw into the jail.

Then comes a disturbing last scene. Popeye is in a policewoman's uniform as the department is lined up to honor him. The female sergeant, played by Possum Pearl (see *Hill-billing and Cooing*), makes him an honorary officer. Popeye's skirt exposes his ugly legs, and socks held up by garters. As the gorgeous doll female officers giggle, Popeye turns red and tries to pull his skirt down. He says, "This is embarraskin!" Well yeah, Popeye, when a man dresses in a skirt and is made an honorary woman, it usually is!

A Job For A Gob (1955)

Director: Seymour Kneitel. *Animation:* Al Eugster, George Germanetti. *Story:* Larz Bourne. *Scenics:* Robert Connavale. *Music:* Winston Sharples.

Vacationing out West, Bluto and Popeye are instantly smitten when they see rancher Olive, who has a great figure and one of the most spectacularly shapely, and realistic-looking, posteriors she's ever been drawn with, bending forward to hang a sign advertising that she needs help. So, of course, the boys compete in slapsticky, cartoony ways at various tasks to determine who will get hired. Bluto keeps trying to get rid of, and best, Popeye, but always fails. Popeye gets the job. And then, in an out-of-character moment of pure pointless evil, Bluto causes a stampede and sets fire to the barn. What is he trying to accomplish here? Will Olive love him after she watches him destroy her ranch? Is he just so angry he wants to wreck everything, like a little kid kicking over a tower of blocks? Or is he, as Olive says, "loco?" At any rate, it's disturbing to watch. Popeye, with

Many cartoons featured Olive unconsciously displaying her assets while just going about her daily life. Though she was being ogled by men, she sweetly didn't know it.

quick thinking and spinach, saves the day. Throughout this cartoon, Bluto keeps getting it in the rear. He sits on a cactus, becomes wedged into a tree, loses his pants, has his branded behind turned into a tic-tac-toe board, and is left to be endlessly paddled by a windmill.

Hill-billing And Cooing (1956)

Director: Seymour Kneitel. *Animation:* Tom Johnson, John Gentilella. *Story:* Jack Mercer. *Scenics:* Robert Connavale. *Music:* Winston Sharples.

In this role reversal cartoon, a woman falls for Popeye and tries to get Olive out of the way. However, the woman is big, burly, mannish, ugly, and uncouth. Popeye doesn't give her a tumble. If this cartoon had been a true role reversal, Olive's antagonist would have been beautiful, charming, and romantic, as the female gym instructor was in the Fleischer film, *Never Kick A Woman*.

This cartoon starts out with Possum Pearl singing about how lonesome she is, spying Popeye and Olive driving through the mountains, and shooting out their rear tire. She then snatches Popeye and knocks Olive through a stone mountain. But Olive rescues Popeye as Pearl is about to kiss him, and the two try to speed away in the car. Pearl turns a covered bridge around, though, grabs Popeye again, and puts him through the bottom of a boat so his arms are trapped at his sides. She says they are going "river smoochin'!" Olive saves him again, but Pearl is right there. Popeye ends up atop a tree that Pearl is chopping down. Pearl drills an interfering Olive into a nearby stump. Popeye is shaken out of the tree and loses his spinach. Pearl drags the unconscious sailor toward the Justice Of The Peace.

But the spinach can has bounced over to Olive. She downs its contents, bursts free of the stump, grows biceps, and tosses Pearl into outer space. Pearl lands on a star and immediately begins chasing the man in the moon.

The cartoon ends with Olive driving the car and singing, "I'll knock the dame sky high who tries to take my guy, Popeye The Sailor Man!" She has the man in question tied securely to the rumble seat.

There's something disturbingly disconcerting about seeing Popeye take a "damsel in distress" role throughout this cartoon and to have him helpless before Pearl. Olive, though, makes a great determined woman and super-powered heroine.

Popeye For President (1956)

Director: Seymour Kneitel. *Animation:* Tom Johnson, Frank Endres. *Story:* Jack Mercer. *Scenics:* Robert Connavale. *Music:* Winston Sharples.

Even though Olive is cute in this cartoon, Bluto has no romantic interest in her. He and Popeye each need her vote to break the tie between them to determine who will be President. But Olive can't go to the polls until her farm chores are done. So, the candidates compete to finish the work and win her vote. Every time Bluto tries to do Popeye in, it backfires and the dirty trick helps Popeye finish a task. The Sailorman wins Olive's vote, so Bluto punches him through a tractor and grabs Olive to drive her to the polls and force her to vote his way. But, of course, there's spinach growing on Olive's farm. Popeye wins the day and the election. As he and Olive are riding in the back of a convertible making victory gestures to the crowd watching the parade, their arms accidentally slip around each other, and they suddenly realize an attraction and share a cute, tender moment as the cartoon ends.

The promising title of this film notwithstanding, this is mostly just a typical "Popeye and Bluto compete to do stunts" cartoon, and is, therefore, somewhat disappointing.

Out To Punch (1956)

Director: Seymour Kneitel. *Animation:* Tom Johnson, John Gentilella. *Story:* Carl Meyer. *Scenics:* John Zago. *Music:* Winston Sharples.

Though Olive is a cutie in this cartoon, Bluto shows no romantic interest in her at all. Instead, his goal is to win a prizefight with Popeye, and Bluto is worried that Popeye will beat him. (Since when did Bluto ever think that!) So he first sabotages Popeye's training, or at least he tries to, but his schemes keep backfiring and he winds up taking physical punishment. But as Popeye is doing road work on the way to the arena, Bluto puts oil, and then wet cement, on the highway ahead of him. An exhausted Popeye, with cement blocks on his feet, arrives for the fight. A muscular Bluto, smoking a cigar, basically uses Popeye as a punching bag, then knocks him into the rafters and through the floor of the ring. As Popeye is being counted out, Olive feeds him his spinach. A restored Popeye's jaw morphs into a cement block. Bluto shreds his boxing gloves while hitting it. Then Bluto tries to clobber Popeye with a steel pole. It has no effect. Popeye's super-punch does, though, and Bluto goes flying out of the ring and into the hospital.

Once again, one must ask, "Why doesn't Popeye eat spinach before he starts fighting?"

Assault and Flattery (1956)

Director: I. Sparber. *Animation:* Al Eugster, Wm. P. Pattengill. *Story:* I. Klein. *Scenics:* Joseph Dommerque. *Music:* Winston Sharples.

Popeye and Bluto appear before Judge Wimpy because Bluto is charging The Sailorman with Assault And Battery. Bluto tells his story, via clips from *The Farmer And The Belle* and *How Green Is My Spinach*, to make his case. A weeping Wimpy tells him his story is very touching. But actually Wimpy is slicing onions for the hamburgers he's continually eating. Popeye responds with clips from *A Balmy Swami*. Wimpy pronounces Popeye innocent. Bluto attacks The Sailorman, out pops the spinach, and you know the rest.

This cartoon demonstrates that what happens in the films is real to the characters. This helped to make everything seem real to those of us who grew up watching these cartoons, too. Also, we see that Popeye and Bluto, being only human, have selective memories and "spin doctor" the events of the past to justify themselves.

Insect to Injury (1956)

Director: Dave Tendlar. *Animation:* Morey Reden, Thomas Moore. *Story:* I. Klein. *Scenics:* Anton Loeb. *Music:* Winston Sharples.

A laugh-filled cartoon that contains gags worthy of Warner Brothers, as Popeye versus anthropomorphic (and creepy looking) termites that want to eat the new house he's building. It's a battle of wits, slapstick, and cartoon universe physics. And the orchestra plays a memorable "termites on the march" theme.

One of the few times Famous Studios let Popeye get the best of tiny creatures; here the termites are defeated.

Finally, the bugs eat everything wooden Popeye has. The sailor eats spinach and quickly constructs an all-metal home. The termites break their teeth and knock themselves silly trying to consume it.

I Don't Scare (1956)

Director: I. Sparber. *Animation:* Tom Johnson, Frank Endres. *Story:* Jack Mercer. *Scenics:* Robert Owen. *Music:* Winston Sharples.

Bluto discovers that Olive is superstitious, so he changes her calendar to read "Fri 13." Olive then refuses to go out on a date with Popeye, fearing bad luck. Popeye tries to debunk her beliefs, but Bluto secretly keeps making it seem that Olive's fortunes have taken a turn for the worse. She gets electrocuted, trapped in a piano, and encased in a fish bowl. The latter mishap was actually Popeye's fault. He brings a mirror over to her so she can see how funny she looks. A sensitive boyfriend Popeye is not! Bluto pulls the rug out from under him, and Popeye smashes the mirror over Olive's head. Olive declares in a shocked and appealing voice, "Breaking a mirror is seven years bad luck!" She then kicks Popeye out of the house, saying she never wants to see him again.

Bluto, not able to keep himself from ruining the good thing he has going, sticks the real calendar page on a dejected Popeye's pipe, thereby alerting Popeye to what's been happening. Bluto then picks up Olive, telling her that it's really Thursday the 12th. The two stroll off arm-in-arm with Olive giving Bluto an adoring look, because, let's remember, in the Famous Studios cartoons, Olive has a relationship with Bluto and likes being alone with him.

But Popeye throws a horseshoe in Bluto's path, and when the big guy picks it up, Popeye uses a magnet to force Bluto's head into the rungs of a ladder. Then he smashes Bluto down on a box of dynamite and lights the three sticks of it which are stuck in Bluto's mouth with one match. Bluto's mouth is blown right off his face! His body goes soaring in the air. Popeye forms the number 13 with his bicep and punches Bluto into a weight and fortune machine.

Then Popeye walks with Olive — but not arm-in-arm. Popeye's not as romantic as Bluto! When they pass a telephone pole on opposite sides, Popeye hurries back and says, "Bread and butter!" Olive laughs to find out Popeye is superstitious, too. It is amusing, but it also makes Popeye's actions at the beginning of the cartoon seem hypocritical.

A Haul In One (1956)

Director: I. Sparber. *Animation:* Al Eugster, Wm. B. Pattengill. *Story:* Larz Bourne. *Scenics:* Robert Owen. *Music:* Winston Sharples.

Pretty Olive Oyl is smitten with moving men Popeye and Bluto, and vice versa. So the boys have a slapstick competition to see who can impress her the most by packing and loading her things. Even when Bluto tries to sabotage Popeye's efforts, Popeye always comes out on top. The Sailorman seems stronger and more competent than Bluto even before he eats his spinach in this cartoon. Olive says to him, "Bravo! Bravo! You're super, Man!" When Bluto finally squishes Popeye's neck between the halves of a dining room table, Popeye does eat the green veggie. And you can guess the rest of the story.

Nearlyweds (1957)

Director: Seymour Kneitel. *Animation:* Tom Johnson, Frank Endres. *Story:* I. Klein. *Scenics:* John Zago. *Music:* Winston Sharples.

One Internet poster used frames from this cartoon's close-up of Olive Oyl to explain why Popeye and Bluto always fight over her. As he put it, "Olive Oyl is a fox!" And in this film, she is indeed.

Popeye and Bluto both ask Olive Oyl to marry them. Olive decides between the two by going, "Eeny, meeny, meiny, moe." Maybe not the best way to make a momentous life decision, but at least it demonstrates that Olive loves Popeye and Bluto equally. Popeye wins, and Bluto appears to lose gracefully, but we know him better than that, don't we?

As Popeye is getting ready for the wedding the next day, Bluto puts cement in his bath, nails his shoes to the floorboards, glues his bottom to a chair, and causes a razor to attack him and shred his tux. The result is that Popeye hurries over to Olive's wearing a barrel!

Meanwhile, a curvy Olive is taking a cue from Scarlet O'Hara and getting her veil literally right out of the window. When Popeye shows up, she's understandably horrified. She thinks he's playing a sick joke on her and slams the door on him. Bluto, coming by in a tux, flicks his cigar ashes into Popeye's mouth. Then Bluto rings Olive's doorbell. She's delighted to see him. He tells her that he just happened by and was hoping she'd changed her mind. "I most certainly have!" The handsome Bluto and Olive, whose dress shows off her beautiful body and shapely legs, stroll past Popeye arm-in-arm on their way to the Justice Of The Peace.

As a happy wedding march is heard on the sound track, they arrive. The creators obviously don't think Olive marrying Bluto is such a bad thing. The Justice begins a singsong list of all the things Bluto will have to do, and give up, as a married man. Bluto decides domestic life isn't for him and, crashing through the wall, runs away. Olive is in hot pursuit to get him to come back. We then see that the Justice is really a laughing Popeye in disguise.

Both Bluto and Popeye are idiots in this cartoon. Bluto could have been honeymooning with the sexiest girl in his animated universe. But no!!! And Popeye thinks it's funny that the girl he wants to marry is chasing after another groom? Maybe Olive deserves someone better than either of them.

The Crystal Brawl (1957)

Director: Seymour Kneitel. *Animation:* Al Eugster, Wm. B. Pattengil. *Story:* Carl Meyer. *Scenics:* Joe Dommerque. *Music:* Winston Sharples.

Most of this cartoon is made up of reedited footage from *Alpine For You* and *Quick On The Vigor*. There's a new scene with a muscular Bluto and pretty Olive, in the outfits they wore in *Alpine for You*, included as well.

Bluto gets Popeye out of the way and goes off on the date The Sailorman was supposed to have with Olive at the fair. But Popeye poses as a fortune teller and shows Olive scenes, via the aforementioned footage, of what Bluto will do to her in the future. She rejects Bluto. Bluto realizes the mystic is Popeye and traps him with farm tools. Then, an enraged Bluto chases Olive into the Tunnel Of Love, but with violence, not romance, apparently on his mind. Fortunately, Popeye eats spinach and Bluto winds up hanging over a fire pit in a Tunnel exhibit labeled "Hades" while getting his buns toasted.

Patriotic Popeye (1957)

Director: I. Sparber. *Animation:* Tom Johnson, Frank Endres. *Story:* Carl Meyer. *Scenics:* Robert Owen. *Music:* Winston Sharples.

Popeye won't let his nephews have fireworks on the Fourth of July because they are too dangerous. Popeye wants to be safe and sane. But aren't safe and sane the antithesis of what cartoon characters are supposed to be? The nephews try to get Popeye out of the way using a bull, a hornet's nest, and other dangers. They finally get their fireworks and guess what? Popeye was right! The little brats are almost launched into orbit before Popeye eats his spinach and rescues them.

Spree Lunch (1957)

Director: Seymour Kneitel. *Animation:* Tom Johnson, Frank Endres. *Story:* Jack Mercer. *Scenics:* Joe Dommerque. *Music:* Winston Sharples.

Wimpy didn't appear often in the Famous Studios cartoons, but when he did, he was completely in character.

Popeye and Bluto both own diners and compete for Wimpy's business in this amusing cartoon. (Evidently Wimpy's non-payment policy doesn't bother them.) The film ends with Popeye and Bluto hurtling cooking appliances, utensils, furnishings, and food at one another. Wimpy calmly plucks the items out of the air that he needs and enjoys a sit-down dinner.

Spooky Swabs (1957)

Director: I. Sparber. *Animation:* Tom Johnson, Frank Endres. *Story:* Larz Bourne. *Scenics:* John Zago. *Music:* Winston Sharples.

Popeye and a cute and curvy Olive are once again adrift on a raft at sea, as ominous music plays to open the cartoon. Fortunately, Popeye spots a ship. Unfortunately, it's a literal ghost ship. British ghosts, who look like the ghostly trio of *Casper* fame, haunt the duo, causing "accidents." They even almost make Olive walk the plank. Finally, the ghosts reveal themselves to Ms. Oyl, but Popeye tells her there's no such thing as ghosts. Wrong again, Sailorman! The ghosts charge them, brandishing swords. Fleeing, Popeye finds "Ye King's Spinach" in the galley. It enables him to turn invisible and uppercut each spirit into a wall, where they go as limp as sheets. Olive then sews them together to make a sail for the ship. That Olive is always industrious!

Popeye and Olive sing together, hug, and sail off into the sunset, a fitting end to their careers as theatrical cartoon stars, and to the Famous Studious Popeye era.

APPENDIX A

The Paramount KFS Popeye Cartoons

In 1960, King Features Syndicate, the distributors of the Popeye comic strip, commissioned several different animation studies to produce made-for-TV Popeye cartoons. These films were aimed at children, so many of the elements that had made the theatrical releases so popular had to be toned way down. And Popeye's main foe was now Brutus. (King Features Syndicate mistakenly believed that they didn't own the character of Bluto, so the name and look had to be changed somewhat.) Still, Paramount Cartoon Studios was one of the groups that got the assignment, and Paramount was actually Famous Studios renamed. Therefore, the same creators from the Famous Studios years kept working on Popeye cartoons. And so, some of the magic of Famous Studios trickled into the new product, albeit in watered-down form. Here's a quick look at a few of the cartoons from Paramount which reflected the Famous Studios aura.

Motor Knocks

Popeye and Olive, out for a drive in Popeye's car, run out of gas and end up at a service station owned and operated by Brutus. The proprietor proceeds to come on to Ms. Oyl big time, saying that Olive will be his inspiration as he pursues his real career, songwriting. At one point, as the two seem destined for that magic kiss, Popeye has to stick a sign between them which says "Stop Check Your Brakes." Popeye, it should be said, is more consciously proactive in trying to keep Brutus and Olive apart in the KFS cartoons than he was in the Famous Studios films. When Popeye goes to punch Brutus for spraying oil all over him, Olive stops him because Brutus said he was sorry. Here we have the classic "Popeye looks like a jerk while the villain seems innocent" theme. While Popeye cleans up, Brutus and Olive get to be alone. Brutus later sabotages Popeye's car so that it won't be able to make it up "Suicide Hill." Now, there's a name to make young viewers shudder! Then he comes to the stranded Popeye and Olive's rescue in his tow truck. He gallantly carries the dreamily acquiescent and happy Olive to the cab of the truck, telling Popeye it will be safer for her there. Popeye's riding in the towed car. At the top of Suicide Hill, Brutus makes the car crash into the truck, breaking the towing cable, so that the damaged car and the injured Popeye plunge down Suicide Hill. Though Olive expresses concern that they are losing Popeye, she doesn't protest when Brutus says that that's the whole idea. She never yells for help or tries to escape, riding away quietly instead with Brutus in the undamaged truck. She mustn't think that losing Popeye and being alone with an amorous Brutus is such a bad prospect, after all. Certainly, he's more romantic and ambitious than The Sailorman is in this entire cartoon. But, of course, Popeye has a can of spinach in the dash of his car. He soon catches up to the tow truck, and you can guess the rest!

Medicine Man

A doctor (Brutus playing a role) tries to eliminate Popeye, the owner of a traveling medicine show, so he can move in on Popeye's cute partner, Olive Oyl. Though the doc uses some cartoony things on The Sailorman, like sneezing powder, jumping beans, and horse radish, the whole idea of a physician purposely giving "treatments" to someone in order to incapacitate him is pretty horrible and among the grossest the Famous Studios gang ever came up with. Not to mention that the doctor also uses a sleeping pill, tries to kill Popeye in a plane crash, and pushes the helpless and hapless sailor in a wheelchair down a steep hill. Popeye spends the majority of the cartoon hiccuping, sneezing, snoring, twitching, and convulsing, unable to do much else. He always looks sick or comatose. And the crafty doctor has played a trick so that neither Popeye nor Olive will trust spinach any more, and he has made himself appear the hero to Olive, as the one who is trying to save Popeye. After he has seemingly secretly dispatched Popeye for good, he and Olive are alone in his office where she seriously considers his offer to be his new partner. She never rejects him or yells for help. And after accidentally ingested spinach restores Popeye and he rushes into the scene and begins dealing out retribution, she first looks concerned, not joyful.

Voo-Doo To You Too

The Sea Hag makes Olive her slave and binds the arms of a Popeye doll with a hair, so that the real Popeye can't fight back. She then has her vulture dispose of the doll, but Popeye finds it with the help of the magical Jeep. However, even after Popeye eats spinach, the spell stays in place and he can't move his arms! The spinach has failed! The Sea Hag's magic is too powerful! Kids watching on TV just about fainted! But the doll is fed the spinach and it bursts free of the hair, destroying the dark sorcery.

Gem Jam

The Sea Hag hypnotizes Olive, causing her to steal a cursed gem from an idol's crown. The idol shoots a lightning bolt at her which causes the ground to open beneath her in an earthquake. Popeye saves her, but is trapped in the crevice without his spinach as it closes back up on him. This cartoon plays right into the fears of falling, earthquakes, getting crushed, and being buried alive! Luckily, Olive pours some spinach down a small crack and then eats the rest of the can herself so she can attack the witch. After Popeye and Olive return the gem, the idol sends out another lightning bolt which makes Olive jump into The Sailorman's arms. But the idol winks at them. It just wanted them to have a romantic moment as a reward.

Operation Ice-Tickle

At the North Pole, Brutus pounds Popeye through the ice cap into the arctic waters, which freeze him into an insensate, maybe dead, block of cold ice. A chilling scene for kids in more ways than one. Brutus prepares to return to civilization and a date with Olive. Popeye will be stranded forever! The exhaust from Brutus' rocket melts Popeye, though, who then downs his spinach.

My Fair Olive

Popeye and Olive Oyl tour a museum where the curator/owner/tour guide (Brutus playing a role again) falls for Ms. Oyl. Popeye gets mad as the two flirt, and the ever-carried-away-by-romantic-fantasies Olive suggests they settle things like in the olden days and joust for her hand. In a possibly risqué pun, Brutus says he will be her big knight. He looks dashing in his armor atop a magnificent horse, but Popeye is wearing a potbellied stove and riding a small, uncooperative donkey. Brutus actually wins the duel and, by all rights, Olive! But he did it in too violent a fashion to suit Olive. She rejects him, he chases her, Popeye eats spinach, you know the rest.

Kiddie Kapers

Olive lets Popeye know she wants to get married. He just puts her off with a lame joke. A rejected Olive then rejects Popeye, telling him he's too old for her anyway and that she wants someone young and handsome. Brutus, overhearing this, goes to the Sea Hag and gets a youth potion. It transforms him into a good-looking, well-built Latin lover. Popeye and Olive are sitting way apart on a porch swing, angry at each other and going through a breakup. Introducing himself as Don Juan, Brutus sits between them and begins wooing a smitten Olive. Popeye realizes that this is Brutus, though, takes the bottle of youth potion, and swigs some of it himself. He has taken too much and it turns him into a baby. Brutus begins giving him quite a spanking, revealing his true cruel identity to Olive. Olive gives Baby Popeye spinach and the day is saved, I guess. Popeye still rejected Olive in a cruel way at the beginning of the cartoon, though. And the young Brutus was quite the suave guy in action!

Brutus shares the weakness of his predecessor, Bluto.

Butler Up

Olive, wearing a slinky black evening gown which shows off her curves, and a different hairstyle which accentuates her pretty face, wants to impress her old college boyfriend — Brutus! (Olive and Brutus were alone together for four years with no Popeye in sight!?!?) So she asks Popeye to pose as her butler. This hampers Popeye, as he tries to keep the couple from ultimately reuniting. He can't slug Brutus, but he can keep interrupting the couple, which he does. And Brutus keeps disposing of him by embedding him into a wall, tangling him up in a coat, and propelling the serving tray he's carrying, and him, away from the table. Finally, Popeye acts as though he has given up. He's off by himself sadly washing the dishes while Brutus is winning Olive back with tales of his glory days as a sports star. Olive really gives Brutus the goo-goo, "come here big boy," alluring eyes and tells him that he was her football hero. But Brutus, as impatient as Bluto always was, grabs Popeye and tries to use him as a prop in the seduction of Olive, while getting rid of him for good at the same time. Talk about killing two birds with one stone! Brutus scrunches Popeye into a football shape as he finishes the story for Olive of how he won an important game with a field goal, and then kicks The Sailorman through Olive's window into the stratosphere, soaring miles away from Olive. Olive is shocked at Brutus. Popeye looks completely out of it. Brutus drops all pretense and becomes animalistic, letting us know exactly what he wants. (A kiss, right, kids?) Olive has to hold him off using a chair as though she was a lion tamer (or maybe that should be "wolf tamer!"). Fortunately for her, Popeye comes to and eats his spinach.

Oil's Well That Ends Well

Brutus tries to gyp Olive out of her prize money by selling her a phony oil well. Popeye tumbles to the con, though. Brutus backhands Popeye into a derrick where a steel bar catches The Sailorman in the throat. Then Brutus runs Popeye over with his car two times. Popeye eats spinach before Brutus can finish him with a third attempt. (Using a car to kill someone is just a tad too realistic for a kiddie cartoon!) Olive rewards Popeye by covering him in kisses via footage from the Famous Studios cartoon *Fright to the Finish*.

APPENDIX B
Under The Influence

Stories about love triangles and tales that feature extreme violence and/or cause one to ask questions have been around seemingly since the dawn of time. Therefore, it's hard to say for sure how much Famous Studios Popeye cartoons influenced the entertainment media, but I'll mention some works that seem to me to have been inspired by the Famous Studios films.

First, appropriately enough, an animated cartoon. In *Real Gone Woody*, a Woody Woodpecker cartoon from Walter Lantz in 1954, Woody and Buzz Buzzard brawl with each other and try to get rid of each other as they vie for a date to the sock hop with cute bird Winnie. Their antics remind one of Popeye and Bluto. Buzz even puts Woody in a final trap that's worthy of Famous Studios in its strangeness, creepiness, and its ability to conjure up feelings we can't even name. And it seems as though it should have spelled curtains for Woody. Buzz engulfs Woody in a mound of pottery clay. He then keeps working it and working it through his fingers, until it's obvious that there's nothing left of it, or the absorbed Woody! When Winnie asks about Woody, hepcat Buzz says that he's gone, real gone. He then takes the happily flirting, smitten miss for a ride. Woody reappears, with no explanation of how he survived. (Maybe he found some spinach in whatever limbo of nonexistence he was transported to?) He dresses in drag, like Popeye in *Popeye and the Pirates* and *Popeye's Pappy*, to play a trick on Buzz. The cartoon ends with Winnie going off with the singer from the band, and Woody and Buzz commiserating together as Popeye and Bluto did in *Shape Ahoy* and *Shaving Muggs*.

In the live-action motion picture realm, *Honeymoon In Vegas* has always seemed to me like one long Famous Studios Popeye cartoon, only just not as enjoyable. What's fun for six minutes can be very uncomfortable and disturbing when stretched out to feature length. James Caan, millionaire mobster, falls for Nicholas Cage's fiancée, Sarah Jessica Parker, because she looks like his dead wife and like, well, Sarah Jessica Parker. He tricks Cage, a gullible and frankly unlikable sad sack, into letting him spend the weekend with her, and the he proceeds to dazzle and woo her. It seems like he's winning her! Cage can't catch up to them to interrupt because of obstacles of his own making, and those put in his path by Caan. Sweet Parker comes to doubt that Cage cared for her at all. Still Cage perseveres and arrives to save the day. (He should have eaten some spinach as he parachuted.) Caan has shown his true colors and has become insistent and abusive with Parker, and she has had to flee from him. Popeye and Olive, er, I mean, Cage and Parker, find each other and have a happy ending. Bluto, er, I mean, Caan, not so much. Even though we think the sweet and sexy Parker should have done better than Popeye, er, I mean Cage, at least he never got rough with her like Bluto, er, I mean Caan did.

And many cartoons and live-action movies feature scenes where a hero's superpowers, or source of his abilities, are taken away. For example, Felix The Cat would have his Magic Bag stolen, and Lex Luthor's men beat on a Kryptonite-irradiated Superman in *Superman Returns*.

Let's turn now to the realm of comic books, and first to Popeye comic books themselves. Though the characters in them always looked like they did in the comic strips, they sometimes acted, and were treated, like they were the Famous Studios cast.

In *Popeye*, volume 1, No. 45 (July-Sept. 1958) from Dell, in a story titled, *Girl Guard*, Popeye appoints Swee'Pea to stay with Olive while he works on his boat because he knows guys will try to beat his time with her. Sure enough, Bluto (though unnamed in this story) shows up at Olive's with flowers and a smooth line. Olive is overwhelmed. Bluto sits on Swee'Pea and tells Olive the tyke is taking a nap. The two go off to the park together and soon Bluto takes Olive rowing out on the lake. Swee'Pea swims underwater and drills a hole in their boat. But this only gives Bluto a chance to save Olive's life and be her big, strong hero. Hearts are flying around Olive. In order to dry off from this dousing in the water, Olive and Bluto take a playful jog around the lake. Swee'Pea yells for help from Popeye because, "A big swab is chasing Olive through the park!" A spinach-powered Popeye punches Bluto and beats him up — for no reason! Olive punches Popeye, calling him, "Cad!" Then Bluto lays on the grass across Olive's lap as she says to him, "You poor boy...did that nasty sailor brute damage you?" A disgusted Popeye carries Swee'Pea off. And Olive is together with Bluto at the end of the story! Finally! Every Famous Studios fan's wish come true!

Popeye The Sailor, No. 147 (June 1979) from Western Publishing, which reprints an earlier Dell issue, finds Popeye ruining Olive's birthday and inadvertently setting her up to be won over by restaurateur Bluto (unnamed in this story as well) who pours on the charm. Soon he's Olive's new boyfriend, and Olive never wants to see Popeye again. She warns Popeye that Bluto is bigger than him and that he'll smash Popeye if The Sailorman tries to see Olive again. A dejected Popeye believes this! Popeye was never lower than this in any Famous

Studios cartoon. Then he says he's going to try and commit suicide! It turns out he only wants to gain Olive's sympathy, but he fails when he dives off the pier at low tide and lands in mud. Wimpy tells Popeye he will only win Olive back if he has a better restaurant than Bluto. After eating spinach, Popeye builds a restaurant next to Bluto's in 47 minutes. But he only serves spinach there, so he has to knock out his customer and paint a smiling face on him so Olive will think the customer is satisfied. But Bluto comes in and challenges Popeye to satisfy him. Popeye force-feeds him spinach and then realizes he's made a mistake. Bluto has developed "spinach muscles" and he and Popeye fight for hours, destroying their restaurants in the process. Olive goes off arm-in-arm with Wimpy! He's taking her to a picnic and — get this — he's bringing the food! Has the world been turned upside-down? It seems that Wimpy, like all males in the Popeye universe, is interested in Olive Oyl! And he wins her!

In *Popeye*, Vol. 6, No. 118 (February 1973) from Charlton Comics, there's a story that doesn't have Popeye in it at all! Instead, it features Brutus and Olive on a romantic winter date. But disasters keep interrupting the romance, which they are both enjoying. They go up the ski lift and a scared Olive yells, "Hold me tight, Brutus!" Then Olive, climbing on Brutus out of fear at the top of the mountain, sends them down before Brutus is ready. They go over a ski jump, while a frightened Brutus wants Olive to hold him. It turns out Olive enjoyed it all and wants to do it again. Brutus wants her to teach him to knit. All the jokes notwithstanding, this is a story focused on Olive and Brutus alone together, enjoying each other's company, and being in love.

A text piece in *Popeye*, Vol. 9, No. 137 (October 1976) from Charleton Comics, entitled *Snow Me Down*, has Popeye going skiing with Olive for the first time. She already knows how. Brutus is the local ski instructor. He tells Popeye that the most important thing about skiing is to keep your eyes closed. And Popeye falls for it! Brutus then pushes Popeye down a treacherous hill and off a ski jump. He crashes into a snow bank and is being turned into a human icicle. Brutus takes Olive in his arms and goes for a kiss. Olive yells and begs Popeye to help her. Popeye gets burning mad, uses his pipe as a blowtorch to melt the snowdrift, eats a can of spinach, and is transformed into Super Skier. He saves the day, of course. The story reads like it was one of the animated cartoons.

Switching to another company and other characters, a story I read in Archie, #249, December 1975, reminded me of Famous Studios Popeye cartoons because it has attractive characters, a hot romance, deception, and enough strangeness to make one feel a little creepy after reading it. A beautiful Veronica Lodge is excitedly telling Archie that a movie star is staying at her mansion. Veronica is very Olive Oyl and Betty Boop-like in this story, the very picture of the sweet young miss caught up in a fantasy. It turns out that the star is a young, muscular, handsome action/adventure hero and one of Veronica's favorites. His name is Brandy Wine. And he wants to get rid of Archie. He first crushes Archie's hand when the two rivals shake (much as Bluto did to Popeye in several cartoons), and knocks Archie to the ground while giving him a "friendly" slap on the back. He says his superhuman strength often gets him in trouble. When Archie starts to get mad, Veronica tells Arch that he shouldn't make a movie star apologize. Not matter how Archie responds, it will be wrong. Popeye was in a similar fix in *The Royal Four-Flusher*, as Olive defended The Count. Brandy Wine tells Archie he will show him how Hollywood stages a fight scene. But Archie lands in wet cement, ruining Mr. Lodge's project and his shoes. Veronica tells him to leave. The star lends Archie his shoes. After Archie is gone, the star takes an eager, smitten, acquiescent Veronica in his arms and says he will show her how they do love scenes. And he does!! Reggie spies the two of them and tells a defeated Archie that he wishes he was in Brandy Wine's shoes. So Archie sells him the shoes. The story ends with Veronica's two usual beaus, Archie and Reggie, alone and frustrated while another guy has his way with the sweet young miss. Popeye and Bluto were left high and dry, and another guy ended up with Olive Oyl in several cartoons, too. But we kind of root for Brandy and Veronica to end up together, while at the same time lamenting what's happened to our good friend, the outclassed Archie, in the same way viewers used to enjoy seeing Olive and another guy get romantic, while fearing for Popeye. Now for the creepiness. Veronica's father, Mr. Lodge, has evidently gone off, sent the household staff away, and left his gorgeous, nubile daughter alone at the mansion with her idol, a libidinous handsome hunk. What kind of father is he? And Brandy Wine is portrayed as being somewhat older than Veronica and Archie. So a 20-something guy is making out with a teenager and this is our happy ending!!!! But just as we Popeye fans tried to harmonize and justify the plots of the animated films and place them in some kind of continuity, so many Archie fans say that stories like this one must take place after the characters are out of high school. This minimizes the creepiness factor and allows us to enjoy them.

APPENDIX C
Sources

E.C. Segar *Popeye* comic strips culled from various collections.

Back issues of the *Official Popeye Fan Club News-Magazine*. Order at *www.popeyethesailor.com* or 618-826-4567 or Official Popeye Fan Club, 1001 State Street, Chester, IL 62233.

Books by Fred Grandinetti:
He Am What He Am! Jack Mercer the Voice of Popeye, BearManor Media, 2008.
Popeye: An Illustrated Cultural History, Second Edition, McFarland & Company, 2004.
Popeye the Collectible, Krause Publications, 1990.

The Cartoon Music Book, edited by Daniel Goldmark and Yuval Taylor, A Cappella Books, 2002.

Of Mice and Magic: A History Of American Animated Cartoons, Revised Edition, by Leonard Maltin, Penguin Books, 1987.

Numerous websites and message boards, including The Internet Movie Database *(us.imdb.com)*, The Big Cartoon Database *(www.bcdb.com)*, Animation Show Forums *(www.animationshow.com/forums/index)*, YouTube *(www.youtube.com)*, GAC forums *(forums.goldenagecartoons.com)*, Popeye Animator ID *(popeyeanimators.blogspot.com)*, Wikipedia *(en.wikipedia.org)*, and The Rough House Café *(roughhousecafe.proboards56.com)*.

APPENDIX D
Availability

At the time of this writing, Warner Home Video is in the process of releasing all the theatrical Popeye cartoons on DVD in chronological order. Warner has also announced that they will eventually release all of the King Features Syndicate made-for-TV cartoons as well. For details contact Warner Home Video at *classiccartoonsdvd.com* and *warnervideo.com* or at Warner Home Video, 4000 Warner Blvd., Burbank, CA 91522.

KOCH Vision released 85 of the KFS made-for-TV cartoons in its *Popeye 75th Anniversary Celebration Collector's Edition* DVD set. The set includes some of the best ones from Paramount Studios. KFS cartoons can also be found on old video tape releases.

The following Famous Studios Popeye cartoons are now in the public domain (their copyrights weren't renewed) and can be found on numerous DVDs and video tapes from various companies:

Me Musical Nephews	*Popeye for President*
Shuteye Popeye	*Out to Punch*
Big Bad Sindbad	*Assault and Flattery*
Ancient Fistory	*Insect to Injury*
Floor Flusher	*Parlez Vous Woo*
Popeye's 20th Anniversary	*I Don't Scare*
Taxi-Turvy	*A Haul in One*
Bride and Gloom	*Nearlyweds*
Greek Mirthology	*The Crystal Brawl*
Fright To The Finish	*Patriotic Popeye*
Private Eye Popeye	*Spree Lunch*
Gopher Spinach	*Spooky Swabs*
Cookin' With Gags	

At the time of this writing, Popeye cartoons are shown on the Boomerang! satellite TV network in the USA, and some can be downloaded from YouTube and other websites.

ENDNOTES

Introduction

1. When I was growing up, there were Popeye cartoons from three different producers shown on TV. The Fleischer Studios films, the Famous Studios cartoons, and the made-for-TV cartoons commissioned by King Features Syndicate. The Fleischer films featured the characters in all of their ugly comic strip glory and seemed mostly to take place in a surreal, run down, ghetto world. The Famous Studios cartoons softened Popeye's appearance and made Olive Oyl and Bluto over into good-looking, romantic leads. The adventures took place in cleaner, more modern, more "realistic" environments. The King Features Syndicate (KFS) cartoons featured a mostly heroic Popeye, a cute Olive Oyl, and a darker, rotund antagonist, named Brutus.

Chapter One

1. Popeye made his screen debut in the Betty Boop cartoon, *Popeye The Sailor* (1933), produced by Fleischer Studios and supervised by brothers Max and Dave Fleischer. The Fleischers were in charge of Popeye's animated career until the middle of 1942, when they lost their studio to Paramount. Paramount changed the studio's name to "Famous Studios," using the name of the corporation's music publishing arm.
2. Spinach was introduced in the comic strip by Segar because it was being widely touted as a good source of iron and as an important element of a healthy diet.
3. Segar wasn't interested in strict continuity.
4. But unlike the Famous Studios cartoons, the Fleischer films never let Bluto get very far with Olive Oyl.
5. The fact that Popeye and Bluto became servicemen in World War II explains why they changed outfits. Instead of donning their black, generic sailor duds, in the last Fleischer films and in the Famous Studios cartoons, they would usually wear white or blue uniforms when they were dressed as sailors.
6. When Paramount Pictures ousted Max and Dave Fleischer and took control of their studio in 1942, renaming it Famous Studios, the company kept the creative talent Max and Dave had employed.
7. Yes, folks, Popeye commits murder for the sake of a "joke"? Talk about being out of character!
8. Near the beginning of this film, sexual norms are set on their ears as we see Popeye painting his toenails to get ready for a date with Olive!
9. Later in the film, we find out that it is actually her costume that has the figure, or is it? As she clings to the main tent pole, we see that her body has some curves.

Chapter Two

1. Spinach makes Bluto beat up Popeye when The Sailorman wants to be injured in order to get Olive's attention and sympathy in *For Better Or Nurse* and *Beaus Will Be Beaus*, and turns the brute into a ship building machine in *Too Weak To Work*.

2. Our hearts also go out to the nephews. More on that later in this chapter.

3. In the early 1960's, Jack Kinney produced a made-for-TV cartoon for King Features Syndicate entitled *Spinach Shortage*, in which Popeye, deprived of his spinach, acts just like a drug addict desperately wanting his next hit. He becomes totally weak, goes into a trance-like state, and he even breaks into a warehouse to steal some spinach! It's easy to see where the idea for this cartoon came from. Just watch the Famous Studios films!

4. In *Popeye And The Pirates*, Popeye sprouts chest hairs after eating his spinach near the end of the cartoon. Does eating spinach symbolize the coming of manhood?

5. In the Famous Studios cartoons, it is often other characters, not Popeye, who move the plots ahead. They are proactive. He is reactive. They have goals in mind. He does not. He's just there.

6. "More realistic," of course, being a relative term.

7. Segar's tough guy version of Popeye dressed in drag a couple of times, but was hilarious, not creepy, when he did so. And he wasn't trying to seduce anyone! Once, he put on a skirt to join a mothers group so he could learn how to care for his adopted "boy kid" Swee'Pea. Another time, he disguised himself as a little old lady to humiliate a gang of bullies. When the bullies picked on "her," the "little old lady" bopped them good.

Chapter Three

1. At least on television screens. The Olive in the comic strips and comic books remained traditionally homely, though. While the comic strips and comic books had their own appeal, looking at pretty people (namely Olive Oyl and Bluto) was one of the reasons viewers tuned in when the Famous Studios Popeye cartoons were shown on TV.

2. Some of these guys were Bluto in disguise, but for most of those cartoons, Bluto would act just like the character he was pretending to be, so it was easy to believe that he was the character and that the character was falling for Olive, romancing her in the way the character would. So, "Superman" saves her from falling, "Santa Claus" tells her a sexy version of *'Twas The Night Before Christmas*, "The International" kisses her hand, etc. More on the many faces of Bluto and Popeye's other rivals in the next chapter.

3. There will be more about Popeye's treatment of Olive and his suitability, or lack thereof, to be her mate, in Chapter Six.

4. There are those few cartoons where Olive's sudden rejection of her new beau is seemingly inexplicable (ex. *Safari So Good, Symphony In Spinach, Vacation With Play*). But because these films were the exception, rather than the rule, viewers often justified Olive's actions in their minds, conditioned as they were to thinking that Olive always had good reasons for doing what she did.

5. "Too violent and mean" being, of course, relative terms when it comes to animated cartoons!

6. Contrary to popular belief, the Famous Studios Olive Oyl wasn't adverse to kissing and getting physical. She just didn't want to be rushed, pressured, or forced. She would give her hand to guys, but she didn't want them to try to snatch it from her.

7. The Fleischer Olive Oyl ate spinach in the popular *Never Kick A Woman* when a gorgeous blonde women's self-defense instructor put the moves on Popeye. The spinach transformed Olive into a fighting hellcat. In the King Features Syndicate made-for-TV cartoons which came after the Famous Studios films, a cute version of Olive ate the spinach more often. This was because the KFS cartoons used Segar's Sea Hag as a continuing villainess, and Popeye's code of ethics wouldn't allow him to hit a woman. So, Olive would take over the fighting. The KFS Olive also ate the green veggie to stop Popeye from being ensnared by a beautiful, magical siren. When the KFS Olive would swallow spinach, she sometimes would gain biceps, or other parts of her body would temporarily swell, giving the visual impression that she was gaining strength.

Chapter Four

1. Actually, Olive has already described the Famous Studios Bluto in the quote from *Abusement Park* which is the title of this chapter.

2. How did he get those, by the way? Does he spend all of his time crumpling newspapers or twisting the lids off jars?

3. Grimek was brought out to Hollywood and recruited by several major studios but, after a few months, did a very Segar Popeye-esque thing — he told them where to get off and returned to his home town of York, PA and his humble job in a steel mill.

4. Observe how he treats Olive in *Beaus Will Be Beaus* and *Mister And Mistletoe.*

5. There will be more about Bluto's romantic side in Chapter Six.

Chapter Five

1. For example, Famous Studios made the ultra-violent Herman and Katnip cartoons which inspired *The Simpsons* own cat and mouse pair, Itchy and Scratchy.

2. Multi-talented Jack Mercer's life and career is covered in Fred Grandinnetti's book *He Yam What He Yam! Jack Mercer: The Voice Of Popeye* (Bear Manor Media, 2008). Included in the book is an essay by me about Mercer's work as Popeye.

3. Once again, as in Chapter Four, I'm using the name "Bluto" in this chapter to stand for all of Popeye's male rivals who embodied the spirit of Bluto.

4. There will be more about the moral ambiguity of the Famous Studios Popeye cartoons in Chapter Seven.

Chapter Six

1. Some Baby Boomers were first introduced to these popular songs through watching Popeye cartoons on TV

2. Once again, I'm using the name "Bluto" to refer to all of Popeye's male rivals for Olive Oyl.

3. Also, we know that Bluto is such a raging hormonal type of guy that it is doubtful that he will stop and be content with just one "little kiss."

4. Those scenes occur in *Tops In The Big Top, Pre-Hysterical Man,* and *Alpine For You.*

5. A case could be made that the straitjacket in *The Royal Four-Flusher* was also going too far.

6. For a fuller explanation, see the chapters in Part II on each of these cartoons.

7. More examples of pushing the envelope and tweaking the noses of the censors will be found in Part II of this book.

8. All of this is accompanied by a saucy, daring, jaunty score on the soundtrack.

Chapter Seven

1. Once again, I'm using the name "Bluto" in this chapter to refer to all of Popeye's male enemies.

2. Technically, Popeye helped with this rescue.

3. Some would say that Bluto isn't very heroic in *Pitchin' Woo At The Zoo* because he takes the time to don a suit of armor before entering the cage to save Olive. But consider that Popeye was "spinached up" when went into cage. So, actually, both Bluto and Popeye were relying on outside help to enhance their abilities as they undertook Olive's rescue.

Chapter Eight

1. Another character voiced by Jackson Beck in non-Popeye Famous Studios cartoons. Buzzy talked like a minstrel show character and would be offensive to audiences today.

2. Those last lines might also be:

> "Yet he'd sign for
> some Hidey-Ho-Oh
> Poor Robinson Crusoe!"

3. It's Bluto playing a role in this cartoon.

4. See Chapter Three for an explanation of O.O.O.P.S.

5. In cartoons such as this one, the Famous Studios Popeye is very much like his Segar counterpart and a Timex watch in that he takes a lickin' and keeps on tickin'!

6. The Famous Studios writers loved to use the word "phony" as a disparaging term, even when it didn't make sense. In this cartoon, how was the island a "phony?"

Chapter Nine

1. Remember the red hat. It will be important later.

2. Watch the kissing sequence in slow motion to really appreciate it.

3. How he can hear her when she's so far away, or even knows where she is, are just two of those unsolved cartoon mysteries.

4. Despite all she goes through in the cartoons, Olive's hair usually stays in place. In *Symphony In Spinach*, however, it is mussed up after she has spent time at the piano trying to fend off an amorous Bluto.

5. Squirrels will help him come to Olive's rescue in *Vacation With Play*.

Chapter Ten

1. See Chapter Three for an explanation of O.O.O.P.S.

2. Translation: "Enter, if you please, My Dear One."

3. Ah, those mysterious, powerful Arabians of our mythic past who could tame and command such creatures!

4. The whole bird gag was first used in Fleischer Studios' film, *Popeye the Sailor Meets Sindbad the Sailor*.

Chapter Eleven

1. See Chapter Three for an explanation of O.O.O.P.S.

2. "What beautiful eyes you got, Olive!" Get it?

3. The interior of the Trading Post is drawn in a very detailed way throughout the cartoon.

4. This line has stayed with viewers through the years, not only because it's a fun pun, but also because the covering and uncovering of bare skin and/or the threat thereof seems to be a theme of the cartoon.

5. Being eaten also plays into the childhood fears of the cartoons' audiences. Think of how many fairy tales, fables, folk tales, and children's stories center around kids, small animals, and even Johnny Cakes and Gingerbread Men facing the threat of being eaten by witches, ogres, bigger predators, dragons, etc.!

Chapter Twelve

1. See Chapter Three for an explanation of O.O.O.P.S.

2. Some fans stop their tapes or turn off their TVs as Olive is enjoying the piano music. Leaving she and Bluto there in love, before things get nasty, seems a more satisfying ending to the cartoon that the one the creators gave us. You gotta love the cartoon's last Popeye versus Bluto sequence, though!

3. He and his instrumentalists really got a workout with this cartoon!

Chapter Thirteen

1. See Chapter Three for an explanation of O.O.O.P.S.

2. The soundtrack from *Snow Place Like Home* is reused here, including even the squeaky licks of Olive's tongue against the ice cream cones from that cartoon. But there aren't any ice cream cones or tongues in the current scene! Uh, oh, a blooper!

3. Maybe the object was supposed to be the lifeguard's hat flying off his head, and the string was supposed to be speed lines, but his hat stays in place the whole scene.

4. We do notice, though, that Olive is looking at Mr. Lifeguard more than she looks at Popeye and that she flirts with the lifeguard using her face and eyes whenever she's near him in the tug-of-war. She's not as neutral as she thinks she is!

5. Incidentally, the lifeguard uses his ears for oars. This guy is much stronger than Popeye. Popeye had to use his feet!

Chapter Fifteen

1. A definition of O.O.O.P.S. can be found in Chapter Three.

2. Unlike Popeye, Mr. Instructor is very thoughtful and considerate of Olive Oyl.

3. It's interesting that the spinach seems to be controlling and directing Popeye here, sending him off in the right direction before he can even be totally aware of what needs to be done. It's really the squirrels and the spinach, not Popeye, that save Olive's virtue in this cartoon.

Chapter Sixteen

1. Or maybe Olive's just oblivious to things going on around her as cartoon characters often need to be so the plot can advance.

2. In this cartoon, the creators applied the old cliche, "You're beautiful when you're angry," to Olive. But the prettiest, and most appealing, ticked-off Olive comes later in the film.

3. See Chapter Three for an explanation of O.O.O.P.S.

4. Moments like these in the cartoons can lead one to daydream about what Bluto and Olive are like when Popeye isn't around. They obviously have a thing for each other, have fun being together, are compatible, know a lot about each other, and don't mind getting intimate. So, wouldn't they date if Popeye was absent? And what would happen on those dates? Where would they go, what would they say, what would they do? And wouldn't the date end with a kiss, or twenty? What would happen if Bluto were to propose? Popeye wasn't always hanging around Olive. We saw cartoons where he was on a mission at sea, or taking a vacation by himself, or spending the day with his nephews or sitting with them at night, or trying to catch a nap, or working in his spinach garden, or visiting the orphanage, or prize fighting, or going for a drive in the country, or being kidnapped by aliens, or participating in an across the USA auto race. And we also know that Olive, being who she is, wouldn't exactly sit home by herself while all of this was going on. She'd be out with her "other boyfriend," or even another suitor besides Bluto. So, one can have fun with this provocative concept. The later, made-for-TV, KFS cartoons did, too. They revealed that Brutus and Olive had been a couple in college *(Butler Up)*, let Popeye show up at Olive's only to discover that she had already made a date with Brutus *(Coffee House)*, had Brutus and Olive spending quality time together while Popeye is in a space capsule for 90 days *(Astro-Nut)*, and sent a potentate's henchmen to kidnap Olive for a bride while Popeye was off with the Foreign Legion *(Insultin' The Sultan)*. So did the Fleischer cartoons when Popeye returned from voyages only to discover that Olive had moved out west to be with her "new" boyfriend, Cowboy Bluto *(Me Feelin's Is Hurt)*, or joined the circus to partner with the daring young man on the flying trapeze *(The Man On The Flying Trapeze)*.

5. If this has never happened to you while diving, it's because you're not a cartoon character.

6. Many of us completed Beaus in our minds so that the couple did stay together — forever!

Chapter Seventeen

1. Whatever happened to the fourth one is just one of the mysteries associated with the boys in this cartoon.

2. The mantle piece and hearth are drawn very realistically, as is the staircase the boys race up and the upper floor that wraps around it.

3. Maybe Bluto's delight isn't faked, for, as we shall see, he's about to get rid of Popeye.

4. Not to mention how Olive's jeopardy plays into Humankind's questionings and deep fears: If spiritual and mythological and powerful forces exist out there, are they benign or malevolent?

5. It's interesting that Popeye felt he needed spinach to handle Bluto, especially since we saw The Sailorman exhibit super strength, stamina, and recuperative powers without it earlier in the cartoon. Bluto must be one tough customer!

Chapter Eighteen

1. For an explanation of O.O.O.P.S., see Chapter Three.

2. The International is a spoof of "The Continental," a character who appeared on CBS in the early '50s reading love poems to the women in the viewing audience.

3. Bluto's French accent is a little cheesier than his TV counterpart's, and Bluto uses some Pepe Le Pew-level phony French. But both Bluto and the real International are voiced by Jackson Beck.

4. Bluto doesn't know French very well, does he?

INDEX OF CARTOONS MENTIONED IN THIS BOOK

*Pages where the cartoon is the main focus are in **boldface**.*

Famous Studios Popeye Cartoons

A Balmy Swami (1949) 25, 28, 61, 62, 68, 69, **256-257,** 291
A Haul In One (1956) **293,** 309
A Hull Of A Mess (1942) **213-214**
A Job For A Gob (1955) **288-289**
A Jolly Good Furlough (1943) **216**
A Wolf In Sheik's Clothing (1948) 36, 37, 44, 47, 61, 63, 68, 69, **101-120**
Abusement Park (1947) 46, **239-240,** 313
All's Fair At The Fair (1947) 35, 44, 45, 62, 69, **245-246**
Alona On The Sarong Seas (1942) 14, **213**
Alpine For You (1951) 45, 62, 67, **267-268,** 294, 313
Ancient Fistory (1953) **275,** 309
Assault And Flattery (1956) **291,** 309
Baby Wants A Battle (1953) **278**
Baby Wants Spinach (1950) **262-263**
Barking Dogs Don't Fite (1949) **259-260**
Beach Peach (1950) 26, 27, 34, 37, 38, 42, 44, 46, 47, 63, 68, **141-155**
Beaus Will Be Beaus (1955) 26, 38, 39, 67, 68, 70, **181-191,** 312, 313
Big Bad Sinbad (1952) **275,** 309
Bride And Gloom (1954) 24, **282,** 309
Car-Azy Drivers (1955) 69, **286-287**
Cartoons Ain't Human (1943) **218**
Child Sockology (1953) **276**
Cookin' With Gags (1955) 38, 46, 67, 68, **284-285,** 309
Cops Is Tops (1955) 27, 28, 34, 69, **287-288**
Double-Cross-Country Race (1951) 44, **269**
Fireman's Brawl (1953) 40, 68, **278-279**
Floor Flusher (1954) **280-281,** 309
For Better Or Nurse (1945) **228-229,** 312
Friend Or Phony (1952) 22, 23, 27, **273-274**

Fright To The Finish (1954) 68, **283,** 301, 309
Gift Of Gag (1955) **286**
Gopher Spinach (1954) 22, **284,** 309
Greek Mirthology (1954) 22, 25, **282-283,** 309
Gym Jam (1950) 27, 62, **261-262**
Happy Birthdaze (1943) 16, 17, 60, **217**
Her Honor The Mare (1943) 15, 26, **218**
Hill-billing And Cooing (1956) 40, 288, **289-290**
Hot Air Aces (1949) **255**
House Tricks? (1946) **230**
How Green Is My Spinach (1950) 23, 46, 70, 71, **260-261,** 291
I Don't Scare (1956) **292-293,** 309
I'll Be Skiing Ya (1947) 39, 62, 68, **240-241,** 273
Insect To Injury (1956) **291-292,** 309
Jitterbug Jive (1950) 24, 25, 26, 28, 39, 47, 62, 67, 68, 69, **157-166**
Klondike Casanova (1946) 44, 47, 62, 64, 103, **231-235**
Let's Stalk Spinach (1951) **270**
Lumberjack And Jill (1949) 62, 68, **254-255**
Lunch With A Punch (1952) 46, **271-272**
Me Musical Nephews (1942) 25, **214,** 265, 309
Mess Production (1945) 31, 32, **229-230**
Mister And Mistletoe (1955) 25, 35, 38, 58, **193-202,** 313
Moving Aweigh (1944) **223**
Nearlyweds (1957) 39, 46, 68, 71, **293-294,** 309
Nurse To Meet Ya (1955) 26, **285**
Olive Oyl For President (1948) 35, 69, **246-247**
Out To Punch (1956) **290-291,** 309
Parlez Vous Woo (1956) 24, 26, 28, 29, 33, 34, 37, 38, 54, 60, 61, 69, **203-209,** 281, 309
Patriotic Popeye (1957) 22, 26, **295,** 309
Peep In The Deep (1946) **235**
Penny Antics (1955) **286**
Pilgrim Popeye (1951) **269-270**

Pitchin' Woo At The Zoo (1944) 16, 67, 68, **222**, 314
Popalong Popeye (1952) **274**
Popeye And The Pirates (1947) 23, 26, 27, 28, 68, 103, **241-242**, 303, 312
Popeye For President (1956) **290**, 309
Popeye Makes A Movie (1950) 25, **262**
Popeye Meets Hercules (1948) 27, 37, 42, 44, **251-252**
Popeye, The Ace Of Space (1953) 23, **279**
Popeye's 20th Anniversary (1954) **281**, 309
Popeye's Mirthday (1953) **276**
Popeye's Pappy (1952) 28, **271**, 303
Popeye's Premiere (1949) **253**
Pop-Pie A La Mode (1945) 9, 16, 52, 103, **225-226**, 252
Pre-Hysterical Man (1948) 9, 36, 42, 62, 63, 68, 70, **248-251**, 313
Private Eye Popeye (1954) **283-284**, 309
Punch And Judo (1951) 22, 23, **270-271**
Puppet Love (1944) 16, 28, 38, 60, **221**
Quick On The Vigor (1950) 25, 42, 62, 69, **263-265**, 294
Ration Fer The Duration (1943) 16, **216-217**
Riot In Rhythm (1950) 25, **265**
Robin Hood-Winked (1948) 22, 62, 63, **253**
Rocket To Mars (1946) 9, 22, **236**
Rodeo Romeo (1946) 23, 24, 25, 28, 46, 47, 62, **236-237**, 281
Safari So Good (1947) 42, 62, 68, **243-245**, 312
Scrap The Japs (1942) **214**
Seein' Red, White, 'N' Blue (1943) 13, 69, **215-216**
Service With A Guile (1946) **231**
Shape Ahoy (1945) 38, 42, **228**, 303
Shaving Muggs (1953) 43, **280**, 303
She-Sick Sailors (1944) 16, 42, 69, **223-224**, 252
Shuteye Popeye (1952) **275**, 309
Silly Hillbilly (1949) 62, 67, **258-259**, 286
Snow Place Like Home (1948) 42, 44, 47, 62, 68, 103, **121-132**, 315
Spinach Fer Britain (1943) **215**
Spinach-Packin' Popeye (1944) **220-221**
Spinach vs. Hamburgers (1948) 25, **252-253**
Spooky Swabs (1957) **296**, 309
Spree Lunch (1957) **295**, 309
Swimmer Take All (1952) 42, 68, **272-273**
Symphony In Spinach (1948) 37, 62, **133-139**, 312, 314

Tar With A Star (1949) 63, 117, 273, **257-258**
Taxi-Turvy (1954) 46, **281-282**, 309
The Anvil Chorus Girl (1944) 16, 36, 38, 48, 62, **220**, 252
The Crystal Brawl (1957) 38, 68, **294**, 309
The Farmer And The Belle (1950) 38, **266**, 291
The Fistic Mystic (1946) 60, 62, 68, **238-239**, 286
The Fly's Last Flight (1949) **260**
The Hungry Goat (1943) **217**
The Island Fling (1946) 9, 25, 34, 44, 45, 59, 62, 63, 68, 70, **73-83**
The Marry-Go-Round (1943) 60, **219**
The Royal Four-Flusher (1947) 9, 34, 44, 45, 48, 60, 62, 63, 67, **85-100**, 306, 314
Thrill Of Fair (1951) **267**
Too Weak To Work (1943) 13, 27, **216**, 312
Tops In The Big Top (1945) 16, 42, 46, 62, **226-228**, 281, 313
Toreadorable (1953) 23, 28, 44, 46, **277**
Tots Of Fun (1952) 25, **274**
Vacation With Play (1951) 26, 34, 35, 37, 42, 44, 46, 61, 62, 64, 68, **167-180**, 312, 314
We're On Our Way To Rio (1944) 14, 16, **219-220**
Wigwam Whoopee (1948) 34, 67, 103, **247-248**
Wood-Peckin' (1943) **218**, 286
Wotta Knight (1947) **243**
You're A Sap, Mr. Jap (1942) **212**

Fleischer Popeye Cartoons

Aladdin And His Wonderful Lamp (1939) 253
Blunder Below (1942) 12
Fightin' Pals (1940) 13
Flies Ain't Human (1941) 12
I'll Never Crow Again (1941) 12
Learn Polikeness (1938) 12, 13, 14
Let's Celebrake (1938) 13
Many Tanks (1942) 12
Me Feelin's Is Hurt (1940) 316
Never Kick A Woman (1936) 289, 313
Olive Oyl And Water Don't Mix (1942) 13
Pip-eye, Pup-eye, Poop-eye, and Peep-eye (1942) 12
Popeye The Sailor (1933) 311
Popeye The Sailor Meets Ali Baba's Forty Thieves (1937) 221, 262
Popeye The Sailor Meets Sindbad The Sailor (1936) 221, 275, 315

INDEX OF CARTOONS MENTIONED IN THIS BOOK 321

Shoein' Hosses (1934) 13
The Dance Contest (1934) 12
The Man On The Flying Trapeze (1934) 316
The Mighty Navy (1941) 12
The Spinach Overture (1935) 12

King Features Syndicate (KFS) Popeye Cartoons by year of release

1960
Astro-Nut 316
Coffee House 316
Insultin' The Sultan 316
Spinach Shortage 312
Voo-Doo To You Too 298

1961
Butler Up 300-301, 316
Gem Jam 299
Kiddie Kapers 299-300
Medicine Man 298
Motor Knocks 297-298
My Fair Olive 299
Oil's Well That Ends Well 301
Operation Ice-Tickle 299

Famous Studios Popeye Cartoons in chronological order: 1942-1957

1942
You're A Sap, Mr. Jap
Alona On The Sarong Seas
A Hull Of A Mess
Scrap The Japs
Me Musical Nephews

1943
Spinach Fer Britain
Seein' Red, White, 'N' Blue
Too Weak To Work
A Jolly Good Furlough
Ration Fer The Duration
The Hungry Goat
Happy Birthdaze
Wood-Peckin'
Cartoons Ain't Human
Her Honor The Mare
The Marry-Go-Round

1944
We're On Our Way To Rio
The Anvil Chorus Girl
Spinach-Packin' Popeye
Puppet Love
Pitchin' Woo At The Zoo
Moving Aweigh
She-Sick Sailors

1945
Pop-Pie A La Mode
Tops In The Big Top
Shape Ahoy
For Better Or Nurse
Mess Production

1946
House Tricks?
Service With A Guile
Klondike Casanova
Peep In The Deep
Rocket To Mars
Rodeo Romeo
Fistic Mystic
The Island Fling

1947
Abusement Park
I'll Be Skiing Ya
Popeye And The Pirates
The Royal Four-Flusher
Wotta Knight
Safari So Good
All's Fair At The Fair

1948
Olive Oyl For President
Wigwam Whoopee
Pre-Hysterical Man
Popeye Meets Hercules
A Wolf In Sheik's Clothing
Spinach vs. Hamburgers
Snow Place Like Home
Robin Hood-Winked
Symphony In Spinach

1949
Popeye's Premiere
Lumberjack And Jill

Hot Air Aces
A Balmy Swami
Tar With A Star
Silly Hillbilly
Barking Dogs Don't Fite
The Fly's Last Flight

1950
How Green Is My Spinach
Gym Jam
Beach Peach
Jitterbug Jive
Popeye Makes A Movie
Baby Wants Spinach
Quick On The Vigor
Riot In Rhythm
The Farmer And The Belle

1951
Vacation With Play
Thrill Of Fair
Alpine For You
Double-Cross-Country Race
Pilgrim Popeye
Let's Stalk Spinach
Punch And Judo

1952
Popeye's Pappy
Lunch With A Punch
Swimmer Take All
Friend Or Phony
Tots Of Fun
Popalong Popeye
Shuteye Popeye
Big Bad Sinbad

1953
Ancient Fistory
Child Sockology
Popeye's Mirthday
Toreadorable
Baby Wants A Battle
Fireman's Brawl
Popeye, The Ace Of Space
Shaving Muggs

1954
Floor Flusher
Popeye's 20th Anniversary
Taxi-Turvy
Bride And Gloom
Greek Mirthology
Fright To The Finish
Private Eye Popeye
Gopher Spinach

1955
Cookin' With Gags
Nurse To Meet Ya
Penny Antics
Beaus Will Be Beaus
Gift Of Gag
Car-Azy Drivers
Mister And Mistletoe
Cops Is Tops
A Job For A Gob

1956
Hill-Billing And Cooing
Popeye For President
Out To Punch
Assault And Flattery
Insect To Injury
Parlez-Vous Woo
I Don't Scare
A Haul In One

1957
Nearlyweds
The Crystal Brawl
Patriotic Popeye
Spree Lunch
Spooky Swabs

Fleischer Popeye Cartoons in chronological order: 1942-1957

1933
Popeye The Sailor 311

1934
The Man On The Flying Trapeze 316
Shoein' Hosses 13
The Dance Contest 12

INDEX OF CARTOONS MENTIONED IN THIS BOOK

1935
The Spinach Overture 12

1936
Never Kick A Woman 289, 313
Popeye The Sailor Meets Sindbad The Sailor 221, 275, 315

1937
Popeye The Sailor Meets Ali Baba's Forty Thieves 221, 262

1938
Let's Celebrake 13
Learn Polikeness 12, 13, 14

1939
Aladdin And His Wonderful Lamp 253

1940
Me Feelin's Is Hurt 316
Fightin' Pals 13

1941
Flies Ain't Human 12
I'll Never Crow Again 12
The Mighty Navy 12

1942
Blunder Below 12
Pip-eye, Pup-eye, Poop-eye, and Peep-eye 12
Olive Oyl And Water Don't Mix 13
Many Tanks 12

ABOUT THE AUTHOR

Steve R. Bierly is a lifelong Popeye fan and a columnist for the *Official Popeye Fan Club News-Magazine*. He has also contributed material to two of Fred Grandinetti's Popeye books, and authored the first website dedicated to the Famous Studios and King Features Syndicate *Popeye* cartoons; see it at *http://www.mtcnet.net/~bierly/popeye.htm*. He also owns and moderates an Olive Oyl Yahoo Group at *http://groups.yahoo.com/group/oliveoyl*.

Steve pastors the American Reformed Church in Hull, Iowa, and has written three books and numerous articles about Christianity.

He lives with his wife and daughter, and has a married son. His hobbies include Popeye (of course), collecting comic books, watching, and collecting movies and classic television series, writing, reading, and walking.

Bear Manor Media

Classic Cinema.
Timeless TV.
Retro Radio.

WWW.BEARMANORMEDIA.COM

www.ingramcontent.com/pod-product-compliance
Lightning Source LLC
Chambersburg PA
CBHW071653160426
43195CB00012B/1452